A Guide to the Pensions Act 1995

A Guide to the Pensions Act 1995

Belinda Benney, LL.B,
Solicitor, Partner in Biddle & Co

Butterworths
London, Dublin, Edinburgh
1995

United Kingdom	Butterworths a Division of Reed Elsevier (UK) Ltd, Halsbury House, 35 Chancery Lane, LONDON WC2A 1EL and 4 Hill Street, EDINBURGH EH2 3JZ
Australia	Butterworths, SYDNEY, MELBOURNE, BRISBANE, ADELAIDE, PERTH, CANBERRA and HOBART
Canada	Butterworth Canada Ltd, TORONTO and VANCOUVER
Ireland	Butterworth (Ireland) Ltd, DUBLIN
Malaysia	Malayan Law Journal Sdn Bhd, KUALA LUMPUR
New Zealand	Butterworths of New Zealand Ltd, WELLINGTON and AUCKLAND
Puerto Rico	Butterworth of Puerto Rico, Inc, SAN JUAN
Singapore	Reed Elsevier (Singapore) Pte Ltd, SINGAPORE
South Africa	Butterworths Publishers Pty Ltd, DURBAN
USA	Butterworth Legal Publishers, CARLSBAD, California; SALEM, New Hampshire

All rights reserved. No part of this publication may be reproduced in any material form (including photocopying or storing it in any medium by electronic means and whether or not transiently or incidentally to some other use of this publication) without the written permission of the copyright owner except in accordance with the provisions of the Copyright, Designs and Patents Act 1988 or under the terms of a licence issued by the Copyright Licensing Agency Ltd, 90 Tottenham Court Road, London, England, W1P 9HE. Application for the copyright owner's written permission to reproduce any part of this publication should be addressed to the publisher.

Warning: The doing of an unauthorised act in relation to a copyright work may result in both a civil claim for damages and criminal prosecution.

© Reed Elsevier (UK) Ltd 1995

Belinda Benney has asserted her right under the Copyright, Designs and Patents Act 1988 to be identified as the author of this work

A CIP catalogue record for this book is available from the British Library.

ISBN 0 406 08133 6

Printed and bound in Great Britain by Clays Ltd, St Ives plc

Preface

The purpose of this book is to provide an introductory guide to the Pensions Act 1995. The chapters broadly follow the layout of the Act itself but have been designed to bring together the main principles on each topic which may be scattered throughout the Act.

The Pensions Act 1995 received Royal Assent on 19 July 1995. It is intended to be fully operative by April 1997 and has been designed to be brought into effect in different phases. Many of the recommendations of the Pension Law Review Committee chaired by Professor Goode have been adopted but the Act also equalises pension benefits for men and women in line with European Law and introduces new procedures for pension-splitting on divorce. Substantial changes to the contracting-out system linked to the State Earnings Related Pension Scheme and an equalised state retirement pension are also implemented.

When the Pensions Bill was introduced into the Houses of Parliament, it was heralded as establishing 'six lines of defence' against fraud and misuse of pension scheme assets. This six-sided fortress consists of: (1) member-nominated trustees; (2) redefinition of the powers and duties of trustees; (3) new regulatory duties for appointed professional advisers; (4) minimum funding requirements backed by financial controls; (5) a pensions regulator; and (6) a compensation scheme as a fail-safe mechanism. The weakest link is the watered-down minimum funding requirement. Words are cheap and a paper pension promise is only as good as the money behind it.

This commentary is not intended to be the 'Key to all Mythologies' of the Pensions Act 1995. We no longer live in the leisured age of George Eliot's 'Middlemarch'. The Pensions Act was urgently required and has been run throughout to a very tight timetable. In the time available and with 35 sets of Regulations promised to add the vital detail to the already complex framework of the Act, a detailed analysis of the total structure was impracticable. For those who require more detail of the history leading up to the Act, the Report of the Pension Law Review Committee and the Government's White Paper (Security, Equality, Choice: The Future for Pensions) are recommended. Those who are looking to the future will already be preparing their comments on the first sets of draft Regulations.

In some areas, interpretation of the Pensions Act 1995 has proved difficult. The views put forward are my own but I am grateful for the work done by my colleagues in the Association of Pension Lawyers and by the National Association of Pension Funds.

Belinda Benney
August 1995

Contents

		Page
Preface		v
Table of Statutes		ix
1	Introduction	1
2	Occupational pensions regulatory authority ('OPRA')	8
3	Trustees	17
4	Dispute resolution	27
5	Professional advisers and 'whistleblowing'	30
6	Indexation	35
7	Minimum funding requirement and financial controls	39
8	Equal treatment	43
9	Modification of scheme rules	48
10	Winding-up priorities and transfers	51
11	Pensions compensation board	58
12	Divorce, assignment and forfeiture	63
13	Contracting-out and state scheme changes	68
14	Money purchase schemes and personal pensions	72

Appendix

Pensions Act 1995 (with annotations)   79

Index   257

Table of statutes

References to *Statutes* are to Halsbury's Statutes of England (Fourth Edition) showing the volume and page at which the annotated text of the Act will be found.

	PARA
Administration of Estates Act 1925 (4 *Statutes* 686)	1.8
Attachment of Earnings Act 1971 (22 *Statutes* 337)	12.16
Bankruptcy (Scotland) Act 1985 (4 *Statutes* 706)	
s 36	12.18
Company Directors Disqualification Act 1986 (8 *Statutes* 781)	2.14, 2.17
Equal Pay Act 1970 (16 *Statutes* 76)	8.2, 8.8, 8.9, 8.10, 8.11, 8.13
European Communities Act 1972 (17 *Statutes* 34)	
s 2(2)	8.10
Family Law (Scotland) Act 1985	12.1
s 167	12.3
Finance Act 1970 (24 *Statutes* 509)	1.3
Financial Services Act 1986 (30 *Statutes* 162)	3.25
s 191(2)	3.26
Income and Corporation Taxes Act 1988 (44 *Statutes* 1)	1.1, 1.3
Sch 22	6.16; 9.9
Insolvency Act 1986 (4 *Statutes* 717)	5.9; 12.16
s 342	12.18
Law of Property Act 1925 (37 *Statutes* 72)	1.8
Matrimonial Causes Act 1973 (27 *Statutes* 734)	12.1
s 25B	12.3, 12.9, 12.19
25C	12.7
25D	12.7, 12.9
(8)	12.9
Parliamentary and other Pensions Act 1972 (33 *Statutes* 496)	
s 27	13.18
Pensions Act 1995	1.1, 1.5, 1.8, 1.11, 1.15, 1.16, 1.18, 1.19; 2.1, 2.12; 3.32; 4.5; 6.3
Pt I (ss 1–125)	1.23, 1.25; 2.13, 2.28, 2.29, 2.40
s 1	2.2
(3)	2.3
2	2.9
3	2.13, 2.14, 2.17, 2.19, 2.37; 3.11, 3.21, 3.31; 4.2; 5.3, 5.6, 5.10; 6.17; 7.11; 10.19; 14.7

	PARA
Pensions Act 1995—*contd*	
s 3(2)(c)–(e)	2.13
4	2.14, 2.17, 2.19
5	2.15
6	2.26
(3), (4)	2.18, 2.27
7	2.22
(5)(b)	2.24
9	2.25
10	1.24; 2.30, 2.33, 2.37; 3.11, 3.21, 3.31; 5.5, 5.6, 5.17; 6.17; 7.11; 10.19, 10.28; 14.7
11, 12	2.38
13	2.34
14	2.34; 6.17
15	2.35, 2.37
(2), (3)	2.36
16	1.25; 3.1
(3), (5)	3.9
(7)	3.5, 3.6
(8)	3.7
17	1.25; 3.1
(4)(a), (b)	3.6
(5)	3.11
18	3.3, 3.4
(3)	3.9
(b)	3.4
(5)	3.9
(6)	3.7
(7)	3.10
(8)	3.3
19	3.3
(5)	3.11
20	3.1, 3.8
(3)	3.9
(5)	3.8
21	3.1, 3.8
(1), (2), (4)	3.11
(6)	3.10
(8)(a)	3.8
22	2.23; 3.12, 3.13
(2)	3.14
23	2.23; 3.12, 3.15
24, 25	2.23; 3.12; 3.16
26	3.12; 5.19
27	5.8, 5.19
(1), (2)	5.9
28	5.10

Table of statutes

	PARA
Pensions Act 1995—*contd*	
s 29	2.17, 2.19
(3)	2.18, 2.19, 2.21
(4)	2.17, 2.18, 2.21
30	2.18
(2)	2.20, 2.25
(3)	2.20
(5), (6)	2.18
(7)	2.21
31	2.33
32	3.21
(2)(b)	3.21
33	3.24
34	3.23, 3.24, 3.27; 5.2
(2)	3.26
(a)	3.28
(4)	3.24, 3.28
(5)	3.24
35	3.29
(4), (5)	3.29
36	3.31
(6)(a)	3.31
37	6.4, 6.14, 6.15, 6.17
(2)	6.15
(3)	6.16
(4)(c)	6.15
(5)	6.16
(8), (9)	6.17
(10)	6.16
38	10.20
(2), (3)	10.20
39	3.20
40	3.32
41(5)	5.7
47	5.7
(1), (2)	5.2
(3)	5.2, 5.3, 5.4
(4)	5.1
(5)	5.7
(8)	5.5
(9)	5.6
48	5.11, 5.12
(4)	5.13
(5)	5.14
(7), (8), (11)-(13)	5.17
49(5)	2.35
(8)	7.18; 14.6
50	4.1, 4.2
51	6.2, 6.4, 6.5, 6.6, 6.11
52	6.2, 6.4, 6.10
53	6.2, 6.4, 6.10
(3)	2.18
54	6.2, 6.4, 6.8
55	6.12
56	14.8

	PARA
Pensions Act 1995—*contd*	
s 56(4)	7.7
57	7.7; 14.8
(1)(b)	7.15
(6)	7.7
(7)	7.11
58	7.12, 7.15; 14.2, 14.8
(3)	7.13
(4)	7.13
(b)	7.14
(6)	7.15
(8)	7.11
59	14.8
(1)	7.16; 14.4
(2)	7.18; 14.5
(3)	7.17
(4)	7.11
60	7.19; 14.8
(4)	7.20
(8)	7.11
61	7.4
62	8.1
(5)	8.3
63	8.1, 8.3
(2)	8.3
(3)	8.5
(4)	8.9
(5), (6)	8.10
64	8.1, 8.6
(2)	8.6
(3)	8.6
(4)	1.24
65	8.1, 8.7; 9.6
(2)	8.7
66	8.1, 8.8; 12.7
(2)	8.8
(4)	8.13
67	9.1, 9.4, 9.14
(2)	9.4
(3)	9.2, 9.4
(4)	9.4
68	9.6
(2)(a)	9.7
(3)	9.7
(b)	10.18
(6)	9.5
69	5.15; 9.8, 9.12
(3)(a)	9.9
(b)	9.10
(c)	9.11; 10.7
70(2), (3)	9.12
71	9.12
72	9.13
73	10.3
(3)	10.7

Table of statutes

Pensions Act 1995—*contd*	PARA	Pensions Act 1995—*contd*	PARA
s 73(3)(a)	10.5	s 91(4), (6)	12.14
(b)	10.6	92	12.12, 12.16, 12.18
(5)	10.15	(4), (5)	12.16
(6)	10.19	93	12.12, 12.17
(9)	10.3	(2), (5)	12.17
74	10.22	94	12.12
(3)(d)	10.22	(3)	12.18
75	10.12; 14.8	95	12.12, 12.18
76	6.4, 6.14; 10.13, 10.14, 10.15, 10.17	96	2.16, 2.40; 5.17
(2)	10.14	(6)	2.40
(3)	10.14	97	5.17
(b)	10.15	(6)	2.40
(6), (7)	10.19	98	2.41
77	6.4, 6.14; 9.10; 10.13, 10.16, 10.18, 10.19	99	2.42; 11.20
(4)(a)	10.17	100	2.42; 11.20
(5)	10.19	(4)	2.42
78	11.2	101	2.42
(2)	11.3	102	2.41
(4)	11.15	103	2.44
(5)	11.4	104–109	2.45; 11.23
(6)	1.24	110	11.19
79	11.8	111	11.21
80	11.9	112	11.19
(5)	11.9	113	11.22
81	11.10, 11.13	114	11.23
(2)	11.11	(1), (3)	11.24
(3)(d)	11.14	(7)	4.9; 11.23
(7)	11.10	115	2.28
82	11.10, 11.12	116	2.29
(5)	11.12	(1)	1.24
83	11.10, 11.14	117	1.25
(2)	11.16	118	1.23
(3)	11.15	119, 120	1.23; 3.12
84	11.4, 11.10, 11.13, 11.14	121–122	3.12
(3)	11.13	123	1.22; 5.9
85	11.17	124	3.7, 3.29; 5.2, 5.9
(3)	11.18	(1)	3.13
86	11.11	(2)	9.3
87	7.4; 14.1, 14.2, 14.8	(b)	9.3
(2)(b)	14.10	125	3.7
(4)	14.3	Pt II (ss 126–134)	1.21
(5)	14.7	s 126	8.15
88	14.1, 14.8	127	13.12
(1)	14.4	128	13.13
(2)	14.5	129–134	13.15
(3)	14.6	Pt III (ss 135–151)	8.12; 13.1
(4)	14.7	s 135	13.1
89(1), (2)	14.8	136	13.2, 13.3
90	14.9	137	14.11, 14.12
91	12.12, 12.13, 12.14, 12.16, 12.18, 12.19	138	14.13
		140	13.4
		141	13.4, 13.5
		142, 143	2.39; 14.21
(3)	12.18	144	14.21

Table of statutes

	PARA
Pensions Act 1995—*contd*	
s 146	13.7, 13.8
147	5.19
148	13.9
149	1.24; 13.8
150	2.4
151	13.10
152	10.24
153	10.27
155	2.32
156	4.10
157	4.4, 4.5
158	4.8
159	4.9
160	4.7
161	2.39; 9.13
162	6.4, 6.13; 14.15
163	14.15
164	14.16
165	2.10; 11.6; 14.10
(4)	11.6
166	12.2, 12.3, 12.19
167	12.2
168	1.21; 12.10
168A	2.32
169	12.10
170	1.21; 13.18
171	1.21; 8.14
172	14.19
174	1.24
(1)	1.24
175	1.24
176	1.22
177	1.26
178, 179	1.21
180	1.20; 11.12
(1)	1.20
(2)	12.10
Sch 1	2.9
para 2	11.4
6(1), (2)	2.6
7(1)	2.6
8	2.8
11	2.7
13, 14, 16	2.9
17	4.8
18	9.8
19	2.2
Sch 2	
para 10, 11	11.7
12	11.7, 11.8
13	11.7
18	4.8
19	11.2

	PARA
Pensions Act 1995—*contd*	
Sch 3	3.32; 6.4; 8.4; 9.13; 10.7; 12.12, 12.13
para 41	12.16
Sch 4	
para 2	13.16
4	13.17
Pt II	13.15, 13.16
para 6	13.14
Sch 5	2.4; 14.16, 14.18
para 36	14.17
37	13.11
39	13.10
Sch 6	
para 2-6	10.28
Sch 7	1.26
Pension (Increase) Act 1971 (33 *Statutes* 414)	1.26; 8.14
Pension Schemes Act 1993	1.1, 1.2; 2.4, 2.10, 2.13, 2.32; 4.5; 6.3; 9.13; 10.28; 14.16
s 12A	13.2
12B	13.3
26, 27	5.19
28	5.19, 14.21
28A	14.25
29	5.19, 14.21
30	5.19
31	5.19; 14.16
(1)	14.17
32	5.19
32A	13.7
33A	5.19
(2)	5.20
37	13.10, 13.11
41, 42	14.11
42A, 42B	14.12
44	14.16
45, 45A	14.13
45B	14.14
48A	13.4
55	13.5
77	12.12, 12.13
78	12.12, 12.16
79	12.12, 12.14
80	12.12
93	10.24
93A	10.27
94(1)	10.27
99	10.28
102	6.4
103	6.2, 6.4
104	6.2, 6.4
105-107	6.4
108	6.4, 6.14

Table of statutes

	PARA
Pension Schemes Act 1993—*contd*	
s 109	6.11, 6.12
112	3.32
118	8.4, 8.10
123	11.10
124	14.9
(3)(b)	14.9
136-141	9.13
145(4)	4.10
146	4.4
(4), (8)	4.5
147, 148	4.4
149(3)	4.8
(5)-(7)	4.9
150, 151	4.4
159	12.16, 12.18, 12.19
175	2.10; 11.6
178	4.5
Pt X (ss 145-152)	4.3
Sch 2	13.5
para 5	13.6
Pensions Appeal Tribunals Act 1943 (33 *Statutes* 369)	12.10
Policyholders Protection Act 1975 (22 *Statutes* 81)	11.11
Settled Land Act 1925 (48 *Statutes* 409):	1.8
Sex Discrimination Act 1975 (6 *Statutes* 753)	8.2, 8.8
Social Security Act 1973 (40 *Statutes* 73)	6.1
Social Security Act 1986 (40 *Statutes* 367)	6.1
Social Security Act 1989 (40 *Statutes* 429)	1.1
Sch 5	8.1, 8.2, 8.5
Social Security Act 1990 (40 *Statutes* 466)	6.1, 6.2, 6.3
Social Security Administration Act 1992 (40 *Statutes* 786)	13.15
Social Security Contributions and Benefits Act 1992 (40 *Statutes* 492)	13.15
s 43	8.6
44	8.6
45	8.6; 13.12
Sch 1	13.9
Sch 5	13.14
Social Security Pensions Act 1975 (40 *Statutes* 134)	8.4
Superannuation Act 1972 (33 *Statutes* 453)	14.19
Trustee Act 1925 (48 *Statutes* 257)	1.1, 1.8; 2.12, 2.13; 3.27
s 25	3.26
30(2)	2.24
61	3.28
Trustee Investments Act 1961 (48 *Statutes* 368)	3.23; 11.18

xiii

1 Introduction

BACKGROUND TO THE 1995 ACT

Previous UK pensions legislation

1.1 A substantial growth in defined benefit (final salary) occupational pension schemes in the UK has taken place since the Second World War. The tax reliefs offered to employers and employees in connection with provision of funded pension benefits coupled with a sophisticated trust law heritage under the common law has meant that pension schemes are governed by three distinct regimes—

(a) statutory legislation such as the Social Security Act 1989, the consolidating Pension Schemes Act 1993 and the Income and Corporation Taxes Act 1988;

(b) the practice and discretion of the Inland Revenue embodied in the Practice Notes[1] and Memoranda; and

(c) the Trustee Act 1925, the equitable doctrine of trust law and the body of case law.

---

[1] IR12 (1991) Occupational Pension Schemes Practice Notes (2nd edition revised January 1995).

STATUTORY LEGISLATION

1.2 The complex system of interrelated state pension and welfare benefits is set out in various statutes. The most important source for pension benefits is the Pension Schemes Act 1993 which consolidated a variety of different aspects of pensions legislation covering the previous 20 years. The 1993 Act covers the revaluation, preservation and transfer rights of early leavers; indexation; the role of the Pensions Ombudsman in facilitating dispute resolution; the detailed protections that fall into place automatically on the insolvency of the sponsoring employer of a pension scheme leading to the appointment of an independent trustee; the contracting-out requirements as an alternative to the State Earnings Related Pension Scheme; and the duties of trustees as to disclosure of information to scheme members.

1.3 The Income and Corporation Taxes Act 1988 replaced the pensions provisions of the Finance Act 1970 and sets out detailed methods of obtaining exempt approved status for occupational pension schemes and personal pension schemes (including retirement annuity contracts). It also covers the tax treatment of funded or unfunded unapproved schemes which, prior to 1988, had not been encouraged.

REVENUE PRACTICE

1.4 The Practice Notes contain detailed guidance as to the form of exempt-approved pension schemes. They cover the procedures for establishing a new scheme,

1.4 *Introduction*

winding-up a scheme and/or transferring or merging it. An extremely complicated set of rules has developed over the years known as Revenue limits (or Revenue maxima) to limit the tax relief granted. These limits cover pensions accrual, spouses' pensions, index-linking, size of contributions and the employer funding rate. The most significant restriction imposed on the pensions industry as a whole in 1989, and reflected in Revenue limits, was the introduction of the 'earnings cap' on final remuneration. This was originally set at the figure of £60,000 per year with the intention that it would increase each year by the increase in the retail prices index. The Government then froze the earnings cap for two years, although it now stands at the rate of £78,600 for the year 1995–96. The fact that the earnings cap does not increase with wages inflation means that an increasingly large proportion of the working population will be affected after the year 2000 and will be unable to pension their full earnings through traditional occupational pension schemes.

1.5 The Practice Notes are supplemented by Memoranda issued by the Inland Revenue through the Pension Schemes Office. (These were originally known as Joint Office Memoranda when they were issued jointly by the Pension Schemes Office, under its previous name of the Superannuation Funds Office, and the Occupational Pensions Board.) The Occupational Pensions Board will be phased out once the Pensions Act 1995 comes into force.

1.6 The difficulty with the Practice Notes and the Memoranda is that they are constantly changing and being updated. Some of the changes represent relaxations and simplifications but many, such as the earnings cap, are restrictive. The wishes of the Government to honour 'previous expectations' and to avoid retrospective changes have led to serious complexity with three different regimes of Revenue limits dependent on the date of joining a scheme (or its predecessor in certain circumstances). By their nature, the Practice Notes and Memoranda do not cover all circumstances, and practitioners frequently have to apply for individual rulings in cases of doubt or uncertainty.

THE LAW OF TRUSTS AND CASE LAW

1.7 The English legal system has developed over the centuries but, from an early date, recognised the concept of the trust which is absent from many civil law jurisdictions. By the end of the Victorian era, a substantial body of case law had developed around the operation of private family trusts and the duties and obligations of trustees. As the trust divorced legal and equitable ownership, these cases were brought in the Chancery Division under its equitable jurisdiction. This emphasised the duty of trustees to 'do the right thing' and take a more prudent and cautious attitude in dealing with trust matters than with their own personal affairs.

1.8 The Trustee Act 1925 formed part of an important grouping of statutes covering all aspects of ownership of assets and land (the Settled Land Act 1925, the Administration of Estates Act 1925 and the Law of Property Act 1925 completing the group). These key statutes have formed a long-lasting and worthy foundation that has stood the test of time remarkably well. They sought to consolidate and update earlier disparate pieces of legislation as interpreted by case law to give clear guidance in what had become an extremely complex area. The similarities with the 1995 Act will be obvious.

1.9 Although there have been many cases over the last 50 years covering private trusts and estates, these have often been tax driven. Nevertheless, helpful analogies can be drawn from this private client database and applied to the difficulties facing pension fund trustees as the assets under their control matured into funds worth millions of pounds, often representing substantial surpluses. The economic recovery of the 1980s led to a climate of hostile take-over bids and diversification with its attendant culture of 'get rich quick'. The blatant asset-stripping of pension scheme surpluses led in turn to defence mechanisms such as the insertion of 'poison pills' into pension scheme documentation to counteract forced mergers. It had suddenly been realised that in many cases the slumbering giant of the occupational pension scheme was worth more than the sponsoring employer.

THE MAXWELL PENSION SCHEMES

1.10 Favourable investment returns in the 1980s coupled with high unemployment and redundancies contributed towards the development of substantial surplus funds in pension schemes. The 'contribution holiday' (which allows employers to suspend ongoing employer contributions to their pension schemes by diminishing surplus internally within the scheme) improved cash flow for employers. Generous pension provision for a few years appeared to cost nothing and the accounting standard SSAP 24 has only partially changed this perception.

1.11 Apart from the contribution holiday, employers in 1986 were allowed, for the first time, to take a refund of surplus from an ongoing pension scheme, subject to payment of tax. The vexed question of 'who owns the surplus?' is still being asked today in negotiations about use of surplus between employers, trade unions and scheme members. The 1995 Act does not seek to give a definitive answer.

1.12 The spectacular performances and highly geared expansions of the late 1980s were followed by equally spectacular crashes of major businesses affecting the commercial sector (Polly Peck and Brent Walker), the investment industry (Barlow Clowes) and banking (BCCI). There were rumours of pension scheme insolvencies resulting from injudicious loans to employers but no-one was prepared for the discovery, shortly after Robert Maxwell's death in November 1991, that over £400 million was missing from pension schemes in the Maxwell group of companies. Pension scheme assets had been wrongfully used in a variety of ways and some schemes had to seek Government assistance to enable them to maintain payment of pensions to current pensioners. The shock of the vulnerability of the Maxwell pensioners and the Government's refusal to provide immediate compensation threatened the credibility of occupational pension schemes to deliver benefits as promised.

THE PENSION LAW REFORM COMMITTEE

1.13 Even before the Maxwell scandal, the House of Commons Select Committee on Social Security had been investigating the idea of setting up a committee of experts from the pensions industry to make proposals for pensions reform. After Maxwell, the Government hastily promoted the idea and, in June 1992, set up the

1.13   Introduction

Pension Law Review Committee ('PLRC') chaired by Professor Roy Goode. The Committee of 12 represented unions, employers, the investment industry, pension lawyers, actuaries and auditors. It sought the views of the pensions industry and produced a substantial consultation document. This was followed on 30 September 1993 by a two volume Report[1] which made 218 detailed recommendations for change. It was stressed by the PLRC that their Report represented both a compromise and a package. The pro-active role of the new Pensions Regulator was central to the whole concept which contained its own system of checks and balances.

---

[1]   Pension Law Reform: The Report of The Pension Law Review Committee Vols I & II Cm 2342-1.

THE GOVERNMENT WHITE PAPER

1.14   The Department of Social Security gave itself a strict timetable to report on the PLRC proposals. The White Paper[1] produced in June 1994 again consisted of two volumes but concentrated on the PLRC proposals without background material. Each proposal was considered in turn and either rejected, accepted or modified. Brief reasons were given for the conclusions on each proposal. The main change to the PLRC model was to change the role of the Pensions Regulator from a pro-active watchdog to a reactive bureaucrat. The Government had been keen to reduce the administrative burden on pension schemes by dropping the proposal for pension schemes to submit detailed annual returns to the Pensions Regulator. The unfortunate side effect of this is that the Pensions Regulator is deprived of information and therefore made less able to fulfil a protective role.

---

[1]   Security, Equality, Choice: The Future for Pensions Vols I & II Cm 2594 - I & II.

THE PENSIONS BILL AND THE PENSIONS ACT 1995

1.15   The Pensions Bill unusually commenced its passage through the Houses of Parliament in the House of Lords in December 1994 and was heavily debated. The 1995 Act implements the bulk of the recommendations of the PLRC and concentrates on building the six-sided fortress of protection detailed in the Preface. The Government also took the opportunity to introduce legislation to equalise pension benefits and retirement ages for men and women and to amend the contracting-out system. It was forced to insert new wording in a number of areas, the most important being pension-splitting on divorce (which it had wished to postpone pending further consultation).

1.16   Much of the 1995 Act sets up a general framework that will have to be fleshed out by over 30 sets of Regulations. Having seen the substantial volume of Regulations already in existence (about 150), there is concern that important issues will be left for the Regulations which will not be subject to the same debate and scrutiny as the Act itself. This is particularly relevant to the sections dealing with the minimum funding requirement, winding-up priorities and the changes to the contracting-out system.

THE EFFECTS OF EC MEMBERSHIP

1.17 The UK's membership of the European Community in 1973 has only slowly affected occupational pension schemes, but it is likely to be of growing importance. Case law from the European Court of Justice in the mid-1970s and 1980s was specialised and largely ignored until the *Barber*[1] case in 1990 which highlighted the effect of the Treaty of Rome, Art 119 on occupational pension schemes. Article 119 was confirmed to have direct effect in the UK without the need for national legislation. The judgment held that pensions form part of pay and required normal retirement ages for men and women to be equalised (with effect from 17 May 1990 only as was later confirmed by the Maastricht Protocol in 1993). As many occupational pension schemes mirrored the state retirement ages of 65 (men) and 60 (women), this created major problems in both financial and trust law terms. The later European Court of Justice decision in *Avdel*[2] in September 1994 compounded the financial problems by reiterating the EC concept that benefits for the disadvantaged sex should be levelled-up to those of the advantaged sex in order to achieve equality (although they could subsequently be levelled-down for both sexes). The Pensions Act 1995 attempts to assist trustees and pension schemes by giving them national statutory authority to effect equality and override protective trust law provisions which in some cases have made equalisation impossible or difficult to achieve.

---

[1] *Barber v Guardian Royal Exchange* (C-262/88) [1990] ECR I–1889, ECJ.
[2] *Smith v Avdel Systems Ltd* (C-408/92) [1994] ECR I–4435, ECJ.

POLITICAL IMPLICATIONS

1.18 There are two schools of thought on the political implications of the 1995 Act. The first is that trustees, employers and scheme advisers now need clear statutory guidance as to how they should handle specialist pension scheme matters instead of being forced to rely on outdated trust and case law. While it is impossible to stop a determined fraudster, a formal regulated system with criminal and civil penalties and sanctions should make malpractice both more difficult and more obvious. The second, more cynical, view is that the 1995 Act will impose excessive bureaucratic controls over matters that are best left flexible. One of the reasons why trust law has remained such a strong force is its foundation in equity and its ability to adjust the law to changing circumstances and times. The increased costs of compliance, the levies required to pay for the Pensions Regulator and the compensation scheme coupled with the restriction of employer freedom in many areas might indirectly have the effect of pushing employers towards the personal pension market. This would be to the obvious benefit of banks, building societies and the insurance sector. The threat of pension scheme trustees of the major funds exercising their powerful voting rights with pension scheme shares (which is compulsory in the USA) could have a major influence on corporate governance and supports the second view.

1.19 The long-term effect of the 1995 Act will depend on a number of factors such as how quickly it is amended, whether the Pensions Regulator can be seen to be operating effectively, how trustees and administrators will respond to a steady flow of detailed Regulations continually imposing new regulatory requirements, and whether the criminal, civil and disqualification penalties are seen to be a deterrent to

1.19 *Introduction*

maladministration and malpractice. The underlying structure of trust law has been confirmed in the 1995 Act but not removed. It is to be hoped that the 1995 Act will strengthen and clarify the position of pension scheme trustees and restore faith that the pensions promise in the UK is secure and really will deliver.

IMPLEMENTATION

Timetable

1.20 Section 180 sets out the timetable for implementation of the 1995 Act which has been designed to come into force in phases. The Government has planned for it to be in full effect by April 1997. Implementation will be made by statutory instrument by order of the Secretary of State (s 180(1)) except for the divorce provisions for England and Wales (but not Scotland) which will come into force on a day appointed by the Lord Chancellor.

1.21 The only sections of the 1995 Act that came into effect on 19 July 1995 were those contained in Pt II (changes to state pensions and benefits), the improvements to war widows' pensions (s 168), the provisions covering pensions for dependants of the Prime Minister and equal treatment for official pensions (ss 170, 171) and a special derogation for corresponding provisions in Northern Ireland (s 179). The other provisions relating to Northern Ireland contained in s 178 which bring limited parts of the 1995 Act into force in Northern Ireland have not yet been brought into effect.

Interpretation

1.22 Section 176 contains brief definitions used throughout the 1995 Act. The main definitions covering interpretation of Pt I are found in ss 124 and 125. Insolvency terminology used in the 1995 Act is defined separately in s 123.

Regulations

1.23 There are detailed provisions in ss 118–120 about the making of Regulations under the 1995 Act. The power of the Government to alter the basic structure established by the 1995 Act is extensive and these provisions do little to redress that balance. For example, the Secretary of State only has to consult 'such persons as he considers appropriate' before making Regulations under Pt I (s 120).

1.24 Sections 174 and 175 provide more details on subordinate legislation generally. The numerous powers to make Regulations dotted throughout the 1995 Act must be exercised by statutory instrument (s 174(1)). Section 175 provides that a draft statutory instrument must be approved by both Houses of Parliament in only five cases. These cover the equal treatment rule (s 64(4)), the amount which the Compensation Board can borrow under s 78(6), the introduction of new criminal offences for breach of Pt I (s 116(1)), implementation of two different contracting-out methods in one scheme (s 149) and increases to the civil penalty fines under s 10.

Overriding legislation

1.25 Section 117 provides that any provisions of Pt I of the 1995 Act, any subordinate legislation giving effect to that Part or any member-nominated trustee arrangements under ss 16 or 17 will be overriding.

Repeals

1.26 Section 177 implements the repeals contained in Sch 7 to the 1995 Act. These are required as a consequence of the new primary legislation. Only one repeal in the Pension (Increase) Act 1971 has been made with immediate effect from 19 July 1995.

2 Occupational Pensions Regulatory Authority

THE CREATION OF THE OCCUPATIONAL PENSIONS REGULATORY AUTHORITY

2.1 The Occupational Pensions Regulatory Authority ('OPRA') is a totally new statutory authority and is referred to throughout the Pensions Act 1995 as 'the Authority'. In the pensions industry, however, it seems likely that the acronym 'OPRA' will be used as a descriptive term.

2.2 The PLRC Report stressed it was vital for a Pensions Regulator to oversee the proposed new regulatory structure to improve the security of occupational pension schemes. The office of Regulator was intended to be held on a full-time basis by an individual supported by an advisory committee. Section 1 instead establishes OPRA as a body corporate, and the reference to 'members' implies that it will be a company limited by guarantee. Schedule 1, para 19 confirms that OPRA will execute documents by use of a company seal.

2.3 The Board of OPRA will be appointed by the Secretary of State and will consist of a Chairman and at least six other members. The other members (also to be appointed by the Secretary of State) have to cover five separate categories set out in s 1(3)—
- (a) a representative of employers;
- (b) a representative of employees;
- (c) a person knowledgeable about life assurance business;
- (d) a person with experience of management or administration of occupational pension schemes; and
- (e) two persons knowledgeable about occupational pension schemes.

This leaves it open for the Chairman to be a career civil servant, a senior figure from the pensions industry or an appointment from the legal or commercial sector.

DISSOLUTION OF OCCUPATIONAL PENSIONS BOARD

2.4 Section 150 provides for the dissolution of the Occupational Pensions Board ('OPB') on an appointed day. Any residual duties or functions will pass to OPRA, the Secretary of State or the Department of Health and Social Services for Northern Ireland. Schedule 5 contains appropriate statutory amendments to other pieces of legislation (mainly the Pension Schemes Act 1993) to repeal or amend references to the OPB and the accompanying changes to the contracting-out legislation.

2.5 The role of the OPB in dealing with the preservation of the rights of early leavers is switched to OPRA while its supervision of the contracting-out legislation passes to the Department of Social Security.

MANAGEMENT OF OPRA

Personnel

2.6 The Chairman may at any time be removed from office by the Secretary of State (Sch 1, para 6(1)) by notice in writing but without reasons being given. Removal as Chairman brings automatic removal as a member of the Board (Sch 1, para 6(2)). The other members of the Board can only be removed by the Secretary of State (Sch 1, para 7(1)) if they—
  (a) have been absent from meetings of OPRA for more than three consecutive months without OPRA's permission;
  (b) have become bankrupt (or became subject to sequestration in Scotland) or made an arrangement with creditors; or
  (c) are unable or unfit to discharge the functions of a Board member.

2.7 Schedule 1, para 11 sets out the procedures for appointment of the next management tier down from the Board. This will comprise a Chief Executive and other employees. The first Chief Executive (and the level of remuneration) will be chosen by the Secretary of State but replacements will be chosen by OPRA with the approval of the Secretary of State. The other employees are chosen by OPRA although the Secretary of State has to agree minimum and maximum numbers. The Secretary of State can second additional staff or make available other facilities from time to time at his discretion.

Budget

2.8 Schedule 1, para 8 provides for the Secretary of State to grant a budget to OPRA and to agree remuneration packages for the Board. The remuneration packages and terms and conditions of employment of other staff will be set by OPRA with the approval of the Secretary of State. The Government estimates that OPRA will have an initial staff of 200 with a start-up cost of £2 million and annual cost of about £10 million (see Appendix 3 of the White Paper).

Administration

2.9 Schedule 1 also sets out the operating procedures and duties of OPRA such as production of accounts (Sch 1, para 16) and the running of meetings and delegation of duties (Sch 1, para 14). The Secretary of State is given power to make Regulations governing the procedures to be followed by OPRA in the exercise of its functions and in particular as to the form of hearings and the taking of evidence (Sch 1, para 13). Section 2 of the 1995 Act requires OPRA to submit an annual report to the Secretary of State 'as soon as practicable' after each year end. The Secretary of State has a duty to present the report to Parliament.

Levy

2.10 Recommendation 212 of the PLRC Report intended the costs of the Regulator to be met by the state. The main reason was that protection of individual rights should be a function of Government and that the 'disinterested status' of the Regulator would be best protected by Government funding. The introduction of a compensation scheme to be funded by a levy from the pensions industry was another reason given for not overburdening pension schemes. Section 165 ignores this recommendation and extends the existing levy mechanism set up to finance the Pensions Registry and the Pensions Ombudsman by the Pension Schemes Act 1993, s 175. A new s 175 is substituted so that prescribed occupational pension schemes and personal pension schemes will now have to finance the setting up and running costs of OPRA.

2.11 The cost of the new Pensions Compensation Board will be covered by a different levy payable to the Compensation Board (rather than to the Secretary of State) and is payable in respect of prescribed occupational pension schemes by the trustees or other prescribed persons. The deliberate exclusion of personal pension schemes from the text means that personal pension schemes will not have to contribute to the Compensation Board as they have their own separate compensation systems depending on the status of the personal pension provider.

TRUSTEES

Removal of trustees

2.12 Prior to the Pensions Act 1995, the statutory power of appointment and removal of trustees was governed by the Trustee Act 1925. These statutory provisions were usually overridden in the trust deed and rules of most pension schemes so as to give the principal employer the power to appoint and remove trustees at will (whereas the statutory provisions made the trustees as a group self-appointing). In the event of a dispute, or circumstances where an employer was unable or unwilling to act, a court application would often be required.

2.13 Section 3 will supplement the Trustee Act 1925 and override the trust deeds and rules of pension schemes to allow OPRA to prohibit a person from being a trustee. A prohibition order will have the effect of removing the trustee from office. An order can be made in three main circumstances—
   (a) if the trustee has been in serious or persistent breach of any duties under Pt I of the 1995 Act (except for the indexation provisions, the equal treatment rule and the provisions regarding gathering of information for the Compensation Board) or under the registration, transfer values, information and levy requirements of the Pension Schemes Act 1993; or
   (b) if OPRA is satisfied that, while being a trustee of the scheme, s 3 has applied to the person by virtue of any other provision of Pt I; or
   (c) in any other circumstances to be prescribed by Regulations.

The removal powers are extended in s 3(2)(c)–(e) to cover corporate trustees, partnerships in Scotland and directors of a corporate trustee.

Suspension

2.14 Section 4 gives OPRA a new power to suspend a trustee from acting as a trustee pending consideration of a prohibition order under s 3 or in the following circumstances, where—
   (a) proceedings have been instituted against the trustee for an offence involving dishonesty or deception;

(b) a bankruptcy or sequestration petition has been presented against the trustee;
(c) a winding-up petition has been presented against a corporate trustee;
(d) an application has been made against the trustee for a disqualification order under the Company Directors Disqualification Act 1986 (this covers matters such as fraudulent and wrongful trading and persistent breaches of company legislation).

The initial suspension period is either 12 months or the conclusion of the proceedings (which might then lead to disqualification as a trustee) although OPRA can grant an extension. It is still unclear how OPRA will get to know of these circumstances as there is no requirement for a trustee to seek removal or suspension in those situations.

2.15 Section 5 requires OPRA to give trustees one month's prior notice of the threat of removal and immediate notice of suspension. OPRA is also required to inform co-trustees before the removal order is made and as soon as practicable after a suspension order has been made. Trustees threatened with removal must be invited to make representations to OPRA (which has a statutory duty to consider them before the notice period expires).

2.16 The removal powers of OPRA go further than existing case law or statute, and avoid the need for a court hearing. It is notable that there is no right of appeal to the courts against a prohibition or suspension order made by OPRA, except on a point of law under s 96. The suspension provisions should give OPRA the chance to investigate fully before they proceed to removal. There is no requirement for a 'fit and proper person' test to be applied to the appointment of trustees generally. OPRA will only step in with a prohibition order or suspension once a breach of trust, statutory duty or other financial or corporate disqualification has occurred.

Disqualification

2.17 The interaction of the prohibition and removal provisions of s 3, and the suspension and temporary 'freezing' provisions of s 4, is further complicated by the disqualification and effective removal provisions of s 29. This follows up the 'pending' suspension activities with automatic disqualification if the trustee concerned is finally declared bankrupt (or his estate is sequestrated), he is convicted of an offence involving dishonesty or deception, or is disqualified under the Company Directors Disqualification Act 1986. A disqualification order can also be made by OPRA if the trustee is incapable of acting as such by reason of mental disorder or is a company that has gone into liquidation (s 29(4)).

2.18 No order is required to effect disqualification except where OPRA has to intervene under s 29(3) or (4). The effect, under s 30, of a trustee becoming disqualified is for him to 'cease to be a trustee'. It is unfortunate that different wording is used here from s 3(3), which provides that the making of a prohibition order against a trustee 'has the effect of removing him'. The net result of both provisions seems to be identical, ie removal. This view is supported by s 30(5) and (6) which contain the same provisions with regard to acting as a purported trustee and liability as s 6(3) and (4) covering prohibition and suspension.

2.19 Section 29(3) contains one of the most far-reaching punishment provisions in the 1995 Act. The thrust of ss 3, 4 and 29 is to prohibit, suspend or disqualify a person from acting as a trustee of 'a particular trust scheme'. If a person is the subject

2.19 Occupational Pensions Regulatory Authority

of a prohibition order under s 3, or has been removed as trustee of a scheme by court order, OPRA may by order disqualify the person from being a trustee if in its opinion it is not desirable for that person to be a trustee of any trust scheme.

2.20 Section 30(2) gives OPRA the power to transfer pension scheme assets on a change in trusteeship resulting from disqualification. Acting while disqualified is a criminal offence under s 30(3), liable to a fine and/or imprisonment.

2.21 OPRA is required by s 30(7) to keep a register of persons disqualified from acting as a trustee of any pension scheme by OPRA under s 29(3) or (4) (but not trustees who have just been removed, suspended or automatically disqualified). The public can ask OPRA to disclose whether a specified person is included on the register as disqualified in respect of a named scheme but do not appear entitled to make a general search.

Appointment of trustees

2.22 Section 7 gives OPRA the power to appoint a trustee to replace one that it has removed or a disqualified trustee (but not a suspended trustee). In addition, OPRA can appoint a new trustee in four other circumstances—
- (a) to secure that the trustees have the necessary knowledge and skill for the proper administration of the scheme;
- (b) to secure that the number of trustees is sufficient for the proper administration of the scheme;
- (c) to secure the proper use or application of the assets of the scheme; or
- (d) in other circumstances prescribed by Regulations.

2.23 The new trustee will usually have the same powers and duties as the continuing trustees, but the order made by OPRA can extend or restrict the powers of the new trustee (s 8). If the appointment replaces an independent trustee, the replacement trustee must satisfy the special requirements set out in ss 22–25.

2.24 Section 7(5)(b) allows a new trustee appointed by OPRA to be paid fees and expenses out of the scheme's resources if the order so requires. Section 8 goes further and allows such expenses to be treated as a debt on the employer. Both these provisions are new. They override the common law and statutory principles that a trustee must not profit from his trust without an express charging clause in the trust instrument and that trustee expenses are met from the scheme assets under the Trustee Act 1925, s 30(2) unless the trust instrument otherwise provides.

2.25 Section 9 of the Pensions Act 1995 allows OPRA to vest trust property in, or transfer pension scheme assets to, trustees as a result of appointment or removal by OPRA. It matches s 30(2) which gives similar powers on disqualification of a trustee.

PENALTIES

Criminal offences

2.26 A person who continues to act as a trustee after removal or suspension by OPRA will be guilty of an offence and liable, on summary conviction, to a fine of up to the current statutory maximum (currently £5,000). On conviction on indictment, the penalty is imprisonment or an unlimited fine, or both (s 6). The explanatory memorandum to the Pensions Bill (ordered to be printed on 15 December 1994) indicated that the maximum term of imprisonment would be two years.

2.27 If such a person continues to act as a trustee, his acts will not be invalid merely because of the prohibition or suspension. Similarly, such a person will not be able to use the fact that he has been removed or suspended as a defence to avoid liability as a trustee (s 6(3), (4)). The intention here is clearly to discourage 'tainted' trustees from seeking to interfere in the pension scheme. It also gives statutory effect to the old case law concept of an 'executor de son tort' where intermeddling with an estate when not so entitled treats a third party as an executor. The only difficulty with this dual approach is that a trustee who has been removed as a result of a prohibition order may still sometimes be treated as a trustee (for example, if he signed a document after removal that would otherwise be invalid for lack of quorum).

2.28 Section 115 provides that where an offence under Pt I of the 1995 Act has been committed by a body corporate, and any director, manager, secretary or other similar officer (or a person purporting to act in such capacity) is implicated in consent, connivance or neglect, that person is guilty of the offence as well as the body corporate. The members of a company limited by guarantee will be liable in a similar way. Partners in a Scottish partnership may also be liable as well as the partnership.

2.29 Section 116 provides that Regulations made under the authority of Pt I of the 1995 Act can create criminal offences subject, on summary conviction, to a fine not exceeding level 5 on the standard scale.

Civil offences

2.30 Section 10 contains a 'catch-all' provision allowing OPRA to impose a fine for civil offences incurred in connection with breaches of other provisions of the 1995 Act. The levels of fine must differentiate between individual and corporate offenders and will be set by Regulations. The maximum penalties are £5,000 for an individual and £50,000 for a company or firm. They can be increased by order of the Secretary of State. OPRA has a duty to recover these penalties and pay them to the Secretary of State.

2.31 The civil offences will be covered in more detail later, but include—
   (a) the failure to set a formal investment policy;
   (b) trustees not appointing an actuary or auditor to the pension scheme;
   (c) the failure to establish a disputes procedure;
   (d) the breach of the valuation and certification procedures required for the minimum funding test;
   (e) the failure to agree schedules of contribution payments with the employer and to disclose non-payment;
   (f) the failure of professionals to 'whistleblow' in breach of new statutory duties; and
   (g) the breach of the new member-nominated trustee procedures.

Offences under the Pension Schemes Act 1993

2.32 Section 155 of the 1995 Act replaces the limited provisions of the Pension Schemes Act 1993, s 168 by substituting two new sections. The new s 168 allows

2.32 Occupational Pensions Regulatory Authority

Regulations to make certain contraventions of provisions of the Pension Schemes Act 1993 a criminal offence subject, on summary conviction, to a fine not exceeding level 5 on the standard scale. Alternatively, Regulations may impose civil penalties and fines that must be paid to OPRA. The new s 168A creates a new criminal offence of providing false or misleading information to the Registrar punishable by a fine up to the statutory maximum and/or imprisonment.

Non-reimbursement

2.33 Section 31 does not allow a trustee to reimburse himself from scheme assets for any fine or penalty or for the scheme to pay for insurance to guard against such risk. Breach of this rule is a criminal offence leading to a further fine and/or imprisonment for the person receiving reimbursement. Any trustee involved in making such a payment risks a prohibition/removal order under s 3 or a civil fine under s 10.

Injunctions and restitution

2.34 Section 13 allows OPRA to apply to the High Court (or the Court of Session in Scotland) for grant of an injunction (or interdict) to restrain a person from misusing or misappropriating scheme assets. Under s 14, OPRA can also apply to the court for restitution where trustees have inappropriately made a loan to the employer (or some other form of self-investment) or made a refund to the employer from surplus in contravention of the provisions of the 1995 Act. The restitution order can be made against the employer or any other person who appears to the court to have been knowingly concerned in the contravention. Section 14 considerably extends the legal and equitable remedies available to pension schemes for tracing missing assets.

Directions

2.35 Section 49(5) requires Regulations to be made to force employers to pay benefits into a separate bank account if payments of benefit to members are supposed to be made by the employer, and it has not complied within a prescribed period. Section 15 allows OPRA to direct the trustees to make arrangements for payment to the members of the missing benefits, presumably from the bank account if the employer has segregated the funds, but otherwise from scheme assets. These provisions only seem likely to arise if the employer is acting as the paying agent of the trustees, for example where pensions are added to the staff pay-roll system.

2.36 OPRA can direct trustees to provide scheme members with a copy of a statement prepared by OPRA either in the next annual report or direct to scheme members (s 15(2), (3)).

2.37 Non-compliance with s 15 by trustees can lead to a prohibition/removal order under s 3 or a civil fine under s 10.

WINDING-UP SCHEMES

2.38 Section 11 allows OPRA to direct or authorise the winding-up of any occupational pension scheme if it is in the best interests of the scheme members to do so. OPRA can also wind-up a non-public service scheme if it believes it should be replaced or is no longer required, but only if the trustees or managers of the scheme, any other person with a power to amend the scheme or the employer, have applied for such an order. Section 12 gives similar powers to wind-up a public service scheme to the Minister of the Crown or Government department with responsibility for the public service scheme. These winding-up provisions are specifically stated to override the trust deed and rules of the pension scheme and statutory enactments covering public service schemes.

2.39 Section 161 provides for the repeal of the Pension Schemes Act 1993, ss 142, 143 which gave similar winding-up powers to the Occupational Pensions Board.

REVIEW OF DECISIONS

2.40 The decisions of OPRA are binding (s 96) although individuals affected by the more serious prohibition, disqualification or penalty orders can insist on a formal review. OPRA can also review its decisions at a later date on the application of 'a person appearing to them to be interested' if it believes there has been a change of circumstances or a mistake of fact or law. Further, OPRA can review its own decision for any reason within six months of that decision. The time period can be extended and OPRA can review its own decisions without an application at any time (s 96(6)). OPRA's review powers include power to vary, revoke or substitute orders. Questions of law only arising from the exercise of OPRA's powers of determination or any matter covered by Pt I of the 1995 Act can be referred to court if OPRA thinks fit or a person does not agree with OPRA's review or refusal to review. The decision of the court in the first instance will be binding (s 97(6)) so no appeal to the Court of Appeal can be made.

INVESTIGATIVE POWERS

2.41 Section 98 gives OPRA the power to force trustees, managers, professional advisers, employers or any person appearing to hold (or likely to hold) written information relevant to the discharge of its functions, to produce any such documents. Notice must be given in writing and any period for compliance will be stated in the notice. Section 102 does not require compliance if it would incriminate the individual or his or her spouse or if the documents are subject to legal professional privilege (or its equivalent in Scotland).

2.42 OPRA is given power by s 99 to send an inspector to enter premises at any reasonable time to make enquiries, search for documents or interview people. The inspector must believe that members of the scheme are employed at the premises or that the scheme administration is undertaken there or that scheme documents are kept on the premises. The right to entry does not extend to a private dwelling-house without a warrant issued by a justice of the peace. Section 100 contains detailed provisions for the issue of search warrants, the seizure of relevant documents and to require persons named in a warrant to provide an explanation of documents or to

2.42 *Occupational Pensions Regulatory Authority*

disclose their location. Any documents seized can be retained by OPRA for six months or until the end of legal proceedings (s 100(4)).

2.43 Failure to comply with the requirement to produce documents leads to a criminal penalty with a fine. Provision of false or misleading information or tampering with evidence involves a fine up to the statutory maximum and/or imprisonment (s 101).

DISCLOSURE OF INFORMATION

2.44 Section 103 allows OPRA to publish a report of an investigation of any case and its decision (which is absolutely privileged against defamation). This report will usually be in general terms because of the detailed restrictions on publishing confidential material.

2.45 Sections 104–109 deal with the disclosure of 'restricted information'. Generally, OPRA will not be able to disclose information it has obtained that is not already in the public domain without the consent of the person to whom it relates and, if different, the person from whom OPRA obtained it. The same restrictions apply to any person who receives such information from OPRA. This duty of confidentiality is lifted to cover disclosure—
- (a) for the purpose of enabling or assisting OPRA to discharge its functions (including obtaining legal advice);
- (b) with a view to the institution of, or assistance in, criminal or certain disciplinary proceedings;
- (c) to the Secretary of State and other listed regulators to assist them in discharging their duties (s 107); and
- (d) to the Secretary of State or the Department of Health and Social Services for Northern Ireland if it appears to be desirable or expedient in the interests of members of occupational pension schemes or in the public interest (s 108).

Section 109 specifically allows the Inland Revenue to disclose tax information to OPRA in certain circumstances.

3 Trustees

MEMBER-NOMINATED TRUSTEES AND DIRECTORS

Appointment and exemptions

3.1 Sections 16–21 of the 1995 Act set out the new provisions giving pension scheme members the right to appoint trustees for the first time. Recommendations 36–38 of the PLRC suggested mandatory appointment for final salary schemes of at least one-third of the trustees by scheme members with the employer being entitled to appoint the remainder. The recommendation for money purchase schemes was for two-thirds of the trustees to be member-nominated. These proposals have been weakened substantially. Member-nominated trustees are not now required for schemes—
  (a) where the employer has made a proposal for the continuance of existing arrangements, or adoption of new arrangements, for selection of trustees which has been accepted by active and pensioner members (and deferred pensioners if the trustees decide to include them in the vote);
  (b) within a 'prescribed class'; or
  (c) where the individual trustees consist of all the members.

3.2 The belief that the employer retains ultimate control of the trustee board through its power to appoint two-thirds of the trustees is hard to dislodge. The 1995 Act has not attempted to change the underlying rule of trust law that trustees have a duty to act on behalf of all the members of the scheme, whether they are nominated from management or represent trade unions or members generally. It would have been helpful if the 1995 Act had emphasised the duty to act impartially as part of the member trustee procedures. Nevertheless, the mere fact of the compulsory presence of member-nominated trustees should be of practical help in ensuring that trustees are told formally about proposals in their capacity as trustees rather than as management.

Corporate trustees

3.3 At a late stage in the passage of the Pensions Bill through Parliament, new provisions were introduced to cover the election by members of their own representatives where there is a corporate trustee connected with the company (ss 18, 19). Independent trustee companies are thus excluded. Section 18 creates the matching concept of 'member-nominated directors' within the corporate trustee who will be subject to the same election procedures as for member-nominated trustees. Section 18(8) provides that where a corporate trustee is a wholly-owned subsidiary of the sponsoring employer of two or more group pension schemes, the members are rolled into one big constituency for the purpose of electing their director candidates.

3.4 Section 18 is easy to apply where there is only one corporate trustee of a pension scheme. Some schemes, however, operate with a mixture of a corporate trustee and individual trustees and sometimes with two corporate trustees. Section 18

3.4 *Trustees*

applies 'where a company is a trustee of a trust scheme', not just where it is the sole trustee. The interaction of ss 16 and 18 is unclear where the corporate trustee is not acting alone. It is also difficult to see how the provisions for election and removal of member-nominated directors will fit with normal company law procedures where shareholders (often the sponsoring employer and a nominee) have an ultimate right to dismiss the directors. Articles of association will need to be re-examined for corporate trustees, but attempts to entrench member-nominated directors to comply with s 18(3)(b) will be difficult.

Equal status

3.5 The new regime for appointing member-nominated trustees will not affect existing entrenched non-statutory independent trustee appointments as much as was originally feared when the proposal for member nominations was coupled with an overriding right for the employer to select the balance. The main difficulty now for independent trustees, in particular 'protector trustees' given a casting vote in key circumstances such as a vote on the refund of surplus or admission of new employers, will arise from s 16(7). This provides that the member trustee arrangements must not provide for the functions of individual member-nominated trustees to differ from those of any other trustee except where OPRA makes an appointment or the statutory independent trustee rules apply. Interestingly, there is no similar provision for directors of a corporate trustee so 'golden votes' which are sometimes used in predator-proofing could be retained.

Small self-administered schemes

3.6 Pensioneer trustees with a limited role in small self-administered schemes may also have to become 'full' trustees to enable their scheme to comply with s 16(7), unless an exemption is prescribed for small self-administered schemes under s 17(4)(b). The exemption in s 17(4)(a) excludes a pension scheme from the member-nominated trustee requirements but only if 'the trustees of the scheme consist of all the members'. This exemption seems designed for small self-administered schemes, but the pensioneer trustee is usually not a member of the scheme but rather an independent external trustee unconnected with the business of the sponsoring employer. A wider exemption, excluding a scheme from these requirements if all the members were trustees, would have been more helpful if this was the intention.

Numbers

3.7 If the members wish to appoint member-nominated trustees or directors, there must be at least two (or one if the scheme has less than 100 members) and at least one-third of the total number of trustees. For the purpose of this numbers headcount, 'member' is defined in s 124 to include active members, deferred pensioners and pensioners, although Regulations could be made under s 125 to extend or restrict the meaning. Final salary and money purchase schemes are treated in an identical way. The members can ask to appoint more member-trustees but the employer is free to give or withhold approval to a greater number (ss 16(6), 18(6)).

Selection

3.8 A member-nominated trustee does not have to be a member of the scheme, which would allow a professional independent trustee to be appointed (although s 20(5) gives the employer a right to veto the appointment of a non-member). Section 21 envisages a prescribed 'statutory consultation procedure' to seek the active or passive approval of active and pensioner members to member-nominations or the approved statutory alternative. Deferred pensioners can only be consulted if the trustees decide to include them (s 21(8)(a)). Apart from the prescribed 'statutory consultation procedure' required to obtain the views of scheme members, the member trustee provisions will also take the form of the rather vague 'appropriate rules' described in s 20. These must either be approved under the statutory consultation procedure or prescribed, and have to 'make the provision required or authorised by' s 20 covering procedures for nomination and selection of member trustees.

Period of office

3.9 A member-nominated trustee or director must have a period of office lasting not less than three nor more than six years (ss 16(5), 18(5)). Re-selection at the end of the term is permitted by s 20(3) so 12 year (or longer) appointments are not ruled out. Sections 16(3) and 18(3) provide that a member-nominated trustee or director may only be removed by the unanimous agreement of all the other trustees or directors.

3.10 Sections 16(8) and 18(7) provide that ceasing to be a member of the scheme (which would result from opting-out or leaving service coupled, in both cases, with a transfer-out) triggers instant removal if the member-nominated trustee or director was a member of the scheme when appointed. Leaving the service of the employer but remaining a deferred pensioner in its scheme will not lead to removal. Retirement is also not a reason for removal. The PLRC debated the issue of pensioner-nominated trustees but rejected the idea of compulsion in favour of encouragement (Recommendation 37). The 1995 Act allows the member-nominated trustee category to include pensioner representatives but does not require one or more to be appointed. There is scope, however, for compulsory pensioner representation in the future as s 21(6) gives a wide power to modify all these provisions.

Compliance

3.11 Regulations made under s 21(4) will be required to set out time limits for the various stages of appointment of member-nominated trustees or directors, or agreement to the statutory permitted alternative. The employer will be liable to a civil penalty under s 10 if an alternative method is suggested but the statutory consultation procedure is ignored (ss 17(5), 19(5)). The trustees or directors have a duty to implement the statutory procedures or the permitted alternative (if chosen by the members) and will be liable to removal under s 3 and/or civil penalties under s 10 if they fail to comply (s 21(1), (2)).

INDEPENDENT TRUSTEES

3.12 Sections 22–26 broadly repeat the independent trustee provisions contained in the Pension Schemes Act 1993, ss 119–122 which are repealed by Sch 3. This protective legislation was introduced in 1990 following cases such as *Icarus*[1] and *Mettoy*[2] where liquidators were obliged to seek court guidance in view of conflicts of interest on winding-up pension schemes of insolvent employers.

3.12   *Trustees*

[1]   *Icarus (Hertford) Ltd v Driscoll* [1990] PLR 1.
[2]   *Mettoy Pension Trustees Ltd v Evans* [1991] 2 All ER 513.

3.13 The independent trustee provisions previously only applied if the pension scheme concerned was set up by trust deed. The words 'trust scheme' used in s 22 are defined more widely in s 124(1) to mean 'an occupational pension scheme established under a trust'. This could now include a pension scheme set up by deed, deed poll, company resolution or declaration.

3.14 The previous legislation required the insolvency practitioner to appoint an independent trustee on the insolvency of a company or individual who is 'the employer of persons in the description or category of employment to which the scheme relates'. The requirement to have an independent trustee was then lifted if another employer took over the business so as to satisfy that definition, even if it did not assume responsibility for the scheme (which could then be left in a conflict situation without an independent trustee). Section 22(2) of the 1995 Act confirms that the independent trustee requirement is lifted only where the new employer acts as such 'in relation to the scheme'.

3.15 Section 23 requires the insolvency practitioner to appoint an independent trustee (if one does not already exist) 'as soon as reasonably practicable' and within any prescribed period. The previous legislation had no time limit so appointments were frequently delayed for several months at a critical period for the pension scheme concerned.

3.16 Section 24 repeats the previous legislation permitting members of the scheme to apply to court for appointment of an independent trustee by the insolvency practitioner if no action is taken within the new time limit.

3.17 Section 25 automatically removes the employer as trustee of a scheme if, on appointment of the independent trustee, it was the sole trustee of the scheme. It also provides for the exercise of trustee and employer powers by the independent trustee to the exclusion of those other parties. Unfortunately, the wording has not been clarified to assist interpretation of which powers an employer exercises 'at his discretion but only as trustee of the power'.

3.18 The insolvency practitioner or official receiver continues to be required under s 26 to give information to the trustees in response to a request if it is reasonably required for scheme administration. The trustees may be required to cover some of the expenses of such an exercise out of the scheme if they cannot otherwise be recovered by the insolvency practitioner.

PERSONAL BENEFIT OF TRUSTEES

3.19 Many pension schemes contain a rule allowing trustees who are also members of their pension scheme to benefit from the trust by drawing their own basic scale entitlements as well as including themselves in any improvements granted at their discretion. This has been seen as a hang-over from the law of private family trusts, where the duty of a trustee not to profit from his own position tended to cause more problems and temptations. Many modern pension scheme documents do not include such a power on the basis that it would be implied as members do not choose to become trustees. It would certainly be a nonsense if a trustee who was also a member could not draw his own basic scale entitlement because of such a rule.

3.20 The cases of *British Coal*[1] and *Drexel Burnham Lambert*[2] cast doubt on the implied protections for trustees in situations where their interests and duty conflict and on the efficacy of any protective powers granted by the trust instrument. Pressure was brought to bear on the Government to create a statutory exemption to put the position beyond doubt before the new compulsory member trustee provisions came into force. Section 39 was eventually inserted at a late stage in the passage of the Pensions Bill. The difficulty in drafting the section lay between giving a blanket mandate to trustees to benefit themselves without breach of trust in all circumstances, and protecting trustees in connection with a reasonable exercise of their duties which incidentally benefited themselves. The wording of s 39 is intended to leave open the possibilities of a breach of trust claim under the common law rules as set out in *Drexel* in cases of flagrant abuse, but otherwise to allow trustees to run their scheme normally even if they receive a personal benefit in the same way as other members through the exercise of their discretionary powers. The message is that each case must be looked at on its own merits.

[1] *British Coal Corpn v British Coal Staff Superannuation Scheme Trustees Ltd* [1995] 1 All ER 912.
[2] *Manning v Drexel Burnham Lambert Holdings Ltd* [1994] PLR 75.

VOTING

3.21 The trustees of a pension scheme are given a new overriding power by s 32 to act by majority vote in different circumstances and to set a quorum unless the scheme rules require unanimity. This is unlikely to upset carefully drafted predator-proofing measures inserted in a trust deed and rules to maintain the balance of power between employer and trustees. If majority vote is allowed, there is a new statutory requirement (s 32(2)(b)) that notice of meetings must be given. Details of the method of notification and timing will be prescribed by Regulations. The threat of removal as a trustee under s 3 and/or civil penalties under s 10 will apply if the notification procedures are not followed.

3.22 There are exceptions to these majority vote provisions covering special appointments of trustees by OPRA, removal of member-nominated trustees (which must always require the agreement of all the other trustees) and the powers of independent trustees appointed by an insolvency practitioner. These voting provisions do not appear to govern the meetings of directors of a corporate trustee.

INVESTMENTS

New investment powers

3.23 Section 34 of the 1995 Act gives trustees of a pension scheme a new statutory power to make an investment of any kind as if they were absolutely entitled to the

3.23   *Trustees*

assets of the scheme. This can be restricted by the terms of the trust deed and rules of a particular scheme. The previous statutory powers of investment were contained in the cautious list of investments permitted by the Trustee Investments Act 1961 (which is not repealed by the 1995 Act). In view of its limited scope, most occupational pension schemes contain a rule with more detailed and wider-ranging investment powers, often including power to invest in modern products and activities such as the derivatives market, stock lending and sub-underwriting which are not always classed as investments. The use in s 34 of the word 'investment' will no doubt be further analysed in the courts.

Duty of skill and care

3.24   Section 33 does not impose a new statutory duty for trustees or investment managers to take care or to exercise skill in the performance of their investment duties. It merely states that where such an obligation exists under 'any rule of law', it cannot be excluded or restricted by the pension scheme documentation. The duty of trustees to exercise care and skill in the performance of their duties would normally extend to the delegation of those functions to an investment manager. Section 33 will limit the effect of the standard exoneration and indemnity clauses found in many pension schemes which attempt to relieve the trustees from liability for wrongdoing unless the trustees are guilty of wilful default. Those exoneration clauses have not been tested in the courts but will now be of no assistance in the investment area. Either the new statutory exoneration in s 34(4) will apply, or the trustees will be unprotected against their own negligence or that of their agents under s 34(5).

Delegation

3.25   The provisions of s 34 were subject to considerable debate and change during the passage of the Pensions Bill. The interaction of the new restricted power to delegate and the improved protection for trustees from the acts of their agents did not at first sit happily with the terms of the Financial Services Act 1986 ('FSA'). When the FSA was brought into force in July 1988 to coincide with the major changes to city financial institutions and the new system of self-regulation, it was made clear that trustees should become authorised under the FSA or delegate their investment powers to an FSA-authorised manager. Trustees tended to divorce themselves from giving investment advice both to scheme members about general pensions and savings options and with regard to day-to-day management of scheme investments. This led to a tightening-up of custodian services and formal written investment management agreements. The FSA could in some ways be held partly responsible for the mis-selling of personal pensions which were launched at the same time and the loss of control many trustees felt through being effectively excluded from the investment process. The only areas left for non-FSA authorised trustees to take decisions on investment matters relate to 'strategic' investment decisions, and asset allocation between different classes of investments. Even those duties are often delegated to the actuary or investment manager.

3.26   Trustees will be strictly governed by s 34(2) with regard to delegation of their investment decisions. They must delegate their investment powers to a fund manager authorised under s 191(2) of FSA (which includes overseas and exempted persons) unless—

    (a)   they delegate their powers to a sub-committee of trustees (which must consist of two trustees as a minimum);

(b) they are absent abroad and delegate their discretionary powers to another person by power of attorney under the Trustee Act 1925, s 25; or

(c) a non-FSA authorised fund manager is not advising the trustees by way of 'investment business' as defined in the FSA (which is normally interpreted as not running a business for profit or dealing with assets excluded from the FSA).

Commercial property and cash are outside the definition of 'investments' for FSA purposes. This is causing concern, particularly for property managers who fear that big institutional investors will be forced to re-invest in commercial property funds rather than owning property direct. The emphasis of the minimum funding requirement (see below paras 7.1–7.20) on gilts and equities is also seen as discouraging direct investment in property.

Sub-delegation

3.27 The Trustee Act 1925 does not give trustees a statutory power to sub-delegate which explains why such powers are frequently contained in the trust deed and rules of pension schemes. Section 34 was amended at the very last stage of the passage of the Pensions Bill to extend its provisions to the delegation and sub-delegation of the trustees' investment function. This was done to cover the position under many common investment funds where the trustees of two or more pension schemes in the same group pool their investments under the control of an administrator which is often a different entity from the trustees. Trustees participating in common investment funds will still need to look at the pooling documentation carefully so as to ensure that they retain responsibility for appointment (or delegated appointment) of the investment manager for the pooled fund.

Exoneration

3.28 The importance of the distinction between delegating to a FSA-authorised fund manager and delegating to the trustee body or a non-authorised person is highlighted in s 34(4). This exonerates the trustees from responsibility for the act or default of any fund manager appointed under s 34(2)(a), subject to the trustees checking the FSA-authorised manager has the appropriate knowledge and experience, is carrying out his work competently and is complying with the other investment-related requirements of the 1995 Act. This protection does not indemnify the pension scheme from any losses caused by a defaulting fund manager, but it does relieve the trustees from personal liability for making good the loss. Under the previous law, trustees would have needed to apply to court under the Trustee Act 1925, s 61 to request such an exoneration or test the efficacy of an exoneration contained in their trust deed and rules. The new statutory exoneration will be helpful to trustees although the price for that safety net is that trustees are being forced more than ever to delegate their investment powers to an FSA-regulated investment manager.

Statement of investment principles

3.29 The requirement of s 35 for trustees to prepare a written statement of investment principles governing decisions about investments in their pension scheme is an attempt to clarify the grey area of asset allocation and strategic investment decisions. These important matters are still left unregulated by the FSA, but the 1995

3.29 *Trustees*

Act seeks to impose a structure at the most basic level covering the need for diversification and suitability and compliance with the new minimum funding requirement as well as risk. The statement must be made after the trustees have considered the written advice of a person they believe to be qualified to advise them and after consulting the employer (s 35(5)). The need to consult the employer means that there must be a dialogue, although the trustees can ignore the employer's wishes. Section 35(4) was inserted at a very late stage in the passage of the Pensions Bill to emphasise that the employer cannot interfere at all with the selection of investments. The final decision must rest with the trustees. The definition of 'employer' in s 124 means all the employers participating in the scheme with active members. So this consultation process could be quite lengthy for a multi-employer scheme and even worse for an industry-wide scheme.

3.30 The preparation of the written statement of investment principles will be of limited effect if it results in standardised 'pieces of paper' being prepared by fund managers. As an attempt to bring the important question of asset allocation into greater prominence, it is helpful, although it does reinforce the artificial divide between investment management (which trustees are strongly encouraged to delegate to obtain the new statutory exoneration) and asset allocation (where they are forced to take an active role).

Choosing investments

3.31 If the trustees of a pension scheme or their FSA-authorised or exempted fund manager chooses an investment, they must check that it complies with the statement of investment principles, vet it for suitability generally and consider the need for diversification. Section 36 brings these trust law concepts into statutory form and ties them in with the new statement of investment principles. If the trustees are making the decision themselves (rather than delegating their powers to a fund manager) they must additionally seek advice in advance on suitability and diversification from a person authorised or exempted under the FSA (complying with the list set out in s 36(6)(a) of the 1995 Act) or a suitably qualified person if the advice is not investment business within the FSA. This implies that even where trustees are authorised themselves under the FSA, they must seek independent advice each time an investment decision is taken and also from time to time to justify retaining investments. The professional advice must be given to trustees (or subsequently confirmed) in writing. Breach of these requirements can lead to a prohibition/removal order under s 3 or a civil penalty under s 10.

Self-investment

3.32 The limit on self-investment in employer-related investments first introduced by Social Security Act 1990 is maintained in the Pensions Act 1995, s 40. The Pension Schemes Act 1993, s 112 is repealed by Sch 3 to the 1995 Act. One of the problems with the previous legislation was that there was no penalty for non-compliance other than a claim by members for breach of trust. Section 40 is now enforced by the threat of a prohibition/removal order against the trustees and civil or criminal penalties.

3.33 It is unfortunate that the 1995 Act has not considered the effect of *Wright v Ginn*[1] which held that the Trustee Act 1925, s 4 allows trustees to ignore statutory restrictions (at present 5% of the assets of the pension scheme) in certain circumstances. The implication must be that the Government intends the 5% restriction to be strictly observed although OPRA and the courts could presumably exercise some discretion in enforcement proceedings.

1   *Wright and Others v Ginn and Another* [1994] OPLR 83.

DISCLOSURE AND RECORD KEEPING

Disclosure Regulations

3.34   The 1995 Act leaves in place the Pension Schemes Act 1993, ss 113, 115 covering disclosure of information to members but, strangely, repeals s 114 and replaces it with s 41 in the 1995 Act. It is most unfortunate that the disclosure requirements are now scattered between this new s 41, the Pension Schemes Act 1993, ss 113, 115 and separate Regulations made under both Acts. Section 41 is in similar terms to the Pension Schemes Act 1993, s 114 (covering provision of audited accounts and actuarial valuations to members) but has been expanded to cover the new minimum funding requirement certificates and reports prepared by the actuary or the trustees or managers. This seems to be the only reason for including these provisions in the 1995 Act, rather than amending the Pension Schemes Act 1993.

3.35   One of the main criticisms of the disclosure of information requirements currently set out in Regulations made under the Pension Schemes Act 1993, ss 113, 114, is that there are no sanctions for non-compliance by trustees apart from a court order to comply with a notice issued by the Secretary of State or an aggrieved person. There are still no criminal or civil penalties imposed for non-compliance with the disclosure requirements, but trustees will be liable to a prohibition/removal order under s 3.

Records of meetings

3.36   Section 49 provides for new Regulations to require trustees to keep records of their meetings and 'sub-committee' meetings and books and records relating to 'prescribed transactions'. These duties might also be extended by Regulations to require participating employers and advisers or administrators to keep books and records relating to prescribed transactions.

Bank account

3.37   Section 49(1) forces trustees to run a separately named bank account for their pension scheme at an institution authorised under the Banking Act 1987. The obscure provisions of s 49(5) concerning segregation of funds by the employer into a separate bank account have been covered earlier (see above para 2.35).

Member contributions

3.38   Section 49(8) imposes a new strict liability criminal offence punishable by a fine and/or imprisonment (for company directors) if the employer deducts member

3.38 *Trustees*

contributions from payroll and fails to pay them over to the trustees within a period to be prescribed by Regulations. This is an extremely valuable protection for scheme members in theory although it remains to be seen how it will be policed and enforced.

TIME OFF WORK AND TRAINING

3.39 The mandatory imposition of member-nominated trustees has created a greater need for trustee training and paid time off work to carry out trustee duties if trustees are no longer drawn primarily from management. The new arrangements for trustees to perform their duties are formalised in ss 42–46. These allow all trustees to take paid time off work to perform trustee duties or be trained. Trustee training is not, however, made compulsory. Trustees will have to decide for themselves whether they think basic or updating trustee training is needed and review courses available. The cost will presumably be met under the normal expenses rule of the pension scheme concerned and treated as a trustee expense. The time taken must be 'reasonable' bearing in mind the effect on the employer's business.

3.40 The failure of the employer to allow a trustee to take time off work, or to pay him or her for that period of absence, must be pursued by an industrial tribunal complaint by the trustee within three months. A longer period is permitted if the tribunal considers the delay has been reasonable and justified (s 44). The industrial tribunal can make a compensation award against the employer under s 45 on both counts.

3.41 Section 46 was inserted at the final stages of the passage of the Pensions Bill to protect the employment position of member-nominated trustees and directors. All trustees will be given employment protection so that dismissal or redundancy will be treated as unfair under the Employment Protection (Consolidation) Act 1978 if the principal reason for it was performance by the employee of trustee functions.

CROWN APPLICATION

3.42 Section 121 confirms that all the provisions of Pt I of the 1995 Act apply to an occupational pension scheme managed by or on behalf of the Crown. References to 'trustees or managers' are to be treated as including the Crown (or a person acting on behalf of the Crown) in that capacity.

4 Dispute resolution

COMPLAINTS PROCEDURE

4.1 Pension schemes will be required to set up a formal complaints procedure under s 50 of the 1995 Act although most of the detail will not be known until Regulations are published. The Government indicated in its response to PLRC recommendation 148 that small schemes with less than twelve members would be excluded.

4.2 The trustees or managers of a pension scheme must nominate a person to arbitrate on any complaint, and review any decision given by that person if the complainant is still dissatisfied. The complaint and all decisions must be put in writing although reasons for decisions do not have to be given. The trustees or managers are liable to a civil fine under s 10 for failure to set up such an arrangement. Strictly, a prohibition/removal order under s 3 could apply, although this has been deliberately excluded from the wording of s 50.

PENSIONS OMBUDSMAN

Expanded jurisdiction

4.3 The 1995 Act considerably expands the role of the Pensions Ombudsman by amending Pt X of the Pension Schemes Act 1993. Under the original legislation, the Pensions Ombudsman could only investigate complaints of injustice in consequence of maladministration in connection with the acts or omissions of the trustees or managers of an occupational or personal pension scheme, or any dispute of fact or law between the trustees or managers of a scheme and an 'authorised complainant'. These individuals were limited to scheme members, spouses or dependants of a deceased member, and persons querying their status as potential members or beneficiaries.

4.4 Section 157 amends the Pension Schemes Act 1993, ss 146–151 by widening the Pensions Ombudsman's powers to investigate and determine—
   (a) claims of maladministration from persons responsible for the management of a scheme against someone else who is responsible for management of the scheme. 'Persons responsible for the management of a scheme' is defined as the trustees or managers of the scheme and the employer. It will therefore now be possible for the trustees to refer allegations of maladministration by the employer to the Pensions Ombudsman or vice versa;
   (b) claims by trustees or managers of one scheme alleging maladministration by the trustees or managers of another scheme;
   (c) disputes of fact or law between trustees or managers of a scheme and the employer of the same scheme; and
   (d) disputes of fact or law between trustees or managers of one scheme and trustees or managers of another scheme.

4.5 *Dispute resolution*

4.5 It should be noted that the definition of 'managers' is different in the 1995 Act and the Pension Schemes Act 1993. For the purposes of the new jurisdiction of the Pensions Ombudsman, 'trustees and managers' can be specified by Regulations made by the Secretary of State under the Pension Schemes Act 1993, s 178. The term is also given a special meaning in the Pension Schemes Act 1993, s 146(8) where the scheme's administrators are specifically covered but only in relation to public service pension schemes or those in Northern Ireland. The case of *Century Life PLC*[1] appealed against a ruling of the Pensions Ombudsman that an insurance company came within the Pensions Ombudsman's jurisdiction as a 'manager'. Although the term 'manager' is still not helpfully defined under the Pension Schemes Act 1993, the new s 146(4) (inserted by s 157 of the 1995 Act) will allow Regulations to be made to include within the Pensions Ombudsman's jurisdiction a person or body if it 'is concerned with the financing or administration of, or the provision of benefits under, the scheme'. This would extend beyond trustees, managers or employers and could cover investment managers, custodians, benefit consultants and in-house pensions administrators, if interpreted widely by Regulations.

1 *Century Life plc v Pensions Ombudsman* [1995] PLR 135.

4.6 The concept of the 'authorised complainant' has been replaced by the phrase 'actual or potential beneficiaries'. The Government indicated in its White Paper, in response to the PLRC's recommendation 150, that it was considering extending the Pensions Ombudsman's jurisdiction to collective disputes but this does not seem to have been done.

Interest

4.7 The main sanction of the Pensions Ombudsman continues to be the power to direct persons responsible for the management of the scheme (trustees or managers and employers) to take or refrain from taking any action he thinks appropriate to resolve the complaint. The 1995 Act still gives no power to the Pensions Ombudsman to award costs like a court. Section 160, however, inserts a new Pension Schemes Act 1993, s 151A. This gives the Pensions Ombudsman a new power to direct interest to be paid in respect of any benefit under the scheme which he rules should have been paid earlier. The interest will be at a prescribed rate.

Costs and expenses

4.8 Section 158 amends the Pension Schemes Act 1993, s 149(3), thus allowing the Pensions Ombudsman to pay such travelling expenses (and compensation for loss of remunerative time) as are determined by the Secretary of State to claimants, their advisers and witnesses who are requested to attend any oral hearing. This provision matches both Sch 1, para 17 and Sch 2, para 18 which give OPRA and the Pensions Compensation Board similar powers to reimburse expenses.

Disclosure

4.9 Section 159 (which adds the Pension Schemes Act 1993, s 149(5)–(7)) gives the Pensions Ombudsman new powers to disclose information to listed regulatory bodies if he considers it would assist in the discharge of their functions. The list is similar, but not identical to, the list permitted for disclosure by the Pensions Compensation Board under s 114(7).

Staff

4.10 Section 156 amends the Pension Schemes Act 1993, s 145(4). The Pensions Ombudsman is given similar powers to OPRA and the Compensation Board to appoint his own staff and to delegate his duties to them (apart from determination of disputes and complaints). Previously, all staff for the Pensions Ombudsman's office had to be 'made available' by the Secretary of State.

5 Professional advisers and "whistleblowing"

PROFESSIONAL ADVISERS

Duty to appoint auditor, actuary and fund manager

5.1 Most occupational pension schemes are serviced by an auditor, actuary and investment manager and frequently have their own legal advisers. Under s 47(4) of the 1995 Act the auditor, actuary, fund manager, legal adviser and any other person exercising any 'prescribed functions' in relation to a particular pension scheme are grouped together (but only if they are appointed by the trustees or managers) and defined as 'professional advisers'. Until now, however, the appointments of professional advisers were often made by the employer who made the advice available to the trustees, or by reference to the name of the scheme, leaving the identity of the client vague.

5.2 Section 47(1) contains a new statutory duty requiring the trustees or managers of a pension scheme to appoint an auditor and an actuary for their pension scheme. 'Managers' is defined in s 124 to mean the persons responsible for the management of the scheme, but only where the pension scheme is not established under trust, so this duty will normally fall on trustees. Section 47(2) extends this duty to appointment by the trustees (or managers) of a separate fund manager to tie in with the requirements of s 34 where the pension scheme has 'investments' within the FSA (which will cover most pension schemes unless they are invested in cash and property only). The actuary appointment must be given to a named individual (not a firm or company), presumably because of the need for individual professional guidance controls. The auditor and investment manager can be named individuals or a firm. There is no statutory requirement for trustees to appoint a legal adviser but, by virtue of s 47(3), they are at risk if they accept legal advice from another source.

Penalties

5.3 Section 47(3) states that if the auditor, actuary, fund manager or legal adviser is appointed by someone other than the trustees or managers (usually by the sponsoring employer or possibly by the members or a trade union which has sought independent advice), the trustees will be liable to removal under s 3 if they place reliance on the skill or judgment of that person. Both trustees and managers will also be liable to a civil penalty under s 10.

5.4 The purist view is that s 47(3) means that trustees must appoint their own professional advisers in all circumstances, who must be different from the advisers appointed by the employer or any other party. In difficult situations, such as a conflict over the refund of surplus, the trustees and employer will frequently seek separate advice. But it seems odd that the trustees are supposed to ignore any advice given to the employer which they may be shown and would normally take into consideration in reaching their own view. The more realistic interpretation of s 47(3) is that trustees can use the same legal advisers as the employer, members or unions, provided that first the advisers are formally appointed by the trustees as well as by the employer, and secondly it is made clear in the terms of the written appointment that in the event of a conflict between the two parties, the professional adviser will only act for one named party. This view is endorsed by Recommendation 87 of the PLRC concerning appointment of auditors (but not actuaries) and by the Department of Social Security, but if trustees wish to err on the side of caution, they will appoint their own independent professional advisers.

5.5 Section 47(8) provides that the failure to appoint an auditor, actuary or fund manager renders trustees liable to a prohibition/removal order under s 3 and a civil penalty under s 10. Managers are also liable to a civil penalty under s 10 but cannot be removed by OPRA.

Disclosure

5.6 Regulations made under s 47(9) may force the employer, and its own auditor or appointed actuary, to disclose information to the trustees or managers of a pension scheme and to the scheme's professional advisers. The trustees or managers also have a new statutory duty to disclose information and documents to the scheme's professional advisers appointed by them. The penalties for non-disclosure are civil fines under s 10 plus the threat of a prohibition/removal order for trustees under s 3.

Exceptions

5.7 Section 47(5) provides for Regulations to make exceptions to these appointment rules, and to specify the qualifications and experience or approval required for appointment as a professional adviser. The 1995 Act also plans for separate Regulations to be issued under s 41(5) to prescribe the persons who may act as auditor or actuary, or their qualifications and experience, for pension schemes otherwise exempted from s 47. This reinforces the requirement that a pension scheme must have its own designated actuary and auditor even if they are not appointed by the trustees or managers.

Ineligibility

5.8 Section 27 creates a new category of persons who are ineligible to act as a trustee or professional adviser. Ineligible persons can be differentiated from disqualified persons who were originally allowed to be trustees but whose conduct has led to automatic or OPRA-driven disqualification.

5.9 Section 27(1) provides that a trustee (or any person connected with, or an associate of, such a trustee) is ineligible to act as an auditor or actuary of the same pension scheme. Section 27(2), however, provides a big exception to this rule for actuaries (but not, strangely, for auditors). A person will still be able to act as actuary of a pension scheme under s 27(2) if any other director, partner or employee of his firm is a trustee of the same scheme. 'Firm' is defined in s 124 to mean a body corporate or partnership while s 123 defines connected and associated persons by reference to the Insolvency Act 1986. There is an allowance for certain 'prescribed' exceptions from this rule.

5.10 *Professional advisers and "whistleblowing"*

5.10 The penalty for acting as an auditor or actuary when ineligible is a criminal offence punishable by a fine and/or imprisonment under s 28. In addition, a trustee who acts as auditor or actuary is liable to removal under s 3. If a connected or associated person acts as auditor or actuary when ineligible, the trustee is again liable to removal under s 3.

BLOWING THE WHISTLE

Auditor and actuary

5.11 The duly appointed auditor and actuary (but not the fund manager or legal adviser) have a new statutory duty under s 48 to report certain irregularities to OPRA. Section 48 is itself called 'Blowing the Whistle'. This was criticised in Standing Committee as being unsatisfactory as a technical term but was defended by the Government on the basis that the term had no legal effect but helped people understand what the section was about. Alternative descriptions would be 'shop the client' or, less controversially, 'duty to inform'.

5.12 Section 48 provides that the scheme auditor or actuary must give a written report to OPRA if he has reasonable cause to believe that any duty relevant to the administration of the scheme imposed by statute or 'rule of law' has been ignored by the trustees or managers, the employer or any professional adviser, and that non-compliance is likely to be of material significance in the exercise by OPRA of its functions. This is a heavy burden for auditors and actuaries, particularly given the subjective nature of the various tests and the guesswork involved. The individual will have to decide if certain facts point to a breach of a material nature and then whether such a breach will be seen as such by OPRA.

Other professional advisers

5.13 At a late stage in the passage of the Pensions Bill through Parliament a new requirement was inserted (now s 48(4)). This encourages professional advisers (other than the auditor and actuary), the trustees, managers or persons involved in the administration of the scheme (but not members), to 'blow the whistle' and submit a written report to OPRA if they believe there has been material non-compliance. It does not impose a duty.

Statutory protection

5.14 Section 48(5) applies to any persons with a mandatory or voluntary power under the 1995 Act to 'blow the whistle' in connection with an occupational pension scheme. It gives them a statutory protection from breach of duty to their clients where they have provided a written report to OPRA. There are exceptions for legal advisers who will not be protected if they choose to disclose documents or information covered by legal professional privilege (or its equivalent in Scotland). It is not entirely clear how widely a court would interpret s 48(5) with regard to any 'duty' to which a professional adviser is subject. The duty presumably covers confidentiality but would not necessarily extend to give protection for breach of a general duty of care or negligence.

5.15 The need for the professional adviser to double check information before making a report to OPRA could alert an employer to the possibility of discovery of malpractice. The statutory protection against the consequences of disclosure unfortunately ignores the real world where such disclosures are likely to be perceived as hostile by the trustees or employer. Whistleblowing may well lead to dismissal as professional adviser, particularly if the breach reported is technical and has been put right by the time OPRA investigates. Instead of increasing awareness among professional advisers, the requirement to 'blow the whistle' may mean that trustees and employers will involve them less in the administration of the pension scheme and be more wary of raising, or admitting to, problems.

5.16 The whistleblowing requirements impose a new positive obligation on auditors and actuaries to inform OPRA of their suspicions of malpractice in a pension scheme based on a subjective analysis of facts or information received. This seems to mark a growing trend of the Government to require individuals to take action rather than standing by and waiting to be found out. Self-assessment for income tax returns is an obvious example. The extension of the confidentiality protections for other professional advisers and parties such as custodians, administrators and trustees or fund managers in return for voluntary reporting of suspicions to OPRA is helpful.

Penalties

5.17 Failing to 'blow the whistle' by an auditor or actuary invokes s 48(7) and makes the adviser liable to a civil penalty under s 10. OPRA also has wide powers under s 48(8)–(13) to disqualify the auditor or actuary from acting for the particular scheme concerned and to extend this to a total ban on acting for any pension scheme. This is potentially a very severe penalty as it could prevent an individual from carrying on his normal occupation without the involvement of his professional body. A disqualification order brings with it instant removal from office as the named scheme auditor or actuary (s 48(11)). Continuing to act in defiance is a criminal offence under s 48(12) leading to a fine and/or imprisonment. The rights of the auditor or actuary to a review of OPRA's decision on disqualification are less wide than for a trustee who is disqualified. A review under s 96 will only apply as of right if the auditor or actuary has been fined under s 10 for failure to 'blow the whistle'. Otherwise, the only appeal possible from OPRA's decision is on a point of law under s 97.

Whistleblower Protection Bill

5.18 A new Bill just introduced into Parliament has all-party support. The Whistleblower Protection Bill would give 'whistleblowers' new legal rights against dismissal or reprisal. It is intended to protect employees who report their employers to regulators. Employers would be encouraged to set up internal mechanisms for monitoring serious concerns raised by staff although employees could by-pass such processes if the complaint was urgent. This type of protection could be of assistance to pension scheme members who report suspected pensions malpractice by their employer to OPRA.

5.19   *Professional advisers and "whistleblowing"*

Personal pensions

5.19   Section 147 applies the concept of 'blowing the whistle' to personal pension schemes, although here it is described as 'monitoring'. The provisions only apply to appropriate (ie contracted-out) personal pension schemes. Section 147 inserts the Pension Schemes Act 1993, s 33A. This provides that if any person acting as an auditor or actuary to an appropriate scheme has reasonable cause to believe that it is in breach of any of the certification requirements set out in the Pension Schemes Act 1993, ss 26–32 (such as failing to identify protected rights), a written report must immediately be given to the Secretary of State. Again, the auditor or actuary need only make the report if they believe failure to satisfy the requirement is likely to be of material significance in the exercise by the Secretary of State of his supervisory functions over appropriate schemes.

5.20   Statutory protection from breach of duty to their clients in connection with provision of a written report to the Secretary of State by the auditor or actuary is given in the Pension Schemes Act 1993, s 33A(2).

6 Indexation

PRESERVATION AND REVALUATION PRECEDENTS

6.1 The unfairness of the position of the early leaver in a final salary scheme led to the introduction of the preservation legislation in the Social Security Act 1973 (with a compulsory deferred pension after five years' qualifying service which was then reduced to a two year period by the Social Security Act 1986 with effect from 6 April 1988). The severe effects of high inflation on the final salary pension promise were eventually counteracted in the Social Security Act 1986. This introduced revaluation (at an annual rate calculated in line with the increase in the retail prices index up to a maximum of five per cent) to limit the devaluation of deferred pensions. It was limited to revaluation of pensions accrued after 1 January 1985 until the Social Security Act 1990 extended revaluation to all service for members who left service after 1 January 1991.

LIMITED PRICE INDEXING

6.2 The improved protection of the deferred pensions of early leavers from the effects of inflation led to the Government's wish to protect the value of pensions in payment in a similar way to preserve purchasing power. The Social Security Act 1990 introduced the concept of limited price indexing ('LPI') which would require pensions in payment (as well as in deferment) to be increased at an annual rate calculated in line with the retail prices index up to a maximum of five per cent. This was a logical extension of revaluation but brought with it further expense for employers. In view of uncertainty about the financial implications of the *Barber*[1] judgment in the European Court of Justice and equalisation of normal retirement ages for men and women, the Government postponed the start date for the new requirements to apply LPI to pensions accrued after an 'appointed day'. The Pension Schemes Act 1993, s 103 was in fact never brought into force and is now replaced by ss 51–54 of the 1995 Act. The Government also intended to force final salary schemes in surplus to use those funds to grant retrospective LPI increases to pensions accrued before the 'appointed day'. Again, the Pension Schemes Act 1993, s 104 was not brought into force for the same *Barber* reason and has now been dropped completely.

---

[1] *Barber v Guardian Royal Exchange* (C-262/88) [1990] ECR I–1889, ECJ.

6.3 The one part of the Social Security Act 1990 LPI package that was brought into immediate effect was consolidated to become the Pension Schemes Act 1993, s 108. It provided that no surplus could be refunded to an employer on a winding-up, or while the scheme was ongoing, without the grant of LPI covering all pensionable service. This has been carried forward into the 1995 Act and made even more stringent.

6.4 *Indexation*

NEW INDEXATION PROVISIONS

Repeals and scope

6.4   Schedule 3 to the 1995 Act repeals the Pension Schemes Act 1993, ss 102–108 which are replaced by ss 51–54 and parts of ss 37, 76 and 77 (covering payments of surplus to an employer). The new indexation provisions are wider as they cover money purchase schemes (s 51) and some personal pensions (s 162). The only exceptions are for public service pension schemes (which already provide full index-linking) and pensions deriving from free-standing AVC schemes ('FSAVCs') and other in-house additional voluntary contributions ('AVCs').

Final salary schemes

6.5   Benefits in an exempt approved (or potentially exempt approved) final salary occupational pension scheme accruing in respect of service after the indexation provisions are brought into force (likely to be 6 April 1997 to match the changes to guaranteed minimum pensions) must now be increased automatically by LPI (s 51). As a result of the changes to the contracting-out system, guaranteed minimum pensions will not accrue after April 1997. This gave the Government its chance to withdraw its own index-linking on the guaranteed minimum pension element of pensions in payment for the future, and switch the entire cost of indexation on post-1997 accruals to private sector schemes. There is now a symmetry between statutory revaluation in deferment and indexation to pensions in payment but there will be a matching increase in future service costs for some employers. In Appendix 5 to the White Paper, however, the Government said that only four per cent of members are in pension schemes which do not provide increases to pensions in payment and more than half of scheme members are already granted LPI or more favourable increases.

Money purchase schemes

6.6   LPI is specifically extended for the first time by s 51 to cover exempt approved (or potentially exempt approved) money purchase schemes where a pension is attributable to payments in respect of employment on or after the indexation provisions are brought into force.

6.7   The crucial difference for employers is that the members bear the cost of their own LPI in a money purchase scheme whereas the employer may be forced to improve the benefit structure at its own expense by awarding LPI in a final salary scheme. The cost-saving options for final salary scheme employers are to change the basic accrual rate to a less favourable basis to allow for the effect of LPI (for example, by cutting an accrual rate of $\frac{1}{60}$th for each year of pensionable service without LPI to $\frac{1}{80}$th with LPI), to increase the member contribution rate (or make a non-contributory scheme contributory) or to convert the scheme to a money purchase basis.

6.8   Section 54 sets out the basis for calculating LPI by reference to the rate set by the Secretary of State each year for revaluation purposes under the Pension Schemes Act 1993.

Additional voluntary contributions

6.9 At a very late stage in the passage of the Pensions Bill, all pensions deriving from the payment of AVCs and FSAVCs were exempted from the requirement to provide LPI.

Early retirement

6.10 Section 52 provides that no LPI increases have to be paid if a member takes early retirement until the member reaches age 55. Once the member reaches age 55, any 'missing' LPI increases have to be calculated. The pension from age 55 must then be paid at the level which would have applied if LPI had been awarded throughout (but without arrears). There is an exception for members who retire on grounds of ill-health when LPI must be awarded from the date of retirement if under age 55.

Set-offs

6.11 A member's pension can be increased in any tax year above the new LPI statutory requirement set by s 51 (and the increase for pre-April 1997 contracted-out service preserved in the Pension Schemes Act 1993, s 109). If so, the excess can be carried forward. Any increase in excess of the legal minimum can be used to offset the LPI increase required in the next tax year under s 53.

CONTRACTING-OUT

6.12 Section 55 amends the Pension Schemes Act 1993, s 109. Final salary occupational pension schemes only have liability to pay three per cent increases to guaranteed minimum pensions in payment accrued between the tax year 1988-89 (when the State gave up liability for full indexation on guaranteed minimum pensions in line with the retail prices index by making schemes pay the first three per cent) and the date in 1997 when the new contracting-out regime commences. Schemes will have to pay LPI on all pensions in payment in respect of accruals after that date in 1997.

PERSONAL PENSIONS

6.13 Section 162 extends the LPI provisions to the protected rights element of an appropriate (ie contracted-out) personal pension but again only in respect of contributions made after the 'appointed day' when the legislation comes into effect. This means that 'rebate only' appropriate personal pensions which have to be used solely for the provision of protected rights (the money purchase equivalent of a guaranteed minimum pension) must force the member to purchase an annuity with LPI on retirement. If the member has contributed more than the rebate, only the protected rights annuity has to be bought with LPI. This ensures that national insurance rebates received as a result of contracting-out of the State Earnings Related Pension Scheme are used to provide pensions with LPI, whether in a final salary or money purchase occupational pension scheme or an appropriate personal pension. It

6.13 *Indexation*

does, however, limit member choice and creates a new distinction between occupational pension schemes and personal pensions. An individual with a contracted-in personal pension can choose not to buy an annuity with LPI whereas a member of a contracted-in money purchase occupational pension scheme will have to pay for LPI increases himself out of his accumulated fund.

REFUNDS OF SURPLUS AND INDEXATION

6.14 Section 37 partially replaces the Pension Schemes Act 1993, s 108 with regard to the indexation requirements if a refund of surplus is taken by an employer from an ongoing pension scheme. It goes further, however, by imposing greater protections for scheme members although money purchase benefits and guaranteed minimum pensions remain excluded from LPI as under s 108. Also, by virtue of ss 76, 77 of the 1995 Act, refund of surplus from a scheme in wind-up is subject to mandatory provision of LPI (see below paras 10.13–10.18).

6.15 If a pension scheme is ongoing and there is power to make a refund of surplus to the employer, s 37 will apply. If there is no such power, an application would have to be made to OPRA under s 69 for a modification of the rules before s 37 would apply (see below para 9.9). Where the employer has power to direct the trustees to make a refund, this is overridden by s 37(2) which switches the power to the trustees (but subject to any restrictions in the trust deed and rules of the particular scheme). The employer's only control over the situation is that it could change its mind and refuse to accept a refund under s 37(4)(c).

6.16 If the employer wants to take a refund, the proposal has to be approved by the Inland Revenue under the Income and Corporation Taxes Act 1988, Sch 22. Notice also has to be given to scheme members in advance in prescribed form and LPI has to be granted to all pensions in payment and deferred pensions. Guaranteed minimum pensions and money purchase benefits are excluded. In addition, the trustees have to be satisfied that it is in the interests of the members that the power to take a refund is exercised in the manner proposed. This is going to make refunds much more difficult as it will rarely be in the interests of members to allow a refund without matching or higher value benefit improvements being granted. Section 37(3), (5) leave open the possibility of Regulations bringing in OPRA to review the refund or further tests for compliance, although s 37(10) suggests Regulations may also create exceptions for certain schemes.

6.17 If the trustees make a refund in contravention of s 37, they become liable to removal under s 3 and to civil penalties under s 10 (s 37(8)). If any other person purports to exercise the power to make a refund, a civil penalty under s 10 will be imposed (s 37(9)). OPRA can apply to court for a restitution order against the employer or other person which received the refund under its powers in s 14 once it has become aware of the position.

7 Minimum funding requirement and financial controls

THE PLRC RECOMMENDATIONS

7.1 A central part of the PLRC proposal was for the pensions promise to be protected in a practical way by the introduction of a 'minimum solvency requirement' for all funded pension schemes. An annual certificate of solvency was recommended with a requirement for trustees to demand extra funds if the level fell below 90%.

7.2 The brutal reality was that the level of the minimum solvency requirement would either lead to higher costs for employers or reduced benefits. The PLRC recommendations have in fact been considerably watered down by the Government in the face of lobbying from the actuarial profession and employers. The actuarial profession was deeply concerned that the term 'minimum solvency requirement' would be misinterpreted by the public as implying a high level of safety and protection with a guarantee that pension schemes would be solvent on discontinuance. The term was accordingly changed to 'minimum funding requirement' ('MFR'). The actuaries feel this term is more accurate although the semantic difference is unlikely to placate the public when they discover the limited effect of these new provisions. Historically, the ultimate solvency test on the winding-up of a scheme has been whether there would be sufficient assets to purchase annuities for all members. The PLRC accepted that the emphasis on the volatile and shrinking annuity market was unrealistic. It was agreed that the MFR would only require cash equivalents (calculated on the same basis as early leaver transfers) to be provided for active and deferred members instead of annuities although these are effectively retained for pensioner liabilities.

7.3 The move towards cash equivalents instead of annuities has been negotiated further by the larger pension schemes (with liabilities of hundreds of millions of pounds). They have been told by the Government that they can extend the less expensive method of calculation to the younger pensioners also. As the MFR will require underlying assets to match the liability promise, this frees the larger schemes to continue investing substantial proportions of their assets in equities rather than in the safer but traditionally lower-performing asset category of gilt-edged securities and bonds.

MINIMUM FUNDING REQUIREMENT

7.4 The skeleton procedures governing MFR are set out in s 56 of the 1995 Act and only apply to final salary occupational pension schemes. There are different funding requirements for money purchase schemes in s 87. The basic principle is that the value of the assets of the scheme must not be less than the amount of its liabilities. The key issue of how the assets and liabilities are to be calculated will be decided by Regulations and guidance notes issued by the Institute and Faculty of Actuaries. Section 61 allows Regulations to be made to modify the whole MFR structure in prescribed circumstances which is a disturbingly wide-ranging power.

7.5 Minimum funding requirement and financial controls

7.5 Preliminary indications are that the cash equivalent transfer values to be used for valuing the liabilities of active members and deferred pensioners will in future be based on UK equity returns moving towards gilt returns for members within ten years of retirement. This would produce smaller cash equivalents than the present gilt-based method for younger members. The valuation method for pensioner liabilities for medium and smaller schemes would be calculated by reference to gilt returns to match annuity purchase costs (with up to a 25% equity allowance for the very large schemes). Discretionary benefits would be excluded.

7.6 Asset valuations are likely to use market values averaged over a period of months rather than reflecting market values on a particular day. Self-investment up to five per cent is likely to be included. Overseas equities and property portfolios do not feature in the MFR portfolio but most schemes will not follow a fully matched strategy so they will remain useful for diversification purposes.

7.7 Section 56(4) contains an interesting loophole. It provides that any provision of a scheme that limits the amount of its liabilities by reference to the amount of its assets is to be disregarded when calculating liabilities. This may have unforeseen effects for final salary schemes with a money purchase underpin where the employer never really intends to meet the generous final salary target of Revenue maxima.

VALUATIONS AND CERTIFICATES

7.8 All schemes subject to the MFR must obtain an initial actuarial valuation within a prescribed period and subsequent valuations at prescribed intervals (s 57). The trustees or managers will also have to obtain a certificate from the scheme actuary on prescribed occasions (probably annually). The certificate must state whether the actuary considers the contributions payable to the scheme are adequate to satisfy the MFR test throughout 'the prescribed period' or, if the scheme fails the MFR test, that it will pass by the end of the prescribed period. 'The prescribed period' should logically be from the date of the certificate until the next one or until a full actuarial valuation falls due, but it will probably be linked to the periods that the Government proposes to allow for remedying a deficiency (between one and five years). The actuary also has a duty to show any relevant changes that have occurred since the last full actuarial valuation.

7.9 The precise form of the actuarial valuation and certificate will be prescribed by Regulations. The trustees or managers must make the valuation and certificates available to the sponsoring employer within seven days of receipt by them (s 57(6)).

7.10 If the actuary's certificate shows that the current level of contributions, if maintained, puts (or will put) the scheme into deficit so that it fails the MFR test at that time (or will do so before the end of the prescribed period), the trustees or managers must obtain a full actuarial valuation. This must be done within six months. Alternatively, they can postpone the valuation until it next falls due if the assets are at or above 90% of the liabilities and they revise the scheme's schedule of contributions.

7.11 The penalties for not obtaining the appropriate valuations or certificates and failing to take appropriate remedial action are a prohibition/removal order under s 3 for trustees, and a civil fine under s 10 for trustees or managers (ss 57(7), 58(8), 59(4), 60(8)).

SCHEDULE OF CONTRIBUTIONS

Rates of contributions

7.12 Section 58 will force trustees or managers of occupational pension schemes subject to the MFR to prepare a schedule of contributions. This has to show the rates of contributions payable by the employer(s) and members (if it is a contributory scheme) and the dates on which they are payable. Further points of detail may be imposed by Regulations (and it is to be hoped that a requirement for monthly payment will be introduced so that any problems in late payment will be relatively small-scale). The schedule of contributions will introduce discipline into an area which has been subject to deliberate abuse or general vagueness in the past and is to be welcomed as a major protection for members.

Timetable

7.13 Regulations will set out the timetable for production and revision of the schedule of contributions (s 58(3)). The first Schedule will follow the signing of the first actuarial valuation of the scheme. The next one will follow each subsequent valuation but there is scope for revision between these dates if the trustees or managers and the employer agree. There is a drafting flaw here in that there is no reference to revision if the trustees and employer fail to agree as contemplated by s 58(4). All schedules of contributions or revisions must be certified by the scheme actuary.

Agreement

7.14 If the trustees or the managers cannot reach agreement with the employer(s) on the schedule of contributions, the contribution rates will be set to meet the MFR as a maximum under s 58(4)(b). The schedule of contributions will effectively override any provisions in the trust deed and rules of the scheme where the employer alone decides on the contributions payable, at least so far as the MFR is concerned.

Certification

7.15 The actuary will have to prepare two certificates, one under s 57(1)(b) in connection with MFR compliance, and the second under s 58 to approve the schedule of contributions. Before the actuary signs the certification for the schedule of contributions, he must consider whether, in his opinion, the MFR is met and must only sign if he believes the rates are also adequate to maintain the MFR throughout the prescribed period. If the MFR is not achieved, the actuary must not certify the Schedule unless he thinks the rates are adequate to meet the MFR at the end of the prescribed period (s 58(6)). The schedule cannot be certified at all if the actuary believes that the MFR is not achieved and the rates would not bring the funding up to 100% of the MFR by the end of the prescribed period.

Notice of breach

7.16 If the schedule of contributions is not honoured, the trustees or managers are required under s 59(1) to give notice to OPRA and to the scheme members within a

7.16   Minimum funding requirement and financial controls

prescribed period. This should be a useful early warning system provided the prescribed period is kept short (not more than one month) and the Regulations insist on a realistic timetable for payment of contributions.

7.17 Section 59(3) contains an obscure provision requiring the trustees to prepare a report giving 'the prescribed information' if the MFR is not met at the end of any prescribed period. Only the Regulations will be able to explain the purpose of such a report and to whom it must be given.

Debt on employer

7.18 If contributions remain unpaid, 'whether payable by the employer or not', they are treated as a debt due from the employer to the trustees or managers (s 59(2)). This was often the position at common law for trustees, although it is helpful to have statutory confirmation. Once the schedule of contributions has been contravened, each employer acquires responsibility for unpaid member contributions even if it was not directly responsible for paying them to the trustees. This provision matches the new criminal penalty for non-payment of member contributions under s 49(8).

SERIOUS UNDERPROVISION

7.19 If an actuarial valuation shows that the value of the scheme assets is less than 90% of the amount of the scheme liabilities on the MFR basis, the employer has primary responsibility to make good the shortfall by making an appropriate payment to the trustees or managers to bring the value of the scheme assets back up to 100% (s 60). The Government has indicated that it will give a scheme one year (instead of the PLRC's three months) to get back to the 90% level. This can be done by a payment of cash or possibly in the form of a loan or bank guarantee. 100% compliance with the MFR would have to be achieved over a five year period.

7.20 If the employer does not take the appropriate action within the prescribed time limits so the scheme is still underfunded, the trustees or managers must within 14 days (or a longer period if prescribed), give written notice to OPRA and to the scheme members (s 60(4)). The shortfall will then become a debt due from the employer to the trustees or managers. A winding-up would probably need to be considered.

8 Equal treatment

THE SOCIAL SECURITY ACT 1989

8.1 The EC Council Directive 86/378[1] of 24 July 1986 on the implementation of the principle of equal treatment for men and women in occupational social security schemes led the Government to introduce the Social Security Act 1989, Sch 5 as a mechanism for UK compliance. The $Barber^2$ case in 1990 with its shock disclosure that normal retirement ages for men and women had to be equalised in occupational pension schemes in advance of equalisation of state retirement ages led to postponement. Even now, Sch 5 has only been partly brought into force when the provisions governing maternity and family leave were activated in 1994. Schedule 5 is only partially repealed by the 1995 Act itself although it will in fact be completely superseded by ss 62–66 on equal treatment.

---

[1] Council Directive 86/378 OJ L225 p 40.
[2] *Barber v Guardian Royal Exchange* (C-262/88) [1990] ECR I-1889, ECJ.

NEW EQUAL TREATMENT RULE

8.2 The Social Security Act 1989, Sch 5 was based on the Sex Discrimination Act 1975. This approach has been abandoned as incompatible with the *Barber* judgment which emphasised that pensions should be treated as pay for the purposes of the Treaty of Rome, Art 119. The Government has seized the opportunity presented by the 1995 Act to dismantle the restrictions in the Equal Pay Act 1970 applying to pensions. This is achieved by the statutory importation into an occupational pension scheme of an 'equal treatment rule' analogous to the 'equality clause' imported into contracts of employment under the Equal Pay Act 1970.

8.3 Section 62 deems an occupational pension scheme to have an equal treatment rule so that terms relating to access and benefits must be no less favourable for women than the corresponding provisions applicable to them in like work, work rated as equivalent, or work of equal value in the same employment. The equal treatment must apply to the exercise of a discretion by the trustees or managers (s 62(5)) and to benefits for dependants (s 63). Discrimination on grounds of marital status is specifically covered in s 63(2).

8.4 The limited equal access rules introduced by the Social Security Pensions Act 1975 and consolidated in the Pension Schemes Act 1993, s 118 are repealed by Sch 3 to the 1995 Act.

EXCEPTIONS

8.5 The equal treatment rule will not operate where the trustees or managers of a scheme can prove that the difference in treatment is genuinely due to a material

8.5 Equal treatment

factor which is a material difference between the woman's case and the man's case (other than sex). Section 63(3) also allows a scheme to implement the maternity and family leave provisions of the Social Security Act 1989, Sch 5 that otherwise would be discriminatory.

8.6 Section 64 contains two other exceptions to the equal treatment rule, although they will only apply when brought into force by Regulations. The first exception allows variations between pensions attributable to differences in state retirement pensions. Section 64(2) permits discrimination attributable to differences between men's and women's benefits payable under the Social Security Contributions and Benefits Act 1992, ss 43–55. Those sections cover the conditions of payment of Category A and B state retirement pensions. This would appear to protect bridging pensions in line with the ruling of the European Court of Justice in the *Birds Eye Walls Ltd v Roberts*[1] decision in 1993 although the scope of the exception is unclear. The second exception covers variations between men's and women's occupational pensions attributable to the use of sex-based actuarial factors for calculation of contributions to a scheme by employers or for calculation of benefits (s 64(3)). This supports the decision of the European Court of Justice in the case of *Neath v Hugh Steeper Ltd*[2] in 1993, which allowed sex-based actuarial factors to be used in a final salary scheme since they related to scheme funding. The situation of actuarial factors used in money purchase schemes is still unclear following the *Coloroll*[3] judgment in 1994. This may be why the Government has left itself room for considerable manoeuvre in s 64(4) to add to the list of exceptions or to repeal or amend the two existing ones (which even now cannot be used until Regulations prescribe exactly how they are to operate).

---

[1] *Birds Eye Walls Ltd v Roberts* (C-132/92) [1994] ICR 338, ECJ.
[2] *D Neath v Hugh Steeper Ltd* (C-152/91) [1993] ECR I-6935, ECJ.
[3] *Coloroll Pension Trustees Ltd v Russell* (C-200/91) [1994] ECR I-4389, ECJ.

IMPLEMENTATION

8.7 The trustees or managers of an occupational pension scheme are given a unilateral discretion to amend their scheme documentation by resolution to ensure that equality is achieved (s 65). This only applies if the scheme's own amendment procedures are inadequate, complex or protracted, or it is difficult to obtain member consents. The power was presumably intended to clarify the trustees' interpretation of their new overriding equal treatment rule for scheme members and employers. In fact, there can be no arguments as the equal treatment rule would always require levelling-up to the benefits of the advantaged sex in all cases. Section 65, on its own wording, can never be used by trustees to implement levelling-down of benefits, even if it post-dates a levelling-up exercise to comply with the decision of the European Court of Justice in *Avdel Engineering*[1]. This held that benefits accrued from 17 May 1990 up to the date of equalisation must always be levelled-up although there was scope for equalised levelling-down subsequently (subject to national trust and employment law constraints in each member state). The alterations can have retrospective effect (s 65(2)).

---

[1] *Smith v Avdel Systems Ltd* (C-408/92) [1994] ECR I-4435, ECJ.

INTERACTION WITH EMPLOYMENT LEGISLATION

8.8 Section 66 makes it clear that the equality clause implied by the Equal Pay Act 1970 does not extend to cover pensions where the 1995 Act would not imply an equal treatment rule. The Equal Pay Act 1970 can also be applied by Regulations to equal treatment rules with prescribed modifications. The Sex Discrimination Act 1975 is also amended so that discrimination is permitted under that legislation if an equal treatment rule would not be deemed to apply under the 1995 Act. The protections against victimisation for staff bringing sex discrimination claims is extended by s 66(2) to cover claims under the new equal treatment rule.

BRINGING A CLAIM

8.9 Section 63(4) applies the Equal Pay Act 1970 enforcement procedures to the new equal treatment rule, but specifically alters the parties, from the traditional employer versus employee, to trustees versus member. Claims can also only be made through an industrial tribunal. This will give rise to the unsatisfactory prospect of the trustees or managers of a scheme having to defend themselves by attempting to prove matters relating to the employment contract in an industrial tribunal. It remains unclear whether a claim can be brought by a third party (such as a widow or widower) in respect of a member.

8.10 The time limits under the Equal Pay Act 1970 for the bringing of claims and the procedures for doing so have already been applied to equal treatment issues in advance of the 1995 Act by The Occupational Pension Schemes (Equal Access to Membership) Amendment Regulations 1995[1]. The Government felt obliged to act quickly in clarifying the position in view of the substantial number of claims from part-timers made following the European Court of Justice decisions in *Vroege*[2] and *Fisscher*[3] in September 1994. Those cases allowed national time limits to be used to limit claims for admission of part-timers to occupational pension schemes which otherwise could be backdated under EC law to 8 April 1976. The Regulations had to be issued under both the Pension Schemes Act 1993, s 118 (the existing equal access rule) and the European Communities Act 1972, s 2(2), as they amend s 118 itself to widen its scope to cover equalisation of benefits as well as access. Replacement Regulations are contemplated under s 63(5). The new time limits imposed by the 1995 Regulations are the same as under the Equal Pay Act 1970. Claims must be brought within six months of termination of employment and with a two year limit on back service. Since the 1995 Regulations came into effect on 31 May 1995, it is difficult to see how the two year period can be reconciled with the statement in s 63(6) that the equal treatment rule covers pensionable service after 17 May 1990 unless this is intended to limit retrospectively claims brought before 31 May 1995.

---

[1] The Occupational Pension Schemes (Equal Access to Membership) Amendment Regulations 1995, SI 1995/1215.
[2] *AA Vroege v NCIV Instituut Voor Volkshuisvesting BV & Stichting Pensioenfonds NCIV* (C-57/93) [1994] ECR I–4541, ECJ.
[3] *Fisscher v Voorhuis Hengelo BV* (C-128/93) [1994] ECR I–4583, ECJ.

8.11 It is also unclear whether an individual bringing a claim for breach of the new equal treatment rule must be able to produce a comparator of the opposite sex

8.11   *Equal treatment*

(which is required under the Equal Pay Act 1970). This comparator requirement is more stringent than for sex discrimination claims and may be incompatible with EC law.

CONTRACTING-OUT

8.12 Part III of the 1995 Act will abolish the requirement for contracted-out schemes to pay a guaranteed minimum pension, probably with effect from April 1998. There are no changes proposed to the discriminatory method (based on unequal state retirement ages) of calculating guaranteed minimum pensions for service between 17 May 1990 and the date the new quality test is introduced in its place. The equal treatment rule also contains no exemptions for guaranteed minimum pensions. It follows that all contracted-out schemes will be in breach of the new equal treatment rule once it is brought into force, even if they otherwise equalised normal retirement ages before 17 May 1990. The only way round this would be to give the more favourable of the male and female guaranteed minimum pension calculations.

COST

8.13 Section 66(4) provides for Regulations to be made requiring employers to make contributions to the pension scheme once the Equal Pay Act 1970 has been given effect in relation to terms of employment relating to membership of, or rights under, an occupational pension scheme. The Occupational Pension Schemes (Equal Access to Membership) Amendment Regulations 1995 already provide (by amendment to the Occupational Pension Schemes (Equal Access to Membership) Regulations 1976, regs 12, 13[1]) that the employer has to pay the full cost of compliance for backdated membership for periods after 31 May 1995 even if it is a contributory scheme. The position of contributions on claims made before 31 May 1995 (of which there are at least 50,000) is not covered by the 1995 Regulations. Under EC law, members can be asked to contribute towards the cost of back-dated entry to a contributory scheme.

---

[1]   The Occupational Pension Schemes (Equal Access to Membership) Regulations 1976, SI 1976/142 (as amended by SI 1994/1062).

EQUAL TREATMENT FOR OFFICIAL PENSIONS

8.14 Section 171 of the 1995 Act amends the Pensions (Increase) Act 1971 to make its terms non-discriminatory. Section 171 is one of the few brought into immediate effect on 19 July 1995. It operates retrospectively for pensions commencing after 17 May 1990 but only in relation to pensions referable to service after that date.

STATE PENSION AGE EQUALISATION

8.15 State pension age will be equalised at age 65 for men and women. The increase for women will be made in stages from 60 to 65 over the period 2010–2020 (s 126). The detailed provisions are set out in Sch 4.

8.16 Women born before 6 April 1950 will retain a state pension age of 60. The sliding scale in the Table in Sch 4 shows a gradual monthly increase so that women born after 5 April 1955 will attain state pension age at 65. Men's state pension age remains unchanged throughout at age 65.

9 Modification of scheme rules

DETRIMENTAL AMENDMENTS

9.1 Recommendation 55 of the PLRC was that amendments to pension schemes which detrimentally affect the accrued rights of scheme members should not generally be permitted. The only exception to this was if the Regulator gave approval in exceptional circumstances. Section 66 reflects this general principle but switches the provision for approval in exceptional circumstances by the Regulator to certification by the scheme actuary.

9.2 Section 67 restricts the operation of any amendment power in a non-public service pension scheme. It cannot be exercised in a way which would or might affect any entitlement, or accrued right, of any member of the scheme acquired before the power is exercised unless special requirements set out in s 67(3) are satisfied.

ACCRUED RIGHTS

9.3 The distinction between an 'entitlement' and an 'accrued right' is not easy to draw in dictionary terms. 'Entitlement' is not defined but in contrast to 'accrued rights' seems to cover rights which are available without reference to the length of pensionable service such as lump sum death benefit. The term 'accrued rights', however, is specifically defined in s 124(2) and contemplates calculation at a particular point in time. They are the rights which have accrued at that time to, 'or in respect of', the member (so would include the contingent rights of spouses or dependants) to future benefits. It is made clear in s 124(2)(b), that a past service reserve basis taking account of projected future salary increases on the basis of reasonable assumptions is not on offer (apart from statutory revaluation and indexation). Accrued rights are limited in a final salary scheme to the leaving service cash equivalent available if the member had opted out. There was considerable lobbying of the Government and within the pensions industry to clarify this wording.

SPECIAL CIRCUMSTANCES

9.4 If there is even a possibility that the amendment power might affect any entitlement or accrued right, then it cannot be exercised unless the trustees have satisfied themselves that either the certification requirements or the member consent procedures have been followed. They must also give formal approval if they are not responsible for exercising the amendment power. The value judgment on possible infringement under s 67(2) and (3) therefore falls on the trustees, not the employer.

9.5 The certification requirements in s 67(4) will be prescribed by Regulations. An actuary will have to certify whether, in his opinion, the proposed amendment would be in breach of s 67 and adversely affect a member without consent. The alternative is for the trustees to obtain member consents to the amendments. This would cover the situation where a package of benefit improvements is offered in return for loss of some accrued rights or entitlements but which overall is favourable to the member. It is not clear if the actuary's certificate could cover this situation. Again, the precise details of the consent procedures will be set out in Regulations. Section 67(6) contemplates that Regulations may have to deem consent to have been given where, for example, deferred pensioners cannot be contacted at their last known address.

OVERRIDING AMENDMENTS

9.6 Section 68 extends the powers of trustees to make certain amendments to a scheme by resolution to comply with the 1995 Act. This is in addition to the separate power under s 65 to implement an equal treatment rule. Trustees can amend their scheme to cover the appointment of member-nominated trustees, to comply with the contribution requirements imposed by the new Compensation Board, to enable the scheme to comply with the new provisions governing repayment of surplus (both in an ongoing scheme and on a winding-up) and to implement the new anti-assignment and forfeiture provisions. Regulations can prescribe other specific purposes since this is not a general power to amend.

9.7 Section 68(2)(a) allows the trustees to make an amendment by resolution to extend the class of persons who may receive benefits under the scheme on a member's death. This is the only power that also requires the consent of the employer (s 68(3)).

AMENDMENT BY OPRA

9.8 If an application is made by the trustees (or the trustees, the employer or the person with power to amend the scheme rules in cases concerning contracting-out), OPRA can authorise a modification for (or directly modify) a non-public service scheme (s 69). This important power can only be used for three purposes. Schedule 1, para 18 for the first time contemplates charging pension schemes for this service. Regulations made by the Secretary of State may authorise OPRA to charge fees for any modification including preparing a formal order.

9.9 Section 69(3)(a) allows trustees to apply to OPRA where their scheme is in statutory surplus (above 105% on the basis set out in the Income and Corporation Taxes Act 1988, Sch 22). If the employer has power to block amendments, trustees sometimes had no option but to risk losing tax relief on the surplus assets. This new provision would allow them to approach OPRA with a package of benefit improvements to see if OPRA will authorise appropriate amendments. If these include a refund to the employer from an ongoing scheme, s 37 will also apply with its compulsory limited price indexing. It is notable that the employer cannot make such an application under s 69(4)(a). Removal of the power of an employer to block benefit improvements where there is a statutory surplus will be a major change for many schemes.

9.10 Section 69(3)(b) contains the second important area for amendment. The trustees can apply to OPRA for an amendment to allow surplus funds to be returned

9.10 *Modification of scheme rules*

to the employer at the end of a winding-up. This will be particularly useful for schemes which converted from the pre-1970 Old Code and were allowed to retain winding-up rules that were silent as to what happened if funds exceeded Revenue maxima for all members. The alternatives of a resulting trust to the original settlor or the funds going to the Crown as bona vacantia had created difficulties. Again, the employer cannot make such an application. The inter-relationship of s 69(3)(b) and s 77, which covers almost identical ground, remains to be clarified by Regulations.

9.11 The least controversial amendment which can be authorised by OPRA is to enable a pension scheme to be treated as contracted-out retrospectively. Section 69(3)(c) would enable late or incorrect contracting-out procedures or documentation to be rectified following the dissolution of the Occupational Pensions Board. The request can be made by the trustees, the employer or any other person with power to alter the scheme rules.

9.12 OPRA can only get involved in scheme amendments if it is satisfied that the amendment cannot be achieved in any other way, or would involve undue complexity or delay or difficulty in obtaining member consents. It is intended to be a power of last resort, but s 70(2) does give OPRA considerable discretion once it has become involved. OPRA must also always be satisfied that it is reasonable in all the circumstances to make an order (s 70(3)). Any order made by OPRA under s 69 can be retrospective in effect (s 71) and overrides the scheme amendment power and any other rules of law or statutory provisions.

9.13 The extensive powers of the Occupational Pensions Board ('OPB') to modify scheme rules, which had developed over the years into a series of detailed instructions, seem intended to remain in force as long as the OPB exists to serve them, although small amendments are made by Sch 3 to remove its powers to implement the equal access legislation. Section 161 will ultimately provide for the repeal of the Pension Schemes Act 1993, ss 136–141 once the OPB has been discontinued. The powers of OPRA to modify schemes are much more extensive then those of the OPB. Some of the OPB's current powers, however, seem destined to disappear once s 161 comes into force (such as those relating to perpetuities and voluntary contributions in the Pension Schemes Act 1993, s 136).

PUBLIC SERVICE SCHEMES

9.14 Section 72 contains special provisions for modification of public service schemes which are excluded from OPRA's powers under s 67. Instead, very similar powers are given to 'the appropriate authority' in relation to a public service scheme. This will be the Minister of the Crown or Government department designated by the Treasury as having responsibility for the scheme. The powers of the appropriate authority extend to modifying the scheme or the statute which governs its creation.

10 Winding-up priorities and Transfers

WINDING-UP PRIORITIES

Reasons for change

10.1 The unexpected and sudden insolvency of the Maxwell pension schemes led the pensions industry to query the fairness of the time-honoured list of priorities contained in the winding-up rules of most pension schemes. These typically gave money purchase additional voluntary contributions ('AVCs') top priority followed by pensions in payment. Apart from the unfairness for AVCs calculated on a final salary 'added years' basis, the absolute pensioner priority also created anomalies. Pensioners who had taken early retirement were treated preferentially to those who opted for normal retirement. The difference for a Maxwell deferred pensioner one year off retirement whose cash equivalent was potentially nil and a pensioner who had just retired and retained his full pension plus annual indexation was stark.

10.2 The PLRC recognised this difficulty and tried to accommodate it within their minimum solvency requirement proposals for increased use of cash equivalents representing the rights of all classes of member (Recommendations 65 and 66). They did not reach consensus on indexation (Recommendation 191) but the Government has taken the winding-up provisions forward to make them overriding and to reflect its decision to extend limited price indexing ('LPI') to future accruals.

Preferential liabilities on winding-up

10.3 Section 73 sets out a list of preferential liabilities for salary related occupational pension schemes subject to the minimum funding requirement which are in winding-up. Section 73(9) also intends the preferential liabilities to apply on a partial winding-up. The list of winding-up priorities is fairly similar to that contained in many scheme rules but with some crucial additions and exceptions. If the scheme assets are insufficient to cover the preferential liabilities in full, they must be applied towards the priorities at the top of the list before those at the bottom. If any group of liabilities cannot be satisfied in full, the liabilities must be partially satisfied in the same proportions. The preferential liabilities set out in s 73(3) in order are as follows—

    (a) pensions or other benefits derived from payment by any member of AVCs;

    (b) pensions or other benefits (including contingent spouses' or dependants' pensions) which have already arisen but excluding any pension increases;

    (c) pensions or other benefits (including contingent survivors' pensions again) for any other member of the scheme and refunds of contributions for members with less than two years' pensionable service but excluding any pension increases; and finally

    (d) increases to pensions counting as preferential liabilities (but not to benefits deriving from AVCs).

10.4 Winding-up priorities and Transfers

AVC priorities

10.4 The priority granted to AVCs has been a controversial subject. For contracting-out purposes, AVCs could only be given priority if they were 'separately identifiable and isolated from' other assets. This effectively limited them to segregated money purchase arrangements. The requirement that a pension scheme had to offer an AVC facility at all only came into effect on 6 April 1988. The difficulty of amending winding-up priorities generally meant that this was sometimes overlooked in scheme documentation so even segregated money purchase AVCs did not always get priority. This led to the nightmare scenario in an insolvent scheme where the non-priority AVCs of active members were used to fund the benefits of pensioners while the active members themselves might receive nothing as they were lower down the list of priorities.

10.5 The wording of what is now s 73(3)(a) on AVCs was changed at a late stage in the passage of the Pensions Bill. The test for priority is that the trustees have to decide whether any liabilities are 'derived from' the payment by a member of AVCs. This wide wording does not now require the AVCs to be held 'distinct' from the other assets of the scheme. This means that the top priority covers money purchase and final salary 'added years' AVCs paid in before retirement and that part of a pension in payment deriving from AVCs. The wording also seems wide enough to catch transfers-in of AVCs from other schemes. These changes substantially reflect representations made by the National Association of Pension Funds.

Entitlement to pension already arisen

10.6 Section 73(3)(b) gives second priority to pensions in payment and benefits for members who have passed normal retirement date but opted for late retirement. Contingent survivors' pensions are also included. Pension increases on those scale pensions are excluded.

Active members and deferred pensioners

10.7 Active members are effectively converted into deferred pensioners once a winding-up commences and both classes are covered in the third order of priority in s 73(3)(c). Individuals with less than two years' service are only given a refund of their own contributions (without interest). It is unclear whether trustees have a choice of giving a cash equivalent reflecting member and employer contributions to members with less than two years' pensionable service if their scheme is more generous than the preservation legislation and offers immediate accrual of benefits from day one. The White Paper in its response to PLRC Recommendation 66 said that minimum benefits on winding-up would be cash equivalents calculated on the same basis as the minimum funding requirement. There is a procedure for calculation in a manner prescribed by Regulations in s 73(3).

Pension increases

10.8 The splitting-off of pension increases from the underlying benefits to form the fourth priority under s 73(3)(d) was intended to reduce the absolute priority of pensioners over other scheme members on an insolvent winding-up. This will create problems for schemes which have bought-out annuities with indexation for pensioners when they retired in the name of the trustees so the pensioners are still members of the scheme. It would be very difficult to reverse the purchase of such annuities on an insolvent winding-up. If this provision leads to purchase of annuities on retirement in the names of the pensioners themselves, this would exclude them from future discretionary increases as their membership of the scheme would have terminated. The Government was aware of this problem so it is to be hoped that it will soon be covered by Regulations under s 73(7) which can modify the preferential liabilities.

Interaction with scheme rules

10.9 If assets remain after satisfying the preferential liabilities, the scheme rules with their own different priority list will apply (s 73(4)). The first priority in most schemes is payment of winding-up expenses. It is not made clear whether these expenses take priority over preferential liabilities or not. A practical interpretation of s 73(1) is that it only affects the order in which the assets of the scheme are to be applied towards satisfying liabilities 'in respect of pensions and other benefits'. This would leave other liabilities such as winding-up expenses untouched by the statutory priorities.

10.10 Section 73(5) overrides scheme rules so that only the trustees or managers can use any power contained in the scheme documentation to 'apply' scheme assets in respect of pensions or other benefits. It is a pity that the wording of this provision is so vague, but it seems to take any discretion to augment away from the employer and give it to the trustees. This is a very significant change to employer expectations. If there is no augmentation power at all, then the trustees are not given any new powers.

Guaranteed minimum pensions ('GMPs')

10.11 The contracting-out legislation insisted that GMPs and associated state scheme premiums were given a fairly high degree of priority on a winding-up. The 1995 Act replaces this with the minimum funding requirement certification procedure by actuaries and the new winding-up preferential liabilities. These do not prioritise GMPs as such but treat them as 'wrapped-up' in the underlying scale benefit. GMPs have effectively been downgraded, particularly with regard to future increases.

DEFICIT ON WINDING-UP

10.12 The Pension Schemes Act 1993, s 144 (formerly the Social Security Pensions Act 1975, s 58B) containing the 'employer debt' and deficiency contribution provisions is repealed by Sch 3. It is reproduced with minor drafting changes in s 75. It should be noted that these provisions continue to apply to final salary schemes only and not to money purchase schemes at all.

SURPLUS ON WINDING-UP

10.13 Sections 76 and 77 deal with the position where a scheme (which need not necessarily be a final salary scheme, but must be an exempt approved scheme) winds-up in surplus.

10.14 *Winding-up priorities and Transfers*

10.14 Section 76 will apply to most schemes winding-up in surplus where the provisions of the scheme contain a power for the employer or the trustees to distribute assets to the employer. That power is frozen under s 76(2) until all the conditions in s 76(3) are satisfied and any additional prescribed requirements. There are four conditions—
    (a) the liabilities of the scheme must have been fully discharged;
    (b) any power to distribute assets to any person other than the employer has been exercised or a decision made not to exercise it;
    (c) LPI increases have been granted to all pensions and prospective pensions; and
    (d) prior notice has been given to members of the proposal to refund surplus to the employers.

10.15 The reference in s 76(3)(b) to the exercise of a power to 'distribute assets to any person other than the employer' is obscure. It may be intended to allow a discretionary payment to a principal employer (such as a holding company) that has no employers participating in the scheme. If it does, it would appear to bypass the purpose of s 76 and effectively allow a refund of surplus to a participating employer without member augmentations or LPI. An alternative explanation is that it is a clumsy reference to any augmentation power, although assets would not be distributed 'to any person' but rather used for their benefit or in respect of them. If the augmentation power is intended, then the effect of s 73(5) must not be overlooked as this effectively puts the power into the hands of the trustees. If the augmentation power is not intended, it is hard to see where the scheme's own augmentation provisions would fit in with the checklist set out in s 76.

10.16 Section 77 contains similar provisions for those schemes without power to distribute assets to the employer(s) at all at the end of the winding-up which cannot amend their rules because of a prohibition on refunds being made to the employer in the amendment rule. These will usually be 'Old Code' schemes set up before 1970 which only partially converted to 'New Code'.

10.17 The situation is more favourable to members than s 76 in these circumstances. Once LPI has been granted, s 77(4)(a) requires the trustees to use any remaining surplus to increase benefits or provide additional benefits (within prescribed limits, which will probably mean Revenue limits). Once that threshold has been reached, the trustees are then given a discretion to refund the remaining assets to the employer(s). This means that the trustees could still consider the option of a resulting trust or payment to the Crown as bona vacantia if they felt that was more appropriate.

10.18 The interaction of s 77 and s 69(3)(b) is not clear. Section 77 appears to operate without requiring a modification order from OPRA in similar circumstances to s 69(3)(b) but requires the grant of LPI and mandatory augmentations to members before surplus is refunded to an employer. It is most unhelpful to have two different approaches for handling the same situation.

Penalties

10.19 The penalties for non-compliance with the new winding-up provisions are a prohibition/removal order for trustees under s 3 and a civil penalty under s 10 for trustees, managers or other persons in contravention (ss 73(6), 76(6), (7), 77(5)) except that no civil penalty applies for breach of s 77.

CLOSED FUNDS

10.20 Section 38 was inserted into the Pensions Bill at a late stage. It contains a new overriding power for trustees to operate their pension scheme as a closed fund instead of putting the scheme into winding-up. The trustees cannot allow new members to join the scheme, but the negative wording of s 38(2) implies that the scheme can otherwise continue to demand contributions from the members and employers in return for future accrual of benefits unless the trustees decide to freeze the scheme completely. In that event, they would stop accepting normal contributions and active members would become deferred pensioners.

10.21 This power to run a closed fund does not apply to a money purchase scheme or a scheme prescribed by Regulations (s 38(3)). It seems to have been intended to give final salary schemes which are temporarily below the minimum funding requirement a chance to meet that test over the prescribed 'top-up' period but it goes further. A secondary aspect is that it greatly increases the bargaining position of trustees in a final salary scheme where the employer is threatening to wind-up the scheme in the hope of securing a refund of surplus, especially as the trustees can both continue the scheme and offer future accruals to existing members.

STATUTORY DISCHARGE

10.22 Section 74 contains provisions which enable the trustees or managers of a final salary scheme subject to the minimum funding requirement to obtain a new type of statutory discharge, but only on winding-up. Members' liabilities can be secured in a number of prescribed ways. These include transferring the liabilities to another occupational pension scheme, acquiring rights for the members under a personal pension scheme or by purchasing an annuity from an insurance company. All these recipients of a transfer must satisfy 'prescribed requirements' and there is scope for the list to be extended in s 74(3)(d). Member choice or consent is not required for exercise of these options and a transfer payment can be split between one or more of the methods.

10.23 The possibility of transfer without member consent to a personal pension (which converts final salary benefits to money purchase) is significant. In an era when the minimum funding requirement will not necessarily ensure that final salary schemes have sufficient assets to purchase immediate and deferred annuities on winding-up, it has proved necessary to dilute members' security further in this way.

TRANSFERS

Extension of transfer rights

10.24 Section 152 extends the scope of statutory transfer rights to all members (unless they are within one year of normal pension age). This is done by amending the Pension Schemes Act 1993, s 93. The previous position was that members who left service before 1 January 1986 did not have a statutory right to a cash equivalent or a transfer. If trustees were permitted by their scheme documentation to make transfers for this class of member, they did not obtain a statutory discharge. Most schemes however, have permitted transfers out for all members regardless of this distinction. Section 152 opens up the right to a statutory transfer payment to all members whose pensionable service terminated before 1 January 1986. It should be noted that this extension can be modified by Regulations to exclude members of final salary schemes which satisfy 'prescribed requirements' if they left pensionable service before 1 January 1986. This implies that some restrictions on transfers may remain but there are no exceptions for pure money purchase schemes (although hybrid schemes may be treated differently). The Department of Social Security in a consultation paper published in July 1995 have indicated that Regulations will exclude all final salary schemes which have fully revalued the deferred benefits of pre-1986 early leavers in line with increases in the Retail Prices Index.

10.25 Recommendation 73 of the PLRC said that if a scheme was fully funded, transfer values should be calculated on a basis no less favourable to the departing member than the basis used in assessing the minimum solvency of the scheme. It also recommended that where the scheme was not fully funded, the transfer value should be capable of proportionate reduction. Details of the minimum funding requirement have not yet been finalised but it seems clear that the new basis (which will be less generous that the current basis for younger members) will be applied to calculation of cash equivalents for transfer purposes also. The extension of the statutory right to transfer paves the way for uniformity in calculating transfer values on the same cash equivalent basis for all members.

Guaranteed cash equivalents

10.26 Changes have been made to the timing of calculation of cash equivalents to reflect the difficulties which arose in practice under the previous legislation. This required trustees to calculate the cash equivalent on the date the trustees received the member's instructions to pay the transfer value. The member could only make a decision, however, on the basis of an earlier transfer value quotation which could be out of date by the time the instruction to transfer was made. Many schemes voluntarily held open cash equivalent figures for a fixed period (often three months) to avoid preparing two calculations and to give the member certainty of a minimum figure.

10.27 The revised procedures only apply to final salary schemes. Section 153 inserts the Pension Schemes Act 1993, s 93A. Trustees or managers of final salary schemes will have to provide a 'statement of entitlement' showing the amount of a member's cash equivalent fixed on the particular 'guarantee date'. This date will be set by Regulations but will be within a fixed period after the date of application by the member. Section 154 then amends the Pension Schemes Act 1993, s 94(1) to give the member a 'guaranteed cash equivalent' of the amount in the statement of entitlement which will be held for three months.

Time limits

10.28 Schedule 6, paras 2–6 make detailed modifications to the Pension Schemes Act 1993 to include references to the new guaranteed cash equivalent for final salary schemes. The main effect is to change various time limits included in the statute so that they relate to the guarantee date rather than the date upon which the application is first received by the trustees. Schedule 6, para 6 amends the Pension Schemes Act 1993, s 99 so that trustees will have to implement a transfer request within six months of the new guarantee date (or of the date they receive the application for money purchase schemes and personal pensions). The trustees previously had a 12 month period for compliance. OPRA may be allowed by Regulations to extend the period. If the six month deadline is not met, the trustees or managers must notify OPRA and civil penalties may apply under s 10 if the trustees have failed to take 'all such steps as are reasonable' to ensure that the transfer was processed.

11 Pensions Compensation Board

NEW COMPENSATION SCHEME

11.1 Recommendations 120 and 121 of the PLRC promoted the establishment of an industry-wide compensation scheme to protect members of occupational pension schemes against the defaults of those dealing with the pension fund assets. An important limitation on the scheme was that it was only to apply to losses resulting from fraud, theft and other misappropriation. Compensation for genuine mistakes and losses arising from poor or unlucky investment decisions or simple underfunding would not be covered. The PLRC also recommended that the cost of the compensation scheme should be met by schemes themselves. Recommendation 133 stressed that contributions levied from money purchase schemes should be met by the scheme but that the employer should have to reimburse the cost of such contributions. The Government accepted nearly all the PLRC's proposals in the form of the new Pensions Compensation Board.

CREATION OF PENSIONS COMPENSATION BOARD

11.2 Section 78 establishes the Pensions Compensation Board ('the Compensation Board') as a body corporate and the reference to 'members' implies that it will be a company limited by guarantee. Schedule 2, para 19 confirms that the Compensation Board will execute documents by use of a company seal.

11.3 The Compensation Board will be appointed by the Secretary of State and will consist of a Chairman and at least two other members. All the non-Chairman members must be appointed by the Secretary of State after consultation with the Chairman. One member must be appointed after consultation with organisations that the Secretary of State considers to be representative of employers and another after consultation with organisations representative of employees (s 78(2)).

MANAGEMENT OF THE COMPENSATION BOARD

Special powers

11.4 Section 78(5) gives the Compensation Board a specific power to borrow money from any institution authorised under the Banking Act 1987 but only up to a prescribed limit. This ties in with the fact that the PLRC recommended the raising of funding by a post-event levy on schemes so interim payments under s 84 might have to be funded by borrowing. This is in direct contrast with OPRA which is not allowed to borrow money in any circumstances (Sch 1, para 2).

11.5 The Compensation Board is allowed to 'do anything which is calculated to facilitate the discharge of their functions', including the giving of guarantees or indemnities or entering into settlement agreements (Sch 2, para 2). These flexible powers have presumably been inserted to reflect the claims and recovery experience of the Maxwell pensions unit.

Budget and levy

11.6 Unlike OPRA, the Compensation Board will not receive a budget from the Secretary of State. This is presumably because the levy under s 165 that will finance its operation is payable direct to the Compensation Board. Section 165 amends the Pension Schemes Act 1993, s 175. The new s 175(4) provides for Regulations to impose a levy on prescribed occupational pension schemes only (not on prescribed personal pension schemes as for the OPRA levy). The rate will be flexible and can take account of estimated expenditure. In view of the Government's agreement to the PLRC proposal for a post-event levy, schemes should not expect to contribute to a 'sinking fund'.

Administration

11.7 Schedule 2 sets out the operating procedures and duties of the Compensation Board. Staff can be appointed by the Compensation Board with the approval of the Secretary of State as to numbers and terms and conditions of employment (Sch 2, para 10). The Secretary of State and the Pensions Ombudsman can second additional staff. Decisions of the Compensation Board must be taken by majority vote (Sch 2, para 14) but the Board only has to meet once a year (Sch 2, para 13).

11.8 The Secretary of State is given power to make Regulations governing the procedures to be followed by the Compensation Board in the exercise of its functions (Sch 2, para 12). Section 79 requires the Compensation Board to submit an annual report to the Secretary of State 'as soon as practicable' after each year end. The Secretary of State has a duty to present the report to Parliament.

REVIEW OF DECISIONS

11.9 The decisions of the Compensation Board are intended to be final and binding (s 80). It can review its own decisions on the application of 'a person appearing to them to be interested' if the Compensation Board is satisfied that there has been a relevant change in circumstances or a mistake of fact or law, or for any reason within three months of its decision. The time period can be extended and the Compensation Board can also review its own decisions at any time without a formal application (s 80(5)).

COMPENSATION PROVISIONS

Qualifying schemes

11.10 The Compensation Board will not be able to act on its own initiative. It can only consider making a compensation payment to trustees under ss 83 or 84 if it receives a formal application from a 'prescribed person' under s 82. An application can only be made in respect of an occupational pension scheme which satisfies all the conditions set out in s 81. The pension scheme must be established under a trust and the employer must be insolvent (as defined in the Pension Schemes Act 1993, s 123). There must also be a reduction in the value of the assets of the scheme and reasonable grounds for believing this was caused by a 'prescribed offence' (likely to be limited to fraud, theft or other misappropriation). For a final salary scheme, the reduction must have reduced assets to below 90% of the liabilities calculated on the minimum funding requirement basis (s 81(7)). Finally, it must be reasonable for the scheme members to be assisted by the Compensation Board although it is unclear who has to make this subjective judgment.

Excluded schemes

11.11 Section 81(2) provides an exception for pension schemes falling within a prescribed class or description. This may be intended to exclude insured schemes by Regulations as they have their own separate arrangements under the Policyholders Protection Act 1975, although PLRC recommendations 123 suggested they should be included. The Government stated in the White Paper that exemptions would not be applied to individual schemes but only to general groupings where adequate protection for members was provided in other ways. Section 86 contemplates a modification of the compensation scheme (rather than a total exemption) for schemes falling within a prescribed class or description which may be used for this purpose.

Time limits

11.12 The procedure for making a formal application to the Compensation Board are set out in s 82. The Compensation Board will decide the form of the application which must be made by the prescribed person in the 'qualifying period'. This is a 12 month period from the later of the date upon which the sponsoring employer of the scheme became insolvent or the date when the auditor, actuary or trustees of the scheme knew (or should have known) that assets were missing due to a prescribed offence. In each case, the relevant event must take place after the date when the compensation scheme provisions are brought into force under s 180. The Compensation Board can otherwise extend the time limit one or more times at its discretion (s 82(5)).

Amount of compensation

11.13 Section 84 allows interim payments to be made to trustees where the Compensation Board believes that the qualifying conditions are (or will be) met and the trustees would not be able to meet prescribed liabilities (such as pensioner payroll, lump sum death benefits or possibly transfer requests). This useful provision would allow the Compensation Board to provide compensation for hardship cases in the lengthy period which it will normally take before the final size of any deficit is known. These interim payments can be recovered by the Compensation Board if the s 81 conditions are not ultimately met or the payments turn out to have been excessive, perhaps following asset recovery litigation (s 84(3)).

11.14 Section 83 will cover the final amount of the compensation paid to scheme trustees on the 'settlement date' which should then enable the scheme involved to finalise its winding-up. The long-stop 'settlement date' is defined in s 81(3)(d) as the date chosen by the Compensation Board, after consulting the trustees, after which further asset recoveries are unlikely to be made without disproportionate cost and within a reasonable time scale. The final payment made will take account of any interim 'drip feed' payments made under s 84.

11.15 The compensation payment must be determined in accordance with Regulations but cannot exceed 90% of the shortfall calculated on the MFR basis at the application date plus an allowance for interest at a prescribed rate (s 83(3)). There is a further test for final salary schemes so that the 90% figure is recalculated using assets and liabilities as at the settlement date (which is likely to be several years on from the application date). Payments made by the Compensation Board can be outright grants or made on such terms and conditions (including terms requiring repayment in whole or in part) as it thinks appropriate (s 78(4)).

Notification

11.16 The Compensation Board will be under an obligation to give written notice of its decision to the person who made the original application for compensation and, if different, the trustees of the scheme (s 83(2)).

SURPLUS FUNDS

11.17 Section 85 contains contingency measures in the unlikely event of the Compensation Board being overfunded. The Secretary of State, after consultation with the Compensation Board, could order funds to be distributed by it 'among occupational pension schemes'.

11.18 The Compensation Board is given power to invest any funds under its control in the limited range of conservative investments permitted by the Trustee Investments Act 1961 or in any investment prescribed by Regulations (s 85(3)).

INVESTIGATIVE POWERS

11.19 Section 110 gives the Compensation Board power to force trustees, professional advisers, employers or any person appearing to hold (or likely to hold) written information relevant to the discharge of its functions to produce any such documents. Notice must be given in writing and any period for compliance will be stated in the notice. Section 112 does not require compliance if it would incriminate the individual or his or her spouse or if the documents are subject to legal professional privilege (or its equivalent in Scotland).

11.20 The Compensation Board is not given any powers to search premises or take evidence from individuals in search of information (unlike the powers given to OPRA under ss 99, 100).

11.21 Failure to comply with the requirements to produce documents to the Compensation Board leads to a criminal penalty with a fine. Provision of false or

11.21 *Pensions Compensation Board*

misleading information or tampering with evidence involves a fine up to the statutory maximum and/or imprisonment (s 111).

DISCLOSURE OF INFORMATION

11.22 Section 113 allows the Compensation Board to publish a report of any investigation it may undertake and the result, which will presumably show the amount of compensation awarded on an interim or final basis. The report will be absolutely privileged against defamation but will usually be in general terms because of the restrictions on publishing confidential material.

11.23 The provisions governing disclosure of information to, and by, the Compensation Board are set out in s 114. They are considerably less detailed than the provisions governing OPRA in this area (ss 104–109) and it is not clear why the two bodies have been treated differently.

11.24 Section 114(7) contains a list of public servants and regulatory bodies who are authorised under s 114(1) to disclose information to the Compensation Board to assist it in its functions. There is a special exception for information acquired by the Inland Revenue which can only be disclosed if authorised by the Commissioners of Inland Revenue and can only be further disclosed by the Compensation Board with a fresh authority or for the purposes of criminal proceedings. Section 114(3) limits the Compensation Board's powers to disclose information it has acquired to the same list of authorised public servants and regulatory bodies to assist it in performing its own duties or to enable them to discharge their functions.

12 Divorce, assignment and forfeiture

DIVORCE

The historic position

12.1 The Government was remarkably unwilling to tackle the issue of pension-splitting on divorce in the 1995 Act and the first edition of the Pensions Bill did not propose any changes to the current law. In England and Wales, the Matrimonial Causes Act 1973 allows the court to have regard to pensions in reaching a divorce settlement but does not require pensions to be considered. The situation is different in Scotland where divorce is covered by the Family Law (Scotland) Act 1985. This requires the court to take pensions into consideration and to include them in the total value of the matrimonial assets. The difficulty in treating pensions fairly is that there is no power in England and Wales or Scotland for part of a pension to be transferred from one party to the other after a divorce. If there are insufficient non-pension assets to compensate for the pension loss, it has to be ignored.

12.2 The independent Working Group on Pensions and Divorce appointed by the Pensions Management Institute in agreement with the Law Society was set up in January 1992 and recommended pension-splitting on divorce as a matter of urgency in its report of May 1993. The PLRC fully endorsed its view (Recommendation 172) and debate in Parliament on the Pensions Bill eventually forced the Government to insert ss 166, 167.

Earmarking

12.3 Section 166 (inter alia) inserts the Matrimonial Causes Act 1973, s 25B to govern pension-splitting on divorce in England and Wales. A similar variation is made to the Family Law (Scotland) Act 1985 by s 167 to cover Scotland. The court will have a new duty in England and Wales to consider loss of pension rights in a divorce settlement. The crucial change, however, is that a court order may now require the trustees or managers of the pension scheme in question, if at any time any payment in respect of any benefits under the scheme becomes due to the party with pension rights, to make a payment for the benefit of the other party to the marriage. This will give courts the power to 'earmark' all or part of a member's pension, commuted tax-free lump sum or lump sum death benefit for direct payment to his or her ex-spouse who will become a member of the scheme by proxy.

12.4 The reason for the Government's insistence on this deferred maintenance approach is cost. Under the 'earmarking' procedure, the whole pension will still be taxed as the member's income even if part of it is paid to the ex-spouse. This would match the checks imposed by Revenue limits on pension benefits and contributions and avoids splitting a pension between two personal tax allowances and loss of higher rate tax. Pension-splitting which created two separately taxed pension entitlements (whether retained in the original scheme or transferred-out) would lead to a tax loss of £300 million a year according to Government estimates. A further problem for the Government concerns the substantial potential liabilities of unfunded public service

12.4 Divorce, assignment and forfeiture

schemes which might face a substantial drain on their resources if pension-splitting at the time of divorce were suddenly permitted (estimated at £500 million per year).

Pension splitting

12.5 The main drawback to the 'earmarking' or deferred maintenance approach is that it makes a clean break in personal as well as financial terms impossible for the couple concerned. The death in service of the member subject to the court order means that the earmarked benefit could be lost completely as the ex-spouse would not qualify for a spouse's pension after divorce in his or her own right. The court could only cover this by allocating the lump sum death benefit. It seems as though an allocation of pension would also have to terminate when the member dies after retirement. The ex-spouse would also be subject to the member's choice of early, normal, late or ill-health retirement dates before payment under the court order would begin. The member would also still be free to transfer a final salary pension into a money purchase or personal pension scheme when the 'earmarking' under the court order would seem to have to switch to the new scheme. The advantages of a clean break achieved through pension-splitting at the time of divorce (whether within the pension scheme or by compulsory transfer payment) were clearly presented to the Government. It can only be hoped that further amendments will be made when the impracticality of 'earmarking' becomes obvious in practice.

Calculation

12.6 The new divorce procedures contemplate the issue of Regulations to make provision for the value of any benefits under a pension scheme to be calculated and verified in a prescribed manner, probably in accordance with guidance from the actuarial profession approved by the Secretary of State. It seems likely that the calculation of the ex-spouse's share will be based on the cash equivalent. This has the advantage of avoiding arguments over assumptions about projected salary increases for final salary schemes which has caused problems in other jurisdictions such as Canada.

Costs and disclosure

12.7 Section 166 (which also inserts the Matrimonial Causes Act 1973, ss 25C, 25D) provides that Regulations can be made under the new s 25D(2) to make provision for the recovery of the administrative expenses of complying with divorce orders where pension scheme trustees have to make two pension payments (to the member and his or her ex-spouse) instead of one, or have to provide information about the value of any benefits (which they can also be required to do by Regulations). The costs can be awarded against the scheme member or the ex-spouse.

Personal pension schemes and policies

12.8 The new divorce provisions will apply to all occupational pension schemes and to personal pension schemes and retirement annuity contracts. An order can also be made against the insurer or provider of an insurance policy or annuity contract purchased or transferred to give effect to rights under a pension scheme.

Retrospection

12.9 It appears from the new Matrimonial Causes Act 1973, s 25D(6) that the courts will not be able to re-open court orders made before the section comes into force to include 'earmarking' of pension. The Government has indicated that ss 25B–25D will become effective in divorce settlements from 6 April 1996 in respect of payments of pension made from 6 April 1997.

WAR WIDOWS' PENSIONS

12.10 Following a Government defeat in the House of Lords, s 168 was inserted so that about 16,500 war widows who lost their pensions as a result of remarriage will have their pensions restored if their second marriage has come to an end. This could be through judicial separation, divorce, annulment or bereavement. The cost of this change is estimated at £400 million each year. This section is one of the few provisions of the 1995 Act to have been brought into effect from 19 July 1995 but will not operate retrospectively or lead to payment of arrears (s 180(2)). Section 169 was inserted into the Pensions Bill at the last stage to amend the Pensions Appeal Tribunals Act 1943 to update provisions relating to war pension claims.

ASSIGNMENT AND FORFEITURE

Previous position

12.11 The PLRC (Recommendation 159) stressed that the inalienability of pension rights should be made a rule of general application, not merely a condition of exempt approval for taxation purposes or a rule confined to short service benefits, guaranteed minimum pensions and protected rights payments. Recommendations 163 and 167 suggested changes to forfeiture provisions on bankruptcy and immunity from creditors while Recommendation 165 proposed changes to forfeiture provisions for ex-employees found guilty of misconduct. All these recommendations were accepted by the Government in its White Paper (although the total immunity from creditors for pension rights on bankruptcy has been limited). No attempt has been made in the 1995 Act to simplify these concepts. The basic philosophy behind all of these provisions is the paternalistic one that a pension (with its attendant tax reliefs and personal nature) should not be transferable or capable of assignment.

New provisions

12.12 Schedule 3 repeals the Pension Schemes Act 1993, ss 77–80 covering assignment, forfeiture and charges, liens and set-offs applied to short service benefit. Similar but extended provisions are found in ss 91–95 of the 1995 Act.

Assignment

12.13 The Pension Schemes Act 1993, s 77 (which will be repealed by Sch 3) provides that a pension scheme must contain rules preventing assignment of short

12.13 *Divorce, assignment and forfeiture*

service benefit and surrender or commutation except in specified circumstances. Section 91 broadly replaces s 77 although it does not contain a requirement for its provisions to be included in scheme rules. The assignment of all pension benefits will be forbidden except assignment or surrender in favour of a widow or widower or dependant, normal commutation on retirement (but only if prescribed by Regulations which may be an indication of the Government's ultimate intention to abolish the tax-free lump sum) or a charge on a pension.

12.14   Employers or trustees can take a charge, lien or set-off against the member's pension to enable them to recover funds lost through a criminal, negligent or fraudulent act by the member. The amount recovered cannot exceed the value of the benefits due to the member under the scheme (s 91(6)). The member must also be given a certificate showing the amount of the charge. If there is a dispute, the charge cannot be exercised without a court order or arbitration award. These provisions are very similar to the Pension Schemes Act 1993, s 79 (to be repealed), although the provisions allowing trustees to impound a member's pension are new. As before, transfers-in are excluded from the employer's right of set-off although they will be available to trustees who can also impose a charge or set-off for breach of trust if the member is a trustee. The PLRC recommended that a lien or charge should not be used against the benefits due to a surviving spouse (Recommendation 166). This has been covered by use in s 91 of the phrase 'the person in question' so that a spouse would only be subject to the lien or charge if he or she was guilty of wrongdoing personally as well as the member.

Attachment of earnings

12.15   There is an important new exception to the anti-assignment provisions which prevent a court making an order which would act as an assignment and deprive the member of pension. Section 91(4) allows pensions to be made the subject of an attachment of earnings order under the Attachment of Earnings Act 1971 or an income payments order under the Insolvency Act 1986. The Pension Schemes Act 1993, s 159 is amended by Sch 3, para 41 to maintain the priority status of guaranteed minimum pensions and protected rights against assignment, but to allow the making of an order under the Attachment of Earnings Act 1971. The making of an attachment of earnings order has the effect of an assignment, but can be seen as the involuntary act of the member. Although the member will have committed an offence for which the order has been made, an attachment of earnings order is never the sole remedy of the court, which has a discretion as to the method of recovering a debt or fine. The member cannot influence the court's discretion to make such an order.

Forfeiture

12.16   Section 92 deals with the forfeiture of members' benefits in very similar terms to the repealed Pension Schemes Act 1993, s 78. Forfeiture is still permitted for assignment or purported assignment contrary to s 91 or on the bankruptcy (or sequestration) of the member or the beneficiary. The trustees are given new discretionary powers to pay a forfeited benefit to the scheme member, his spouse, widow or widower, dependant or any other prescribed person. Forfeiture is also permitted if the member has been found guilty of a serious offence against the state (s 92(4)) or if the member has failed to claim his pension for more than six years (s 92(5)).

12.17 Section 93 contains a new power for a member's pension to be forfeited if he owes a monetary obligation to the employer as a result of a criminal, negligent or fraudulent act or omission. Again, the amount recovered cannot exceed the value of the benefits due to the member under the scheme (s 93(2)) or the size of the monetary obligation. In the event of a dispute, a court order or arbitration award is required to authorise the forfeiture. The trustees are given an important new power to pay 'an amount not exceeding the amount forfeited' to the employer which means that a capital sum or monthly refunds could be made to the employer (s 93(5)).

Bankruptcy

12.18 Section 94(3) provides that the bankruptcy and assignment terms used in ss 91 and 92 will also apply to Scotland but using the appropriate terminology. Accrued rights are generally prevented from passing to a member's creditors on bankruptcy under s 91(3) but s 95 contains a new detailed exception. It inserts lengthy provisions into the Insolvency Act 1986, s 342 and the Bankruptcy (Scotland) Act 1985, s 36 to enable a trustee in bankruptcy to recover, on the court's authority, up to five years' worth of contributions made to a pension scheme. The court also has a power to order the trustees to reduce the member's benefit or that of any dependants. This can only be done if the court is satisfied that the pension contributions made before the bankruptcy were excessive and have unfairly prejudiced the individual's creditors. This new provision is specifically stated to override the general prohibitions on assignment of pensions in s 91 and in the Pension Schemes Act 1993, s 159 (protecting guaranteed minimum pensions and protected rights).

Divorce

12.19 Section 166(4) disapplies the anti-assignment provisions of s 91 of the 1995 Act for the purposes of allowing a court to assign pension benefits to a divorced spouse when they come into payment. The Pension Schemes Act 1993, s 159 has not been disapplied by contrast with the specific override for bankruptcy. This would leave the divorced member with a guaranteed minimum pension or protected rights in all circumstances in a contracted-out scheme.

13 Contracting-out and state scheme changes

NEW CERTIFICATION REQUIREMENTS

13.1 Part III of the 1995 Act, when brought into force, will set up a new regime for contracting-out of the State Earnings Related Pension Scheme ('SERPS'). All the new provisions will apply from the 'principal appointed day' (probably 6 April 1997) when an Order will be made under s 180 designating the start date (s 135).

13.2 With effect from the 'principal appointed day', contracted-out final salary schemes must provide pensions which are 'broadly equivalent to, or better than, the pensions which would be provided' under a reference scheme as certified by the scheme actuary (the Pension Schemes Act 1993, s 12A, as inserted by s 136(5) of the 1995 Act).

Reference scheme

13.3 The 'reference scheme' is a notional scheme with a level of benefits satisfying the new quality test for contracting-out which replaces guaranteed minimum pensions ('GMPs'). It will have a normal pension age of 65 and an accrual rate of $\frac{1}{80}$th of average qualifying earnings in the last three tax years preceding the end of service for each year of service (not exceeding 40). Qualifying earnings are 90% of that part of the member's earnings which exceed 52 times the weekly lower earnings limit and do not exceed 53 times the weekly upper earnings limit. If the member dies, the reference scheme would provide a surviving spouse's pension of 50% of the actual or prospective pension payable to the member (the Pension Schemes Act 1993, s 12B, as inserted by s 136(5) of the 1995 Act). These provisions may be modified by Regulations.

BREAKING THE LINK WITH SERPS

13.4 Under the present contracting-out system, the state makes a top-up payment to GMPs (or notional GMPs where protected rights accrue) to the full amount of the SERPS benefit. The link between contracted-out schemes and SERPS will be broken for the future. Section 140 inserts a new Pension Schemes Act 1993, s 48A to make it clear that if an individual pays reduced rate National Insurance contributions, no SERPS entitlement will accrue. The only exceptions will be where a Contributions Equivalent Premium ('CEP') is paid to reinstate an early leaver with less than two years' qualifying service in a final salary contracted-out scheme, who has not become entitled to a deferred pension under the scheme rules, or on an insolvent winding-up (s 141).

State scheme premiums

13.5 State scheme premiums will be completely abolished by s 141 (which amends the Pension Schemes Act 1993, s 55, Sch 2) once the new contracting-out regime starts except for the limited CEP described above. Schemes will need to consider whether to contract-in before this happens if they do not wish to retain pre-April 1997 GMP liabilities indefinitely.

13.6 Apart from the CEP, there is only other way of reinstating a member of a contracted-out scheme into SERPS. Under the Pension Schemes Act 1993, Sch 2, para 5 (as amended) the Secretary of State can treat a person as contracted-in to SERPS if a scheme's resources are insufficient to meet all or part of the member's cash equivalent on an insolvent winding-up. These provisions are subject to Regulations being made to bring them into force. The amount required to restore the member's SERPS entitlement will be a debt due from the trustees or managers to the Secretary of State.

13.7 Section 146 inserts a new Pension Schemes Act 1993, s 32A to provide additional methods of giving effect to protected rights on the winding-up of a contracted-out money purchase scheme by taking out, or assuring, one or more appropriate policies of insurance. The current position is that protected rights must be bought back within SERPS if the member does not wish to transfer. That option will cease in April 1997.

HYBRID SCHEMES

13.8 It has been possible for some years for a pension scheme to have both a contracted-in and a contracted-out section. It has not, however, been possible for a scheme to operate with two contracted-out sections with one offering protected rights and the other offering GMPs. Section 149 was inserted at a very late stage into the Pensions Bill to make this possible if Regulations are issued. The effect will be for the two sections to be treated like separate schemes.

13.9 Section 148 makes detailed changes to the Social Security Contributions and Benefits Act 1992, Sch 1 to cover the position of earners employed in more than one employment where the different employments may involve membership of schemes contracted-out on the final salary or protected rights basis or contracted-in membership.

RULE CHANGES

13.10 Section 151 is the enabling section for Sch 5 which makes numerous changes to the contracting-out legislation to reflect the introduction of the new quality test. Schedule 5, para 39 is particularly important. It amends the Pension Schemes Act 1993, s 37 to provide that it will not be possible to alter the rules of a contracted-out scheme unless the alteration is of a 'prescribed description'. The amendment will otherwise be void.

13.11 Schedule 5, para 37 amends the Pension Schemes Act 1993, s 34 to give the Secretary of State power to cancel a contracting-out certificate if the employer or actuary fail to provide documentation to prove that it is in compliance with the new quality test regime for contracting-out.

13.12 *Contracting-out and state scheme changes*

CHANGES TO STATE PENSIONS

Family credit or disability working allowance

13.12 Section 127 inserts the Social Security Contributions and Benefits Act 1992, s 45A. Family credit and disability working allowance will be counted as earnings for calculating both the state basic and SERPS pensions. This will only apply to pensions coming into payment from 5 April 1999 onwards.

Calculation of surplus in earnings factors

13.13 Section 128 amends the Social Security Contributions and Benefits Act 1992, s 44. The calculation of surplus in earnings factors for SERPS will be altered so that the earnings factor is compared each year with the lower earnings limit for that year. At present, the revalued earnings factor at the pensioner's retirement date is compared with the lower earnings limit at that date. The proposed change brings the SERPS test in line with the GMP test so that the lower earnings limit and the revalued earnings factor are not increased in different ways.

Flexible deferment of retirement pension

13.14 Schedule 4, para 6 (which amends the Social Security Contributions and Benefits Act 1992, Sch 5) provides that state retirement pensions will be increased by $\frac{1}{5}$% for each week they are drawn after state pensionable age (10.4% for a year) rather than $\frac{1}{7}$% each week (7.4% for a year). The five year upper limit on the number of years by which pension can be deferred will be removed to give added flexibility. These changes will not apply until after 6 April 2010.

Contribution conditions

13.15 Sections 129–134 make various amendments to the Social Security Contributions and Benefits Act 1992 (and the Social Security Administration Act 1992) which are beyond the scope of this work. They broadly cover up-rating of pensions, graduated retirement benefit, the treatment of contributions paid in error and the extension of Christmas bonus for pensioners. Equalisation of certain benefits is also covered in Sch 4, Pt II.

Pension increases for dependent spouses

13.16 Schedule 4, para 2 equalises the conditions for dependency increases so that they will be payable when the first spouse reaches state pensionable age (subject to earnings limits). It will not be operative until 6 April 2010.

Home responsibilities protection

13.17 Home responsibilities protection is covered in Sch 4, para 4 so as to extend SERPS entitlement to individuals precluded from regular employment by responsibilities at home.

Changes to state pensions 13.18

Official and public service pensions

13.18 Section 170 amends the Parliamentary and Other Pensions Act 1972, s 27 relating to the calculation of pensions for dependants of the Prime Minister and Speaker of the House of Commons and pension increases. This is one of the few sections of the 1995 Act brought into immediate effect on 19 July 1995.

14 Money purchase schemes and Personal Pensions

MONEY PURCHASE SCHEMES

Payment schedules

14.1 Money purchase schemes are excluded from the full rigours of the minimum funding requirement as the nature of the defined contribution pensions promise makes future funding much more straightforward. The simplistic solution to underfunding is to ensure that member and employer contributions are paid regularly and invested promptly after payment. Sections 87, 88 of the 1995 Act cover the payment of contributions but there is no requirement for timely investment of funds generally (apart from the existing rules for money purchase schemes contracted-out on the protected rights basis).

14.2 Section 87 provides details of a 'payment schedule' which is very similar to the 'schedule of contributions' required for final salary schemes as part of the minimum funding requirement under s 58. The trustees or managers of a money purchase scheme must draw up and regularly review a payment schedule. This must show the current contribution rates payable by the employer and the active members as well as any other payments that may be prescribed. These other payments could cover the cost of insured benefits where the employer is responsible for the premiums or the levy for the Compensation Board or OPRA. The payment schedule must also show the dates when these payments fall due and satisfy any prescribed requirements.

Agreement of contribution rates

14.3 The Government seems to intend money purchase scheme rules to cover the matters shown in the payment schedule. Contribution rates for employers and employees will normally be fixed but it is less usual to see a timetable for payment. If the rules do not cover all these matters, they must be agreed by the employer and the trustees or managers before the payment schedule is prepared. If no agreement is reached, the decision of the trustees or managers is final (s 87(4)). As the scheme will usually set the contribution rates in its rules, the trustees' discretion is really only extended to setting the timetable for collection of contributions.

Notice of breach

14.4 If the payment schedule is not honoured, the trustees or managers are required under s 88(1) to give notice to OPRA and to the scheme members within a prescribed period. As with s 59(1) for final salary schemes (see above para 7.16), this will be a useful early warning system provided the prescribed period is kept short.

Debt on employer

14.5 If contributions remain unpaid, they are treated as a debt due from the employer to the trustees or managers (s 88(2)). As with s 59(2) for final salary schemes (see above para 7.18), this was often the position at common law for trustees, although it is helpful to have statutory confirmation. The debt will include member and employer contributions.

Penalties

14.6 The employer becomes liable to a civil penalty under s 10 for late payment of contributions (s 88(3)). There is no equivalent penalty for final salary schemes. In addition, the new criminal penalty for non-payment of member contributions under s 49(8) may apply.

14.7 The penalties for failing to prepare, agree or review the payment schedule, or to notify OPRA and the scheme members in the event of a breach of it, are a prohibition/removal order under s 3 for trustees and a civil fine under s 10 for trustees or managers (ss 87(5), 88(4)).

Serious underprovision

14.8 The statutory debt on the employer for asset deficiencies which arises in the case of a final salary scheme under s 75 (see above para 10.12) on an insolvent winding-up or on the liquidation of the employer does not apply to money purchase schemes. But s 89(2) contemplates possible application of those principles to money purchase schemes by Regulations, with appropriate modifications, plus extension of the statutory debt to cover any deficit (as opposed to unpaid contributions for a particular period) even if the scheme is not being wound-up and the employer is solvent. Such Regulations would effectively extend the minimum funding requirements with appropriate adaptations to money purchase schemes. This possibility is repeated again in s 89(1) which would specifically allow Regulations to apply ss 56–60 to money purchase schemes and to amend ss 87, 88.

14.9 Section 90 contains a small amendment to the Pension Schemes Act 1993, s 124. This provides that the Secretary of State must pay certain unpaid employer and employee contributions to an occupational or personal pension scheme due from the last 12 months before the sponsoring employer became insolvent. The Pension Schemes Act 1993, s 124 is amended with regard to money purchase schemes so as to avoid the reference in s 124(3)(b) to valuation by the actuary of final salary liabilities.

Levy

14.10 Recommendation 133 of the PLRC was for the post-event levy required to fund the Compensation Board to be financed in the form of an additional contribution funded by the employer for money purchase schemes. The scheme would pay the levy but the employer would reimburse the scheme for the same amount. The Government accepted this recommendation in the White Paper but neither the levy provisions for the Compensation Board (or OPRA) in s 165 nor the payment schedule requirements cover this expressly. It is possible, however, that the payment schedule is intended to cover this as s 87(2)(b) makes reference to 'such other amounts payable towards the scheme as may be prescribed'.

14.11   *Money purchase schemes and Personal Pensions*

AGE RELATED REBATES

14.11   Section 137 amends the Pension Schemes Act 1993, ss 41, 42, covering payment of reduced rate National Insurance contributions for contracting-out purposes. The introduction of age-related National Insurance rebates for contracted-out money purchase and personal pension schemes (but not final salary schemes) is new.

Money purchase schemes

14.12   Section 137 also inserts the Pension Schemes Act 1993, ss 42A, 42B. These broadly provide that members of contracted-out money purchase schemes will qualify for age-related National Insurance rebates (probably with effect from 6 April 1997). The National Insurance contributions of both employer and employee will be reduced by a flat-rate percentage (different from the specified flat-rate percentage set out in the new Pension Schemes Act 1993, s 41 for final salary schemes). The Department of Social Security will also contribute an additional age-related percentage. The estimated total age-related rebates for contracted-out money purchase schemes lie between 3% for younger members and over 13% after age 60. The Government's announcement that age-related rebates will be capped at 9% would be likely to affect members within ten years of retirement. The Pension Schemes Act 1993, s 42B will require a five yearly review of the rates of contributions and rebates applicable to money purchase contracted-out schemes by the Government Actuary.

Personal pension schemes

14.13   Section 138 amends the Pension Schemes Act 1993, s 45 to make members of appropriate (ie contracted-out) personal pension schemes subject to a flat-rate and age-related rebates also, although these will be different from those applying to contracted-out money purchase schemes as different timing and expenses assumptions will be used. The estimated total age-related rebates for appropriate personal pensions lie between 3.8% for younger members and over 13% after age 60. The 9% cap would be likely to affect those within ten years of retirement. The Pension Schemes Act 1993, s 45A will require a five yearly review of the rates of contributions and rebates applicable to appropriate personal pension schemes by the Government Actuary.

Verification of ages

14.14   The introduction of age-related rebates means that establishing the correct date of birth of members before retirement will be critical. Section 139 inserts the Pension Schemes Act 1993, 45B to allow Regulations to be made to help schemes to verify an individual's age. It also allows the Secretary of State to disclose information held about an individual's age (perhaps for the purpose of claiming state welfare benefits) to the trustees or managers of schemes in receipt of age-related rebates and to other prescribed persons.

PERSONAL PENSIONS

Indexation

14.15   As mentioned earlier (see above para 6.13), the biggest change in the 1995 Act for personal pensions is the new requirement in ss 162, 163 for the protected rights element of appropriate personal pensions to be compulsorily index-linked. The annuity deriving from protected rights must be purchased with limited price indexing on retirement once these provisions come into force.

Control over personal pension providers

14.16 Schedule 5 contains numerous amendments to the Pension Schemes Act 1993, some of which relate to contracted-out personal pensions. Section 164 specifically amends the Pension Schemes Act 1993, s 44 which gives the trustees or managers of an appropriate personal pension scheme, and the proposed member, a right to direct the payment of the National Insurance rebate payable in respect of the proposed member to a personal pension. The Secretary of State is given a new power to reject such a direction if the Pension Schemes Act 1993, s 31(5) (as inserted by Sch 5, para 36) is not being followed. This would be the case if money purchase benefits were not being applied in the prescribed manner or the Secretary of State considered it inexpedient to allow the scheme to be chosen by future members in view of breach of other provisions of the Pension Schemes Act 1993. This power should be seen as a further safeguard for individuals in making their own pension provision rather than as a restriction on the individual's freedom of choice.

14.17 Schedule 5, para 36 also repeals the Pension Schemes Act 1993, s 31(1). This removes reference to directions of the Occupational Pensions Board but also means that appropriate personal pension schemes will have more freedom in the way in which funds representing protected rights can be invested.

14.18 It is generally unclear why some of the changes relating to personal pensions have been inserted in the main text of the 1995 Act whereas others are tucked away in Sch 5 and presented in a piecemeal fashion.

Mis-selling of personal pensions

14.19 What is now s 172 was introduced into the Pensions Bill at a late stage to enable public service schemes governed by the Superannuation Act 1972 to recover expenses from personal pension providers or independent financial advisers accused of mis-selling personal pensions. The expenses would cover the extra costs those schemes may incur in supplying information or processing admissions or readmissions and calculating the size of restitution payments. Section 172 only applies in respect of costs connected with individuals who were eligible to join a public service scheme and who instead contributed to a personal pension scheme. It is limited to administrative expenses and does not attempt to govern the financial compensation which the public service schemes may negotiate towards reinstatement. The intention seems to have been to ensure that public service schemes are not put to additional trouble in dealing with these claims at the taxpayer's expense. Nothing similar is provided for private sector occupational pension schemes. This is presumably on the basis that the trustees will be free to negotiate reinstatement terms as they wish even if it is at the employer's expense.

Annuity deferral for personal pensions

14.20 In the White Paper, the Government recognised the difficulties caused by volatile annuity rates to members of money purchase schemes on retirement. Flexibility

14.20 *Money purchase schemes and Personal Pensions*

as to choice of retirement date was, however, only proposed for personal pension schemes and not for occupational money purchase schemes. The Government proposed to allow members of a personal pension scheme to be allowed to delay retirement up to age 75 and postpone annuity purchase accordingly and to draw a direct income from the personal pension fund in the interim subject to strict annual limits.

14.21 Sections 142–144 amend the Pension Schemes Act 1993, ss 28, 29 and insert ss 28A, 28B. These provisions only affect the protected rights element of appropriate personal pensions. Similar provisions in respect of other non-protected rights personal pension benefits have already been brought into force by the Finance Act 1995, s 58, Sch 11 which received Royal Assent on 1 May 1995.

14.22 The new Pension Schemes Act 1993, s 28 (as amended by s 142) allows interim arrangements to be set up to put protected rights into payment at any time after age 60 without the purchase of an annuity until it becomes compulsory at age 75. This upper age limit of 75 applies to the member's own benefits and to the age of the surviving spouse where a widow's or widower's pension is provided.

14.23 Section 143 inserts the Pension Schemes Act 1993, s 28A, setting out the requirements for the interim income arrangements. The first rule is that benefits must be paid at intervals not exceeding 12 months. In the first 12 month period and each successive year, payments of income must not be greater than the annual amount of the annuity which could have been purchased for the member on a specified date or less than a minimum percentage of that amount (currently 35% under the Finance Act 1995). The specified 'reference date' is the start date for the income payments and each third anniversary of that date.

14.24 The new Pension Schemes Act 1993, s 28B (also inserted by s 143) requires the trustees or managers of the personal pension scheme to disclose to the Secretary of State documents relevant to the level of income payments made under an interim arrangement or the value of protected rights subject to such an arrangement.

14.25 The Pension Schemes Act 1993, s 28A provides for the protected rights annuity to be calculated using statutory factors provided by the Government Actuary. The Pension Schemes Office has also been working to produce a set of model rules to be grafted onto existing personal pension scheme documentation so the new facility can be offered.

14.26 Section 144 amends the age requirements under the Pension Schemes Act 1993, s 29 with which pensions and annuities giving effect to protected rights must comply to reflect the new flexible annuity provisions for personal pensions.

14.27 It is possible that the flexible annuity regime may be extended to occupational pension schemes. At present there is no flexibility except for small self-administered schemes which are subject to their own flexible retirement provisions and regular reviews. Section 145 allows the Secretary of State to make Regulations modifying ss 142–144 so that they apply to specified occupational pension schemes.

Appendix

Pensions Act 1995

Pensions Act 1995

(1995 c 26)

ARRANGEMENT OF SECTIONS

PART I

OCCUPATIONAL PENSIONS

Occupational Pensions Regulatory Authority

Section
1 The new authority.
2 Reports to Secretary of State.

Supervision by the Authority

3 Prohibition orders.
4 Suspension orders.
5 Removal of trustees: notices.
6 Removal or suspension of trustees: consequences.
7 Appointment of trustees.
8 Appointment of trustees: consequences.
9 Removal and appointment of trustees: property.
10 Civil penalties.
11 Powers to wind up schemes.
12 Powers to wind up public service schemes.
13 Injunctions and interdicts.
14 Restitution.
15 Directions.

Member-nominated trustees and directors

16 Requirement for member-nominated trustees.
17 Exceptions.
18 Corporate trustees: member-nominated directors.
19 Corporate trustees: exceptions.
20 Selection, and eligibility, of member-nominated trustees and directors.
21 Member-nominated trustees and directors: supplementary.

Independent trustees

22 Circumstances in which following provisions apply.
23 Requirement for independent trustee.
24 Members' powers to apply to court to enforce duty.
25 Appointment and powers of independent trustees: further provisions.
26 Insolvency practitioner or official receiver to give information to trustees.

Trustees: general

27 Trustee not to be auditor or actuary of the scheme.
28 Section 27: consequences.
29 Persons disqualified for being trustees.
30 Persons disqualified: consequences.
31 Trustees not to be indemnified for fines or civil penalties.

Functions of trustees

32 Decisions by majority.
33 Investment powers: duty of care.

34 Power of investment and delegation.
35 Investment principles.
36 Choosing investments.
37 Payment of surplus to employer.
38 Power to defer winding up.
39 Exercise of powers by member trustees.

Functions of trustees or managers

40 Restriction on employer-related investments.
41 Provision of documents for members.

Employee trustees

42 Time off for performance of duties and for training.
43 Payment for time off.
44 Time limit for proceedings.
45 Remedies.
46 Right not to suffer detriment in employment or be unfairly dismissed.

Advisers

47 Professional advisers.
48 "Blowing the whistle".

Receipts, payments and records

49 Other responsibilities of trustees, employers, etc.

Resolution of disputes

50 Resolution of disputes.

Indexation

51 Annual increase in rate of pension.
52 Restriction on increase where member is under 55.
53 Effect of increases above the statutory requirement.
54 Sections 51 to 53: supplementary.
55 Section 51: end of annual increase in GMP.

Minimum funding requirement

56 Minimum funding requirement.
57 Valuation and certification of assets and liabilities.
58 Schedules of contributions.
59 Determination of contributions: supplementary.
60 Serious underprovision.
61 Sections 56 to 60: supplementary.

Equal treatment

62 The equal treatment rule.
63 Equal treatment rule: supplementary.
64 Equal treatment rule: exceptions.
65 Equal treatment rule: consequential alteration of schemes.
66 Equal treatment rule: effect on terms of employment, etc.

Modification of schemes

67 Restriction on powers to alter schemes.
68 Power of trustees to modify schemes by resolution.

69   Grounds for applying for modifications.
70   Section 69: supplementary.
71   Effect of orders under section 69.
72   Modification of public service pension schemes.

Winding up

73   Preferential liabilities on winding up.
74   Discharge of liabilities by insurance, etc.
75   Deficiencies in the assets.
76   Excess assets on winding up.
77   Excess assets remaining after winding up: power to distribute.

The Pensions Compensation Board

78   The Compensation Board.
79   Reports to Secretary of State.
80   Review of decisions.

The compensation provisions

81   Cases where compensation provisions apply.
82   Applications for payments.
83   Amount of compensation.
84   Payments made in anticipation.
85   Surplus funds.
86   Modification of compensation provisions.

Money purchase schemes

87   Schedules of payments to money purchase schemes.
88   Schedules of payments to money purchase schemes: supplementary.
89   Application of further provisions to money purchase schemes.
90   Unpaid contributions in cases of insolvency.

Assignment, forfeiture, bankruptcy, etc

91   Inalienability of occupational pension.
92   Forfeiture, etc.
93   Forfeiture by reference to obligation to the employer.
94   Sections 91 to 93: supplementary.
95   Pension rights of individuals adjudged bankrupt etc.

Questioning the decisions of the Authority

96   Review of decisions.
97   References and appeals from the Authority.

Gathering information: the Authority

98   Provision of information.
99   Inspection of premises.
100   Warrants.
101   Information and inspection: penalties.
102   Savings for certain privileges etc.
103   Publishing reports.

Disclosure of information: the Authority

104   Restricted information.
105   Information supplied to the Authority by corresponding overseas authorities.

Pensions Act 1995

106 Disclosure for facilitating discharge of functions by the Authority.
107 Disclosure for facilitating discharge of functions by other supervisory authorities.
108 Other permitted disclosures.
109 Disclosure of information by the Inland Revenue.

Gathering information: the Compensation Board

110 Provision of information.
111 Information: penalties.
112 Savings for certain privileges.
113 Publishing reports.
114 Disclosure of information.

General

115 Offences by bodies corporate and partnerships.
116 Breach of regulations.
117 Overriding requirements.
118 Powers to modify this Part.
119 Calculations etc under regulations: sub-delegation.
120 Consultations about regulations.
121 Crown application.
122 Consequential amendments.
123 "Connected" and "associated" persons.
124 Interpretation of Part I.
125 Section 124: supplementary.

PART II
STATE PENSIONS

126 Equalisation of pensionable age and of entitlement to certain benefits.
127 Enhancement of additional pension, etc where family credit or disability working allowance paid.
128 Additional pension: calculation of surpluses.
129 Contribution conditions.
130 Uprating of pensions increased under section 52 of the Social Security Contributions and Benefits Act.
131 Graduated retirement benefit.
132 Extension of Christmas bonus for pensioners.
133 Contributions paid in error.
134 Minor amendments.

PART III
CERTIFICATION OF PENSION SCHEMES AND EFFECTS ON MEMBERS' STATE SCHEME RIGHTS AND DUTIES

Introductory

135 The "principal appointed day" for Part III.

New certification requirements applying as from the principal appointed day

136 New requirements for contracted-out schemes.

Reduction in State scheme contributions, payment of rebates and reduction in State scheme benefits

137 State scheme contributions and rebates.
138 Minimum contributions towards appropriate personal pension schemes.

139 Money purchase and personal pension schemes: verification of ages.
140 Reduction in benefits for members of certified schemes.

Premiums and return to State scheme

141 State scheme etc premiums and buyback into State scheme.

Protected rights

142 Interim arrangements for giving effect to protected rights.
143 Requirements for interim arrangements.
144 Interim arrangements: supplementary.
145 Extension of interim arrangements to occupational pension schemes.
146 Discharge of protected rights on winding up: insurance policies.

Miscellaneous

147 Monitoring personal pension schemes.
148 Earner employed in more than one employment.
149 Hybrid occupational pension schemes.
150 Dissolution of Occupational Pensions Board.

Minor and consequential amendments

151 Minor and consequential amendments related to sections 136 to 150.

PART IV

MISCELLANEOUS AND GENERAL

Transfer values

152 Extension of scope of right to cash equivalent.
153 Right to guaranteed cash equivalent.
154 Right to guaranteed cash equivalent: supplementary.

Penalties

155 Breach of regulations under the Pension Schemes Act 1993.

Pensions Ombudsman

156 Employment of staff by the Pensions Ombudsman.
157 Jurisdiction of Pensions Ombudsman.
158 Costs and expenses.
159 Disclosing information.
160 Interest on late payment of benefit.

Modification and winding up of schemes

161 Repeal of sections 136 to 143 of the Pensions Schemes Act 1993.

Personal pensions

162 Annual increase in rate of personal pension.
163 Section 162: supplementary.
164 Power to reject notice choosing appropriate personal pension scheme.

Levy

165 Levy.

Pensions on divorce, etc

166 Pensions on divorce, etc.
167 Pensions on divorce, etc: Scotland.

War Pensions

168 War pensions for widows: effect of remarriage.
169 Extension of Pensions Appeal Tribunals Act 1943.

Official and public service pensions

170 Pensions for dependants of the Prime Minister etc.
171 Equal treatment in relation to official pensions.
172 Information about public service schemes.

General minor and consequential amendments

173 General minor and consequential amendments.

Subordinate legislation etc

174 Orders and regulations (general provisions).
175 Parliamentary control of orders and regulations.

General

176 Interpretation.
177 Repeals.
178 Extent.
179 Northern Ireland.
180 Commencement.
181 Short title.

SCHEDULES:
    Schedule 1—Occupational Pensions Regulatory Authority.
    Schedule 2—Pensions Compensation Board.
    Schedule 3—Amendments consequential on Part I.
    Schedule 4—Equalisation.
        Part I—Pensionable ages for men and women.
        Part II—Entitlement to certain pension and other benefits.
        Part III—Consequential amendments.
    Schedule 5—Amendments relating to Part III.
    Schedule 6—General minor and consequential amendments.
    Schedule 7—Repeals.
        Part I—Occupational pensions.
        Part II—State pensions.
        Part III—Certification of pension schemes etc.
        Part IV—Miscellaneous and General.

An Act to amend the law about pensions and for connected purposes.

[19 July 1995]

Parliamentary Debates
House of Lords:
2nd Reading 24 January 1995: 560 HL Official Report (5th series) col 974.
Committee (1st Day) 7 February 1995: 561 HL Official Report (5th series) col 106.
Committee (2nd Day) 13 February 1995: 561 HL Official Report (5th series) col 440.
Committee (3rd Day) 16 February 1995: 561 HL Official Report (5th series) col 869.
Committee (4th Day) 20 February 1995: 561 HL Official Report (5th series) col 917.

Committee (5th Day) 21 February 1995: 561 HL Official Report (5th series) col 1036.
Report (1st Day) 13 March 1995: 562 HL Official Report (5th series) col 637.
Report (2nd Day) 14 March 1995: 562 HL Official Report (5th series) col 726.
3rd Reading 21 March 1995: 562 HL Official Report (5th series) col 113.
Commons Amendments 12 July 1995: 565 HL Official Report (5th series) col 1683.
House of Commons:
2nd Reading 24 April 1995: 258 HC Official Report (6th series) col 525.
Committee Stage 2 May–27 June 1995: HC Official Report, SC D (Pensions Bill).
Remaining Stages 4 July 1995: 263 HC Official Report (6th series) col 145; 5 July 1995: 263 HC Official Report (6th series) col 390.

PART I
OCCUPATIONAL PENSIONS

Occupational Pensions Regulatory Authority

1 The new authority

(1) There shall be a body corporate called the Occupational Pensions Regulatory Authority (referred to in this Part as "the Authority").

(2) The Authority shall consist of not less than seven members appointed by the Secretary of State, one of whom shall be so appointed as chairman.

(3) In addition to the chairman, the Authority shall comprise—
   (a) a member appointed after the Secretary of State has consulted organisations appearing to him to be representative of employers,
   (b) a member appointed after the Secretary of State has consulted organisations appearing to him to be representative of employees,
   (c) a member who appears to the Secretary of State to be knowledgeable about life assurance business,
   (d) a member who appears to the Secretary of State to have experience of, and to have shown capacity in, the management or administration of occupational pension schemes, and
   (e) two members who appear to the Secretary of State to be knowledgeable about occupational pension schemes,

and such other member or members as the Secretary of State may appoint.

(4) Neither the Authority nor any person who is a member or employee of the Authority shall be liable in damages for anything done or omitted in the discharge or purported discharge of the functions of the Authority under this Part or the Pension Schemes Act 1993, or any provisions in force in Northern Ireland corresponding to either of them, unless it is shown that the act or omission was in bad faith.

(5) Schedule 1 (constitution, procedure, etc of the Authority) shall have effect.

(6) In this section, "life assurance business" means the issue of, or the undertaking of liability under, policies of assurance upon human life, or the granting of annuities upon human life.

Definitions For "employer", see ss 124(1), 125(3). By virtue of s 124(5), for "employee", see the Pension Schemes Act 1993, s 181(1). By virtue of s 176, for "occupational pension scheme", see s 1 of the 1993 Act. Note as to "the Authority", sub-s (1) above, and as to "life assurance business", sub-s (6) above.
References See paras 2.1–2.3.

2 Reports to Secretary of State

(1) The Authority must prepare a report for the first twelve months of their existence, and a report for each succeeding period of twelve months, and must send

each report to the Secretary of State as soon as practicable after the end of the period for which it is prepared.

(2) A report prepared under this section for any period must deal with the activities of the Authority in the period.

(3) The Secretary of State must lay before each House of Parliament a copy of every report received by him under this section.

Definitions For "the Authority" see s 1(1).
References See para 2.9.

Supervision by the Authority

3 Prohibition orders

(1) The Authority may by order prohibit a person from being a trustee of a particular trust scheme in any of the following circumstances.

(2) The circumstances are—
  (a) that the Authority are satisfied that while being a trustee of the scheme the person has been in serious or persistent breach of any of his duties under—
    (i) this Part, other than the following provisions: sections 51 to 54, 62 to 65 and 110 to 112, or
    (ii) the following provisions of the Pension Schemes Act 1993: section 6 (registration), Chapter IV of Part IV (transfer values), section 113 (information) and section 175 (levy),
  (b) that the Authority are satisfied that, while being a trustee of the scheme, this section has applied to the person by virtue of any other provision of this Part,
  (c) that the person is a company and any director of the company is prohibited under this section from being a trustee of the scheme,
  (d) that the person is a Scottish partnership and any of the partners is prohibited under this section from being a trustee of the scheme, or
  (e) that the person is a director of a company which, by reason of circumstances falling within paragraph (a) or (b), is prohibited under this section from being a trustee of the scheme and the Authority are satisfied that the acts or defaults giving rise to those circumstances were committed with the consent or connivance of, or attributable to any neglect on the part of, the director;

or any other prescribed circumstances.

(3) The making of an order under subsection (1) against a person who is a trustee of the scheme in question has the effect of removing him.

(4) The Authority may, on the application of any person against whom an order under subsection (1) is in force, by order revoke the order, but a revocation made at any time cannot affect anything done before that time.

Definitions For "the Authority", see s 1(1); for "prescribed", "Scottish partnership" and "trust scheme", see s 124(1).
References See paras 2.12, 2.13.

4 Suspension orders

(1) The Authority may by order suspend a trustee of a trust scheme—
  (a) pending consideration being given to the making of an order against him under section 3(1),

(b) where proceedings have been instituted against him for an offence involving dishonesty or deception and have not been concluded,

(c) where a petition has been presented to the court for an order adjudging him bankrupt, or for the sequestration of his estate, and proceedings on the petition have not been concluded,

(d) where the trustee is a company, if a petition for the winding up of the company has been presented to the court and proceedings on the petition have not been concluded,

(e) where an application has been made to the court for a disqualification order against him under the Company Directors Disqualification Act 1986 and proceedings on the application have not been concluded, or

(f) where the trustee is a company or Scottish partnership and, if any director or, as the case may be, partner were a trustee, the Authority would have power to suspend him under paragraph (b), (c) or (e).

(2) An order under subsection (1)—

(a) if made by virtue of paragraph (a), has effect for an initial period not exceeding twelve months, and

(b) in any other case, has effect until the proceedings in question are concluded;

but the Authority may by order extend the initial period referred to in paragraph (a) for a further period of twelve months, and any order suspending a person under subsection (1) ceases to have effect if an order is made against that person under section 3(1).

(3) An order under subsection (1) has the effect of prohibiting the person suspended, during the period of his suspension, from exercising any functions as trustee of any trust scheme to which the order applies; and the order may apply to a particular trust scheme, a particular class of trust schemes or trust schemes in general.

(4) An order under subsection (1) may be made on one of the grounds paragraphs (b) to (e) whether or not the proceedings were instituted, petition presented or application made (as the case may be) before or after the coming into force of that subsection.

(5) The Authority may, on the application of any person suspended under subsection (1), by order revoke the order, either generally or in relation to a particular scheme or a particular class of schemes; but a revocation made at any time cannot affect anything done before that time.

(6) An order under this section may make provision as respects the period of the trustee's suspension for matters arising out of it, and in particular for enabling any person to execute any instrument in his name or otherwise act for him and for adjusting any rules governing the proceedings of the trustees to take account of the reduction in the number capable of acting.

Definitions For "the Authority", see s 1(1); for "Scottish partnership" and "trust scheme", see s 124(1).
References See para 2.14.

5 Removal of trustees: notices

(1) Before the Authority make an order under section 3 against a person without his consent, the Authority must, unless he cannot be found or has no known address, give him not less than one month's notice of their proposal, inviting representations to be made to them within a time specified in the notice.

(2) Where any such notice is given, the Authority must take into consideration any representations made to them about the proposals within the time specified in the notice.

(3) Before making an order under section 3 against a person, the Authority must give notice of their intention to do so to each of the trustees of the scheme, except that person (if he is a trustee) and any trustee who cannot be found or has no known address.

(4) Where the Authority make an order under section 4 against a person, they must—
    (a) immediately give notice of that fact to that person, and
    (b) as soon as reasonably practicable, give notice of that fact to the other trustees of any trust scheme to which the order applies, except any trustee who cannot be found or has no known address.

(5) Any notice to be given to any person under this section may be given by delivering it to him or by leaving it at his proper address or by sending it to him by post; and, for the purposes of this subsection and section 7 of the Interpretation Act 1978 in its application to this subsection, the proper address of any person is his latest address known to the Authority.

Definitions   For "the Authority", see s 1(1); for "trust scheme", see s 124(1).
References   See paras 2.15, 2.16.

6 Removal of suspension of trustees: consequences

(1) A person who purports to act as trustee of a trust scheme while prohibited from being a trustee of the scheme under section 3 or suspended in relation to the scheme under section 4 is guilty of an offence and liable—
    (a) on summary conviction, to a fine not exceeding the statutory maximum, and
    (b) on conviction on indictment, to a fine or imprisonment or both.

(2) An offence under subsection (1) may be charged by reference to any day or longer period of time; and a person may be convicted of a second or subsequent offence under that subsection by reference to any period of time following the preceding conviction of the offence.

(3) Things done by a person purporting to act as trustee of a trust scheme while prohibited from being a trustee of the scheme under section 3 or suspended in relation to the scheme under section 4 are not invalid merely because of that prohibition or suspension.

(4) Nothing in section 3 or 4 or this section affects the liability of any person for things done, or omitted to be done, by him while purporting to act as trustee of a trust scheme.

Definitions   For "trust scheme" see s 124(1).
References   See paras 2.26, 2.27.

7 Appointment of trustees

(1) Where a trustee of a trust scheme is removed by an order under section 3, or a trustee of such a scheme ceases to be a trustee by reason of his disqualification, the Authority may by order appoint another trustee in his place.

(2) Where a trustee appointed under subsection (1) is appointed to replace a trustee appointed under section 23(1)(b), sections 22 to 26 shall apply to the replacement trustee as they apply to a trustee appointed under section 23(1)(b).

(3) The Authority may also by order appoint a trustee of a trust scheme where they are satisfied that it is necessary to do so in order—
    (a) to secure that the trustees as a whole have, or exercise, the necessary knowledge and skill for the proper administration of the scheme,
    (b) to secure that the number of trustees is sufficient for the proper administration of the scheme, or
    (c) to secure the proper use or application of the assets of the scheme.

(4) The Authority may also appoint a trustee of a trust scheme in prescribed circumstances.

(5) The power to appoint a trustee by an order under this section includes power by such an order—
- (a) to determine the appropriate number of trustees for the proper administration of the scheme,
- (b) to require a trustee appointed by the order to be paid fees and expenses out of the scheme's resources,
- (c) to provide for the removal or replacement of such a trustee.

(6) Regulations may make provision about the descriptions of persons who may or may not be appointed trustees under this section.

Definitions For "the Authority", see s 1(1); for "prescribed", "regulations", "resources" and "trust scheme", see s 124(1).
References See paras 2.22, 2.24.

8 Appointment of trustees: consequences

(1) An order under section 7 appointing a trustee may provide that an amount equal to the amount (if any) to which subsection (2) applies is to be treated for all purposes as a debt due from the employer to the trustees.

(2) This subsection applies to any amount which has been paid to the trustee so appointed out of the resources of the scheme and has not been reimbursed by the employer.

(3) Subject to subsection (4), a trustee appointed under that section shall, unless he is the independent trustee and section 22 applies in relation to the scheme, have the same powers and duties as the other trustees.

(4) Such an order may make provision—
- (a) for restricting the powers or duties of a trustee so appointed, or
- (b) for powers or duties to be exercisable by a trustee so appointed to the exclusion of other trustees.

Definitions As to "independent trustee", see s 23(3); for "resources", see s 124(1); for "employer", see ss 124(1), 125(3).
References See paras 2.23, 2.24

9 Removal and appointment of trustees: property

Where the Authority have power under this Part to appoint or remove a trustee, they may exercise the same jurisdiction and powers as are exercisable by the High Court or, in relation to a trust scheme subject to the law of Scotland, the Court of Session for vesting any property in, or transferring any property to, trustees in consequence of the appointment or of the removal.

Definitions For "the Authority", see s 1(1); for "trust scheme", see s 124(1).
References See para 2.25.

10 Civil penalties

(1) Where the Authority are satisfied that by reason of any act or omission this section applies to any person, they may by notice in writing require him to pay, within a prescribed period, a penalty in respect of that act or omission not exceeding the maximum amount.

(2) In this section "the maximum amount" means—
- (a) £5,000 in the case of an individual and £50,000 in any other case, or

(b) such lower amount as may be prescribed in the case of an individual or in any other case,

and the Secretary of State may by order amend paragraph (a) by substituting higher amounts for the amounts for the time being specified in that paragraph.

(3) Regulations made by virtue of this Part may provide for any person who has contravened any provision of such regulations to pay, within a prescribed period, a penalty under this section not exceeding an amount specified in the regulations; and the regulations must specify different amounts in the case of individuals from those specified in other cases and any amount so specified may not exceed the amount for the time being specified in the case of individuals or, as the case may be, others in subsection (2)(a).

(4) An order made under subsection (2) or regulations made by virtue of subsection (3) do not affect the amount of any penalty recoverable under this section by reason of an act or omission occurring before the order or, as the case may be, regulations are made.

(5) Where—
    (a) apart from this subsection, a penalty under this section is recoverable from a body corporate or Scottish partnership by reason of any act or omission of the body or partnership as a trustee of a trust scheme, and
    (b) the act or omission was done with the consent or connivance of, or is attributable to any neglect on the part of, any persons mentioned in subsection (6),

this section applies to each of those persons who consented to or connived in the act or omission or to whose neglect the act or omission was attributable.

(6) The persons referred to in subsection (5)(b)—
    (a) in relation to a body corporate, are—
        (i) any director, manager, secretary, or other similar officer of the body, or a person purporting to act in any such capacity, and
        (ii) where the affairs of a body corporate are managed by its members, any member in connection with his functions of management, and
    (b) in relation to a Scottish partnership, are the partners.

(7) Where the Authority requires any person to pay a penalty by virtue of subsection (5), they may not also require the body corporate, or Scottish partnership, in question to pay a penalty in respect of the same act or omission.

(8) A penalty under this section is recoverable by the Authority.

(9) The Authority must pay to the Secretary of State any penalty recovered under this section.

Definitions For "the Authority", see s 1(1); for "contravention", "prescribed", "regulations", "Scottish partnership" and "trust scheme", see s 124(1). Note as to "the maximum amount", sub-s (2) above.
References See paras 2.30, 2.31.

11 Powers to wind up schemes

(1) Subject to the following provisions of this section, the Authority may by order direct or authorise an occupational pension scheme to be wound up if they are satisfied that—
    (a) the scheme, or any part of it, ought to be replaced by a different scheme,
    (b) the scheme is no longer required, or
    (c) it is necessary in order to protect the interests of the generality of the members of the scheme that it be wound up.

(2) The Authority may not make an order under this section on either of the grounds referred to in subsection (1)(a) or (b) unless they are satisfied that the winding up of the scheme—
- (a) cannot be achieved otherwise than by means of such an order, or
- (b) can only be achieved in accordance with a procedure which—
  - (i) is liable to be unduly complex or protracted, or
  - (ii) involves the obtaining of consents which cannot be obtained, or can only be obtained with undue delay or difficulty,

and that it is reasonable in all the circumstances to make the order.

(3) An order made under this section on either of the grounds referred to in subsection (1)(a) or (b) may be made only on the application of—
- (a) the trustees or managers of the scheme,
- (b) any person other than the trustees or managers who has power to alter any of the rules of the scheme, or
- (c) the employer.

(4) An order under this section authorising a scheme to be wound up must include such directions with respect to the manner and timing of the winding up as the Authority think appropriate having regard to the purposes of the order.

(5) The winding up of a scheme in pursuance of an order of the Authority under this section is as effective in law as if it had been made under powers conferred by or under the scheme.

(6) An order under this section may be made and complied with in relation to a scheme—
- (a) in spite of any enactment or rule of law, or any rule of the scheme, which would otherwise operate to prevent the winding up, or
- (b) except for the purpose of the Authority determining whether or not they are satisfied as mentioned in subsection (2), without regard to any such enactment, rule of law or rule of the scheme as would otherwise require, or might otherwise be taken to require, the implementation of any procedure or the obtaining of any consent, with a view to the winding up.

(7) In the case of a public service pension scheme—
- (a) an order under subsection (1) directing or authorising the scheme to be wound up may only be made on the grounds referred to in paragraph (c), and
- (b) such an order may, as the Authority think appropriate, adapt, amend or repeal any enactment in which the scheme is contained or under which it is made.

Definitions For "the Authority", see s 1(1); for "trustees or managers", see s 124(1); for "employer", see ss 124(1), 125(3); for "member", see ss 124(1), 125(4). By virtue of s 124(1), for "public service pension scheme", and, by virtue of s 176, for "occupational pension scheme", see the Pension Schemes Act 1993, s 1; for "enactment", see s 176.
References See para 2.38.

12 Powers to wind up public services schemes

(1) The appropriate authority may by order direct a public service pension scheme to be wound up if they are satisfied that—
- (a) the scheme, or any part of it, ought to be replaced by a different scheme, or
- (b) the scheme is no longer required.

(2) Subsection (2) of section 11 applies for the purposes of this section as it applies for the purposes of that, but as if references to the Authority were to the appropriate authority.

(3) In this section "the appropriate authority", in relation to a scheme, means such Minister of the Crown or government department as may be designated by the Treasury as having responsibility for the particular scheme.

(4) An order under this section must include such directions with respect to the manner and timing of the winding up as that authority think appropriate.

(5) Such an order may, as that authority think appropriate, adapt, amend or repeal any enactment in which the scheme is contained or under which it is made.

Definitions By virtue of s 124(1), for "public service pension scheme", see the Pension Schemes Act 1993, s 1; for "enactment", see s 176. Note as to "the appropriate authority", sub-s (3) above.
References See para 2.38.

13 Injunctions and interdicts

(1) If, on the application of the Authority, the court is satisfied that—
　　(a) there is a reasonable likelihood that a particular person will do any act which constitutes a misuse or misappropriation of assets of an occupational pension scheme, or
　　(b) that a particular person has done any such act and that there is a reasonable likelihood that he will continue or repeat the act in question or do a similar act,
the court may grant an injunction restraining him from doing so or, in Scotland, an interdict prohibiting him from doing so.

(2) The jurisdiction conferred by this section is exercisable by the High Court or the Court of Session.

Definitions For "the Authority", see s 1(1). By virtue of s 176, for "occupational pension scheme", see the Pension Schemes Act 1993, s 1.
References See para 2.34.

14 Restitution

(1) If, on the application of the Authority, the court is satisfied—
　　(a) that a power to make a payment, or distribute any assets, to the employer, has been exercised in contravention of section 37, 76 or 77, or
　　(b) that any act or omission of the trustees or managers of an occupational pension scheme was in contravention of section 40,
the court may order the employer and any other person who appears to the court to have been knowingly concerned in the contravention to take such steps as the court may direct for restoring the parties to the position in which they were before the payment or distribution was made, or the act or omission occurred.

(2) The jurisdiction conferred by this section is exercisable by the High Court or the Court of Session.

Definitions For "the Authority", see s 1(1); for "contravention" and "trustees or managers", see s 124(1); for "employer", see ss 124(1), 125(3). By virtue of s 176, for "occupational pension scheme", see the Pension Schemes Act 1993, s 1.
References See para 2.34.

15 Directions

(1) The Authority may, where in the case of any trust scheme the employer fails to comply with any requirement included in regulations by virtue of section 49(5), direct the trustees to make arrangements for the payment to the members of the benefit to which the requirement relates.

(2) The Authority may—
  (a) where in the case of any trust scheme an annual report is published, direct the trustees to include a statement prepared by the Authority in the report, and
  (b) in the case of any trust scheme, direct the trustees to send to the members a copy of a statement prepared by the Authority.

(3) A direction under this section must be given in writing.

(4) Where a direction under this section is not complied with, sections 3 and 10 apply to any trustee who has failed to take all such steps as are reasonable to secure compliance.

Definitions For "the Authority", see s 1(1); for "regulations" and "trust scheme", see s 124(1); for "employer", see ss 124(1), 125(3); for "member", see ss 124(1), 125(4).
References See paras 2.35–2.37.

Member-nominated trustees and directors

16 Requirement for member-nominated trustees

(1) The trustees of a trust scheme must (subject to section 17) secure—
  (a) that such arrangements for persons selected by members of the scheme to be trustees of the scheme as are required by this section are made, and
  (b) that those arrangements, and the appropriate rules, are implemented.

(2) Persons who become trustees under the arrangements required by subsection (1) are referred to in this Part as "member-nominated trustees".

(3) The arrangements must provide—
  (a) for any person who has been nominated and selected in accordance with the appropriate rules to become a trustee by virtue of his selection, and
  (b) for the removal of such a person to require the agreement of all the other trustees.

(4) Where a vacancy for a member-nominated trustee is not filled because insufficient nominations are received, the arrangements must provide for the filling of the vacancy, or for the vacancy to remain, until the expiry of the next period in which persons may be nominated and selected in accordance with the appropriate rules.

(5) The arrangements must provide for the selection of a person as a member-nominated trustee to have effect for a period of not less than three nor more than six years.

(6) The arrangements must provide for the number of member-nominated trustees to be—
  (a) at least two or (if the scheme comprises less than 100 members) at least one, and
  (b) at least one-third of the total number of trustees;
but the arrangements must not provide for a greater number of member-nominated trustees than that required to satisfy that minimum unless the employer has given his approval to the greater number.

(7) The arrangements must not provide for the functions of member-nominated trustees to differ from those of any other trustee but, for the purposes of this subsection—
  (a) any provision made by an order under section 8(4), and
  (b) section 25(2),
shall be disregarded.

(8) The arrangements must provide that, if a member-nominated trustee who was a member of the scheme when he was appointed ceases to be a member of the scheme, he ceases to be a trustee by virtue of that fact.

Definitions As to "the appropriate rules", see s 20(1); for "trust scheme", see s 124(1); for "employer", see ss 124(1), 125(3); for "member", see ss 124(1), 125(4). Note as to "member-nominated trustees", sub-s (2) above.
References See paras 3.1–3.11.

17 Exceptions

(1) Section 16 does not apply to a trust scheme if—
  (a) a proposal has been made by the employer for the continuation of existing arrangements, or the adoption of new arrangements, for selecting the trustees of the scheme,
  (b) the arrangements referred to in the proposal are for the time being approved under the statutory consultation procedure, and
  (c) such other requirements as may be prescribed are satisfied.

(2) Where—
  (a) by virtue of subsection (1), section 16 does not apply to a trust scheme, and
  (b) the employer's proposal was for the adoption of new arrangements which, in consequence of subsection (1)(b), are adopted,
the trustees shall secure that the proposed arrangements are made and implemented.

(3) For the purposes of this section, the arrangements for selecting the trustees of a scheme include all matters relating to the continuation in office of the existing trustees, the selection or appointment of new trustees and the terms of their appointments and any special rules for decisions to be made by particular trustees.

(4) Section 16 does not apply to a trust scheme if—
  (a) the trustees of the scheme consist of all the members, or
  (b) it falls within a prescribed class.

(5) Section 10 applies to any employer who—
  (a) makes such a proposal as is referred to in subsection (1)(a), but
  (b) fails to give effect to the statutory consultation procedure.

Definitions For "the statutory consultation procedure", see s 21(7); for "prescribed" and "trust scheme", see s 124(1); for "employer", see ss 124(1), 125(3).
References See paras 3.1–3.11.

18 Corporate trustees: member-nominated directors

(1) Where a company is a trustee of a trust scheme and the employer is connected with the company or prescribed conditions are satisfied, the company must, subject to section 19, secure—
  (a) that such arrangements for persons selected by the members of the scheme to be directors of the company as are required by this section are made, and
  (b) that those arrangements, and the appropriate rules, are implemented.

(2) Persons who become directors under the arrangements required by subsection (1) are referred to in this Part as "member-nominated directors".

(3) The arrangements must provide—
  (a) for any person who has been nominated and selected in accordance with the appropriate rules to become a director by virtue of his selection, and

(b) for the removal of such a person to require the agreement of all the other directors.

(4) Where a vacancy for a member-nominated director is not filled because insufficient nominations are received, the arrangements must provide for the filling of the vacancy, or for the vacancy to remain, until the expiry of the next period in which persons may be nominated and selected in accordance with the appropriate rules.

(5) The arrangements must provide for the selection of a person as a member-nominated director to have effect for a period of not less than three nor more than six years.

(6) The arrangements must provide for the number of member-nominated directors to be—
- (a) at least two or (if the scheme comprises less than 100 members) at least one, and
- (b) at least one-third of the total number of directors;

but the arrangements must not provide for a greater number of member-nominated directors than that required to satisfy that minimum unless the employer has given his approval to the greater number.

(7) The arrangements must provide that, if a member-nominated director who was a member of the scheme when he was appointed ceases to be a member of the scheme, he ceases to be a director by virtue of that fact.

(8) Where this section applies to a company which is—
- (a) a trustee of two or more trust schemes, and
- (b) a wholly-owned subsidiary (within the meaning of section 736 of the Companies Act 1985) of a company which is the employer in relation to those schemes,

the following provisions apply as if those schemes were a single scheme and the members of each of the schemes were members of that scheme, that is: the preceding provisions of this section, section 20 and section 21(8).

Definitions For "the appropriate rules", see s 20(1); for "prescribed" and "trust scheme", see s 124(1); for "employer", see ss 124(1), 125(3); for "member", see ss 124(1), 125(4). Note as to "member-nominated directors", sub-s (2) above.
References See paras 3.1–3.11.

19 Corporate trustees: exceptions

(1) Section 18 does not apply to a company which is a trustee of a trust scheme if—
- (a) a proposal has been made by the employer for the continuation of existing arrangements, or the adoption of new arrangements, for selecting the directors of the company,
- (b) the arrangements referred to in the proposal are for the time being approved under the statutory consultation procedure, and
- (c) such other requirements as may be prescribed are satisfied.

(2) Where—
- (a) by virtue of subsection (1), section 18 does not apply to a company which is a trustee of a trust scheme, and
- (b) the employer's proposal was for the adoption of new arrangements which, in consequence of subsection (1)(b), are adopted,

the company must secure that the proposed arrangements are made and implemented.

(3) For the purposes of this section, the arrangements for selecting the directors of a company include all matters relating to the continuation in office of the existing

Pensions Act 1995, s 19

directors, the selection or appointment of new directors and the terms of their appointments and any special rules for decisions to be made by particular directors.

(4) Section 18 does not apply to a company which is a trustee of a trust scheme if the scheme falls within a prescribed class.

(5) Section 10 applies to any employer who—
    (a) makes such a proposal as is referred to in subsection (1)(a), but
    (b) fails to give effect to the statutory consultation procedure.

Definitions For "the statutory consulation procedure", see s 21(7); for "prescribed" and "trust scheme", see s 124(1); for "employer", see ss 124(1), 125(3)
References See paras 3.1–3.11.

20 Selection, and eligibility, of member-nominated trustees and directors

(1) For the purposes of sections 16 to 21, the appropriate rules are rules which—
    (a) make the provision required or authorised by this section, and no other provision, and
    (b) are for the time being approved under the statutory consultation procedure or, if no rules are for the time being so approved, are prescribed rules;
and the arrangements required by section 16 or 18 to be made must not make any provision which is required or authorised to be made by the rules.

(2) The appropriate rules—
    (a) must determine the procedure for the nomination and selection of a person to fill a vacancy as a member-nominated trustee, and
    (b) may determine, or provide for the determination of, the conditions required of a person for filling such a vacancy.

(3) The appropriate rules must provide for a member-nominated trustee to be eligible for re-selection at the end of his period of service.

(4) Where a vacancy for a member-nominated trustee is not filled because insufficient nominations are received, the appropriate rules must provide for determining the next period in which persons may be nominated and selected in accordance with the rules, being a period ending at a prescribed time.

(5) The appropriate rules must provide that, where the employer so requires, a person who is not a member of the scheme must have the employer's approval to qualify for selection as a member-nominated trustee.

(6) Where section 18 applies to a trust scheme, references in this section to a member-nominated trustee include a member-nominated director.

Definitions For "member-nominated trustee", see s 16(2); for "member-nominated directors", see s 18(2); for "the statutory consulation procedure", see s 21(7); for "prescribed" and "trust scheme", see s 124(1); for "employer", see ss 124(1), 125(3). Note as to the appropriate rules", sub-s (1) above.
References See paras 3.1–3.11.

21 Member-nominated trustees and directors: supplementary

(1) If, in the case of a trust scheme—
    (a) such arrangements as are required by section 16(1) or 17(2) to be made have not been made, or
    (b) arrangements required by section 16(1) or 17(2) to be implemented, or the appropriate rules, are not being implemented,
sections 3 and 10 apply to any trustee who has failed to take all such steps as are reasonable to secure compliance.

(2) If, in the case of a company which is a trustee of a trust scheme—
    (a) such arrangements as are required by section 18(1) or 19(2) to be made have not been made, or
    (b) arrangements required by section 18(1) or 19(2) to be implemented, or the appropriate rules, are not being implemented,
sections 3 and 10 apply to the company.

(3) No such arrangements or rules as are required by section 16(1) or 17(2), or any corresponding provisions in force in Northern Ireland, to be made or implemented shall be treated as effecting an alteration to the scheme in question for the purposes of section 591B of the Taxes Act 1988.

(4) Regulations may make provision for determining the time by which—
    (a) such arrangements (or further arrangements) as are referred to in section 16(1), 17(2), 18(1) or 19(2) are required to be made, and
    (b) trustees or directors are required to be selected in pursuance of the appropriate rules.

(5) Regulations may make provision for determining when any approval under the statutory consultation procedure—
    (a) of the appropriate rules, or
    (b) of arrangements for selecting the trustees of a scheme, or the directors of a company, given on a proposal by the employer,
is to cease to have effect.

(6) The Secretary of State may by regulations modify sections 16 to 20 and this section in their application to prescribed cases.

(7) In sections 16 to 20 and this section, "the statutory consultation procedure" means the prescribed procedure for obtaining the views of members of schemes.

(8) For the purposes of this and those sections—
    (a) approval of the appropriate rules, or of arrangements, under the statutory consultation procedure must be given by—
        (i) the active and pensioner members of the scheme, and
        (ii) if the trustees so determine, such deferred members of the scheme as the trustees may determine,
    taken as a whole, and
    (b) references to the approval of the appropriate rules, or of arrangements under section 17 or 19, by any persons under the statutory consultation procedure are to prescribed conditions in respect of those rules or, as the case may be, arrangements being satisfied in the case of those persons in pursuance of the procedure, and those conditions may relate to the extent to which those persons have either endorsed, or not objected to, the rules or, as the case may be, arrangements.

Definitions For "the appropriate rules", see s 20(1); for "active member", "deferred member", "pensioner member", "prescribed", "regulations" and "trust scheme", see s 124(1); for "employer", see ss 124(1), 125(3); for "member", see ss 124(1), 125(4). By virtue of s 124(5), for "modify", see the Pension Schemes Act 1993, s 181(1). Note as to "the statutory consultation procedure", sub-s (7) above.
References See paras 3.1–3.11.

Independent trustees

22 Circumstances in which following provisions apply

(1) This section applies in relation to a trust scheme—
    (a) if a person (referred to in this section and sections 23 to 26 as "the practitioner") begins to act as an insolvency practitioner in relation to a company which, or an individual who, is the employer in relation to the scheme, or

(b) if the official receiver becomes—
    (i) the liquidator or provisional liquidator of a company which is the employer in relation to the scheme, or
    (ii) the receiver and the manager, or the trustee, of the estate of a bankrupt who is the employer in relation to the scheme.

(2) Where this section applies in relation to a scheme, it ceases to do so—
    (a) if some person other than the employer mentioned in subsection (1) becomes the employer, or
    (b) if at any time neither the practitioner nor the official receiver is acting in relation to the employer;

but this subsection does not affect the application of this section in relation to the scheme on any subsequent occasion when the conditions specified in subsection (1)(a) or (b) are satisfied in relation to it.

(3) In this section and sections 23 to 26—

"acting as an insolvency practitioner" and "official receiver" shall be construed in accordance with sections 388 and 399 of the Insolvency Act 1986,

"bankrupt" has the meaning given by section 381 of the Insolvency Act 1986,

"company" means a company within the meaning given by section 735(1) of the Companies Act 1985 or a company which may be wound up under Part V of the Insolvency Act 1986 (unregistered companies), and

"interim trustee" and "permanent trustee" have the same meanings as they have in the Bankruptcy (Scotland) Act 1985.

Definitions For "trust scheme", see s 124(1); for "employer", see ss 124(1), 125(3). Note as to "the practitioner", sub-s (1)(a) above; and as to "acting as an insolvency practitioner", "bankrupt", "company", "interim trustee", "official receiver" and "permanent trustee", sub-s (3) above.
References See paras 3.12–3.14.

23 Requirement for independent trustee

(1) While section 22 applies in relation to a scheme, the practitioner or official receiver must—
    (a) satisfy himself that at all times at least one of the trustees of the scheme is an independent person, and
    (b) if at any time he is not so satisfied, appoint under this paragraph, or secure the appointment of, an independent person as a trustee of the scheme.

(2) The duty under subsection (1)(b) must be performed as soon as reasonably practicable and, if a period is prescribed for the purposes of that subsection, within that period.

(3) For the purposes of subsection (1) a person is independent only if—
    (a) he has no interest in the assets of the employer or of the scheme, otherwise than as trustee of the scheme,
    (b) he is neither connected with, nor an associate of—
        (i) the employer,
        (ii) any person for the time being acting as an insolvency practitioner in relation to the employer, or
        (iii) the official receiver, acting in any of the capacities mentioned in section 22(1)(b) in relation to the employer, and
    (c) he satisfies any prescribed requirements;

and any reference in this Part to an independent trustee shall be construed accordingly.

(4) Where, apart from this subsection, the duties imposed by subsection (1) in relation to a scheme would fall to be discharged at the same time by two or more persons acting in different capacities, those duties shall be discharged—
    (a) if the employer is a company, by the person or persons acting as the company's liquidator, provisional liquidator or administrator, or
    (b) if the employer is an individual, by the person or persons acting as his trustee in bankruptcy or interim receiver of his property or as permanent or interim trustee in the sequestration of his estate.

(5) References in this section to an individual include, except where the context otherwise requires, references to a partnership and to any debtor within the meaning of the Bankruptcy (Scotland) Act 1985.

Definitions As to "the practitioner", see s 22(1)(a); as to "acting as an insolvency practitioner", "company", "interim trustee", "official receiver" and "permanent trustee", see s 22(3); for "prescribed", see s 124(1); for "employer", see ss 124(1), 125(3). Note as to "an independent trustee", sub-s (3) above; and as to "an individual", sub-s (5) above.
References See para 3.15.

24 Members' powers to apply to court to enforce duty

(1) If—
    (a) section 22 applies in relation to a trust scheme, but
    (b) the practitioner or official receiver neglects or refuses to discharge any duty imposed on him by section 23(1) in relation to the scheme,
any member of the scheme may apply to the appropriate court for an order requiring him to discharge his duties under section 23(1).

(2) In subsection (1) "the appropriate court" means—
    (a) if the employer in question is a company—
        (i) where a winding-up order has been made or a provisional liquidator appointed, the court which made the order or appointed the liquidator,
        (ii) in any other case, any court having jurisdiction to wind up the company, and
    (b) in any other case—
        (i) in England and Wales, the court (as defined in section 385 of the Insolvency Act 1986), or
        (ii) in Scotland, where a sequestration has been awarded or, by virtue of the proviso to section 13(1) of the Bankruptcy (Scotland) Act 1985 (petition presented by creditor or trustee acting under trust deed) an interim trustee has been appointed, the court which made the award or appointment and, if no such award or appointment has been made, any court having jurisdiction under section 9 of that Act.

Definitions As to "the practitioner", see 22(1)(a); as to "company", "interim trustee" and "official receiver", see s 22(3); for "trust scheme", see s 124(1); for "employer", see ss 124(1), 125(3); for "member", see ss 124(1),125(4).
References See para 3.16.

25 Appointment and powers of independent trustees: further provisions

(1) If, immediately before the appointment of an independent trustee under section 23(1)(b), there is no trustee of the scheme other than the employer, the employer shall cease to be a trustee upon the appointment of the independent trustee.

(2) While section 22 applies in relation to a scheme—
    (a) any power vested in the trustees of the scheme and exercisable at their discretion may be exercised only by the independent trustee, and

(b) any power—
  (i) which the scheme confers on the employer (otherwise than as trustee of the scheme), and
  (ii) which is exercisable by him at his discretion but only as trustee of the power,
may be exercised only by the independent trustee,
but if, in either case, there is more than one independent trustee, the power may also be exercised with the consent of at least half of those trustees by any person who could exercise it apart from this subsection.

(3) While section 22 applies in relation to a scheme, no independent trustee of the scheme may be removed from being a trustee by virtue only of any provision of the scheme.

(4) If a trustee appointed under section 23(1)(b) ceases to be an independent person, then—
  (a) he must immediately give written notice of that fact to the practitioner or official receiver by whom the duties under that provision fall to be discharged, and
  (b) subject to subsection (5), he shall cease to be a trustee of the scheme.

(5) If, in a case where subsection (4) applies, there is no other trustee of the scheme than the former independent trustee, he shall not cease by virtue of that subsection to be a trustee until such time as another trustee is appointed.

(6) A trustee appointed under section 23(1)(b) is entitled to be paid out of the scheme's resources his reasonable fees for acting in that capacity and any expenses reasonably incurred by him in doing so, and to be so paid in priority to all other claims falling to be met out of the scheme's resources.

Definitions As to "the practitioner", see s 22(1)(a); as to "official receiver", see s 22(3); as to "independent trustee", see s 23(3); for "resources", see s 124(1); for "employer", see ss 124(1), 125(3).
References See para 3.17.

26 Insolvency practitioner or official receiver to give information to trustees

(1) Notwithstanding anything in section 155 of the Insolvency Act 1986 (court orders for inspection etc), while section 22 applies in relation to a scheme, the practitioner or official receiver must provide the trustees of the scheme, as soon as practicable after the receipt of a request, with any information which the trustees may reasonably require for the purposes of the scheme.

(2) Any expenses incurred by the practitioner or official receiver in complying with a request under subsection (1) are recoverable by him as part of the expenses incurred by him in discharge of his duties.

(3) The practitioner or official receiver is not required under subsection (1) to take any action which involves expenses that cannot be so recovered, unless the trustees of the scheme undertake to meet them.

Definitions As to "the practitioner", see s 22(1)(a); as to "the official receiver", see s 22(3).
References See para 3.18.

Trustees: general

27 Trustee not to be auditor or actuary of the scheme

(1) A trustee of a trust scheme, and any person who is connected with, or an associate of, such a trustee, is ineligible to act as an auditor or actuary of the scheme.

(2) Subsection (1) does not make a person who is a director, partner or employee of a firm of actuaries ineligible to act as an actuary of a trust scheme merely because another director, partner or employee of the firm is a trustee of the scheme.

(3) Subsection (1) does not make a person who falls within a prescribed class or description ineligible to act as an auditor or actuary of a trust scheme.

(4) A person must not act as an auditor or actuary of a trust scheme if he is ineligible under this section to do so.

(5) In this section and section 28 references to a trustee of a trust scheme do not include—
    (a) a trustee, or
    (b) a trustee of a scheme,
falling within a prescribed class or description.

Definitions As to "the actuary" and "the auditor", see s 47(1); for "firm", "prescribed" and "trust scheme", see s 124(1). By virtue of s 124(5), for "employee", see the Pension Schemes Act 1993, s 181(1). Note as to "a trustee of a trust scheme", sub-s (5) above.
References See paras 5.8, 5.9.

28 Section 27: consequences

(1) Any person who acts as an auditor or actuary of a trust scheme in contravention of section 27(4) is guilty of an offence and liable—
    (a) on summary conviction, to a fine not exceeding the statutory maximum, and
    (b) on conviction on indictment, to imprisonment or a fine, or both.

(2) An offence under subsection (1) may be charged by reference to any day or longer period of time; and a person may be convicted of a second or subsequent offence under that subsection by reference to any period of time following the preceding conviction of the offence.

(3) Acts done as an auditor or actuary of a trust scheme by a person who is ineligible under section 27 to do so are not invalid merely because of that fact.

(4) Where—
    (a) a trustee of a trust scheme acts as auditor or actuary of the scheme, or
    (b) a person acts as auditor or actuary of a trust scheme when he is ineligible under section 27 to do so by reason of being connected with, or an associate of, a trustee of the scheme,
section 3 applies to the trustee.

Definitions As to "a trustee of a trust scheme", see s 27(5); for "the actuary" and "the auditor", see s 47(1); for "contravention" and "trust scheme", see s 124(1).
References See para 5.10.

29 Persons disqualified for being trustees

(1) Subject to subsection (5), a person is disqualified for being a trustee of any trust scheme if—
    (a) he has been convicted of any offence involving dishonesty or deception,
    (b) he has been adjudged bankrupt or sequestration of his estate has been awarded and (in either case) he has not been discharged,
    (c) where the person is a company, if any director of the company is disqualified under this section,
    (d) where the person is a Scottish partnership, if any partner is disqualified under this section,

(e) he has made a composition contract or an arrangement with, or granted a trust deed for the behoof of, his creditors and has not been discharged in respect of it, or

(f) he is subject to a disqualification order under the Company Directors Disqualification Act 1986 or to an order made under section 429(2)(b) of the Insolvency Act 1986 (failure to pay under county court administration order).

(2) In subsection (1)—
  (a) paragraph (a) applies whether the conviction occurred before or after the coming into force of that subsection, but does not apply in relation to any conviction which is a spent conviction for the purposes of the Rehabilitation of Offenders Act 1974,
  (b) paragraph (b) applies whether the adjudication of bankruptcy or the sequestration occurred before or after the coming into force of that subsection,
  (c) paragraph (e) applies whether the composition contract or arrangement was made, or the trust deed was granted, before or after the coming into force of that subsection, and
  (d) paragraph (f) applies in relation to orders made before or after the coming into force of that subsection.

(3) Where a person—
  (a) is prohibited from being a trustee of a trust scheme by an order under section 3, or
  (b) has been removed as a trustee of a trust scheme by an order made (whether before or after the coming into force of this subsection) by the High Court or the Court of Session on the grounds of misconduct or mismanagement in the administration of the scheme for which he was responsible or to which he was privy, or which he by his conduct contributed to or facilitated,

the Authority may, if in their opinion it is not desirable for him to be a trustee of any trust scheme, by order disqualify him for being a trustee of any trust scheme.

(4) The Authority may by order disqualify a person for being a trustee of any trust scheme where—
  (a) in their opinion he is incapable of acting as such a trustee by reason of mental disorder (within the meaning of the Mental Health Act 1983 or, as respects Scotland, the Mental Health (Scotland) Act 1984), or
  (b) the person is a company which has gone into liquidation (within the meaning of section 247(2) of the Insolvency Act 1986).

(5) The Authority may, on the application of any person disqualified under this section—
  (a) give notice in writing to him waiving his disqualification,
  (b) in the case of a person disqualified under subsection (3) or (4), by order revoke the order disqualifying him,

either generally or in relation to a particular scheme or particular class of schemes.

(6) A notice given or revocation made at any time by virtue of subsection (5) cannot affect anything done before that time.

Definitions For "the Authority", see s 1(1); for "Scottish partnership" and "trust scheme", see s 124(1).
References See paras 2.17–2.19.

30 Persons disqualified: consequences

(1) A trustee of a trust scheme who becomes disqualified under section 29 shall, while he is so disqualified, cease to be a trustee.

(2) Where—
   (a) a trustee of a trust scheme becomes disqualified under section 29, or
   (b) in the case of a trustee of a trust scheme who has become so disqualified, his disqualification is waived or the order disqualifying him is revoked or he otherwise ceases to be disqualified,

the Authority may exercise the same jurisdiction and powers as are exercisable by the High Court or, in relation to a trust scheme subject to the law of Scotland, the Court of Session for vesting any property in, or transferring any property to, the trustees.

(3) A person who purports to act as a trustee of a trust scheme while he is disqualified under section 29 is guilty of an offence and liable—
   (a) on summary conviction to a fine not exceeding the statutory maximum, and
   (b) on conviction on indictment, to a fine or imprisonment or both.

(4) An offence under subsection (3) may be charged by reference to any day or longer period of time; and a person may be convicted of a second or subsequent offence under that subsection by reference to any period of time following the preceding conviction of the offence.

(5) Things done by a person disqualified under section 29 while purporting to act as trustee of a trust scheme are not invalid merely because of that disqualification.

(6) Nothing in section 29 or this section affects the liability of any person for things done, or omitted to be done, by him while purporting to act as trustee of a trust scheme.

(7) The Authority must keep, in such manner as they think fit, a register of all persons who are disqualified under section 29(3) or (4); and the Authority must, if requested to do so, disclose whether the name of a person specified in the request is included in the register in respect of a scheme so specified.

Definitions For "the Authority", see s 1(1); for "trust scheme", see s 124(1).
References See paras 2.20, 2.21.

31 Trustees not to be indemnified for fines or civil penalties

(1) No amount may be paid out of the assets of a trust scheme for the purpose of reimbursing, or providing for the reimbursement of, any trustee of the scheme in respect of—
   (a) a fine imposed by way of penalty for an offence of which he is convicted, or
   (b) a penalty which he is required to pay under section 10 or under section 168(4) of the Pension Schemes Act 1993.

(2) For the purposes of subsection (1), providing for the reimbursement of a trustee in respect of a fine or penalty includes (among other things) providing for the payment of premiums in respect of a policy of insurance where the risk is or includes the imposition of such a fine or the requirement to pay such a penalty.

(3) Where any amount is paid out of the assets of a trust scheme in contravention of this section, sections 3 and 10 apply to any trustee who fails to take all such steps as are reasonable to secure compliance.

(4) Where a trustee of a trust scheme—
   (a) is reimbursed, out of the assets of the scheme or in consequence of provision for his reimbursement made out of those assets, in respect of any of the matters referred to in subsection (1)(a) or (b), and
   (b) knows, or has reasonable grounds to believe, that he has been reimbursed as mentioned in paragraph (a),

then, unless he has taken all such steps as are reasonable to secure that he is not so reimbursed, he is guilty of an offence.

(5) A person guilty of an offence under subsection (4) is liable—
    (a) on summary conviction, to a fine not exceeding the statutory maximum, and
    (b) on conviction on indictment, to imprisonment, or a fine, or both.

Definitions For "contravention" and "trust scheme", see s 124(1).
References See para 2.33.

Functions of trustees

32 Decisions by majority

(1) Decisions of the trustees of a trust scheme may, unless the scheme provides otherwise, be taken by agreement of a majority of the trustees.

(2) Where decisions of the trustees of a trust scheme may be taken by agreement of a majority of the trustees—
    (a) the trustees may, unless the scheme provides otherwise, by a determination under this subsection require not less than the number of trustees specified in the determination to be present when any decision is so taken, and
    (b) notice of any occasions at which decisions may be so taken must, unless the occasion falls within a prescribed class or description, be given to each trustee to whom it is reasonably practicable to give such notice.

(3) Notice under subsection (2)(b) must be given in a prescribed manner and not later than the beginning of a prescribed period.

(4) This section is subject to sections 8(4)(b), 16(3)(b) and 25(2).

(5) If subsection (2)(b) is not complied with, sections 3 and 10 apply to any trustee who has failed to take all such steps as are reasonable to secure compliance.

Definitions For "prescribed" and "trust scheme", see s 124(1).
References See paras 3.21, 3.22.

33 Investment powers: duty of care

(1) Liability for breach of an obligation under any rule of law to take care or exercise skill in the performance of any investment functions, where the function is exercisable—
    (a) by a trustee of a trust scheme, or
    (b) by a person to whom the function has been delegated under section 34,
cannot be excluded or restricted by any instrument or agreement.

(2) In this section, references to excluding or restricting liability include—
    (a) making the liability or its enforcement subject to restrictive or onerous conditions,
    (b) excluding or restricting any right or remedy in respect of the liability, or subjecting a person to any prejudice in consequence of his pursuing any such right or remedy, or
    (c) excluding or restricting rules of evidence or procedure.

(3) This section does not apply—
    (a) to a scheme falling within any prescribed class or description, or
    (b) to any prescribed description of exclusion or restriction.

Definitions For "prescribed" and "trust scheme", see s 124(1). Note as to "excluding or restricting liability", sub-s (2) above.
References See paras 3.23–3.28.

34 Power of investment and delegation

(1) The trustees of a trust scheme have, subject to any restriction imposed by the scheme, the same power to make an investment of any kind as if they were absolutely entitled to the assets of the scheme.

(2) Any discretion of the trustees of a trust scheme to make any decision about investments—
- (a) may be delegated by or on behalf of the trustees to a fund manager to whom subsection (3) applies to be exercised in accordance with section 36, but
- (b) may not otherwise be delegated except under section 25 of the Trustee Act 1925 (delegation of trusts during absence abroad) or subsection (5) below.

(3) This subsection applies to a fund manager who, in relation to the decisions in question, falls, or is treated as falling, within any of paragraphs (a) to (c) of section 191(2) of the Financial Services Act 1986 (occupational pension schemes: exemptions where decisions taken by authorised and other persons).

(4) The trustees are not responsible for the act or default of any fund manager in the exercise of any discretion delegated to him under subsection (2)(a) if they have taken all such steps as are reasonable to satisfy themselves or the person who made the delegation on their behalf has taken all such steps as are reasonable to satisfy himself—
- (a) that the fund manager has the appropriate knowledge and experience for managing the investments of the scheme, and
- (b) that he is carrying out his work competently and complying with section 36.

(5) Subject to any restriction imposed by a trust scheme—
- (a) the trustees may authorise two or more of their number to exercise on their behalf any discretion to make any decision about investments, and
- (b) any such discretion may, where giving effect to the decision would not constitute carrying on investment business in the United Kingdom (within the meaning of the Financial Services Act 1986), be delegated by or on behalf of the trustees to a fund manager to whom subsection (3) does not apply to be exercised in accordance with section 36;

but in either case the trustees are liable for any acts or defaults in the exercise of the discretion if they would be so liable if they were the acts or defaults of the trustees as a whole.

(6) Section 33 does not prevent the exclusion or restriction of any liability of the trustees of a trust scheme for the acts or defaults of a fund manager in the exercise of a discretion delegated to him under subsection (5)(b) where the trustees have taken all such steps as are reasonable to satisfy themselves, or the person who made the delegation on their behalf has taken all such steps as are reasonable to satisfy himself—
- (a) that the fund manager has the appropriate knowledge and experience for managing the investments of the scheme, and
- (b) that he is carrying out his work competently and complying with section 36;

and subsection (2) of section 33 applies for the purposes of this subsection as it applies for the purposes of that section.

(7) The provisions of this section override any restriction inconsistent with the provisions imposed by any rule of law or by or under any enactment, other than an enactment contained in, or made under, this Part or the Pension Schemes Act 1993.

Definitions For "fund manager" and "trust scheme", see s 124(1); for "enactment", see s 176.
References See paras 3.23–3.28.

Pensions Act 1995, s 35

35 Investment principles

(1) The trustees of a trust scheme must secure that there is prepared, maintained and from time to time revised a written statement of the principles governing decisions about investments for the purposes of the scheme.

(2) The statement must cover, among other things—
   (a) the trustees' policy for securing compliance with sections 36 and 56, and
   (b) their policy about the following matters.

(3) Those matters are—
   (a) the kinds of investments to be held,
   (b) the balance between different kinds of investments,
   (c) risk,
   (d) the expected return on investments,
   (e) the realisation of investments, and
   (f) such other matters as may be prescribed.

(4) Neither the trust scheme nor the statement may impose restrictions (however expressed) on any power to make investments by reference to the consent of the employer.

(5) The trustees of a trust scheme must, before a statement under this section is prepared or revised—
   (a) obtain and consider the written advice of a person who is reasonably believed by the trustees to be qualified by his ability in and practical experience of financial matters and to have the appropriate knowledge and experience of the management of the investments of such schemes, and
   (b) consult the employer.

(6) If in the case of any trust scheme—
   (a) a statement under this section has not been prepared or is not being maintained, or
   (b) the trustees have not obtained and considered advice in accordance with subsection (5),

sections 3 and 10 apply to any trustee who has failed to take all such steps as are reasonable to secure compliance.

(7) This section does not apply to any scheme which falls within a prescribed class or description.

Definitions For "prescribed" and "trust scheme", see s 124(1); for "employer", see ss 124(1), 125(3).
References See paras 3.29, 3.30.

36 Choosing investments

(1) The trustees of a trust scheme must exercise their powers of investment in accordance with subsections (2) to (4) and any fund manager to whom any discretion has been delegated under section 34 must exercise the discretion in accordance with subsection (2).

(2) The trustees or fund manager must have regard—
   (a) to the need for diversification of investments, in so far as appropriate to the circumstances of the scheme, and
   (b) to the suitability to the scheme of investments of the description of investment proposed and of the investment proposed as an investment of that description.

(3) Before investing in any manner (other than in a manner mentioned in Part I of Schedule 1 to the Trustee Investments Act 1961) the trustees must obtain and consider proper advice on the question whether the investment is satisfactory having

regard to the matters mentioned in subsection (2) and the principles contained in the statement under section 35.

(4) Trustees retaining any investment must—
   (a) determine at what intervals the circumstances, and in particular the nature of the investment, make it desirable to obtain such advice as is mentioned in subsection (3), and
   (b) obtain and consider such advice accordingly.

(5) The trustees, or the fund manager to whom any discretion has been delegated under section 34, must exercise their powers of investment with a view to giving effect to the principles contained in the statement under section 35, so far as reasonably practicable.

(6) For the purposes of this section "proper advice" means—
   (a) where giving the advice constitutes carrying on investment business in the United Kingdom (within the meaning of the Financial Services Act 1986), advice—
      (i) given by a person authorised under Chapter III of Part I of that Act,
      (ii) given by a person exempted under Chapter IV of that Part who, in giving the advice, is acting in the course of the business in respect of which he is exempt,
      (iii) given by a person where, by virtue of paragraph 27 of Schedule 1 to that Act, paragraph 15 of that Schedule does not apply to giving the advice, or
      (iv) given by a person who, by virtue of regulation 5 of the Banking Coordination (Second Council Directive) Regulations 1992, may give the advice though not authorised as mentioned in sub-paragraph (i) above.
   (b) in any other case, the advice of a person who is reasonably believed by the trustees to be qualified by his ability in and practical experience of financial matters and to have the appropriate knowledge and experience of the management of the investments of trust schemes.

(7) Trustees shall not be treated as having complied with subsection (3) or (4) unless the advice was given or has subsequently been confirmed in writing.

(8) If the trustees of a trust scheme do not obtain and consider advice in accordance with this section, sections 3 and 10 apply to any trustee who has failed to take all such steps as are reasonable to secure compliance.

Definitions For "fund manager" and "trust scheme", see s 124(1). Note as to "proper advice", sub-s (6) above.
References See para 3.31.

37 Payment of surplus to employer

(1) This section applies to a trust scheme if—
   (a) apart from this section, power is conferred on any person (including the employer) to make payments to the employer out of funds which are held for the purposes of the scheme,
   (b) the scheme is one to which Schedule 22 to the Taxes Act 1988 (reduction of pension fund surpluses in certain exempt approved schemes) applies, and
   (c) the scheme is not being wound up.

(2) Where the power referred to in subsection (1)(a) is conferred by the scheme on a person other than the trustees, it cannot be exercised by that person but may be exercised instead by the trustees; and any restriction imposed by the scheme on the exercise of the power shall, so far as capable of doing so, apply to its exercise by the trustees.

(3) The power referred to in subsection (1)(a) cannot be exercised unless the requirements of subsection (4) and (in prescribed circumstances) (5), and any prescribed requirements, are satisfied.

(4) The requirements of this subsection are that—
- (a) the power is exercised in pursuance of proposals approved under paragraph 6(1) of Schedule 22 to the Taxes Act 1988,
- (b) the trustees are satisfied that it is in the interests of the members that the power be exercised in the manner so proposed,
- (c) where the power is conferred by the scheme on the employer, the employer has asked for the power to be exercised, or consented to it being exercised, in the manner so proposed,
- (d) the annual rates of the pensions under the scheme which commence or have commenced are increased by the appropriate percentage, and
- (e) notice has been given in accordance with prescribed requirements to the members of the scheme of the proposal to exercise the power.

(5) The requirements of this subsection are that the Authority are of the opinion that—
- (a) any requirements prescribed by virtue of subsection (3) are satisfied, and
- (b) the requirements of subsection (4) are satisfied.

(6) In subsection (4)—
- (a) "annual rate" and "appropriate percentage" have the same meaning as in section 54, and
- (b) "pension" does not include—
  - (i) any guaranteed minimum pension (as defined in section 8(2) of the Pension Schemes Act 1993) or any increase in such a pension under section 109 of that Act, or
  - (ii) any money purchase benefit (as defined in section 181(1) of that Act).

(7) This section does not apply to any payment to which, by virtue of section 601(3) of the Taxes Act 1988, section 601(2) of that Act does not apply.

(8) If, where this section applies to any trust scheme, the trustees purport to exercise the power referred to in subsection (1)(a) by making a payment to which this section applies without complying with the requirements of this section, sections 3 and 10 apply to any trustee who has failed to take all such steps as are reasonable to secure compliance.

(9) If, where this section applies to any trust scheme, any person, other than the trustees, purports to exercise the power referred to in subsection (1)(a) by making a payment to which this section applies, section 10 applies to him.

(10) Regulations may provide that, in prescribed circumstances, this section does not apply to schemes falling within a prescribed class or description, or applies to them with prescribed modifications.

Definitions For "the Authority", see s 1(1); for "prescribed", "regulations" and "trust scheme", see s 124(1); for "employer", see ss 124(1), 125(3); for "member", see ss 124(1), 125(4). By virtue of s 124(5), for "modifications", see the Pension Schemes Act 1993, s 181(1).
References See paras 6.14–6.17.

38 Power to defer winding up

(1) If, apart from this section, the rules of a trust scheme would require the scheme to be wound up, the trustees may determine that the scheme is not for the time being to be wound up but that no new members are to be admitted to the scheme.

(2) Where the trustees make a determination under subsection (1), they may also determine—
- (a) that no further contributions are to be paid towards the scheme, or

(b) that no new benefits are to accrue to, or in respect of, members of the scheme;

but this subsection does not authorise the trustees to determine, where there are accrued rights to any benefit, that the benefit is not to be increased.

(3) This section does not apply to—
    (a) a money purchase scheme, or
    (b) a scheme falling within a prescribed class or description.

Definitions   For "prescribed" and "trust scheme", see s 124(1); for "accrued rights", see s 124(2); for "member", see ss 124(1), 125(4). By virtue of s 124(5), for "money purchase scheme", see the Pension Schemes Act 1993, s 181(1).
References   See paras 10.20, 10.21.

39 Exercise of powers by member trustees

No rule of law that a trustee may not exercise the powers vested in him so as to give rise to a conflict between his personal interest and his duties to the beneficiaries shall apply to a trustee of a trust scheme, who is also a member of the scheme, exercising the powers vested in him in any manner, merely because their exercise in that manner benefits, or may benefit, him as a member of the scheme.

Definitions   For "trust scheme", see s 124(1); for "member", see ss 124(1), 125(4).
References   See paras 3.19, 3.20.

Functions of trustees or managers

40 Restriction on employer-related investments

(1) The trustees or managers of an occupational pension scheme must secure that the scheme complies with any prescribed restrictions with respect to the proportion of its resources that may at any time be invested in, or in any description of, employer-related investments.

(2) In this section—
    "employer-related investments" means—
        (a) shares or other securities issued by the employer or by any person who is connected with, or an associate of, the employer,
        (b) land which is occupied or used by, or subject to a lease in favour of, the employer or any such person,
        (c) property (other than land) which is used for the purposes of any business carried on by the employer or any such person,
        (d) loans to the employer or any such person, and
        (e) other prescribed investments,
    "securities" means any asset, right or interest falling within paragraph 1, 2, 4 or 5 of Schedule 1 to the Financial Services Act 1986.

(3) To the extent (if any) that sums due and payable by a person to the trustees or managers of an occupational pension scheme remain unpaid—
    (a) they shall be regarded for the purposes of this section as loans made to that person by the trustees or managers, and
    (b) resources of the scheme shall be regarded as invested accordingly.

(4) If in the case of a trust scheme subsection (1) is not complied with, sections 3 and 10 apply to any trustee who fails to take all such steps as are reasonable to secure compliance.

Pensions Act 1995, s 40

(5) If any resources of an occupational pension scheme are invested in contravention of subsection (1), any trustee or manager who agreed in the determination to make the investment is guilty of an offence and liable—
    (a) on summary conviction, to a fine not exceeding the statutory maximum, and
    (b) on conviction on indictment, to a fine or imprisonment, or both.

Definitions For "contravention", "prescribed", "resources" and "trustees or managers", see s 124(1); for "employer", see ss 124(1), 125(3). By virtue of s 176, for "occupational pension scheme", see the Pension Schemes Act 1993, s 1. Note as to "employer-related investments" and "securities", sub-s (2) above.
References See paras 3.32, 3.33.

41 Provision of documents for members

(1) Regulations may require the trustees or managers of an occupational pension scheme—
    (a) to obtain at prescribed times the documents mentioned in subsection (2), and
    (b) to make copies of them, and of the documents mentioned in subsection (3), available to the persons mentioned in subsection (4).

(2) The documents referred to in subsection (1)(a) are—
    (a) the accounts audited by the auditor of the scheme,
    (b) the auditor's statement about contributions under the scheme,
    (c) a valuation by the actuary of the assets and liabilities of the scheme, and a statement by the actuary concerning such aspects of the valuation as may be prescribed.

(3) The documents referred to in subsection (1)(b) are—
    (a) any valuation, or certificate, prepared under section 57 or 58 by the actuary of the scheme,
    (b) any report prepared by the trustees or managers under section 59(3).

(4) The persons referred to in subsection (1)(b) are—
    (a) members and prospective members of the scheme,
    (b) spouses of members and of prospective members,
    (c) persons within the application of the scheme and qualifying or prospectively qualifying for its benefits,
    (d) independent trade unions recognised to any extent for the purposes of collective bargaining in relation to members and prospective members of the scheme.

(5) Regulations may in the case of occupational pension schemes to which section 47 does not apply—
    (a) prescribe the persons who may act as auditors or actuaries for the purposes of subsection (2), or
    (b) provide that the persons who may so act shall be—
        (i) persons with prescribed professional qualifications or experience, or
        (ii) persons approved by the Secretary of State.

(6) Regulations shall make provision for referring to an industrial tribunal any question whether an organisation is such a trade union as is mentioned in subsection (4)(d) and may make provision as to the form and content of any such document as is referred to in subsection (2).

Definitions For the actuary" and "the auditor", see s 47(1); for "prescribed", "regulations" and "trustees or managers", see s 124(1); for "member" and "prospective member", see ss 124(1), 125(4). By virtue of s 124(5), for "independent trade union" and "industrial tribunal", see the Pension Schemes Act 1993, s 181(1). By virtue of s 176, for "occupational pension scheme", see s 1 of the 1993 Act.
References See paras 3.34, 3.35.

Employee trustees

42 Time off for performance of duties and for training

(1) The employer in relation to a trust scheme must permit any employee of his who is a trustee of the scheme to take time off during his working hours for the purpose of—
    (a) performing any of his duties as such a trustee, or
    (b) undergoing training relevant to the performance of those duties.

(2) The amount of time off which an employee is to be permitted to take under this section and the purposes for which, the occasions on which and any conditions subject to which time off may be so taken are those that are reasonable in all the circumstances having regard in particular to—
    (a) how much time off is required for the performance of the duties of a trustee of the scheme and the undergoing of relevant training, and how much time off is required for performing the particular duty or, as the case may be, for undergoing the particular training, and
    (b) the circumstances of the employer's business and the effect of the employee's absence on the running of that business.

(3) An employee may present a complaint to an industrial tribunal that his employer has failed to permit him to take time off as required by his section.

(4) For the purposes of this section, the working hours of an employee are any time when in accordance with his contract of employment he is required to be at work.

Definitions For "trust scheme", see s 124(1); for "employer", see ss 124(1), 125(3). By virtue of s 124(5), for "employee" and "industrial tribunal", see the Pension Schemes Act 1993, s 181(1). Note as to "the working hours of an employee", sub-s (4) above.
References See paras 3.39, 3.40.

43 Payment for time off

(1) An employer who permits an employee to take time off under section 42 must pay him for the time taken off pursuant to the permission.

(2) Where the employee's remuneration for the work he would ordinarily have been doing during that time does not vary with the amount of work done, he must be paid as if he had worked at that work for the whole of that time.

(3) Where the employee's remuneration for the work he would ordinarily have been doing during that time varies with the amount of work done, he must be paid an amount calculated by reference to the average hourly earnings for that work.

(4) The average hourly earnings mentioned in subsection (3) are those of the employee concerned or, if no fair estimate can be made of those earnings, the average hourly earnings for work of that description of persons in comparable employment with the same employer or, if there are no such persons, a figure of average hourly earnings which is reasonable in the circumstances.

(5) A right to be paid an amount under this section does not affect any right of an employee in relation to remuneration under his contract of employment, but—
    (a) any contractual remuneration paid to an employee in respect of a period of time off to which this section applies shall go towards discharging any liability of the employer under this section in respect of that period, and
    (b) any payment under this section in respect of a period shall go towards discharging any liability of the employer to pay contractual remuneration in respect of that period.

(6) An employee may present a complaint to an industrial tribunal that his employer has failed to pay him in accordance with this section.

Definitions For "employer", see ss 124(1), 125(3). By virtue of s 124(5), for "earnings", "employee", "employment" and "industrial tribunal", see the Pension Schemes Act 1993, s 181(1).
References See paras 3.39, 3.40.

44 Time limit for proceedings

An industrial tribunal must not consider a complaint under section 42 or 43 unless it is presented to the tribunal—
    (a) within three months of the date when the failure occurred, or
    (b) where the tribunal is satisfied that it was not reasonably practicable for the complaint to be presented within that period, within such further period as the tribunal considers reasonable.

Definitions For "industrial tribunal", see, by virtue of s 124(5), the Pension Schemes Act 1993, s 181(1).
References See paras 3.39, 3.40.

45 Remedies

(1) Where the tribunal finds a complaint under section 42 is well-founded, it must make a declaration to that effect and may make an award of compensation to be paid by the employer to the employee.

(2) The amount of the compensation shall be such as the tribunal considers just and equitable in all the circumstances having regard to the employer's default in failing to permit time off to be taken by the employee and to any loss sustained by the employee which is attributable to the matters complained of.

(3) Where on a complaint under section 43 the tribunal finds that the employer has failed to pay the employee in accordance with that section, it must order him to pay the amount which it finds to be due.

(4) The remedy of an employee for infringement of the rights conferred on him by section 42 or 43 is by way of complaint to an industrial tribunal in accordance with this Part, and not otherwise.

Definitions For "employer", see ss 124(1), 125(3). By virtue of s 124(5), for "employee" and "industrial tribunal", see the Pension Schemes Act 1993, s 181(1).
References See paras 3.39, 3.40.

46 Right not to suffer detriment in employment or be unfairly dismissed

(1) Subject to subsection (2), an employee has the right not to be subjected to any detriment by any act, or any deliberate failure to act, by his employer done on the ground that, being a trustee of a trust scheme which relates to his employment, the employee performed (or proposed to perform) any functions as such a trustee.

(2) Subsection (1) does not apply where the detriment in question amounts to dismissal, except where an employee is dismissed in circumstances in which, by virtue of section 142 of the Employment Protection (Consolidation) Act 1978 ("the 1978 Act"), section 54 of that Act does not apply to the dismissal.

(3) Sections 22B and 22C of the 1978 Act (which relate to proceedings brought by an employee on the grounds that he has been subjected to a detriment in contravention of section 22A of that Act) shall have effect as if the reference in section 22B(1) to section 22A included a reference to subsection (1).

(4) In the following provisions of the 1978 Act—
  (a) section 129 (remedy for infringement of certain rights),
  (b) section 141(2) (employee ordinarily working outside Great Britain), and
  (c) section 150 and Schedule 12 (death of employee or employer),
any reference to Part II of that Act includes a reference to subsection (1).

(5) The dismissal of an employee by an employer shall be regarded for the purposes of Part V of the 1978 Act as unfair if the reason (or, if more than one, the principal reason) for it is that, being a trustee of a trust scheme which relates to his employment, the employee performed (or proposed to perform any functions as such a trustee.

(6) Where the reason or the principal reason for which an employee was elected for dismissal was that he was redundant, but it is shown—
  (a) that the circumstances constituting the redundancy applied equally to one or more other employees in the same undertaking who held positions similar to that held by him and who have not been dismissed by the employer, and
  (b) that the reason (or, if more than one, the principal reason) for which he was selected for dismissal was that specified in subsection (5),
then, for the purposes of Part V of the 1978 Act, the dismissal shall be regarded as unfair.

(7) Section 54 of the 1978 Act (right of employee not to be unfairly dismissed) applies to a dismissal regarded as unfair by virtue of subsection (5) or (6) regardless of the period for which the employee has been employed and of his age; and accordingly section 64(1) of that Act (which provides a qualifying period and an upper age limit) does not apply to such a dismissal.

(8) Any provision in an agreement (whether a contract of employment or not) shall be void in so far as it purports—
  (a) to exclude or limit the operation of any provision of this section, or
  (b) to preclude any person from presenting a complaint to an industrial tribunal by virtue of any provision of this section.

(9) Subsection (8) does not apply to an agreement to refrain from presenting or continuing with a complaint where—
  (a) a conciliation officer has taken action under section 133(2) or (3) of the 1978 Act (general provisions as to conciliation) or under section 134(1), (2) or (3) (conciliation in case of unfair dismissal) of that Act, or
  (b) the conditions regulating compromise agreements under the 1978 Act (as set out in section 140(3) of that Act) are satisfied in relation to the agreement.

(10) In this section, "dismissal" has the same meaning as in Part V of the 1978 Act.

(11) Section 153 of the 1978 Act (general interpretation) has effect for the purposes of this section as it has effect for the purposes of that Act.

Definitions For "trust scheme", see s 124(1); for "employer", see ss 124(1), 125(3). By virtue of s 124(5), for "age", "employee", "employment" and "industrial tribunal", see the Pension Schemes Act 1993, s 181(1). Note as to "the 1978 Act", sub-s (2) above; and as to "dismissal", sub-s (10) above.
References See para 3.41.

Advisers

47 Professional advisers

(1) For every occupational pension scheme there shall be—
  (a) an individual, or a firm, appointed by the trustees or managers as auditor (referred to in this Part, in relation to the scheme, as "the auditor"), and

(b) an individual appointed by the trustees or managers as actuary (referred to in this Part, in relation to the scheme, as "the actuary").

(2) For every occupational pension scheme the assets of which consist of or include investments (within the meaning of the Financial Services Act 1986) there shall be an individual or a firm appointed by or on behalf of the trustees or managers as fund manager.

(3) If in the case of an occupational pension scheme any person—
 (a) is appointed otherwise than by the trustees or managers as legal adviser or to exercise any prescribed functions in relation to the scheme, or
 (b) is appointed otherwise than by or on behalf of the trustees or managers as a fund manager,

sections 3 and 10 apply to any trustee, and section 10 applies to any manager, who in exercising any of his functions places reliance on the skill or judgement of that person.

(4) In this Part, in relation to an occupational pension scheme—
 (a) the auditor, actuary and legal adviser appointed by the trustees or managers,
 (b) any fund manager appointed by or on behalf of the trustees or managers, and
 (c) any person appointed by the trustees or managers to exercise any of the functions referred to in subsection (3)(a),

are referred to as "professional advisers".

(5) This section does not apply to an occupational pension scheme falling within a prescribed class or description and regulations may—
 (a) make exceptions to subsections (1) to (3),
 (b) specify the qualifications and experience, or approval, required for appointment as a professional adviser.

(6) Regulations may make provision as to—
 (a) the manner in which professional advisers may be appointed and removed,
 (b) the terms on which professional advisers may be appointed (including the manner in which the professional advisers may resign).

(7) Subject to regulations made by virtue of subsection (6), professional advisers shall be appointed on such terms as the trustees or managers may determine.

(8) If in the case of an occupational pension scheme an auditor, actuary or fund manager is required under this section to be appointed but the appointment has not been made, or not been made in accordance with any requirements imposed under this section, sections 3 and 10 apply to any trustee, and section 10 applies to any manager, who has failed to take all such steps as are reasonable to secure compliance.

(9) Regulations may in the case of occupational pension schemes—
 (a) impose duties on any person who is or has been the employer, and on any person who acts as auditor or actuary to such a person, to disclose information to the trustees or managers and to the scheme's professional advisers,
 (b) impose duties on the trustees or managers to disclose information to, and make documents available to, the scheme's professional advisers.

(10) If in the case of an occupational pension scheme a person fails to comply with any duty imposed under subsection (9)(a), section 10 applies to him.

(11) If in the case of an occupational pension scheme any duty imposed under subsection (9)(b) is not complied with, sections 3 and 10 apply to any trustee, and

section 10 applies to any manager, who has failed to take all such steps as are reasonable to secure compliance.

Definitions   For "firm", "fund manager", "prescribed", "regulations", "trust scheme" and "trustees or managers", see s 124(1); for "employer", see ss 124(1), 125(3). By virtue of s 176, for "occupational pension scheme", see s 1 of the 1993 Act. Note as to "the actuary" and "the auditor", sub-s (1) above; and as to "professional advisers", sub-s (4) above.
References   See paras 5.1–5.7.

48   "Blowing the whistle"

(1) If the auditor or actuary of any occupational pension scheme has reasonable cause to believe that—
> (a) any duty relevant to the administration of the scheme imposed by any enactment or rule of law on the trustees or managers, the employer, any professional adviser or any prescribed person acting in connection with the scheme has not been or is not being complied with, and
> (b) the failure to comply is likely to be of material significance in the exercise by the Authority of any of their functions,

he must immediately give a written report of the matter to the Authority.

(2) The auditor or actuary of any occupational pension scheme must, in any prescribed circumstances, immediately give a written report of any prescribed matter to the Authority.

(3) No duty to which the auditor or actuary of any occupational pension scheme is subject shall be regarded as contravened merely because of any information or opinion contained in a written report under this section.

(4) If in the case of any occupational pension scheme any professional adviser (other than the auditor or actuary), any trustee or manager or any person involved in the administration of the scheme has reasonable cause to believe as mentioned in paragraphs (a) and (b) of subsection (1), he may give a report of the matter to the Authority.

(5) In the case of any such scheme, no duty to which any such adviser, trustee or manager or other person is subject shall be regarded as contravened merely because of any information or opinion contained in a report under this section; but this subsection does not apply to any information disclosed in such a report by the legal adviser of an occupational pension scheme if he would be entitled to refuse to produce a document containing the information in any proceedings in any court on the grounds that it was the subject of legal professional privilege or, in Scotland, that it contained a confidential communication made by or to an advocate or solicitor in that capacity.

(6) Subsections (1) to (5) apply to any occupational pension scheme to which section 47 applies.

(7) Section 10 applies to any auditor or actuary who fails to comply with subsection (1) or (2).

(8) If it appears to the Authority that an auditor or actuary has failed to comply with subsection (1) or (2), the Authority may by order disqualify him for being the auditor or, as the case may be, actuary of any occupational pension scheme specified in the order.

(9) An order under subsection (8) may specify the scheme to which the failure relates, all schemes falling within any class or description of occupational pension scheme or all occupational pension schemes.

(10) The Authority may, on the application of any person disqualified under this section who satisfies the Authority that he will in future comply with those

subsections, by order revoke the order disqualifying him; but a revocation made at any time cannot affect anything done before that time.

(11) An auditor or actuary of an occupational pension scheme who becomes disqualified under this section shall, while he is so disqualified, cease to be auditor or, as the case may be, actuary of any scheme specified in the order disqualifying him.

(12) A person who, while he is disqualified under this section, purports to act as auditor or actuary of an occupational pension scheme specified in the order disqualifying him is guilty of an offence and liable—
> (a) on summary conviction, to a fine not exceeding the statutory maximum, and
> (b) on conviction on indictment, to a fine or imprisonment, or both.

(13) An offence under subsection (12) may be charged by reference to any day or longer period of time; and a person may be convicted of a second or subsequent offence under that subsection by reference to any period of time following the preceding conviction of the offence.

Definitions   For "the Authority", see s 1(1); as to "the actuary" and "the auditor", see s 47(1); as to "professional advisers", see s 47(4); for "contravention", "prescribed" and "trustees or managers", see s 124(1); for "employer", see ss 124(1), 125(3). For "enactment", see s 176, and by virtue of that section, for "occupational pension scheme", see the Pension Schemes Act 1993, s 1.
References   See paras 5.11–5.17.

Receipts, payments and records

49 Other responsibilities of trustees, employers, etc

(1) The trustees of any trust scheme must, except in any prescribed circumstances, keep any money received by them in a separate account kept by them at an institution authorised under the Banking Act 1987.

(2) Regulations may require the trustees of any trust scheme to keep—
> (a) records of their meetings (including meetings of any of their number), and
> (b) books and records relating to any prescribed transaction.

(3) Regulations may, in the case of any trust scheme, require the employer, and any prescribed person acting in connection with the scheme, to keep books and records relating to any prescribed transaction.

(4) Regulations may require books or records kept under subsection (2) or (3) to be kept in a prescribed form and manner and for a prescribed period.

(5) Regulations must, in cases where payments of benefit to members of trust schemes are made by the employer, require the employer to make into a separate account kept by him at an institution authorised under the Banking Act 1987 any payments of benefit which have not been made to the members within any prescribed period.'

(6) If in the case of any trust scheme any requirements imposed by or under subsection (1) or (2) are not complied with, sections 3 and 10 apply to any trustee who has failed to take all such steps as are reasonable to secure compliance.

(7) If in the case of any trust scheme any person fails to comply with any requirement imposed under subsection (3) or (5), section 10 applies to him.

(8) Where—
> (a) on making a payment of any earnings in respect of any employment there is deducted any amount corresponding to any contribution payable on behalf of an active member of an occupational pension scheme, and

(b) the amount deducted is not, within a prescribed period, paid to the trustees or managers of the scheme and there is no reasonable excuse for the failure to do so,

the employer is guilty of an offence and liable, on summary conviction, to a fine not exceeding the statutory maximum and, on conviction on indictment, to imprisonment, or a fine, or both.

Definitions For "active member", "prescribed", "regulations", "trustees or managers" and "trust scheme", see s 124(1); for "employer", see ss 124(1), 125(3); for "member", see ss 124(1), 125(4). By virtue of s 124(5), for "earnings" and "employment", see the Pension Schemes Act 1993, s 181(1). By virtue of s 176, for "occupational pension scheme", see the Pension Schemes Act 1993, s 1.
References See paras 2.35, 3.36–3.38.

Resolution of disputes

50 Resolution of disputes

(1) The trustees or managers of an occupational pension scheme must secure that such arrangements as are required by or under this section for the resolution of disagreements between prescribed persons about matters in relation to the scheme are made and implemented.

(2) The arrangements must—
    (a) provide for a person, on the application of a complainant of a prescribed description, to give a decision on such a disagreement, and
    (b) require the trustees or managers, on the application of such a complainant following a decision given in accordance with paragraph (a), to reconsider the matter in question and confirm the decision or give a new decision in its place.

(3) Regulations may make provision about—
    (a) applications for decisions under such arrangements, and
    (b) the procedure for reaching and giving such decisions,
including the times by which applications are to be made and decisions given.

(4) Applications and decisions under subsection (2) must be in writing.

(5) Arrangements under subsection (1) must, in the case of existing schemes, have effect as from the commencement of this section.

(6) If, in the case of any occupational pension scheme, such arrangements as are required by this section to be made have not been made, or are not being implemented, section 10 applies to any of the trustees or managers who have failed to take all such steps as are reasonable to secure that such arrangements are made or implemented.

(7) This section does not apply to a scheme of a prescribed description and subsection (1) does not apply to prescribed matters in relation to the scheme.

Definitions For "prescribed", "regulations" and "trustees or managers", see s 124(1). By virtue of s 176, for "occupational pension scheme", see the Pension Schemes Act 1993, s 1.
References See paras 4.1, 4.2.

Indexation

51 Annual increase in rate of pension

(1) Subject to subsection (6) this section applies to a pension under an occupational pension scheme if—
    (a) the scheme—
        (i) is an approved scheme, within the meaning of Chapter I of Part XIV of the Taxes Act 1988 (retirement benefit schemes approved

by the Commissioners of Inland Revenue) or is a scheme for which such approval has been applied for under that Chapter and not refused, and
    (ii) is not a public service pension scheme, and
  (b) apart from this section, the annual rate of the pension would not be increased each year by at least the appropriate percentage of that rate.

(2) Subject to section 52, where a pension to which this section applies, or any part of it, is attributable to pensionable service on or after the appointed day or, in the case of money purchase benefits, to payments in respect of employment carried on on or after the appointed day—
  (a) the annual rate of the pension, or
  (b) if only part of the pension is attributable to pensionable service or, as the case may be, to payments in respect of employment carried on on or after the appointed day, so much of the annual rate as is attributable to that part,

must be increased annually by at least the appropriate percentage.

(3) Subsection (2) does not apply to a pension under an occupational pension scheme if the rules of the scheme require—
  (a) the annual rate of the pension, or
  (b) if only part of the pension is attributable to pensionable service or, as the case may be, to payments in respect of employment carried on on or after the appointed day, so much of the annual rate as is attributable to that part,

to be increased at intervals of not more than twelve months by at least the relevant percentage and the scheme complies with any prescribed requirements.

(4) For the purposes of subsection (3) the relevant percentage is—
  (a) the percentage increase in the retail prices index for the reference period, being a period determined, in relation to each periodic increase, under the rules, or
  (b) the percentage for that period which corresponds to 5 per cent per annum,

whichever is the lesser.

(5) Regulations may provide that the provisions of subsections (2) and (3) apply in relation to a pension as if so much of it as would not otherwise be attributable to pensionable service or to payments in respect of employment were attributable to pensionable service or, as the case may be, payments in respect of employment—
  (a) before the appointed day,
  (b) on or after that day, or
  (c) partly before and partly on or after that day.

(6) This section does not apply to any pension or part of a pension which, in the opinion of the trustees or managers, is derived from the payment by any member of the scheme of voluntary contributions.

Definitions   For "annual rate", "the appointed day", "appropriate percentage" and "pension", see s 54(3); for "prescribed", "regulations" and "trustee or managers", see s 124(1); for "pensionable service", see s 124(1), (3); for "member", see ss 124(1), 125(4). By virtue of s 124(1), for "public service pension scheme", see the Pension Schemes Act 1993, s 1. By virtue of s 124(5), for "employment" and "money purchase benefits", see s 181(1) of the 1993 Act. By virtue of s 176, for "occupational pension scheme", see s 1 of the 1993 Act.
References   See paras 4.1, 4.2.

52 Restriction on increase where member in under 55

(1) Subject to subsection (2), no increase under section 51 is required to be paid to or for a member of a scheme whose pension is in payment but who has not attained the age of 55 at the time when the increase takes effect.

(2) Subsection (1) does not apply if the member—
   (a) is permanently incapacitated by mental or physical infirmity from engaging in regular full-time employment, or
   (b) has retired on account of mental or physical infirmity from the employment in respect of which, or on retirement from which, the pension is payable.

(3) The rules of a scheme may provide that if, in a case where a pension has been paid to or for a member under the age of 55 at an increased rate in consequence of subsection (2), the member—
   (a) ceases to suffer from the infirmity in question before he attains the age of 55, but
   (b) continues to be entitled to the pension,
any increases subsequently taking effect under section 51 in the annual rate of the pension shall not be paid or shall not be paid in full.

(4) In any case where—
   (a) by virtue only of subsection (1) or (3), increases are not paid to or for a member or are not paid in full, but
   (b) the member attains the age of 55 or, in a case falling within subsection (3), again satisfies the condition set out in subsection (2)(a) or
his pension shall then become payable at the annual rate at which it would have been payable apart from subsection (1) or (3).

Definitions For "annual rate" and "pension", see s 54(3); for "member", see ss 124(1), 125(4). By virtue of s 124(5), for "employment", see the Pension Schemes Act 1993, s 181(1).
References See paras 6.4–6.11.

53 Effect of increases above the statutory requirement

(1) Where in any tax year the trustees or managers of an occupational pension scheme make an increase in a person's pension, not being an increase required by section 109 of the Pension Schemes Act 1993 or section 51 of this Act, they may deduct the amount of the increase from any increase which, but for this subsection, they would be required to make under either of those sections in the next tax year.

(2) Where in any tax year the trustees or managers of such a scheme make an increase in a person's pension and part of the increase is not required by section 109 of the Pension Schemes Act 1993 or section 51 of this Act, they may deduct that part of the increase from any increase which, but for this subsection, they would be required to make under either of those sections in the next tax year.

(3) Where by virtue of subsection (1) or (2) any pensions are not required to be increased in pursuance of section 109 of the Pension Schemes Act 1993 or section 51 of this Act, or not by the full amount that they otherwise would be, their amount shall be calculated for any purpose as if they had been increased in pursuance of the section in question or, as the case may be, by that full amount.

(4) In section 110 of the Pension Schemes Act 1993 (resources for annual increase of guaranteed minimum pension)—
   (a) subsections (2) to (4) are omitted, and
   (b) in subsection (1), for "subsection (2) or (3)" there is substituted "section 53 of the Pensions Act 1995".

Definitions For "pension", see s 54(3); for "trustees or managers", see s 124(1). By virtue of s 124(5), for "tax year", see the Pension Schemes Act 1993, s 181(1). By virtue of s 176, for "occupational pension scheme", see s 1 of the 1993 Act.
References See paras 6.4–6.11.

54 Sections 51 to 53: supplementary

(1) The first increase required by section 51 in the rate of a pension must take effect not later than the first anniversary of the date on which the pension is first paid; and subsequent increases must take effect at intervals of not more than twelve months.

(2) Where the first such increase is to take effect on a date when the pension has been in payment for a period of less than twelve months, the increase must be of an amount at least equal to one twelfth of the amount of the increase so required (apart from this subsection) for each complete month in that period.

(3) In sections 51 to 53 and this section—
"annual rate", in relation to a pension, means the annual rate of the pension, as previously increased under the rules of the scheme or under section 51,
"the appointed day" means the day appointed under section 180 for the commencement of section 51,
"appropriate percentage", in relation to an increase in the whole or part of the annual rate of a pension, means the revaluation percentage for the revaluation period the reference period for which ends with the last preceding 30th September before the increase is made (expressions used in this definition having the same meaning as in paragraph 2 of Schedule 3 to the Pension Schemes Act 1993 (methods of revaluing accrued pension benefits)),
"pension", in relation to a scheme, means any pension in payment under the scheme and includes an annuity.

References   See paras 6.4–6.11.

55 Section 51: end of annual increase in GMP

In section 109 of the Pension Schemes Act 1993 (annual increase of guaranteed minimum pensions)—
   (a) in subsection (2) (increase in rate of that part of guaranteed minimum pension attributable to earnings factors for tax year 1988-89 and subsequent tax years) for "the tax year 1988-89 and subsequent tax years there is substituted "the tax years in the relevant period", and
   (b) after subsection (3) there is inserted—

"(3A) The relevant period is the period—
   (a) beginning with the tax year 1988–89, and
   (b) ending with the last tax year that begins before the principal appointed day for the purposes of Part III of the Pensions Act 1995".

Definitions   For "tax year", see, by virtue of s 124(5), the Pension Schemes Act 1993, s 181(1).
References   See para 6.12.

Minimum funding requirement

56 Minimum funding requirement

(1) Every occupational pension scheme to which this section applies is subject to a requirement (referred to in this Part as "the minimum funding requirement") that the value of the assets of the scheme is not less than the amount of the liabilities of the scheme.

(2) This section applies to an occupational pension scheme other than—
   (a) a money purchase scheme, or
   (b) a scheme falling within a prescribed class or description.

(3) For the purposes of this section and sections 57 to 61, the liabilities and assets to be taken into account, and their amount or value, shall be determined, calculated and verified by a prescribed person and in the prescribed manner.

(4) In calculating the value of any liabilities for those purposes, a provision of the scheme which limits the amount of its liabilities by reference to the amount of its assets is to be disregarded.

(5) In sections 57 to 61, in relation to any occupational pension scheme to which this section applies—
- (a) the amount of the liabilities referred to in subsection (1) is referred to as "the amount of the scheme liabilities",
- (b) the value of the assets referred to in that subsection is referred to as "the value of the scheme assets",
- (c) an "actuarial valuation" means a written valuation prepared and signed by the actuary of the scheme of the assets and liabilities referred to in subsection (1), and
- (d) the "effective date" of an actuarial valuation is the date by reference to which the assets and liabilities are valued.

Definitions As to "the actuary", see s 47(1); for "prescribed", see s 124(1). By virtue of s 176, for "occupational pension scheme", see the Pension Schemes Act 1993, s 1. By virtue of s 124(5), for "money purchase scheme", see s 181(1) of the 1993 Act. Note as to "the minimum funding requirement", sub-s (1) above, and as to "the amount of the scheme liabilities", "the value of the scheme assets", "actuarial valuation" and "effective date", sub-s (5) above.
References See paras 7.4–7.7.

57 Valuation and certification of assets and liabilities

(1) The trustees or managers of an occupational pension scheme to which section 56 applies must—
- (a) obtain, within a prescribed period, an actuarial valuation and afterwards obtain such a valuation before the end of prescribed intervals, and
- (b) on prescribed occasions or within prescribed periods, obtain a certificate prepared by the actuary of the scheme—
  - (i) stating whether or not in his opinion the contributions payable towards the scheme are adequate for the purpose of securing that the minimum funding requirement will continue to be met throughout the prescribed period or, if it appears to him that it is not met, will be met by the end of that period, and
  - (ii) indicating any relevant changes that have occurred since the last actuarial valuation was prepared.

(2) Subject to subsection (3), the trustees or managers must—
- (a) if the actuary states in such a certificate that in his opinion the contributions payable towards the scheme are not adequate for the purpose of securing that the minimum funding requirement will continue to be met throughout the prescribed period or, if it appears to him that it is not met, will be met by the end of that period, or
- (b) in prescribed circumstances,

obtain an actuarial valuation within the period required by subsection (4).

(3) In a case within subsection (2)(a), the trustees or managers are not required to obtain an actuarial valuation if—
- (a) in the opinion of the actuary of the scheme, the value of the scheme assets is not less than 90 per cent of the amount of the scheme liabilities, and
- (b) since the date on which the actuary signed the certificate referred to in that subsection, the schedule of contributions for the scheme has been revised under section 58(3)(b).

(4) If the trustees or managers obtain a valuation under subsection (2) they must do so—
  (a) in the case of a valuation required by paragraph (a), within the period of six months beginning with the date on which the certificate was signed, and
  (b) in any other case, within a prescribed period.

(5) A valuation or certificate obtained under subsection (1) or (2) must be prepared in such manner, give such information and contain such statements as may be prescribed.

(6) The trustees or managers must secure that any valuation or certificate obtained under this section is made available to the employer within seven days of their receiving it.

(7) Where, in the case of an occupational pension scheme to which section 56 applies, subsection (1), (2) or (6) is not complied with—
  (a) section 3 applies to any trustee who has failed to take all such steps as are reasonable to secure compliance, and
  (b) section 10 applies to any trustee or manager who has failed to take all such steps.

Definitions As to "the actuary", see s 47(1); as to "the minimum funding requirement", see s 56(1); as to "actuarial valuation", "the amount of the scheme liabilities" and "the value of the scheme assets", see s 56(5); as to "schedule of contributions", see s 58(1); for "prescribed" and "trustees or managers", see s 124(1); for "employer", see ss 124(1), 125(3). By virtue of s 176, for "occupational pension scheme", see the Pension Schemes Act 1993, s 1.
References See paras 7.8–7.11.

---

58 Schedules of contributions

(1) The trustees or managers of an occupational pension scheme to which section 56 applies must secure that there is prepared, maintained and from time to time revised a schedule (referred to in sections 57 to 59 as a "schedule of contributions") showing—
  (a) the rates of contributions payable towards the scheme by or on behalf of the employer and the active members of the scheme, and
  (b) the dates on or before which such contributions are to be paid.

(2) The schedule of contributions for a scheme must satisfy prescribed requirements.

(3) The schedule of contributions for a scheme—
  (a) must be prepared before the end of a prescribed period beginning with the signing of the first actuarial valuation for the scheme,
  (b) may be revised from time to time where the revisions are previously agreed by the trustees or managers and the employer and any revision in the rates of contributions is certified by the actuary of the scheme, and
  (c) must be revised before the end of a prescribed period beginning with the signing of each subsequent actuarial valuation.

(4) The matters shown in the schedule of contributions for a scheme—
  (a) must be matters previously agreed by the trustees or managers and the employer, or
  (b) if no such agreement has been made as to all the matters shown in the schedule, must be—
    (i) rates of contributions determined by the trustees or managers, being such rates as in their opinion are adequate for the purpose of securing that the minimum funding requirement will continue

to be met throughout the prescribed period or, if it appears to them that it is not met, will be met by the end of that period, and
(ii) other matters determined by the trustees or managers;
and the rates of contributions shown in the schedule must be certified by the actuary of the scheme.

(5) An agreement for the purposes of subsection (4) (a) is one which is made by the trustees or managers and the employer during the prescribed period beginning with the signing of the last preceding actuarial valuation for the scheme.

(6) The actuary may not certify the rates of contributions shown in the schedule of contributions—
(a) in a case where on the date he signs the certificate it appears to him that the minimum funding requirement is met, unless he is of the opinion that the rates are adequate for the purpose of securing that the requirement will continue to be met throughout the prescribed period, and
(b) in any other case, unless he is of the opinion that the rates are adequate for the purpose of securing that the requirement will be met by the end of that period.

(7) The Authority may in prescribed circumstances extend (or further extend) the period referred to in subsection (6).

(8) Where, in the case of any occupational pension scheme to which section 56 applies, this section is not complied with—
(a) section 3 applies to any trustee who has failed to take all such steps as are reasonable to secure compliance, and
(b) section 10 applies to any trustee or manager who has failed to take all such steps.

Definitions For "the Authority", see s 1(1); as to "the actuary", see s 47(1); as to "the minimum funding requirement", see s 56(1); as to an "actuarial valuation", see s 56(5); for "active member", "prescribed" and "trustees or managers", see s 124(1); for "employer", see ss 124(1), 125(3). By virtue of s 176, for "occupational pension scheme", see the Pension Schemes Act 1993, s 1. Note as to "schedule of contributions", sub-s (1) above.
References See paras 7.12–7.15.

59 Determination of contributions: supplementary

(1) Except in prescribed circumstances, the trustees or managers of an occupational pension scheme to which section 56 applies must, where any amounts payable by or on behalf of the employer or the active members of the scheme in accordance with the schedule of contributions have not been paid on or before the due date, give notice of that fact, within the prescribed period, to the Authority and to the members of the scheme.

(2) Any such amounts which for the time being remain unpaid after that date (whether payable by the employer or not) shall, if not a debt due from the employer to the trustees or managers apart from this subsection, be treated as such a debt.

(3) If, in the case of an occupational pension scheme to which section 56 applies, it appears to the trustees or managers, at the end of any prescribed period that the minimum funding requirement is not met, they must prepare a report giving the prescribed information about the failure to meet that requirement.

(4) If in the case of any such scheme, subsection (1) or (3) is not complied with—
(a) section 3 applies to any trustee who has failed to take all such steps as are reasonable to secure compliance, and
(b) section 10 applies to any trustee or manager who has failed to take all such steps.

Definitions For "the Authority", see s 1(1); as to "the minimum funding requirement", see s 56(1); as to "schedule of contributions", see s 58(1); for "active member", "prescribed" and "trustees or managers", see s 124(1); for "employer", see ss 124(1), 125(3); for "member", see ss 124(1), 125(4). By virtue of s 176, for "occupational pension scheme", see the Pension Schemes Act 1993, s 1.
References See paras 7.16–7.18.

60 Serious underprovision

(1) Subsection (2) applies where, in the case of an occupational pension scheme to which section 56 applies, an actuarial valuation shows that, on the effective date of the valuation, the value of the scheme assets is less than 90 per cent of the amount of the scheme liabilities (the difference shown in the valuation being referred to in this section as "the shortfall").

(2) The employer must—
    (a) by making an appropriate payment to the trustees or managers, or
    (b) by a prescribed method,

secure an increase in the value of the scheme assets which, taken with any contributions paid, is not less than the shortfall.

(3) The required increase in that value must be secured—
    (a) before the end of a prescribed period beginning with the signing of the valuation, or
    (b) if the actuarial valuation was obtained by reason of such a statement in a certificate as is referred to in section 57(2), before the end of a prescribed period beginning with the signing of the certificate.

(4) Except in prescribed circumstances, if the employer fails to secure the required increase in value before the end of the period applicable under subsection (3), the trustees or managers must, within the period of fourteen days (or such longer period as is prescribed) beginning with the end of that period, give written notice of that fact to the Authority and to the members of the scheme.

(5) If the employer fails to secure the required increase in value before the end of the period applicable under subsection (3), then so much of the shortfall as, at any subsequent time, has not been met by an increase In value under subsection (2) made—
    (a) by making an appropriate payment to the trustees or managers,
    (b) by a prescribed method, or
    (c) by contributions made before the end of that period,

shall, if not a debt due from the employer to the trustees or managers apart from this subsection, be treated at that time as such a debt.

(6) Where an increase in value is secured by a prescribed method, the increase is to be treated for the purposes of this section as being of an amount determined in accordance with regulations.

(7) The Authority may in prescribed circumstances extend (or further extend) the period applicable under subsection (3).

(8) If subsection (4) is not complied with—
    (a) section 3 applies to any trustee who has failed to take all such steps as are reasonable to secure compliance, and
    (b) section 10 applies to any trustee or manager who has failed to take all such steps.

Definitions For "the Authority", see s 1(1); as to "actuarial valuation", "effective date", "the value of the scheme assets" and "the amount of the scheme liabilities", see s 56(5); for "prescribed", "regulations" and "trustees or managers", see s 124(1); for "employer", see ss 124(1), 125(3); for "member", see ss 124(1), 125(4). By virtue of s 176, for "occupational pension scheme", see the Pension Schemes Act 1993, s 1. Note as to "the shortfall", sub-s (1) above.
References See paras 7.19, 7.20.

61 Section 56 to 60: supplementary

Regulations may modify sections 56 to 60 as they apply in prescribed circumstances.

Definitions For "prescribed" and "regulations", see s 124(1). By virtue of s 124(5), for "modify", see the Pension Schemes Act 1993, s 181(1).
References See para 7.4.

Equal treatment

62 The equal treatment rule

(1) An occupational pension scheme which does not contain an equal treatment rule shall be treated as including one.

(2) An equal treatment rule is a rule which relates to the terms on which—
    (a) persons become members of the scheme, and
    (b) members of the scheme are treated.

(3) Subject to subsection (6), an equal treatment rule has the effect that where—
    (a) a woman is employed on like work with a man in the same employment,
    (b) a woman is employed on work rated as equivalent with that of a man in the same employment, or
    (c) a woman is employed on work which, not being work in relation to which paragraph (a) or (b) applies, is, in terms of the demands made on her (for instance under such headings as effort, skill and decision) of equal value to that of a man in the same employment,

but (apart from the rule) any of the terms referred to in subsection (2) is or becomes less favourable to the woman than it is to the man, the term shall be treated as so modified as not to be less favourable.

(4) An equal treatment rule does not operate in relation to any difference as between a woman and a man in the operation of any of the terms referred to in subsection (2) if the trustees or managers of the scheme prove that the difference is genuinely due to a material factor which—
    (a) is not the difference of sex, but
    (b) is a material difference between the woman's case and the man's case.

(5) References in subsection (4) and sections 63 to 65 to the terms referred to in subsection (2), or the effect of any of those terms, include—
    (a) a term which confers on the trustees or managers of an occupational pension scheme, or any other person, a discretion which, in a case within any of paragraphs (a) to (c) of subsection (3)—
        (i) may be exercised so as to affect the way in which persons become members of the scheme, or members of the scheme are treated, and
        (ii) may (apart from the equal treatment rule) be so exercised in a way less favourable to the woman than to the man, and
    (b) the effect of any exercise of such a discretion;

and references to the terms on which members of the scheme are treated are to be read accordingly.

(6) In the case of a term within subsection (5)(a) the effect of an equal treatment rule is that the term shall be treated as so modified as not to permit the discretion to be exercised in a way less favourable to the woman than to the man.

Definitions For "trustees or managers", see s 124(1); for "member", see ss 124(1), 125(4). By virtue of s 124(5), for "employed", "employment", "modified" and "modifying", see the Pension Schemes Act 1993, s 181(1). By virtue of s 176, for "occupational pension scheme", see the Pension Schemes Act 1993, s 1. Note as to "equal treatment rule", sub-s (2) above, and as to "the term referred to in subsection (2), etc" sub-s (5) above.
References See paras 8.2, 8.3.

63 Equal treatment rule: supplementary

(1) The reference in section 62(2) to the terms on which members of a scheme are treated includes those terms as they have effect for the benefit of dependants of members, and the reference in section 62(5) to the way in which members of a scheme are treated includes the way they are treated as it has effect for the benefit of dependants of members.

(2) Where the effect of any of the terms referred to in section 62(2) on persons of the same sex differs according to their family or marital status, the effect of the term is to be compared for the purposes of section 62 with its effect on persons of the other sex who have the same status.

(3) An equal treatment rule has effect subject to paragraphs 5 and 6 of Schedule 5 to the Social Security Act 1989 (employment-related-benefit schemes: maternity and family leave provisions).

(4) Section 62 shall be construed as one with section 1 of the Equal Pay Act 1970 (requirement of equal treatment for men and women in the same employment); and sections 2 and 2A of that Act (disputes and enforcement) shall have effect for the purposes of section 62 as if—
- (a) references to an equality clause were to an equal treatment rule,
- (b) references to employers and employees were to the trustees or managers of the scheme (on the one hand) and the members, or prospective members, of the scheme (on the other),
- (c) for section 2(4) there were substituted—

"(4) No claim in respect of the operation of an equal treatment rule in respect of an occupational pension scheme shall be referred to an industrial tribunal otherwise than by virtue of subsection (3) above unless the woman concerned has been employed in a description or category of employment to which the scheme relates within the six months preceding the date of the reference", and

- (d) references to Section 1(2)(c) of the Equal Pay Act 1970 were to section 62(3)(c) of this Act.

(5) Regulations may make provision for the Equal Pay Act 1970 to have effect, in relation to an equal treatment rule, with prescribed modifications; and subsection (4) shall have effect subject to any regulations made by virtue of this subsection.

(6) Section 62, so far as it relates to the terms on which members of a scheme are treated, is to be treated as having had effect in relation to any pensionable service on or after 17th May 1990.

Definitions As to "equal treatment rule", see s 62(2); for "prescribed", "regulations" and "trustees or managers", see s 124(1); for "pensionable service", see s 124(1), (3); for "employer", see ss 124(1), 125(3); for "member" and "prospective member", see ss 124(1), 125(4). By virtue of s 124(5), for "modifications", see the Pension Schemes Act 1993, s 181(1).
References See paras 8.2, 8.3, 8.5, 8.9, 8.10.

64 Equal treatment rule: exceptions

(1) An equal treatment rule does not operate in relation to any variation as between a woman and a man in the effect of any of the terms referred to in section 62(2) if the variation is permitted by or under any of the provisions of this section.

(2) Where a man and a woman are eligible, in prescribed circumstances, to receive different amounts by way of pension, the variation is permitted by this subsection if, in prescribed circumstances the differences are attributable only to

differences between men and women in the benefits under sections 43 to 55 of the Social Security Contributions and Benefits Act 1992 (State retirement pensions) to which, in prescribed circumstances, they are or would be entitled.

(3) A variation is permitted by this subsection if—
   (a) the variation consists of the application of actuarial factors which differ for men and women to the calculation of contributions to a scheme by employers, being factors which fall within a prescribed class or description, or
   (b) the variation consists of the application of actuarial factors which differ for men and women to the determination of benefits falling within a prescribed class or description;

and in this subsection "benefits" include any payment or other benefit made to or in respect of a person as a member of the scheme.

(4) Regulations may—
   (a) permit further variations, or
   (b) amend or repeal subsection (2) or (3);

and regulations made by virtue of this subsection may have effect in relation to pensionable service on or after 17th May 1990 and before the date on which the regulations are made.

Definitions As to "equal treatment rule", see s 62(2); for "prescribed" and "regulations", see s 124(1); for "pensionable service", see s 124(1), (3); for "employer", see ss 124(1), 125(3); for "member", see ss 124(1), 125(4).
References See para 8.6.

65 Equal treatment rule: consequential alteration of schemes

(1) The trustees or managers of an occupational pension scheme may, if—
   (a) they do not (apart from this section) have power to make such alterations to the scheme as may be required to secure conformity with an equal treatment rule, or
   (b) they have such power but the procedure for doing so—
      (i) is liable to be unduly complex or protracted, or
      (ii) involves the obtaining of consents which cannot be obtained, or can only be obtained with undue delay or difficulty,

by resolution make such alterations to the scheme.

(2) The alterations may have effect in relation to a period before the alterations are made.

Definitions As to "equal treatment rule", see s 62(2); for "trustees or managers", see s 124(1). By virtue of s 176, for "occupational pension scheme", see the Pension Schemes Act 1993, s 1.
References See para 8.7.

66 Equal treatment rule: effect on terms of employment

(1) In section 6 of the Equal Pay Act 1970 (exclusions), for subsections (1A) and (2) (exclusion for terms related to death or retirement) there is substituted—

> "(1B) An equality clause shall not operate in relation to terms relating to a person's membership of, or rights under, an occupational pension scheme, being terms in relation to which, by reason only of any provision made by or under sections 62 to 64 of the Pensions Act 1995 (equal treatment), an equal treatment rule would not operate if the terms were included in the scheme.
>
> (1C) In subsection (1B), "occupational pension scheme" has the same meaning as in the Pension Schemes Act 1993 and "equal treatment rule" has the meaning given by section 62 of the Pensions Act 1995".

(2) In section 4(1) of the Sex Discrimination Act 1975 (victimisation of complainants etc)—
   (a) in paragraphs (a), (b) and (c), after "Equal Pay Act 1970" there is inserted "or sections 62 to 65 of the Pensions Act 1995", and
   (b) at the end of paragraph (d) there is added "or under sections 62 to 65 of the Pensions Act 1995".

(3) In section 6 of the Sex Discrimination Act 1975 (discrimination against applicants and employees), for subsection (4) there is substituted—

"(4) Subsections (1)(b) and (2) do not render it unlawful for a person to discriminate against a woman in relation to her membership of, or rights under, an occupational pension scheme in such a way that, were any term of the scheme to provide for discrimination in that way, then, by reason only of any provision made by or under sections 62 to 64 of the Pensions Act 1995 (equal treatment), an equal treatment rule would not operate in relation to that term.

(4A) In subsection (4), "occupational pension scheme" has the same meaning as in the Pension Schemes Act 1993 and "equal treatment rule" has the meaning given by section 62 of the Pensions Act 1995".

(4) Regulations may make provision—
   (a) for the Equal Pay Act 1970 to have effect, in relation to terms of employment relating to membership of, or rights under, an occupational pension scheme with prescribed modifications, and
   (b) for imposing requirements on employers as to the payment of contributions and otherwise in case of their failing or having failed to comply with any such terms.

(5) References in subsection (4) to terms of employment include (where the context permits)—
   (a) any collective agreement or pay structure, and
   (b) an agricultural wages order within section 5 of the Equal Pay Act 1970.

Definitions As to "equal treatment rule", see s 62(2); for "prescribed" and "regulations", see s 124(1); for "employer", see ss 124(1), 125(3). By virtue of s 124(5), for "modifications", see the Pension Schemes Act 1993, s 181(1). By virtue of s 176, for "occupational pension scheme", see s 1 of the 1993 Act.
References See paras 8.8, 8.13.

Modification of schemes

67 Restriction on powers to alter schemes

(1) This section applies to any power conferred on any person by an occupational pension scheme (other than a public service pension scheme) to modify the scheme.

(2) The power cannot be exercised on any occasion in a manner which would or might affect any entitlement, or accrued right, of any member of the scheme acquired before the power is exercised unless the requirements under subsection (3) are satisfied.

(3) Those requirements are that, in respect of the exercise of the power in that manner on that occasion—
   (a) the trustees have satisfied themselves that—
      (i) the certification requirements, or
      (ii) the requirements for consent, are met in respect of that member, and
   (b) where the power is exercised by a person other than the trustees, the trustees have approved the exercise of the power in that manner on that occasion.

(4) In subsection (3)—
  (a) "the certification requirements" means prescribed requirements for the purpose of securing that no power to which this section applies is exercised in any manner which, in the opinion of an actuary, would adversely affect any member of the scheme (without his consent) in respect of his entitlement, or accrued rights, acquired before the power is exercised, and
  (b) "the consent requirements" means prescribed requirements for the purpose of obtaining the consent of members of a scheme to the exercise of a power to which this section applies.

(5) Subsection (2) does not apply to the exercise of a power in a prescribed manner.

(6) Where a power to which this section applies may not (apart from this section) be exercised without the consent of any person, regulations may make provision for treating such consent as given in prescribed circumstances.

Definitions   As to "the actuary", see s 47(1); for "prescribed" and "regulations", see s 124(1); for "accrued rights", see s 124(2); for "member", see ss 124(1), 125(4). By virtue of s 124(1), for "public service pension scheme", see the Pension Schemes Act 1993, s 1. By virtue of s 124(5), for "modify", see s 181(1) of that Act. By virtue of s 176, for "occupational pension scheme", see s 1 of the 1993 Act.
References   See paras 9.1–9.5.

68 Power of trustees to modify schemes by resolution

(1) The trustees of a trust scheme may by resolution modify the scheme with a view to achieving any of the purposes specified in subsection (2).

(2) The purposes referred to in subsection (1) are—
  (a) to extend the class of persons who may receive benefits under the scheme in respect of the death of a member of the scheme,
  (b) to enable the scheme to conform with such arrangements as are required by section 16(1) or 17(2),
  (c) to enable the scheme to comply with such terms and conditions as may be imposed by the Compensation Board in relation to any payment made by them under section 83 or 84,
  (d) to enable the scheme to conform with section 37(2), 76(2), 91 or 92, and
  (e) prescribed purposes.

(3) No modification may be made by virtue of subsection (2)(a) without the consent of the employer.

(4) Modifications made by virtue of subsection (2)(b) may include in particular—
  (a) modification of any limit on the number of, or of any category of, trustees, or
  (b) provision for the transfer or vesting of property.

(5) Nothing done by virtue of subsection (2)(d), or any corresponding provisions in force in Northern Ireland, shall be treated as effecting an alteration to the scheme in question for the purposes of section 591B (cessation of approval) of the Taxes Act 1988.

(6) Regulations may provide that this section does not apply to trust schemes falling within a prescribed class or description.

Definitions   For "the Compensation Board", see s 78(1); for "prescribed", "regulations" and "trust scheme", see s 124(1); for "employer", see ss 124(1), 125(3); for "member", see ss 124(1), 125(4). By virtue of s 124(5), for "modification" and "modify", see the Pension Schemes Act 1993, s 181(1).
References   See paras 9.6, 9.7.

69 Grounds for applying modifications

(1) The Authority may, on an application made to them by persons competent to do so, make an order in respect of an occupational pension scheme (other than a public service pension scheme)—
  (a) authorising the modification of the scheme with a view to achieving any of the purposes mentioned in subsection (3), or
  (b) modifying the scheme with a view to achieving any such purpose.

(2) Regulations may make provision about the manner of dealing with applications under this section.

(3) The purposes referred to in subsection (1) are—
  (a) in the case of a scheme to which Schedule 22 to the Taxes Act 1988 (reduction of pension fund surpluses in certain exempt approved schemes) applies, to reduce or eliminate on any particular occasion any excess in accordance with any proposal submitted under paragraph 3(1) of that Schedule, where any requirements mentioned in section 37(4), and any other prescribed requirements, will be satisfied in relation to the reduction or elimination,
  (b) in the case of an exempt approved scheme (within the meaning given by section 592(1) of the Taxes Act 1988) which is being wound up, to enable assets remaining after the liabilities of the scheme have been fully discharged to be distributed to the employer, where prescribed requirements in relation to the distribution are satisfied, or
  (c) to enable the scheme to be so treated during a prescribed period that an employment to which the scheme applies may be contracted-out employment by reference to it.

(4) The persons competent to make an application under this section are—
  (a) in the case of the purposes referred to in paragraph (a) or (b) of subsection (3), the trustees of the scheme, and
  (b) in the case of the purposes referred to in paragraph (c) of that subsection—
    (i) the trustees or managers of the scheme,
    (ii) the employer, or
    (iii) any person other than the trustees or managers who has power to alter the rules of the scheme.

(5) An order under subsection (1)(a) must be framed—
  (a) if made with a view to achieving either of the purposes referred to in subsection (3)(a) or (b), so as to confer the power of modification on the trustees, and
  (b) if made with a view to achieving the purposes referred to in subsection (3)(c), so as to confer the power of modification on such persons (who may include persons who were not parties to the application made to the Authority) as the Authority think appropriate.

(6) Regulations may provide that in prescribed circumstances this section does not apply to occupational pension schemes falling within a prescribed class or description or applies to them with prescribed modifications.

Definitions For "the Authority", see s 1(1); for "prescribed", "regulations" and "trustees or managers", see s 124(1); for "employer", see ss 124(1), 125(3). By virtue of s 124(1), for "public service pension scheme", see the Pension Schemes Act 1993, s 1. By virtue of s 124(5), for "contracted-out employment", see s 8(1) of the 1993 Act, as amended by ss 136(2), 151 of, Sch 5, paras 18, 21(a) to, this Act, and for "employment" and "modification", see s 181(1) of the 1993 Act. By virtue of s 176, for "occupational pension scheme", see s 1 of the 1993 Act.
References See paras 9.8–9.11.

70 Section 69: supplementary

(1) The Authority may not make an order under section 69 unless they are satisfied that the purposes for which the application for the order was made—
- (a) cannot be achieved otherwise than by means of such an order, or
- (b) can only be achieved in accordance with a procedure which—
    - (i) is liable to be unduly complex or protracted, or
    - (ii) involves the obtaining of consents which cannot be obtained, or can only be obtained with undue delay or difficulty.

(2) The extent of the Authority's powers to make such an order is not limited, in relation to any purposes for which they are exercisable, to the minimum necessary to achieve those purposes.

(3) The Authority may not make an order under section 69 with a view to achieving the purpose referred to in subsection (3)(c) of that section unless they are satisfied that it is reasonable in all the circumstances to make it.

Definitions For "the Authority", see s 1(1).
References See para 9.12.

71 Effect of orders under section 69

(1) An order under paragraph (a) of subsection (1) of section 69 may enable those exercising any power conferred by the order to exercise it retrospectively (whether or not the power could otherwise be so exercised) and an order under paragraph (b) of that subsection may modify a scheme retrospectively.

(2) Any modification of a scheme made in pursuance of an order of the Authority under section 69 is as effective in law as if it had been made under powers conferred by or under the scheme.

(3) An order under section 69 may be made and complied with in relation to a scheme—
- (a) in spite of any enactment or rule of law, or any rule of the scheme, which would otherwise operate to prevent the modification being made, or
- (b) without regard to any such enactment, rule of law or rule of the scheme as would otherwise require, or might otherwise be taken to require, the implementation of any procedure or the obtaining of any consent, with a view to the making of the modification.

(4) In this section, "retrospectively" means with effect from a date before that on which the power is exercised or, as the case may be, the order is made.

Definitions For "the Authority", see s 1(1). By virtue of s 124(5), for "modification" and "modify", see the Pension Schemes Act 1993, s 181(1). For "enactment", see s 176. Note as to "retrospectively", sub-s (4) above.
References See para 9.12.

72 Modification of public service pension schemes

(1) The appropriate authority may make such provision for the modification of a public service pension scheme as could be made in respect of a scheme other than a public service pension scheme by an order of the Authority under section 69(1)(b).

(2) In this section "the appropriate authority", in relation to a scheme, means such Minister of the Crown or government department as may be designated by the Treasury as having responsibility for the particular scheme.

(3) The powers of the appropriate authority under this section are exercisable by means of an order—
  (a) directly modifying the scheme (without regard, in the case of a scheme contained in or made under powers conferred by an enactment, to the terms of the enactment or any of its restrictions), or
  (b) modifying an enactment under which the scheme was made or by virtue of which it has effect.

(4) Any such order may adapt, amend or repeal any such enactment as is referred to in paragraph (a) or (b) of subsection (3) as that authority thinks appropriate.

Definitions For "prescribed", "regulations" and "trustees or managers", see s 124(1); for "pensionable service", see s 124(1), (3); for "member", see ss 124(1), 125(4). By virtue of s 124(5), for "modifications", see the Pension Schemes Act 1993, s 181(1). By virtue of s 176, for "occupational pension scheme", see s 1 of the 1993 Act. For "salary-related occupational pension scheme", see s 93(1A) of the 1993 Act, as inserted by s 152(1), (3) of this Act.
References See para 9.14.

Winding up

73 Preferential liabilities on winding up

(1) This section applies, where a salary related occupational pension scheme to which section 56 applies is being wound up, to determine the order in which the assets of the scheme are to be applied towards satisfying the liabilities in respect of pensions and other benefits (including increases in pensions).

(2) The assets of the scheme must be applied first towards satisfying the amounts of the liabilities mentioned in subsection (3) and, if the assets are insufficient to satisfy those amounts in full, then—
  (a) the assets must be applied first towards satisfying the amounts of the liabilities mentioned in earlier paragraphs of subsection (3) before the amounts of the liabilities mentioned in later paragraphs, and
  (b) where the amounts of the liabilities mentioned in one of those paragraphs cannot be satisfied in full, those amounts must be satisfied in the same proportions.

(3) The liabilities referred to in subsection (2) are—
  (a) any liability for pensions or other benefits which, in the opinion of the trustees, are derived from the payment by any member of the scheme of voluntary contributions,
  (b) where a person's entitlement to payment of pension or other benefit has arisen, liability for that pension or benefit and for any pension or other benefit which will be payable to dependants of that person on his death (but excluding increases to pensions),
  (c) any liability for—
    (i) pensions or other benefits which have accrued to or in respect of any members of the scheme (but excluding increases to pensions), or
    (ii) (in respect of members with less than two years pensionable service) the return of contributions,
  (d) any liability for increases to pensions referred to in paragraphs (b) and (c);

and, for the purposes of subsection (2), the amounts of the liabilities mentioned in paragraphs (b) to (d) are to be taken to be the amounts calculated and verified in the prescribed manner.

(4) To the extent that any liabilities, as calculated in accordance with the rules of the scheme, have not been satisfied under subsection (2), any remaining assets of the scheme must then be applied towards satisfying those liabilities (as so calculated) in the order provided for in the rules of the scheme.

(5) If the scheme confers power on any person other than the trustees or managers to apply the assets of the scheme in respect of pensions or other benefits (including increases in pensions), it cannot be exercised by that person but may be exercised instead by the trustees or managers.

(6) If this section is not complied with—
  (a) section 3 applies to any trustee who has failed to take all such steps as are reasonable to secure compliance, and
  (b) section 10 applies to any trustee or manager who has failed to take all such steps.

(7) Regulations may modify subsection (3).

(8) This section does not apply to an occupational pension scheme falling within a prescribed class or description.

(9) This section shall have effect with prescribed modifications in cases where part of a salary related occupational pension scheme to which section 56 applies is being wound up.

Definitions For "prescribed", "regulations", "transfer credits" and "trustees or managers", see s 124(1); for "accrued rights", see s 124(2); for "member", see ss 124(1), 125(4). By virtue of s 124(5), for "insurance company" and "modifications", see the Pension Schemes Act 1993, s 181(1). By virtue of s 176, for "occupational pension scheme" and "personal pension scheme", see s 1 of the 1993 Act. For "salary-related occupational pension scheme", see s 93(1A) of the 1993 Act, as inserted by s 152(1), (3) of this Act.
References See paras 10.1–10.11.

74 Discharge of liabilities by insurance, etc

(1) This section applies where a salary related occupational pension scheme to which section 56 applies, other than a scheme falling within a prescribed class or description, is being wound up.

(2) A liability to or in respect of a member of the scheme in respect of pensions or other benefits (including increases in pensions) is to be treated as discharged (to the extent that it would not be so treated apart from this section) if the trustees or managers of the scheme have, in accordance with prescribed arrangements, provided for the discharge of the liability in one or more of the ways mentioned in subsection (3).

(3) The ways referred to in subsection (2) are—
  (a) by acquiring transfer credits allowed under the rules of another occupational pension scheme which satisfies prescribed requirements and the trustees or managers of which are able and willing to accept payment in respect of the member,
  (b) by acquiring rights allowed under the rules of a personal pension scheme which satisfies prescribed requirements and the trustees or managers of which are able and willing to accept payment in respect of the member's accrued rights,
  (c) by purchasing one or more annuities which satisfy prescribed requirements from one or more insurance companies, being companies willing to accept payment in respect of the member from the trustees or managers,
  (d) by subscribing to other pension arrangements which satisfy prescribed requirements.

(4) If the assets of the scheme are insufficient to satisfy in full the liabilities, as calculated in accordance with the rules of the scheme, in respect of pensions and other benefits (including increases in pensions), the reference in subsection (2) to providing for the discharge of any liability in one or more of the ways mentioned in

subsection (3) is to applying any amount available, in accordance with section 73, in one or more of those ways.

(5) Regulations may provide for this section—
   (a) to have effect in relation to so much of any liability as may be determined in accordance with the regulations, or
   (b) to have effect with prescribed modifications in relation to schemes falling within a prescribed class or description.

Definitions For "prescribed", "regulations", "transfer credits" and "trustees or managers", see s 124(1); for "accrued rights", see s 124(2); for "member", see ss 124(1), 125(4). By virtue of s 124(5), for "insurance company" and "modifications", see the Pension Schemes Act 1993, s 181(1). By virtue of s 176, for "occupational pension scheme" and "personal pension scheme", see s 1 of the 1993 Act. For "salary-related occupational pension scheme", see s 93(1A) of the 1993 Act, as inserted by s 152(1), (3) of this Act.
References See paras 10.22, 10.23.

75 Deficiencies in the assets

(1) If, in the case of an occupational pension scheme which is not a money purchase scheme, the value at the applicable time of the assets of the scheme is less than the amount at that time of the liabilities of the scheme, an amount equal to the difference shall be treated as a debt due from the employer to the trustees or managers of the scheme.

(2) If in the case of an occupational pension scheme which is not a money purchase scheme—
   (a) a relevant insolvency event occurs in relation to the employer, and
   (b) a debt due from the employer under subsection (1) has not been discharged at the time that event occurs,
the debt in question shall be taken, for the purposes of the law relating to winding up, bankruptcy or sequestration as it applies in relation to the employer, to arise immediately before that time.

(3) In this section "the applicable time" means —
   (a) if the scheme is being wound up before a relevant insolvency event occurs in relation to the employer, any time when it is being wound up before such an event occurs, and
   (b) otherwise, immediately before the relevant insolvency event occurs.

(4) For the purposes of this section a relevant insolvency event occurs in relation to the employer —
   (a) in England and Wales—
      (i) where the employer is a company, when it goes into liquidation, within the meaning of section 247(2) of the Insolvency Act 1986, or
      (ii) where the employer is an individual, at the commencement of his bankruptcy, within the meaning of section 278 of that Act, or
   (b) in Scotland—
      (i) where the employer is a company, at the commencement of its winding up, within the meaning of section 129 of that Act, or
      (ii) where the employer is a debtor within the meaning of the Bankruptcy (Scotland) Act 1985, on the date of sequestration as defined in section 12(4) of that Act.

(5) For the purposes of subsection (1), the liabilities and assets to be taken into account, and their amount or value, must be determined, calculated and verified by a prescribed person and in the prescribed manner.

(6) In calculating the value of any liabilities for those purposes, a provision of the scheme which limits the amount of its liabilities by reference to the amount of its assets is to be disregarded.

(7) This section does not prejudice any other right or remedy which the trustees or managers may have in respect of a deficiency in the scheme's assets.

(8) A debt due by virtue only of this section shall not be regarded—
  (a) as a preferential debt for the purposes of the Insolvency Act 1986, or
  (b) as a preferred debt for the purposes of the Bankruptcy (Scotland) Act 1985.

(9) This section does not apply to an occupational pension scheme falling within a prescribed class or description.

(10) Regulations may modify this section as it applies in prescribed circumstances.

Definitions For "prescribed", regulations" and "trustees or managers", see s 124(1); for "employer", see ss 124(1), 125(3). By virtue of s 124(5), for "modify" and "money purchase scheme", see the Pension Schemes Act 1993, s 181(1). By virtue of s 176, for "occupational pension scheme", see s 1 of the 1993 Act. Note as to "the applicable time", sub-s (3) above, and as to "a relevant insolvency event", sub-s (4) above.
References See para 10.12.

76 Excess assets on winding up

(1) This section applies to a trust scheme in any circumstances if—
  (a) it is an exempt approved scheme, within the meaning given by section 592(1) of the Taxes Act 1988,
  (b) the scheme is being wound up, and
  (c) in those circumstances power is conferred on the employer or the trustees to distribute assets to the employer on a winding up.

(2) The power referred to in subsection (1)(c) cannot be exercised unless the requirements of subsections (3) and (in prescribed circumstances) (4), and any prescribed requirements, are satisfied.

(3) The requirements of this subsection are that—
  (a) the liabilities of the scheme have been fully discharged,
  (b) where there is any power under the scheme, after the discharge of those liabilities, to distribute assets to any person other than the employer, the power has been exercised or a decision has been made not to exercise it,
  (c) the annual rates of the pensions under the scheme which commence or have commenced are increased by the appropriate percentage, and
  (d) notice has been given in accordance with prescribed requirements to the members of the scheme of the proposal to exercise the power.

(4) The requirements of this subsection are that the Authority are of the opinion that—
  (a) any requirements prescribed by virtue of subsection (2) are satisfied, and
  (b) the requirements of subsection (3) are satisfied.

(5) In subsection (3)—
  (a) "annual rate" and "appropriate percentage" have the same meaning as in section 54, and
  (b) "pension" does not include—
    (i) any guaranteed minimum pension (as defined in section 8(2) of the Pension Schemes Act 1993) or any increase in such a pension under section 109 of that Act, or
    (ii) any money purchase benefit (as defined in section 181(1) of that Act).

(6) If, where this section applies to any trust scheme, the trustees purport to exercise the power referred to in subsection (1)(c) without complying with the requirements of this section, sections 3 and 10 apply to any of them who have failed to take all such steps as are reasonable to secure compliance.

(7) If, where this section applies to any trust scheme, any person other than the trustees purports to exercise the power referred to in subsection (1)(c) without complying with the requirements of this section, section 10 applies to him.

(8) Regulations may provide that, in prescribed circumstances, this section does not apply to schemes falling within a prescribed class or description, or applies to them with prescribed modifications.

Definitions For "the Authority", see s 1(1); for "prescribed", "regulations" and "trust scheme", see s 124(1); for "employer", see ss 124(1), 125(3); for "member", see ss 124(1), 125(4). By virtue of s 124(5), for "modifications", see the Pension Schemes Act 1993, s 181(1).
References See paras 10.13–10.15.

77 Excess assets remaining after winding up: power to distribute

(1) This section applies to a trust scheme in any circumstances if—
   (a) it is an exempt approved scheme, within the meaning given by section 592(1) of the Taxes Act 1988,
   (b) the scheme is being wound up,
   (c) the liabilities of the scheme have been fully discharged,
   (d) where there is any power under the scheme, after the discharge of those liabilities, to distribute assets to any person other than the employer, the power has been exercised or a decision has been made not to exercise it,
   (e) any assets remain undistributed, and
   (f) the scheme prohibits the distribution of assets to the employer in those circumstances.

(2) The annual rates of the pensions under the scheme which commence or have commenced must be increased by the appropriate percentage, so far as the value of the undistributed assets allows.

(3) In subsection (2)—
   (a) "annual rate" and "appropriate percentage" have the same meaning as in section 54, and
   (b) "pension" does not include—
      (i) any guaranteed minimum pension (as defined in section 8(2) of the Pension Schemes Act 1993) or any increase in such a pension under section 109 of that Act, or
      (ii) any money purchase benefit (as defined in section 181(1) of that Act).

(4) Where any assets remain undistributed after the discharge of the trustees duty under subsection (2)—
   (a) the trustees must use those assets for the purpose of providing additional benefits or increasing the value of any benefits, but subject to prescribed limits, and
   (b) the trustees may then distribute those assets (so far as undistributed) to the employer.

(5) If, where this section applies to a trust scheme, the requirements of this section are not complied with, section 3 applies to any trustee who has failed to take all such steps as are reasonable to secure compliance.

(6) Regulations may modify this section as it applies in prescribed circumstances.

Definitions For "prescribed", "regulations" and "trust scheme", see s 124(1); for "employer", see ss 124(1), 125(3). By virtue of s 124(5), for "modify", see the Pension Schemes Act 1993, s 181(1).
Regulations See paras 10.13, 10.16–10.18.

The Pensions Compensation Board

78 The Compensation Board

(1) There shall be a body corporate called the Pensions Compensation Board (referred to in this Part as "the Compensation Board").

(2) The Compensation Board shall consist of not less than three members appointed by the Secretary of State, one of whom shall be so appointed as chairman.

(3) In addition to the chairman, the Board shall comprise—
    (a) a member appointed after the Secretary of State has consulted—
        (i) organisations appearing to him to be representative of employers, and
        (ii) the chairman,
    (b) a member appointed after the Secretary of State has consulted—
        (i) organisations appearing to him to be representative of employees, and
        (ii) the chairman,
and such other member or members as the Secretary of State may appoint after consultation with the chairman.

(4) Payments made by the Compensation Board may be made on such terms (including terms requiring repayment in whole or in part) and on such conditions as the Board think appropriate.

(5) The Compensation Board may borrow from an institution authorised under the Banking Act 1987 such sums as they may from time to time require for exercising any of their functions.

(6) The aggregate amount outstanding in respect of the principal of any money borrowed by the Compensation Board under subsection (5) must not exceed the prescribed amount.

(7) Neither the Compensation Board nor any person who is a member or employee of the Compensation Board shall be liable in damages for anything done or omitted in the discharge or purported discharge of the functions of the Compensation Board under this Part, or any corresponding provisions in force in Northern Ireland, unless it is shown that the act or omission was in bad faith.

(8) Schedule 2 (constitution, procedure, etc of the Compensation Board) shall have effect.

Definitions For "prescribed", see s 124(1); for "employer", see ss 124(1), 125(3). By virtue of s 124(5), for "employee", see the Pension Schemes Act 1993, s 181(1). Note as to "the Compensation Board", sub-s (1) above.
References See paras 11.1–11.5.

79 Reports to Secretary of State

(1) The Compensation Board must prepare a report for the first twelve months of their existence, and a report for each succeeding period of twelve months, and must send each report to the Secretary of State as soon as practicable after the end of the period for which it is prepared.

(2) A report prepared under this section for any period must deal with the activities of the Compensation Board in the period.

(3) The Secretary of State must lay before each House of Parliament a copy of every report received by him under this section.

Definitions For "the Compensation Board", see s 78(1).
References See para 11.8.

80 Review of decisions

(1) Subject to the following provisions of this section, any determination by the Compensation Board of a question which it is within their functions to determine shall be final.

(2) The Compensation Board may on the application of a person appearing to them to be interested—
- (a) at any time review any such determination of theirs as is mentioned in subsection (1) (including a determination given by them on a previous review), if they are satisfied that there has been a relevant change of circumstances since the determination was made, or that the determination was made in ignorance of a material fact or based on a mistake as to a material fact or was erroneous in point of law, and
- (b) at any time within a period of three months from the date of the determination, or within such longer period as they may allow in any particular case, review such a determination on any ground.

(3) The Compensation Board's powers on a review under this section include power—
- (a) to vary or revoke any determination previously made,
- (b) to substitute a different determination, and
- (c) generally to deal with the matters arising on the review as if they had arisen on the original determination;

and also include power to make savings and transitional provisions.

(4) Subject to subsection (5), regulations may make provision with respect to the procedure to be adopted on any application for a review under this section, or under any corresponding provision in force in Northern Ireland, and generally with respect to such applications and reviews.

(5) Nothing in subsection (4) shall be taken to prevent such a review being entered upon by the Compensation Board without an application being made.

Definitions For "the Compensation Board", see s 78(1); for "regulations", see s 124(1).
References See para 11.9.

The compensation provisions

81 Cases where compensation provisions apply

(1) Subject to subsection (2), this section applies to an application for compensation under section 82 in respect of an occupational pension scheme if all the following conditions are met—
- (a) the scheme is a trust scheme,
- (b) the employer is insolvent,
- (c) the value of the assets of the scheme has been reduced, and there are reasonable grounds for believing that the reduction was attributable to an act or omission constituting a prescribed offence,
- (d) in the case of a salary related trust scheme, immediately before the date of the application the value of the assets of the scheme is less than 90 per cent of the amount of the liabilities of the scheme, and
- (e) it is reasonable in all the circumstances that the members of the scheme should be assisted by the Compensation Board paying to the trustees of the scheme, out of funds for the time being held by them, an amount determined in accordance with the compensation provisions.

(2) Subsection (1) does not apply in respect of a trust scheme falling within a prescribed class or description; and paragraph (c) applies only to reductions in value since the appointed day.

(3) In this Part the "compensation provisions" means the provisions of this section and sections 82 to 85; and below in the compensation provisions as they relate to a trust scheme—
- (a) "the application date" means the date of the application for compensation under section 82,
- (b) "the appointed day" means the day appointed under section 180 for the commencement of this section,
- (c) "the insolvency date" means the date on which the employer became insolvent,
- (d) "the settlement date" means the date determined by the Compensation Board, after consulting the trustees, to be the date after which further recoveries of value are unlikely to be obtained without disproportionate cost or within a reasonable time,
- (e) "the shortfall at the application date" means the amount of the reduction falling within subsection (1)(c) or (if there was more than one such reduction) the aggregate of the reductions, being the amount or aggregate immediately before the application date,
- (f) "recovery of value" means any increase in the value of the assets of the scheme, being an increase attributable to any payment received (otherwise than from the Compensation Board) by the trustees of the scheme in respect of any act or omission—
    - (i) which there are reasonable grounds for believing constituted a prescribed offence, and
    - (ii) to which any reduction in value falling within subsection (1)(c) was attributable.

(4) It is for the Compensation Board to determine whether anything received by the trustees of the scheme is to be treated as a payment received for any such act or omission as is referred to in subsection (3)(f); and in this section "payment" includes any money or money's worth.

(5) Where this section applies to an application for compensation under section 82, the trustees must obtain any recoveries of value, to the extent that they may do so without disproportionate cost and within a reasonable time.

(6) If subsection (5) is not complied with, section 3 applies to any trustee who has failed to take all such steps as are reasonable to secure compliance.

(7) Section 56(3) and (4) applies for the purposes of the compensation provisions as it applies for the purposes of sections 56 to 61.

(8) Section 123 of the Pension Schemes Act 1993 (meaning of insolvency) applies for the purposes of the compensation provisions as it applies for the purposes of Chapter II of Part VII of that Act (unpaid scheme contributions).

Definitions For "the Compensation Board", see s 78(1); for "prescribed" and "trust scheme", see s 124(1); as to "salary related trust scheme", see s 125(1); for "employer", see ss 124(1), 125(3); for "member", see s 124(1), 125(4). By virtue of s 176, for "occupational pension scheme", see the Pension Schemes Act 1993, s 1. Note as to "compensation provisions", "the application date", "the appointed day", "the insolvency date", "the settlement date", "the shortfall at the application date" and "recovery of value", sub-s (3) above; and as to "payment", sub-s (4) above.
References See paras 11.10, 11.11.

82 Applications for payments

(1) Compensation may be paid under section 83 only on an application to which section 81 applies made within the qualifying period by a prescribed person.

(2) An application under this section must be made in the manner, and give the information, required by the Compensation Board.

(3) For the purposes of this section the "qualifying period", subject to subsection (5), is the period expiring with the period of twelve months mentioned in subsection (4).

(4) The period of twelve months referred to in subsection (3) is that beginning with the later of the following times—
  (a) the insolvency date,
  (b) when the auditor or actuary of the scheme, or the trustees, knew or ought reasonably to have known that a reduction of value falling within section 81(1)(c) had occurred,

being, in each case, a time after the appointed day.

(5) The Compensation Board may extend, or further extend, the qualifying period.

Definitions For "the actuary" and "the auditor", see s 47(1); for "the Compensation Board", see s 78(1); as to "the appointed day" and "the insolvency date", see s 81(3); for "prescribed", see s 124(1). Note as to "the qualifying period", sub-s (3) above.
References See paras 11.10, 11.12.

83 Amount of compensation

(1) Where in the opinion of the Compensation Board section 81 applies to an application for compensation under section 82 in respect of a trust scheme, and the Board have determined the settlement date, the Board may make a payment or payments to the trustees of the scheme in accordance with this section.

(2) The amount of any payment must be determined in accordance with regulations and must take account of any payment already made under section 84, and the Compensation Board must give written notice of their determination to the person who made the application under section 82 and (if different) to the trustees.

(3) The amount of the payment or (if there is more than one) the aggregate—
  (a) must not exceed 90 per cent of the shortfall at the application date, together with interest at the prescribed rate for the prescribed period on the shortfall or (if the shortfall comprises more than one reduction in value) on each of the reductions, and also,
  (b) in the case of a salary related scheme, must not exceed the amount which, on the settlement date, is required to be paid to the trustees of the scheme in order to secure that the value on that date of the assets of the scheme is equal to 90 per cent of the amount on that date of the liabilities of the scheme.

Definitions For "the Compensation Board", see s 78(1); as to "the application date", "the settlement date" and "the shortfall at the application date", see s 81(3); for "prescribed", "regulations" and "trust scheme", see s 124(1); as to "salary related scheme", see s 125(1).
References See paras 11.14–11.16.

84 Payments made in anticipation

(1) The Compensation Board may, on an application for compensation under section 82, make a payment or payments to the trustees of a trust scheme where in their opinion—
  (a) section 81 applies, or may apply, to the application, and
  (b) the trustees would not otherwise be able to meet liabilities falling within a prescribed class,

but the Board have not determined the settlement date.

(2) Amounts payable under this section must be determined in accordance with regulations.

(3) Where any payment is made under this section, the Compensation Board may, except in prescribed circumstances—
  (a) if they subsequently form the opinion that section 81 does not apply to the application for compensation in respect of the scheme, or
  (b) if they subsequently form the opinion that the amount of the payment was excessive,
recover so much of the payment as they consider appropriate.

Definitions For "the Compensation Board", see s 78(1); as to "the settlement date", see s 81(3); for "prescribed", "regulations" and "trust scheme", see s 124(1).
References See para 11.13.

85 Surplus funds

(1) If the Secretary of State, after consultation with the Compensation Board, considers that the funds for the time being held by the Board exceed what is reasonably required for the purpose of exercising their functions under this Part, he may by order require them to distribute any of those funds appearing to him to be surplus to their requirements among occupational pension schemes.

(2) A distribution under subsection (1) must be made in the prescribed manner and subject to the prescribed conditions.

(3) The Compensation Board may invest any funds for the time being held by them which appear to them to be surplus to their requirements—
  (a) in any investment for the time being falling within Part I, Part II or Part III of Schedule 1 to the Trustee Investments Act 1961, or
  (b) in any prescribed investment.

Definitions For "the Compensation Board", see s 78(1); for "prescribed", see s 124(1). By virtue of s 176, for "occupational pension scheme", see the Pension Schemes Act 1993, s 1.
References See paras 11.17, 11.18.

86 Modification of compensation provisions

Regulations may modify the compensation provisions in their application to trust schemes falling within a prescribed class or description.

Definitions For "the compensation provisions", see s 81(3); for "prescribed", "regulations" and "trust scheme", see s 124(1). By virtue of s 124(5), for "modify", see the Pension Schemes Act 1993, s 181(1).
References See para 11.11.

Money purchase schemes

87 Schedules of payments to money purchase schemes

(1) This section applies to an occupational pension scheme which is a money purchase scheme, other than one falling within a prescribed class or description.

(2) The trustees or managers of every occupational pension scheme to which this section applies must secure that there is prepared, maintained and from time to time revised a schedule (referred to in this section and section 88 as a "payment schedule") showing—
  (a) the rates of contributions payable towards the scheme by or on behalf of the employer and the active members of the scheme,
  (b) such other amounts payable towards the scheme as may be prescribed, and
  (c) the dates on or before which payments of such contributions or other amounts are to be made (referred to in those sections as "due dates").

(3) The payment schedule for a scheme must satisfy prescribed requirements.

(4) The matters shown in the payment schedule for a scheme—
- (a) to the extent that the scheme makes provision for their determination, must be so determined, and
- (b) otherwise,
   - (i) must be matters previously agreed between the employer and the trustees or managers of the scheme, or
   - (ii) if no such agreement has been made as to all matters shown in the schedule (other than those for whose determination the scheme makes provision), must be matters determined by the trustees or managers of the scheme.

(5) Where in the case of a scheme this section is not complied with—
- (a) section 3 applies to any trustee who has failed to take all such steps as are reasonable to secure compliance, and
- (b) section 10 applies to any trustee or manager who has failed to take all such steps.

Definitions For "active member", "prescribed" and "trustees or managers", see s 124(1); for "employer", see ss 124(1), 125(3). By virtue of s 124(5), for "money purchase scheme", see the Pension Schemes Act 1993, s 181(1). By virtue of s 176, for "occupational pension scheme", see s 1 of the 1993 Act. Note as to "payment schedule" and "due dates", sub-s (2) above.
References See paras 14.1, 14.3, 14.10.

88 Schedules of payments to money purchase schemes: supplementary

(1) Except in prescribed circumstances, the trustees or managers of an occupational pension scheme to which section 87 applies must, where any amounts payable in accordance with the payment schedule have not been paid on or before the due date, give notice of that fact, within the prescribed period, to the Authority and to the members of the scheme.

(2) Any such amounts which for the time being remain unpaid after that date (whether payable by the employer or not) shall, if not a debt due from the employer to the trustees or managers apart from this subsection, be treated as such a debt.

(3) Where any amounts payable in accordance with the payment schedule by or on behalf of the employer have not been paid on or before the due date, section 10 applies to the employer.

(4) If, in the case of an occupational pension scheme to which section 87 applies, subsection (1) is not complied with—
- (a) section 3 applies to any trustee who has failed to take all such steps as are reasonable to secure compliance, and
- (b) section 10 applies to any trustee or manager who has failed to take all such steps.

Definitions For "the Authority", see s 1(1); as to "due date" and "payment schedule", see s 87(2); for "prescribed" and "trustees or managers", see s 124(1); for "employer", see ss 124(1), 125(3); for "member", see ss 124(1), 125(4). By virtue of s 176, for "occupational pension scheme", see the Pension Schemes Act 1993, s 1.
References See paras 14.4–14.7.

89 Application of further provisions to money purchase schemes

(1) In the case of money purchase schemes falling within a prescribed class or description, regulations may—
- (a) provide for any of the provisions of sections 56 to 60 to apply, or apply with prescribed modifications (in spite of anything in those sections), and

(b) provide for any of the provisions of sections 87 and 88 to apply with prescribed modifications or not to apply,

to such extent as may be prescribed.

(2) Regulations may provide for any of the provisions of section 75 to apply, or apply with prescribed modifications, to money purchase schemes to such extent as may be prescribed (in spite of anything in that section), and the power conferred by this subsection includes power to apply section 75 in circumstances other than those in which the scheme is being wound up or a relevant insolvency event occurs (within the meaning of that section).

Definitions For "prescribed" and "regulations", see s 124(1). By virtue of s 124(5), for "modifications" and "money purchase scheme", see the Pension Schemes Act 1993, s 181(1).
References See para 14.8.

90 Unpaid contributions in cases of insolvency

In section 124 of the Pension Schemes Act 1993 (duty of Secretary of State to pay unpaid contributions to schemes), after subsection (3) there is inserted—

"(3A) Where the scheme in question is a money purchase scheme, the sum payable under this section by virtue of subsection (3) shall be the lesser of the amounts mentioned in paragraphs (a) and (c) of that subsection",

and, accordingly, at the beginning of subsection (3) there is inserted "Subject to subsection (3A),".

Definitions For "money purchase scheme", see the Pension Schemes Act 1993, s 181(1).
References See para 14.9.

Assignment, forfeiture, bankruptcy etc

91 Inalienability of occupational pension

(1) Subject to subsection (5), where a person is entitled, or has an accrued right, to a pension under an occupational pension scheme—
  (a) the entitlement or right cannot be assigned, commuted or surrendered,
  (b) the entitlement or right cannot be charged or a lien exercised in respect of it, and
  (c) no set-off can be exercised in respect of it,
and an agreement to effect any of those things is unenforceable.

(2) Where by virtue of this section a person's entitlement, or accrued right, to a pension under an occupational pension scheme cannot, apart from subsection (5), be assigned, no order can be made by any court the effect of which would be that he would be restrained from receiving that pension.

(3) Where a bankruptcy order is made against a person, any entitlement or right of his which by virtue of this section cannot, apart from subsection (5), be assigned is excluded from his estate for the purposes of Parts VIII to XI of the Insolvency Act 1986 or the Bankruptcy (Scotland) Act 1985.

(4) Subsection (2) does not prevent the making of—
  (a) an attachment of earnings order under the Attachment of Earnings Act 1971, or
  (b) an income payments order under the Insolvency Act 1986.

(5) In the case of a person ("the person in question") who is entitled, or has an accrued right, to a pension under an occupational pension scheme, subsection (1) does not apply to any of the following, or any agreement to effect any of the following—

(a) an assignment in favour of the person in question's widow, widower or dependant,
(b) a surrender, at the option of the person in question, for the purpose of—
  (i) providing benefits for that person's widow, widower or dependant, or
  (ii) acquiring for the person in question entitlement to further benefits under the scheme,
(c) a commutation—
  (i) of the person in question's benefit on or after retirement or in exceptional circumstances of serious ill health,
  (ii) in prescribed circumstances, of any benefit for that person's widow, widower or dependant, or
  (iii) in other prescribed circumstances,
(d) subject to subsection (6), a charge or lien on, or set-off against, the person in question's entitlement, or accrued right, to pension (except to the extent that it includes transfer credits other than prescribed transfer credits) for the purpose of enabling the employer to obtain the discharge by him of some monetary obligation due to the employer and arising out of a criminal, negligent or fraudulent act or omission by him,
(e) subject to subsection (6), except in prescribed circumstances a charge or lien on, or set-off against, the person in question's entitlement, or accrued right, to pension, for the purpose of discharging some monetary obligation due from the person in question to the scheme and—
  (i) arising out of a criminal, negligent or fraudulent act or omission by him, or
  (ii) in the case of a trust scheme of which the person in question is a trustee, arising out of a breach of trust by him.

(6) Where a charge, lien or set-off is exercisable by virtue of subsection (5)(d) or (e)—
  (a) its amount must not exceed the amount of the monetary obligation in question, or (if less) the value (determined in the prescribed manner) of the person in question's entitlement or accrued right, and
  (b) the person in question must be given a certificate showing the amount of the charge, lien or set-off and its effect on his benefits under the scheme,
and where there is a dispute as to its amount, the charge, lien or set-off must not be exercised unless the obligation in question has become enforceable under an order of a competent court or in consequence of an award of an arbitrator or, in Scotland, an arbiter to be appointed (failing agreement between the parties) by the sheriff.

(7) This section is subject to section 159 of the Pension Schemes Act 1993 (inalienability of guaranteed minimum pension and protected rights payments).

Definitions For "pension", see s 94(2); for "prescribed","transfer credits" and "trust scheme", see s 124(1); for "accrued rights", see s 124(2); for "employer", see ss 124(1), 125(3). By virtue of s 176, for "occupational pension scheme", see s 1 of the 1993 Act. Note as to "the person in question", sub-s (5) above.
References See paras 12.13–12.16.

92 Forfeiture, etc

(1) Subject to the provisions of this section and section 93, an entitlement, or accrued right, to a pension under an occupational pension scheme cannot be forfeited.

(2) Subsection (1) does not prevent forfeiture by reference to—
  (a) a transaction or purported transaction which under section 91 is of no effect, or
  (b) the bankruptcy of the person entitled to the pension or whose right to it has accrued,
whether or not that event occurred before or after the pension became payable.

(3) Where such forfeiture as is mentioned in subsection (2) occurs, any pension which was, or would but for the forfeiture have become, payable may, if the trustees or managers of the scheme so determine, be paid to all or any of the following—
    (a) the member of the scheme to or in respect of whom the pension was, or would have become, payable,
    (b) the spouse, widow or widower of the member,
    (c) any dependant of the member, and
    (d) any other person falling within a prescribed class.

(4) Subsection (1) does not prevent forfeiture by reference to the person entitled to the pension, or whose right to it has accrued, having been convicted of one or more offences—
    (a) which are committed before the pension becomes payable, and
    (b) which are—
        (i) offences of treason,
        (ii) offences under the Official Secrets Acts 1911 to 1989 for which the person has been sentenced on the same occasion to a term of imprisonment of, or to two or more consecutive terms amounting in the aggregate to, at least 10 years, or
        (iii) prescribed offences.

(5) Subsection (1) does not prevent forfeiture by reference to a failure by any person to make a claim for pension—
    (a) where the forfeiture is in reliance on any enactment relating to the limitation of actions, or
    (b) where the claim is not made within six years of the date on which the pension becomes due.

(6) Subsection (1) does not prevent forfeiture in prescribed circumstances.

(7) In this section and section 93, references to forfeiture include any manner of deprivation or suspension.

Definitions   For "pension", see s 94(2); for "prescribed" and "trustees or managers", see s 124(1); for "accrued rights", see s 124(2); for "member", see ss 124(1), 125(4); for "enactment", see s 176. By virtue of s 176, for "occupational pension scheme", see the Pension Schemes Act 1993, s 1. Note as to "forfeiture", sub-s (7) above.
References   See para 12.16.

93 Forfeiture by reference to obligation to employer

(1) Subject to subsection (2), section 92(1) does not prevent forfeiture of a person's entitlement, or accrued right, to a pension under an occupational pension scheme by reference to the person having incurred some monetary obligation due to the employer and arising out of a criminal, negligent or fraudulent act or omission by the person.

(2) A person's entitlement or accrued right to a pension may be forfeited by reason of subsection (1) to the extent only that it does not exceed the amount of the monetary obligation in question, or (if less) the value (determined in the prescribed manner) of the person's entitlement or accrued right to a pension under the scheme.

(3) Such forfeiture as is mentioned in subsection (1) must not take effect where there is a dispute as to the amount of the monetary obligation in question, unless the obligation has become enforceable under an order of a competent court or in consequence of an award of an arbitrator or, in Scotland, an arbiter to be appointed (failing agreement between the parties) by the sheriff.

(4) Where a person's entitlement or accrued right to a pension is forfeited by reason of subsection (1), the person must be given a certificate showing the amount forfeited and the effect of the forfeiture on his benefits under the scheme.

Pensions Act 1995, s 93

(5) Where such forfeiture as is mentioned in subsection (1) occurs, an amount not exceeding the amount forfeited may, if the trustees or managers of the scheme so determine, be paid to the employer.

Definitions For "forfeiture", see s 92(7); for "pension", see s 94(2); for "prescribed" and "trustees or managers", see s 124(1); for "accrued rights", see s 124(2); for "employer", see ss 124(1), 125(3). By virtue of s 176, for "occupational pension scheme", see the Pension Schemes Act 1993, s 1. Note as to "forfeiture", sub-s (7) above.
Regulations See para 12.17.

94 Sections 91 to 93: supplementary

(1) Regulations may—
    (a) modify sections 91 to 93 in their application to public service pension schemes or to other schemes falling within a prescribed class or description, or
    (b) provide that those sections do not apply in relation to schemes falling within a prescribed class or description.

(2) In those sections, "pension" in relation to an occupational pension scheme, includes any benefit under the scheme and any part of a pension and any payment by way of pension.

(3) In the application of sections 91 and 92 to Scotland—
    (a) references to a charge are to be read as references to a right in security or a diligence and "charged" is to be interpreted accordingly,
    (b) references to assignment are to be read as references to assignation and "assign" is to be interpreted accordingly,
    (c) the reference to a person's bankruptcy is to be read as a reference to the sequestration of his estate or the appointment on his estate of a judicial factor under section 41 of the Solicitors (Scotland) Act 1980,
    (d) the reference to an income payments order under the Insolvency Act 1986 is to be read as a reference to an order under section 32(2) of the Bankruptcy (Scotland) Act 1985, and
    (e) the reference to the making of a bankruptcy order is to be read as a reference to the award of sequestration or the making of the appointment of such a judicial factor.

Definitions For "prescribed" and "regulations", see s 124(1). By virtue of ss 176, 124(1) respectively, for "occupational pension scheme" and "public service pension scheme", see the Pension Schemes Act 1993, s 1. By virtue of s 124(5), for "modify", see the Pension Schemes Act 1993, s 181(1). Note as to "pension", sub-s (2) above.
Regulations See para 12.18.

95 Pension rights of individuals adjudged bankrupt etc

(1) After section 342 of the Insolvency Act 1986 (adjustment of certain transactions entered into by individuals subsequently adjudged bankrupt), there is inserted—

    "342A Recovery of excessive pension contributions

    (1) Where an individual is adjudged bankrupt and—
        (a) he has during the relevant period made contributions as a member of an occupational pension scheme, or
        (b) contributions have during the relevant period been made to such a scheme on his behalf,
    the trustee of the bankrupt's estate may apply to the court for an order under this section.

(2) If, on an application for an order under this section, the court is satisfied that the making of any of the contributions ("the excessive contributions") has unfairly prejudiced the individual's creditors, the court may make such order as it thinks fit for restoring the position to what it would have been if the excessive contributions had not been made.

(3) The court shall, in determining whether it is satisfied under subsection (2), consider in particular—
    (a) whether any of the contributions were made by or on behalf of the individual for the purpose of putting assets beyond the reach of his creditors or any of them,
    (b) whether the total amount of contributions made by or on behalf of the individual (including contributions made to any other occupational pension scheme) during the relevant period was excessive in view of the individual's circumstances at the time when they were made, and
    (c) whether the level of benefits under the scheme, together with benefits under any other occupational pension scheme, to which the individual is entitled, or is likely to become entitled, is excessive in all the circumstances of the case.

342B   Orders under section 342A

(1) Without prejudice to the generality of section 342A(2), an order under that section may include provision—
    (a) requiring the trustees or managers of the scheme to pay an amount to the individual's trustee in bankruptcy,
    (b) reducing the amount of any benefit to which the individual (or his spouse, widow, widower or dependant) is entitled, or to which he has an accrued right, under the scheme,
    (c) reducing the amount of any benefit to which, by virtue of any assignment, commutation or surrender of the individual's entitlement (or that of his spouse, widow, widower or dependant) or accrued right under the scheme, another person is entitled or has an accrued right,
    (d) otherwise adjusting the liabilities of the scheme in respect of any such person as is mentioned in paragraph (b) or (c).

(2) The maximum amount by which an order under section 342A may require the assets of an occupational pension scheme to be reduced is the lesser of—
    (a) the amount of the excessive contributions, and
    (b) the value (determined in the prescribed manner) of the assets of the scheme which represent contributions made by or on behalf of the individual.

(3) Subject to subsections (4) and (5), an order under section 342A must reduce the amount of the liabilities of the scheme by an amount equal to the amount of the reduction made in the value of the assets of the scheme.

(4) Subsection (3) does not apply where the individual's entitlement or accrued right to benefits under the scheme which he acquired by virtue of the excessive contributions (his "excessive entitlement") has been forfeited.

(5) Where part of the individual's excessive entitlement has been forfeited, the amount of the reduction in the liabilities of the scheme required by subsection (3) is the value of the remaining part of his excessive entitlement.

(6) An order under section 342A in respect of an occupational pension scheme shall be binding on the trustees or managers of the scheme.

342C Orders under section 342A: supplementary

(1) Nothing in—
   (a) any provision of section 159 of the Pension Schemes Act 1993 or section 91 of the Pensions Act 1995 (which prevent assignment, or orders being made restraining a person from receiving anything which he is prevented from assigning, and make provision in relation to a person's pension on bankruptcy),
   (b) any provision of any enactment (whether passed or made before or after the passing of the Pensions Act 1995) corresponding to any of the provisions mentioned in paragraph (a), or
   (c) any provision of the scheme in question corresponding to any of those provisions,

applies to a court exercising its powers under section 342A.

(2) Where any sum is required by an order under section 342A to be paid to the trustee in bankruptcy, that sum shall be comprised in the bankrupt's estate.

(3) Where contributions have been made during the relevant period to any occupational pension scheme and the entitlement or accrued right to benefits acquired thereby has been transferred to a second or subsequent occupational pension scheme ("the transferee scheme"), sections 342A and 342B and this section shall apply as though the contributions had been made to the transferee scheme.

(4) For the purposes of this section and sections 342A and 342B—
   (a) contributions are made during the relevant period if—
      (i) they are made by or on behalf of the individual at any time during the period of 5 years ending with the day of presentation of the bankruptcy petition on which the individual is adjudged bankrupt, or
      (ii) they are made on behalf of the individual at any time during the period between the presentation of the petition and the commencement of the bankruptcy, and
   (b) the accrued rights of an individual under an occupational pension scheme at any time are the rights which have accrued to or in respect of him at that time to future benefits under the scheme.

(5) In this section and sections 342A and 342B—
   "occupational pension scheme" has the meaning given by section 1 of the Pension Schemes Act 1993, and
   "trustees or managers", in relation to an occupational pension scheme, means—
      (a) in the case of a scheme established under a trust, the trustees of the scheme, and
      (b) in any other case, the managers of the scheme."

(2) After section 36 of the Bankruptcy (Scotland) Act 1985 there is inserted—

"36A Recovery of excessive pension contributions

(1) Where a debtor's estate has been sequestrated and—
   (a) he has during the relevant period made contributions as a member of an occupational pension scheme; or
   (b) contributions have during the relevant period been made to such a scheme on his behalf;

the permanent trustee may apply to the court for an order under this section.

(2) If, on an application for an order under this section, the court is satisfied that the making of any of the contributions ("the excessive contributions") has

unfairly prejudiced the debtor's creditors, the court may make such order as it thinks fit for restoring the position to what it would have been if the excessive contributions had not been made.

(3) The court shall, in determining whether it is satisfied under subsection (2) above, consider in particular—
- (a) whether any of the contributions were made by or on behalf of the debtor for the purpose of putting assets beyond the reach of his creditors or any of them;
- (b) whether the total amount of contributions made by or on behalf of the debtor (including contributions made to any other occupational pension scheme) during the relevant period was excessive in view of the debtor's circumstances at the time when they were made; and
- (c) whether the level of benefits under the scheme, together with benefits under any other occupational pension scheme, to which the debtor is entitled, or is likely to become entitled, is excessive in all the circumstances of the case.

36B Orders under section 36A

(1) Without prejudice to the generality of subsection (2) of section 36A of this Act, an order under that section may include provision—
- (a) requiring the trustees or managers of the scheme to pay an amount to the permanent trustee;
- (b) reducing the amount of any benefit to which the debtor (or his spouse, widow, widower or dependant) is entitled, or to which he has an accrued right, under the scheme;
- (c) reducing the amount of any benefit to which, by virtue of any assignation, commutation or surrender of the debtor's entitlement (or that of his spouse, widow, widower or dependant) or accrued right under the scheme, another person is entitled or has an accrued right;
- (d) otherwise adjusting the liabilities of the scheme in respect of any such person as is mentioned in paragraph (b) or (c) above.

(2) The maximum amount by which an order under section 36A of this Act may require the assets of an occupational pension scheme to be reduced is the lesser of—
- (a) value (determined in the prescribed manner) of the assets of the scheme which the amount of the excessive contributions; and
- (b) the represent contributions made by or on behalf of the debtor.

(3) Subject to subsections (4) and (5) below, an order under section 36A of this Act must reduce the amount of the liabilities of the scheme by an amount equal to the amount of the reduction made in the value of the assets of the scheme.

(4) Subsection (3) above does not apply where the debtor's entitlement or accrued right to benefits under the scheme which he acquired by virtue of the excessive contributions (his "excessive entitlement") has been forfeited.

(5) Where part of the debtor's excessive entitlement has been forfeited, the amount of the reduction in the liabilities of the scheme required by subsection (3) above is the value of the remaining part of his excessive entitlement.

(6) An order under section 36A of this Act in respect of an occupational pension scheme shall be binding on the trustees or managers of the scheme.

(7) The court may, on the application of any person having an interest, review, rescind or vary an order under section 36A of this Act.

36C Orders under section 36A: supplementary

(1) Nothing in—
  (a) any provision of section 159 of the Pension Schemes Act 1993 or 91 of the Pensions Act 1995 (which prevent assignation, or orders being made restraining a person from receiving anything which he is prevented from assigning, and make provision in relation to a person's pension on sequestration);
  (b) any provision of any enactment (whether passed or made before or after the passing of the Pensions Act 1995) corresponding to any of the provisions mentioned in paragraph (a) above; or
  (c) any provision of the scheme in question corresponding to any of those provisions,
applies to a court exercising its powers under section 36A of this Act.

(2) Where any sum is required by an order under section 36A of this Act to be paid to the permanent trustee, that sum shall be comprised in the debtor's estate.

(3) Where contributions have been made during the relevant period to any occupational pension scheme and the entitlement or accrued right to benefits acquired thereby has been transferred to a second or subsequent occupational pension scheme ("the transferee scheme"), sections 36A and 36B of this Act and this section shall apply as though the contributions had been made to the transferee scheme.

(4) For the purposes of this section and sections 36A and 36B of this Act—
  (a) contributions are made during the relevant period if they are made at any time during the period of 5 years ending with the date of sequestration; and
  (b) the accrued rights of a debtor under an occupational pension scheme at any time are the rights which have accrued to or in respect of him at that time to future benefits under the scheme.

(5) In this section and sections 36A and 36B of this Act—
"occupational pension scheme" has the meaning given by section 1 of the Pension Schemes Act 1993; and
"trustees or managers", in relation to an occupational pension scheme, means—
  (a) in the case of a scheme established under a trust, the trustees of the scheme; and
  (b) in any other case, the managers of the scheme."

Definitions For "creditor", see the Insolvency Act 1986, s 383(1); for "prescribed", see s 384(1) of the 1986 Act; for "the court", "estate" and "the trustee", see s 385(1) thereof. Note as to "the excessiove contributions", s 342A(2) of the 1986 Act, as inserted by sub-s (1) above; as to "excessive entitlement", s 342B(4) of the 1986 Act, as so inserted; as to "the transferee scheme", see s 342C(3) of the 1986 Act, as so inserted; as to "contributions made during the relevant period" and "accrued rights", see s 342C(4) of the 1986 Act, as so inserted; and as to "occupational pension scheme" and "trustees or managers", s 342C(5) of the 1986 Act, as so inserted.
References See para 12.18.

Questioning the decisions of the Authority

96 Review of decisions

(1) Subject to the following provisions of this section and to section 97, any determination by the Authority of a question which it is within their functions to determine shall be final.

(2) The Authority must, on the application of any person ("the applicant") at any time within the prescribed period, review any determination of theirs—

(a) to make an order against the applicant under section 3,
(b) to require the applicant to pay a penalty under section 10 of this Act or section 168(4) of the Pension Schemes Act 1993, or
(c) to disqualify the applicant from being a trustee of any trust scheme under section 29(3) or (4).

(3) The Authority may on the application of a person appearing to them to be interested—
    (a) at any time review any other such determination of theirs as is mentioned in subsection (1) (including a determination given by them on a previous review), if they are satisfied that there has been a relevant change of circumstances since the determination was made, or that the determination was made in ignorance of a material fact or based on a mistake as to a material fact or was erroneous in point of law,
    (b) at any time within a period of six months from the date of the determination, or within such longer period as they may allow in any particular case, review such a determination on any ground.

(4) The Authority's powers on a review under subsection (2) or (3) include power—
    (a) to vary or revoke any determination or order previously made,
    (b) to substitute a different determination or order, and
    (c) generally to deal with the matters arising on the review as if they had arisen on the original determination;
and also include power to make savings and transitional provisions.

(5) Subject to subsection (6), regulations may make provision with respect to the procedure to be adopted on any application for a review under subsection (2) or (3) or under any corresponding provision in force in Northern Ireland and generally with respect to such applications and reviews.

(6) Nothing in subsection (5) shall be taken to prevent such a review being entered upon by the Authority without an application being made.

Definitions For "the Authority", see s 1(1); for "prescribed", "regulations" and "trust scheme", see s 124(1). Note as to "the applicant", sub-s (2) above.
References See para 2.40.

97 References and appeals from the Authority

(1) Any question of law arising in connection with—
    (a) any matter arising under this Part for determination, or
    (b) any matter arising on an application to the Authority for a review of a determination, or on a review by them entered upon without an application,
may, if the Authority think fit, be referred for decision to the court.

(2) If the Authority determine in accordance with subsection (1) to refer any question of law to the court, they must give notice in writing of their intention to do so—
    (a) in a case where the question arises on an application made to the Authority, to the applicant, and
    (b) in any case to such persons as appear to them to be concerned with the question.

(3) Any person who is aggrieved—
    (a) by a determination of the Authority given on a review under section 96, or
    (b) by the refusal of the Authority to review a determination,
where the determination involves a question of law and that question is not referred by the Authority to the court under subsection (1), may on that question appeal from the determination to the court.

(4) The Authority is entitled to appear and be heard on any reference or appeal under this section.

(5) The rules of court must include provision for regulating references and appeals to the court under this section and for limiting the time within which such appeals may be brought.

(6) The decision of the court on a reference or appeal under this section is final, and this subsection overrides any other enactment.

(7) On any such reference or appeal the court may order the Authority to pay the costs or, in Scotland, the expenses of any other person, whether or not the decision is in that other person's favour and whether or not the Authority appear on the reference or appeal.

(8) In this section "the court" means the High Court or the Court of Session.

Definitions For "the Authority", see s 1(1); for "enactment", see s 176. Note as to "the court", sub-s (8) above.
References See para 2.40.

Gathering information: the Authority

98 Provision of information

(1) In the case of any occupational pension scheme—
   (a) a trustee, manager, professional adviser or employer, and
   (b) any other person appearing to the Authority to be a person who holds, or is likely to hold, information relevant to the discharge of the Authority's functions,

must, if required to do so by them by notice in writing, produce any document relevant to the discharge of those functions.

(2) To comply with subsection (1) the document must be produced in such a manner, at such a place and within such a period as may be specified in the notice.

(3) In this section and sections 99 to 101, "document" includes information recorded in any form, and any reference to production of a document, in relation to information recorded otherwise than in legible form, is to producing a copy of the information in legible form.

Definitions For "the Authority", see s 1(1); as to "professional advisers", see s 47(4); for "employer", see ss 124(1), 125(3). By virtue of s 176, for "occupational pension scheme", see the Pension Schemes Act 1993, s 1. Note as to "document", sub-s (3) above.
References See para 2.41.

99 Inspection of premises

(1) An inspector may, for the purposes of investigating whether, in the case of any occupational pension scheme, the regulatory provisions are being, or have been, complied with, at any reasonable time enter premises liable to inspection and, while there—
   (a) may make such examination and inquiry as may be necessary for such purposes,
   (b) may require any person on the premises to produce, or secure the production of, any document relevant to compliance with those provisions for his inspection, and
   (c) may, as to any matter relevant to compliance with those provisions, examine, or require to be examined, either alone or in the presence of another person, any person on the premises whom he has reasonable cause to believe to be able to give information relevant to that matter.

(2) In subsection (1), "the regulatory provisions" means provisions made by or under—
(a) the provisions of this Part, other than the following provisions: sections 51 to 54, 62 to 65 and 110 to 112,
(b) the following provisions of the Pension Schemes Act 1993: section 6 (registration), Chapter IV of Part IV (transfer values), section 113 (information) or section 175 (levy), or
(c) any corresponding provisions in force in Northern Ireland.

(3) Premises are liable to inspection for the purposes of this section if the inspector has reasonable grounds to believe that—
(a) members of the scheme are employed there,
(b) documents relevant to the administration of the scheme are being kept there, or
(c) the administration of the scheme, or work connected with the administration of the scheme, is being carried out there,
unless the premises are a private dwelling-house not used by, or by permission of, the occupier for the purposes of a trade or business.

(4) An inspector applying for admission to any premises for the purposes of this section must, if so required, produce his certificate of appointment.

(5) In this Part "inspector" means a person appointed by the Authority as an inspector.

Definitions For "the Authority", see s 1(1); as to "document", see s 98(3); for "member", see ss 124(1), 125(4). By virtue of s 124(5), for "employed" and "trade or business", see the Pension Schemes Act 1993, s 181(1). By virtue of s 176, for "occupational pension scheme", see s 1 of the 1993 Act. Note as to "inspector", sub-s (5) above.
References See para 2.42.

100 Warrants

(1) A justice of the peace may issue a warrant under this section if satisfied on information on oath given by or on behalf of the Authority that there are reasonable grounds for believing—
(a) that there are on any premises documents whose production has been required under section 98(1) or 99(1)(b), or any corresponding provisions in force in Northern Ireland, and which have not been produced in compliance with the requirement,
(b) that there are on any premises documents whose production could be so required and that if their production were so required the documents would not be produced but would be removed from the premises, hidden, tampered with or destroyed, or
(c) that—
  (i) an offence has been committed under this Act or the Pension Schemes Act 1993, or any enactment in force in Northern Ireland corresponding to either of them,
  (ii) a person will do any act which constitutes a misuse or misappropriation of the assets of an occupational pension scheme,
  (iii) a person is liable to pay a penalty under section 10 of this Act or section 168(4) of the Pension Schemes Act 1993, or any enactment in force in Northern Ireland corresponding to either of them, or
  (iv) a person is liable to be prohibited from being a trustee of a trust scheme under section 3,
and that there are on any premises documents which relate to whether the offence has been committed, whether the act will be done, or whether the

person is so liable, and whose production could be required under section 98(1) or 99(1)(b) or any corresponding provisions in force in Northern Ireland.

(2) A warrant under this section shall authorise an inspector—
    (a) to enter the premises specified in the information, using such force as is reasonably necessary for the purpose,
    (b) to search the premises and take possession of any documents appearing to be such documents as are mentioned in subsection (1) or to take in relation to such documents any other steps which appear necessary for preserving them or preventing interference with them,
    (c) to take copies of any such documents, or
    (d) to require any person named in the warrant to provide an explanation of them or to state where they may be found.

(3) A warrant under this section shall continue in force until the end of the period of one month beginning with the day on which it is issued.

(4) Any documents of which possession is taken by virtue of a warrant under this section may be retained—
    (a) for a period of six months, or
    (b) if within that period proceedings to which the documents are relevant are commenced against any person for any offence under this Act or the Pension Schemes Act 1993, or any enactment in force in Northern Ireland corresponding to either of them, until the conclusion of those proceedings.

(5) In the application of this section in Scotland—
    (a) the reference to a justice of the peace is to be read as a reference to a justice within the meaning of the Criminal Procedure (Scotland) Act 1975, and
    (b) the references to information are to be read as references to evidence.

Definitions For "the Authority", see s 1(1); as to "document", see s 98(3); for "inspector", see s 99(5); for "trust scheme", see s 124(1); for "enactment", see s 176. By virtue of s 176, for "occupational pension scheme", see the Pension Schemes Act 1993, s 1.
References See para 2.42.

101 Information and inspection: penalties

(1) A person who, without reasonable excuse, neglects or refuses to produce a document when required to do so under section 98 is guilty of an offence.

(2) A person who without reasonable excuse—
    (a) intentionally delays or obstructs an inspector exercising any power under section 99,
    (b) neglects or refuses to produce, or secure the production of, any document when required to do so under that section, or
    (c) neglects or refuses to answer a question or to provide information when so required,
is guilty of an offence.

(3) A person guilty of an offence under subsection (1) or (2) is liable on summary conviction to a fine not exceeding level 5 on the standard scale.

(4) An offence under subsection (1) or (2)(b) or (c) may be charged by reference to any day or longer period of time; and a person may be convicted of a second or subsequent offence by reference to any period of time following the preceding conviction of the offence.

(5) Any person who knowingly or recklessly provides the Authority with information which is false or misleading in a material particular is guilty of an offence if the information—
  (a) is provided in purported compliance with a requirement under section 99, or
  (b) is provided otherwise than as mentioned in paragraph (a) above but in circumstances in which the person providing the information intends, or could reasonably be expected to know, that it would be used by the Authority for the purpose of discharging their functions under this Act.

(6) Any person who intentionally and without reasonable excuse alters, suppresses, conceals or destroys any document which he is or is liable to be required under section 98 or 99 to produce to the Authority is guilty of an offence.

(7) Any person guilty of an offence under subsection (5) or (6) is liable—
  (a) on summary conviction, to a fine not exceeding the statutory maximum,
  (b) on conviction on indictment, to imprisonment or a fine, or both.

Definitions For "the Authority", see s 1(1); for "document", see s 98(3); for "inspector", see s 99(5).
References See para 2.43.

102 Savings for certain privileges etc

(1) Nothing in sections 98 to 101 requires a person to answer any question or give any information if to do so would incriminate that person or that person's spouse.

(2) Nothing in those sections requires any person to produce any document to the Authority, or to any person acting on their behalf, if he would be entitled to refuse to produce the document in any proceedings in any court on the grounds that it was the subject of legal professional privilege or, in Scotland, that it contained a confidential communication made by or to an advocate or solicitor in that capacity.

(3) Where a person claims a lien on a document, its production under section 98 or 99 shall be without prejudice to the lien.

Definitions For "the Authority", see s 1(1).
References See para 2.41.

103 Publishing reports

(1) The Authority may, if they consider it appropriate to do so in any particular case, publish in such form and manner as they think fit a report of any investigation under this Part and of the result of that investigation.

(2) For the purposes of the law of defamation, the publication of any matter by the Authority shall be absolutely privileged.

Definitions For "the Authority", see s 1(1).
References See para 2.44.

Disclosure of information: the Authority

104 Restricted information

(1) Except as provided by sections 106 to 108, restricted information must not be disclosed by the Authority or by any person who receives the information directly or indirectly from them, except with the consent of the person to whom it relates and (if different) the person from whom the Authority obtained it.

(2) For the purposes of this section and sections 105 to 108, "restricted information" means any information obtained by the Authority in the exercise of their functions which relates to the business or other affairs of any person, except for information—
> (a) which at the time of the disclosure is or has already been made available to the public from other sources, or
> (b) which is in the form of a summary or collection of information so framed as not to enable information relating to any particular person to be ascertained from it.

(3) Any person who discloses information in contravention of this section is guilty of an offence and liable—
> (a) on summary conviction, to a fine not exceeding the statutory maximum, and
> (b) on conviction on indictment, to a fine or imprisonment, or both.

Definitions For "the Authority", see s 1(1); for "contravention", see s 124(1). Note as to "restricted information", sub-s (2) above.
References See para 2.45.

105 Information supplied to the Authority by corresponding overseas authorities

(1) Subject to subsection (2), for the purposes of section 104, "restricted information" includes information which has been supplied to the Authority for the purposes of their functions by an authority which exercises functions corresponding to the functions of the Authority in a country or territory outside the United Kingdom.

(2) Sections 106 to 108 do not apply to such information as is mentioned in subsection (1), and such information must not be disclosed except—
> (a) as provided in section 104,
> (b) for the purpose of enabling or assisting the Authority to discharge their functions, or
> (c) with a view to the institution of, or otherwise for the purposes of, criminal proceedings, whether under this Act or otherwise.

Definitions For "the Authority", see s 1(1); for "restricted information", see s 104(2)
References See para 2.45.

106 Disclosure for facilitating discharge of functions by the Authority

(1) Section 104 does not preclude the disclosure of restricted information in any case in which disclosure is for the purpose of enabling or assisting the Authority to discharge their functions.

(2) If, in order to enable or assist the Authority properly to discharge any of their functions, the Authority consider it necessary to seek advice from any qualified person on any matter of law, accountancy, valuation or other matter requiring the exercise of professional skill, section 104 does not preclude the disclosure by the Authority to that person of such information as appears to the Authority to be necessary to ensure that he is properly informed with respect to the matters on which his advice is sought.

Definitions For "the Authority", see s 1(1); for "restricted information", see ss 104(2), 105.
References See para 2.45.

107 Disclosure for facilitating discharge of functions by other supervisory authorities

(1) Section 104 does not preclude the disclosure by the Authority of restricted information to any person specified in the first column of the following Table if the Authority consider that the disclosure would enable or assist that person to discharge the functions specified in relation to him in the second column of that Table.

TABLE

Persons	Functions
The Secretary of State.	Functions under the Insurance Companies Act 1982, Part XIV of the Companies Act 1985, the Insolvency Act 1986, the Financial Services Act 1986, Part III of the Companies Act 1989 or Part III of the Pension Schemes Act 1993.
The Treasury.	Functions under the Financial Services Act 1986.
The Bank of England.	Functions under the Banking Act 1987 or any other functions.
The Charity Commissioners.	Functions under the Charities Act 1993.
The Lord Advocate.	Functions under Part I of the Law Reform (Miscellaneous Provisions) (Scotland) Act 1990.
The Pensions Ombudsman and the Registrar of Occupational and Personal Pension Schemes.	Functions under the Pension Schemes Act 1993 or the Pension Schemes (Northern Ireland) Act 1993.
The Compensation Board.	Functions under this Act of any corresponding enactment in force in Northern Ireland.
The Policyholders Protection Board.	Functions under the Policyholders Protection Act 1975.
The Deposit Protection Board.	Functions under the Banking Act 1987.
The Investor Protection Board.	Functions under the Building Societies Act 1986.
The Friendly Societies Commission.	Functions under the enactments relating to friendly societies.
The Building Societies Commission.	Functions under the Building Societies Act 1986.
The Commissioners of Inland Revenue or their officers.	Functions under the Taxes Act 1988 or the Taxation of Chargeable Gains Act 1992.
The Official Receiver, or, in Northern Ireland, the Official Receiver for Northern Ireland.	Functions under the enactments relating to insolvency.

Pensions Act 1995, s 107

Persons	Functions
An inspector appointed by the Secretary of State.	Functions under Part XIV of the Companies Act 1985 or section 94 or 177 of the Financial Services Act 1986.
A person authorised to exercise powers under section 43A or 44 of the Insurance Companies Act 1982, section 447 of the Companies Act 1985, section 106 of the Financial Services Act 1986, Article 440 of the Companies (Northern Ireland) Order 1986, or section 84 of the Companies Act 1989.	Functions under those sections or that Article.
A designated agency or transferee body or the competent authority (within the meaning of the Financial Services Act 1986).	Functions under the Financial Services Act 1986.
A recognised self-regulating organisation, recognised professional body, recognised investment exchange or recognised clearing house (within the meaning of the Financial Services Act 1986).	Functions in its capacity as an organisation, body, exchange or clearing house recognised under the Financial Services Act 1986.
A person administering a scheme for compensating investors under section 54 of the Financial Services Act 1986.	Functions under that section.
A recognised professional body (within the meaning of section 391 of the Insolvency Act 1986).	Functions in its capacity as such a body under that Act.
The Department of Economic Development in Northern Ireland.	Functions under Part XV of the Companies (Northern Ireland) Order 1986, the Insolvency (Northern Ireland) Order 1989, or Part II of the Companies (No 2) (Northern Ireland) Order 1990.
The Department of Health and Social Services for Northern Ireland.	Functions under Part III of the Pension Schemes (Northern Ireland) Act 1993.
An inspector appointed by the Department of Economic Development in Northern Ireland.	Functions under Part XV of the Companies (Northern Ireland) Order 1986.
A recognised professional body within the meaning of Article 350 of the Insolvency (Northern Ireland) Order 1989.	Functions in its capacity as such a body under that Order.

(2) The Secretary of State may after consultation with the Authority—
    (a) by order amend the Table in subsection (1) by—
        (i) adding any person exercising regulatory functions and specifying functions in relation to that person,

(ii) removing any person for the time being specified in the Table, or
(iii) altering the functions for the time being specified in the Table in relation to any person, or
(b) by order restrict the circumstances in which, or impose conditions subject to which, disclosure may be made to any person for the time being specified in the Table.

Definitions For "the Authority", see s 1(1); for "the Compensation Board", see s 78(1); for "restricted information", see ss 104(2), 105; for "enactment", see s 176.
References See para 2.45.

108 Other permitted disclosures

(1) Section 104 does not preclude the disclosure by the Authority of restricted information to—
    (a) the Secretary of State, or
    (b) the Department of Health and Social Services for Northern Ireland,
if the disclosure appears to the Authority to be desirable or expedient in the interests of members of occupational pension schemes or in the public interest.

(2) Section 104 does not preclude the disclosure of restricted information—
    (a) with a view to the institution of, or otherwise for the purposes of, criminal proceedings, whether under this Act or otherwise,
    (b) in connection with any other proceedings arising out of—
        (i) this Act, or
        (ii) the Pension Schemes Act 1993,
    or any corresponding enactment in force in Northern Ireland or any proceedings for breach of trust in relation to an occupational pension scheme,
    (c) with a view to the institution of, or otherwise for the purposes of, proceedings under section 7 or 8 of the Company Directors Disqualification Act 1986 or Article 10 or 11 of the Companies (Northern Ireland) Order 1989,
    (d) in connection with any proceedings under the Insolvency Act 1986 or the Insolvency (Northern Ireland) Order 1989 which the Authority have instituted or in which they have a right to be heard,
    (e) with a view to the institution of, or otherwise for the purposes of, any disciplinary proceedings relating to the exercise of his professional duties by a solicitor, an actuary or an accountant,
    (f) with a view to the institution of, or otherwise for the purposes of, any disciplinary proceedings relating to the discharge by a public servant of his duties,
    (g) for the purpose of enabling or assisting an authority in a country outside the United Kingdom to exercise functions corresponding to those of the Authority under this Act, or
    (h) in pursuance of a Community obligation.

(3) Section 104 does not preclude the disclosure by the Authority of information to the Director of Public Prosecutions, the Director of Public Prosecutions for Northern Ireland, the Lord Advocate, a procurator fiscal or a constable.

(4) Section 104 does not preclude the disclosure by any person mentioned in subsection (1) or (3) of information obtained by the person by virtue of that subsection, if the disclosure is made with the consent of the Authority.

(5) Section 104 does not preclude the disclosure by any person specified in the first column of the Table in section 107 of information obtained by the person by virtue of that subsection, if the disclosure is made—

Pensions Act 1995, s 108

       (a) with the consent of the Authority, and
       (b) for the purpose of enabling or assisting the person to discharge any functions specified in relation to him in the second column of the Table.

    (6) The Authority must, before deciding whether to give their consent to such a disclosure as is mentioned in subsection (4) or (5), take account of any representations made to them by the person seeking to make the disclosure as to the desirability of the disclosure or the necessity for it.

    (7) In subsection (2), "public servant" means an officer or servant of the Crown or of any prescribed authority.

Definitions   For "the Authority", see s 1(1); for "restricted information", see ss 104(2), 105; for "prescribed", see s 124(1); for "member", see ss 124(1), 125(4). For "enactment", see s 176. By virtue of s 176, for "occupational pension scheme", see the Pension Schemes Act 1993, s 1.
References   See para 2.45.

109 Disclosure of information by the Inland Revenue

    (1) This section applies to information held by any person in the exercise of tax functions about any matter relevant, for the purposes of those functions, to tax or duty in the case of an identifiable person (in this section referred to as "tax information").

    (2) No obligation as to secrecy imposed by section 182 of the Finance Act 1989 or otherwise shall prevent the disclosure of tax information to the Authority for the purpose of enabling or assisting the Authority to discharge their functions.

    (3) Where tax information is disclosed to the Authority by virtue of subsection (2), it shall, subject to subsection (4), be treated for the purposes of section 104 as restricted information.

    (4) Sections 106 to 108 do not apply to tax information and such information must not be disclosed except—
       (a) to, or in accordance with authority duly given by, the Commissioners of Inland Revenue or the Commissioners of Customs and Excise, or
       (b) with a view to the institution of, or otherwise for the purposes of, criminal proceedings under this Act or the Pension Schemes Act 1993, or any enactment in force in Northern Ireland corresponding to either of them.

    (5) In this section "tax functions" has the same meaning as in section 182 of the Finance Act 1989.

Definitions   For "the Authority", see s 1(1); for "enactment", see s 176. Note as to "tax information", sub-s (1) above; and as to "tax functions", sub-s (5) above.
References   See para 2.45.

Gathering information: the Compensation Board

110 Provision of information

    (1) In the case of any trust scheme—
       (a) a trustee, professional adviser or employer, and
       (b) any other person appearing to the Compensation Board to be a person who holds, or is likely to hold, information relevant to the discharge of the Board's functions,
must, if required to do so by the Board by notice in writing, produce any document relevant to the discharge of those functions.

(2) To comply with subsection (1) the document must be produced in such a manner, at such a place and within such a period as may be specified in the notice.

(3) In this section and section 111, "document" includes information recorded in any form, and any reference to production of a document, in relation to information recorded otherwise than in legible form, is to producing a copy of the information in legible form.

Definitions   As to "professional advisers", see s 47(4); for "the Compensation Board", see s 78(1); for "trust scheme", see s 124(1); for "employer", see ss 124(1), 125(3). Note as to "document", sub-s (3) above.
References   See paras 11.19, 11.20.

111 Information: penalties

(1) A person who without reasonable excuse neglects or refuses to produce a document when required to do so under section 110 is guilty of an offence.

(2) A person guilty of an offence under subsection (1) is liable on summary conviction to a fine not exceeding level 5 on the standard scale.

(3) An offence under subsection (1) may be charged by reference to any day or longer period of time; and a person may be convicted of a second or subsequent offence by reference to any period of time following the preceding conviction of the offence.

(4) Any person who knowingly or recklessly provides the Compensation Board with information which is false or misleading in a material particular is guilty of an offence if the information is provided in circumstances in which the person providing the information intends, or could reasonably be expected to know, that it would be used by the Board for the purpose of discharging their functions under this Act or any corresponding enactment in force in Northern Ireland.

(5) Any person who intentionally and without reasonable excuse alters, suppresses, conceals or destroys any document which he is or is liable to be required under section 110 to produce to the Compensation Board is guilty of an offence.

(6) Any person guilty of an offence under subsection (4) or (5) is liable—
  (a) on summary conviction, to a fine not exceeding the statutory maximum,
  (b) on conviction on indictment, to imprisonment or a fine, or both.

Definitions   For "the Compensation Board", see s 78(1); for "document", see s 110(3); for "enactment", see s 176.
References   See para 11.21.

112 Savings for certain privileges

Nothing in section 110 or 111 requires a person—
  (a) to answer any question or give any information if to do so would incriminate that person or that person's spouse, or
  (b) to produce any document if he would be entitled to refuse to produce the document in any proceedings in any court on the grounds that it was the subject of legal professional privilege or, in Scotland, that it contained a confidential communication made by or to an advocate or solicitor in that capacity.

References   See para 11.19.

Pensions Act 1995, s 113

113 Publishing reports

(1) The Compensation Board may, if they consider it appropriate to do so in any particular case, publish in such form and manner as they think fit a report of any investigation under this Part and of the result of that investigation.

(2) For the purposes of the law of defamation, the publication of any matter by the Compensation Board shall be absolutely privileged.

Definitions For "the Compensation Board", see s 78(1).
References See para 11.22.

114 Disclosure of information

(1) A person to whom this section applies may disclose to the Compensation Board any information received by him under or for the purposes of any enactment if the disclosure is made by him for the purpose of enabling or assisting the Board to discharge any of their functions.

(2) In the case of information which a person holds or has held in the exercise of functions—
    (a) of the Commissioners of Inland Revenue or their officers, and
    (b) relating to any tax within the general responsibility of the Commissioners,
subsection (1) does not authorise any disclosure unless made in accordance with an authorisation given by the Commissioners.

(3) Subject to subsection (4), the Compensation Board may disclose to a person to whom this section applies any information received by them under or for the purposes of any enactment, where the disclosure is made by the Board—
    (a) for any purpose connected with the discharge of their functions, or
    (b) for the purpose of enabling or assisting that person to discharge any of his functions.

(4) Where any information disclosed to the Compensation Board under this section is so disclosed subject to any express restriction on the disclosure of the information by the Board, the Board's power of disclosure under subsection (3) is, in relation to the information, exercisable by them subject to any such restriction.

(5) In the case of any such information as is mentioned in subsection (2), subsection (3) does not authorise any disclosure of that information by the Compensation Board unless made—
    (a) to, or in accordance with authority duly given by, the Commissioners of Inland Revenue or the Commissioners of Customs and Excise, or
    (b) with a view to the institution of, or otherwise for the purposes of, criminal proceedings under this Act or the Pension Schemes Act 1993, or any enactment in force in Northern Ireland corresponding to either of them.

(6) Nothing in this section shall be construed as affecting any power of disclosure exercisable apart from this section.

(7) This section applies to the following (and, accordingly, in this section "person" shall be construed as including any of them)—
    (a) any department of the Government (including the government of Northern Ireland),
    (b) the Director of Public Prosecutions,
    (c) the Director of Public Prosecutions for Northern Ireland,
    (d) the Lord Advocate,
    (e) any constable,

(f) any designated agency or recognised self-regulating organisation (within the meaning of the Financial Services Act 1986),
(g) a recognised professional body (within the meaning of section 391 of the Insolvency Act 1986),
(h) the Pensions Ombudsman,
(j) the Policyholders Protection Board,
(k) the Authority,
(l) the Registrar of Occupational and Personal Pension Schemes,
(m) the Official Receiver, or, in Northern Ireland, the Official Receiver for Northern Ireland, and
(n) such other persons as may be prescribed.

Definitions   For "the Authority", see s 1(1); for "the Compensation Board", see s 78(1); for "prescribed", see s 124(1); for "enactment", see s 176. Note as to "person", sub-s (7) above.
References   See paras 11.23, 11.24.

General

115 Offences by bodies corporate and partnerships

(1)   Where an offence under this Part committed by a body corporate is proved to have been committed with the consent or connivance of, or to be attributable to any neglect on the part of, a director, manager, secretary or other similar officer of the body, or a person purporting to act in any such capacity, he as well as the body corporate is guilty of the offence and liable to be proceeded against and punished accordingly.

(2)   Where the affairs of a body corporate are managed by its members, subsection (1) applies in relation to the acts and defaults of a member in connection with his functions of management as to a director of a body corporate.

(3)   Where an offence under this Part committed by a Scottish partnership is proved to have been committed with the consent or connivance of, or to be attributable to any neglect on the part of, a partner, he as well as the partnership is guilty of the offence and liable to be proceeded against and punished accordingly.

Definitions   For "Scottish partnership", see s 124(1).
References   See para 2.28.

116 Breach of regulations

(1)   Regulations made by virtue of any provision of this Part may provide for the contravention of any provision contained in any such regulations to be an offence under this Part and for the recovery on summary conviction for any such offence of a fine not exceeding level 5 on the standard scale.

(2)   An offence under any provision of the regulations may be charged by reference to any day or longer period of time; and a person may be convicted of a second or subsequent offence under such a provision by reference to any period of time following the preceding conviction of the offence.

(3)   Where by reason of the contravention of any provision contained in regulations made by virtue of this Part—
  (a) a person is convicted of an offence under this Part, or
  (b) a person pays a penalty under section 10,
then, in respect of that contravention, he shall not, in a case within paragraph (a), be liable to pay such a penalty or, in a case within paragraph (b), be convicted of such an offence.

Definitions   For "contravention" and "regulations", see s 124(1).
References   See para 2.29.

117 Overriding requirements

(1) Where any provision mentioned in subsection (2) conflicts with the provisions of an occupational pension scheme—
- (a) the provision mentioned in subsection (2), to the extent that it conflicts, overrides the provisions of the scheme, and
- (b) the scheme has effect with such modifications as may be required in consequence of paragraph (a).

(2) The provisions referred to in subsection (1) are those of—
- (a) this Part,
- (b) any subordinate legislation made or having effect as if made under this Part, or
- (c) any arrangements under section 16(1) or 17(2).

Definitions By virtue of s 124(5), for "modifications", see the Pension Schemes Act 1993, s 181(1). By virtue of s 176, for "occupational pension scheme", see s 1 of the 1993 Act.
Regulations See para 1.25.

118 Powers to modify this Part

(1) Regulations may modify any provisions of this Part, in their application—
- (a) to a trust scheme which applies to earners in employments under different employers,
- (b) to a trust scheme of which there are no members who are in pensionable service under the scheme, or
- (c) to any case where a partnership is the employer, or one of the employers, in relation to a trust scheme.

(2) Regulations may provide for sections 22 to 26, and section 117 (so far as it applies to those sections), not to apply in relation to a trust scheme falling within a prescribed class or description.

Definitions For "prescribed", "regulations" and "trust scheme", see s 124(1); for "pensionable service", see s 124(1), (3); for "employer", see ss 124(1), 125(3); for "member", see ss 124(1), 125(4). By virtue of s 124(5), for "earner", "employment" and "modify", see the Pension Schemes Act 1993, s 181(1).
References See para 1.23.

119 Calculations etc under regulations: sub-delegation

Regulations made by virtue of section 56(3), 73(3) or 75 may provide for the values of the assets and the amounts of the liabilities there mentioned to be calculated and verified in accordance with guidance—
- (a) prepared and from time to time revised by a prescribed body, and
- (b) approved by the Secretary of State.

Definitions For "prescribed" and "regulations", see s 124(1)
References See para 1.23.

120 Consultations about regulations

(1) Before the Secretary of State makes any regulations by virtue of this Part, he must consult such persons as he considers appropriate.

(2) Subsection (1) does not apply—
- (a) to regulations made for the purpose only of consolidating other regulations revoked by them,
- (b) to regulations in the case of which the Secretary of State considers consultation inexpedient because of urgency,

(c) to regulations made before the end of the period of six months beginning with the coming into force of the provision of this Part by virtue of which the regulations are made, or
(d) to regulations which—
  (i) state that they are consequential upon a specified enactment, and
  (ii) are made before the end of the period of six months beginning with the coming into force of that enactment.

Definitions For "regulations", see s 124(1); for "enactment", see s 176.
References See para 1.23.

121 Crown application

(1) This Part applies to an occupational pension scheme managed by or on behalf of the Crown as it applies to other occupational pension schemes; and, accordingly, references in this Part to a person in his capacity as a trustee or manager of an occupational pension scheme include the Crown, or a person acting on behalf of the Crown, in that capacity.

(2) References in this Part to a person in his capacity as employer in relation to an occupational pension scheme include the Crown, or a person acting on behalf of the Crown, in that capacity.

(3) This section does not apply to any provision made by or under this Part under which a person may be prosecuted for an offence; but such a provision applies to persons in the public service of the Crown as it applies to other persons.

(4) This section does not apply to sections 42 to 46.

(5) Nothing in this Part applies to Her Majesty in Her private capacity (within the meaning of the Crown Proceedings Act 1947).

Definitions For "trustees or managers", see s 124(1); for "employer", see ss 124(1), 125(3). By virtue of s 176, for "occupational pension scheme", see the Pension Schemes Act 1993, s 1.
References See para 3.42.

122 Consequential amendments

Schedule 3 (amendments consequential on this Part) shall have effect.

References See paras 6.4, 12.12.

123 "Connected" and "associated" persons

(1) Sections 249 and 435 of the Insolvency Act 1986 (connected and associated persons) shall apply for the purposes of the provisions of this Act listed in subsection (3) as they apply for the purposes of that Act.

(2) Section 74 of the Bankruptcy (Scotland) Act 1985 (associated persons) shall apply for the purposes of the provisions so listed as it applies for the purposes of that Act.

(3) The provisions referred to in subsections (1) and (2) are—
  (a) section 23(3)(b),
  (b) sections 27 and 28,
  (c) section 40,
but in the case of section 40 the provisions mentioned in subsections (1) and (2) shall apply for those purposes with any prescribed modifications.

Definitions For "modifications", see, by virtue of s 124(5), the Pension Schemes Act 1993, s 181(1).
References See para 1.22.

124 Interpretation of Part I

(1) In this Part—

"active member", in relation to an occupational pension scheme, means a person who is in pensionable service under the scheme,

"the actuary" and "the auditor", in relation to an occupational pension scheme, have the meanings given by section 47,

"the Authority" has the meaning given by section 1(1),

"the Compensation Board" has the meaning given by section 78(1),

"the compensation provisions" has the meaning given by section 81(3),

"contravention" includes failure to comply,

"deferred member", in relation to an occupational pension scheme, means a person (other than an active or pensioner member) who has accrued rights under the scheme,

"employer", in relation to an occupational pension scheme, means the employer of persons in the description or category of employment to which the scheme in question relates (but see section 125(3)),

"equal treatment rule" has the meaning given by section 62,

"firm" means a body corporate or a partnership,

"fund manager", in relation to an occupational pension scheme, means a person who manages the investments held for the purposes of the scheme,

"independent trustee" has the meaning given by section 23(3),

"managers", in relation to an occupational pension scheme other than a trust scheme, means the persons responsible for the management of the scheme,

"member", in relation to an occupational pension scheme, means any active, deferred or pensioner member (but see section 125(4)),

"member-nominated director" has the meaning given by section 18(2),

"member-nominated trustee" has the meaning given by section 16(2),

"the minimum funding requirement" has the meaning given by section 56,

"normal pension age" has the meaning given by section 180 of the Pension Schemes Act 1993,

"payment schedule" has the meaning given by section 87(2),

"pensionable service", in relation to a member of an occupational pension scheme, means service in any description or category of employment to which the scheme relates which qualifies the member (on the assumption that it continues for the appropriate period) for pension or other benefits under the scheme,

"pensioner member", in relation to an occupational pension scheme, means a person who in respect of his pensionable service under the scheme or by reason of transfer credits, is entitled to the present payment of pension or other benefits,

"prescribed" means prescribed by regulations,

"professional adviser", in relation to a scheme, has the meaning given by section 47,

"public service pension scheme" has the meaning given by section 1 of the Pension Schemes Act 1993,

"regulations" means regulations made by the Secretary of State,

"resources", in relation to an occupational pension scheme, means the funds out of which the benefits provided by the scheme are payable from time to time, including the proceeds of any policy of insurance taken out, or annuity contract entered into, for the purposes of the scheme,

"Scottish partnership" means a partnership constituted under the law of Scotland,

"the Taxes Act 1988" means the Income and Corporation Taxes Act 1988,

"transfer credits" means rights allowed to a member under the rules of an occupational pension scheme by reference to a transfer to that scheme of his accrued rights from another scheme (including any transfer credits allowed by that scheme),

"trustees or managers", in relation to an occupational pension scheme, means—
- (a) in the case of a trust scheme, the trustees of the scheme, and
- (b) in any other case, the managers of the scheme,

"trust scheme" means an occupational pension scheme established under a trust.

(2) For the purposes of this Part—
- (a) the accrued rights of a member of an occupational pension scheme at any time are the rights which have accrued to or in respect of him at that time to future benefits under the scheme, and
- (b) at any time when the pensionable service of a member of an occupational pension scheme is continuing, his accrued rights are to be determined as if he had opted, immediately before that time, to terminate that service;

and references to accrued pension or accrued benefits are to be interpreted accordingly.

(3) In determining what is "pensionable service" for the purposes of this Part—
- (a) service notionally attributable for any purpose of the scheme is to be disregarded, and
- (b) no account is to be taken of any rules of the scheme by which a period of service can be treated for any purpose as being longer or shorter than it actually is.

(4) In the application of this Part to Scotland, in relation to conviction on indictment, references to imprisonment are to be read as references to imprisonment for a term not exceeding two years.

(5) Subject to the provisions of this Act, expressions used in this Act and in the Pension Schemes Act 1993 have the same meaning in this Act as in that.

Definitions For "occupational pension scheme", see, by virtue of s 176, the Pension Schemes Act 1993, s 1.
References See para 1.22.

125 Section 124: supplementary

(1) For the purposes of this Part, an occupational pension scheme is salary related if—
- (a) the scheme is not a money purchase scheme, and
- (b) the scheme does not fall within a prescribed class or description,

and "salary related trust scheme" is to be read accordingly.

(2) Regulations may apply this Part with prescribed modifications to occupational pension schemes—
- (a) which are not money purchase schemes, but
- (b) where some of the benefits that may be provided are money purchase benefits.

(3) Regulations may, in relation to occupational pension schemes, extend for the purposes of this Part the meaning of "employer" to include persons who have been the employer in relation to the scheme.

(4) For any of the purposes of this Part, regulations may in relation to occupational pension schemes—
- (a) extend or restrict the meaning of "member",
- (b) determine who is to be treated as a prospective member, and
- (c) determine the times at which a person is to be treated as becoming, or as ceasing to be, a member or prospective member.

Definitions For "prescribed" and "regulations", see s 124(1). By virtue of s 124(5), for "modifications", "money purchase benefits" and "money purchase scheme", see the Pension Schemes Act 1993, s 181(1). By virtue of s 176, for "occupational pension scheme", see s 1 of the 1993 Act.
References See para 1.22.

PART II
STATE PENSIONS

126 Equalisation of pensionable age and of entitlement to certain benefits

Schedule 4 to this Act, of which—
  (a) Part I has effect to equalise pensionable age for men and women progressively over a period of ten years beginning with 6th April 2010,
  (b) Part II makes provision for bringing equality for men and women to certain pension and other benefits, and
  (c) Part III makes consequential amendments of enactments,
shall have effect.

Definitions For "enactments", see s 176.
References See paras 8.15, 8.16.

127 Enhancement of additional pension, etc where family credit or disability working allowance paid

(1) After section 45 of the Social Security Contributions and Benefits Act 1992 (additional pension in a Category A retirement pension) there is inserted—

> **"45A Effect of family credit and disability working allowance on earnings factor**
>
> (1) For the purpose of calculating additional pension under sections 44 and 45 above where, in the case of any relevant year, family credit is paid in respect of any employed earner, or disability working allowance is paid to any employed earner, section 44(6)(a)(i) above shall have effect as if—
>   (a) where that person had earnings of not less than the qualifying earnings factor for that year, being earnings upon which primary Class 1 contributions were paid or treated as paid ("qualifying earnings") in respect of that year, the amount of those qualifying earnings were increased by the aggregate amount (call it "AG") of family credit or, as the case may be, disability working allowance paid in respect of that year, and
>   (b) in any other case, that person had qualifying earnings in respect of that year and the amount of those qualifying earnings were equal to AG plus the qualifying earnings factor for that year.
>
> (2) The reference in subsection (1) above to the person in respect of whom family credit is paid—
>   (a) where it is paid to one of a married or unmarried couple, is a reference to the prescribed member of the couple, and
>   (b) in any other case, is a reference to the person to whom it is paid.
>
> (3) A person's qualifying earnings in respect of any year cannot be treated by virtue of subsection (1) above as exceeding the upper earnings limit for that year multiplied by fifty-three.
>
> (4) Subsection (1) above does not apply to any woman who has made, or is treated as having made, an election under regulations under section 19(4) above, which has not been revoked, that her liability in respect of primary Class 1 contributions shall be at a reduced rate.
>
> (5) In this section—
>   "married couple" and "unmarried couple" (defined in section 137 below) have the same meaning as in Part VII, and
>   "relevant year" has the same meaning as in section 44 above."

(2) Accordingly, in the following provisions of the Social Security Contributions and Benefits Act 1992, for "sections 44 and 45" there is substituted "sections 44 to 45A": sections 39(1) to (3), 50(3) to (5) and 51(2) and (3).

(3) Subject to subsections (4) and (5) below, this section applies to a person ("the pensioner") who attains pensionable age after 5th April 1999 and, in relation to such persons, has effect for 1995–96 and subsequent tax years.

(4) Where the pensioner is a woman, this section has effect in the case of additional pension falling to be calculated under sections 44 and 45 of the Social Security Contributions and Benefits Act 1992 by virtue of section 39 of that Act (widowed mother's allowance and widow's pension), including Category B retirement pension payable under section 48B(4), if her husband—

(a) dies after 5th April 1999, and
(b) has not attained pensionable age on or before that date.

(5) This section has effect where additional pension falls to be calculated under sections 44 and 45 of the Social Security Contributions and Benefits Act 1992 as applied by sections 48A or 48B(2) of that Act (other Category B retirement pension) if—

(a) the pensioner attains pensionable age after 5th April 1999, and
(b) the pensioner's spouse has not attained pensionable age on or before that date.

Definitions For "employed earner", see the Social Security Contributions and Benefits Act 1992, s 2; for "earnings", see ss 3, 4, 112 of that Act; for "upper earnings limit", see ss 5, 122(1) of the 1992 Act; for "prescribe", "qualifying earnings factor" and "tax year", see 122(1) thereof. By virtue of s 122(1) of the 1992 Act, as amended by s 126(b), Sch 4, Pt II, para 13(a) of this Act; for "pensionable age", see Sch 4, para 1 to this Act. Note as to "qualifying earnings", s 45A(1) of the 1992 Act, as inserted by sub-s (1) above, and as to "married couple", "unmarried couple" and "relevant year", s 45A(5) of the 1992 Act, as so inserted. Note as to "the pensioner", sub-s (3) above.
References See para 13.12.

128 Additional pension: calculation of surpluses

(1) In section 44 of the Social Security Contributions and Benefits Act 1992 (Category A retirement pension), for subsection (5) (surplus on which additional pension is calculated) there is substituted—

"(5A) For the purposes of this section and section 45 below—
(a) there is a surplus in the pensioner's earnings factor for a relevant year if that factor exceeds the qualifying earnings factor for that year, and
(b) the amount of the surplus is the amount of that excess, as increased by the last order under section 148 of the Administration Act to come into force before the end of the final relevant year".

(2) In subsection (6) of that section (calculation of earnings factors), for paragraphs (a)(ii) and (b) there is substituted—

"(ii) his earnings factors derived from Class 2 and Class 3 contributions actually paid in respect of that year, or, if less, the qualifying earnings factor for that year; and
(b) where the relevant year is an earlier tax year, to the aggregate of—
(i) his earnings factors derived from Class 1 contributions actually paid by him in respect of that year, and
(ii) his earnings factors derived from Class 2 and Class 3 contributions actually paid by him in respect of that year, or, if less, the qualifying earnings factor for that year."

(3) Section 148 of the Social Security Administration Act 1992 (revaluation of earnings factors) shall have effect in relation to surpluses in a person's earnings factors under section 44(5A) of the Social Security Contributions and Benefits Act 1992 as it has effect in relation to earnings factors.

(4) Subject to subsections (5) and (6) below, this section has effect in relation to a person ("the pensioner") who attains pensionable age after 5th April 2000.

(5) Where the pensioner is a woman, this section has effect in the case of additional pension falling to be calculated under sections 44 and 45 of the Social Security Contributions and Benefits Act 1992 by virtue of section 39 of that Act (widowed mother's allowance and widow's pension), including Category B retirement pension payable under section 48B(4), if her husband—
   (a) dies after 5th April 2000, and
   (b) has not attained pensionable age on or before that date.

(6) This section has effect where additional pension falls to be calculated under sections 44 and 45 of the Social Security Contributions and Benefits Act 1992 as applied by section 48A or 48B(2) of that Act (other Category B retirement pension) if—
   (a) the pensioner attains pensionable age after 5th April 2000, and
   (b) the pensioner's spouse has not attained pensionable age on or before that date.

Definitions As to "the pensioner's earnings factor for any relevant year", see the Social Security Contributions and Benefits Act 1992, s 44(6), as amended by sub-s (2) above; for "relevant year" and "final relevant year", see s 44(7) of the 1992 Act; for "qualifying earnings factor" and "tax year", see 122(1) thereof. By virtue of s 122(1) of the 1992 Act, as amended by s 126(b), Sch 4, Pt II, para 13(a) of this Act, for "pensionable age", see Sch 4, para 1 to this Act. Note as to "a surplus in the pensioner's earnings factor", s 44(5A) of the 1992 Act, as substituted by sub-s (1) above; and as to "the pensioner", sub-s (4) above.
References See para 13.12.

129 Contribution conditions

In Schedule 3 to the Social Security Contributions and Benefits Act 1992 (contribution conditions), in paragraph 5(3)(a) (conditions for widowed mother's allowance, widow's pension and Category A and Category B retirement pension), after "class" there is inserted "or been credited (in the case of 1987–88 or any subsequent year) with earnings".

Definitions For "earnings", see the Social Security Contributions and Benefits Act 1992, ss 3, 4, 112.
References See para 13.15.

130 Up-rating of pensions increased under section 52 of the Social Security Contributions and Benefits Act

(1) For section 156 of the Social Security Administration Act 1992 there is substituted—

> **"156 Up-rating under section 150 above of pensions increased under section 52(3) of the Contributions and Benefits Act**
>
> (1) This section applies in any case where a person is entitled to a Category A retirement pension with an increase, under section 52(3) of the Contributions and Benefits Act, in the additional pension on account of the contributions of a spouse who has died.
>
> (2) Where in the case of any up-rating order under section 150 above—
>   (a) the spouse's final relevant year is the tax year preceding the tax year in which the up-rating order comes into force, but
>   (b) the person's final relevant year was an earlier tax year,

then the up-rating order shall not have effect in relation to that part of the additional pension which is attributable to the spouse's contributions.

(3) Where in the case of any up-rating order under section 150 above—
 (a) the person's final relevant year is the tax year preceding the tax year in which the up-rating order comes into force, but
 (b) the spouse's final relevant year was an earlier tax year,
then the up-rating order shall not have effect in relation to that part of the additional pension which is attributable to the person's contributions."

(2) In section 151(1) of that Act (effect of up-rating orders on additional pensions), after "and shall apply" there is inserted "subject to section 156 and".

Definitions For "tax year", see the Social Security Administration Act 1992, s 191. By virtue of s 192(2) of that Act, for "final relevant year", see the Social Security Contributions and Benefits Act 1992, s 44(7)(b), and for "entitled", see s 122(1) thereof.
References See para 13.15.

131 Graduated retirement benefit

(1) In section 62(1) of the Social Security Contributions and Benefits Act 1992 (graduated retirement benefit), after paragraph (a) there is inserted—

"(aa) for amending section 36(7) of that Act (persons to be treated as receiving nominal retirement pension) so that where a person has claimed a Category A or Category B retirement pension but—
 (i) because of an election under section 54(1) above, or
 (ii) because he has withdrawn his claim for the pension,
he is not entitled to such a pension, he is not to be treated for the purposes of the preceding provisions of that section as receiving such a pension at a nominal weekly rate;".

(2) In section 150(11) of the Social Security Administration Act 1992 (application of up-rating provisions to graduated retirement benefit) for the words following "provisions of this section" there is substituted—

"(a) to the amount of graduated retirement benefit payable for each unit of graduated contributions,
 (b) to increases of such benefit under any provisions made by virtue of section 24(1)(b) of the Social Security Pensions Act 1975 or section 62(1)(a) of the Contributions and Benefits Act, and
 (c) to any addition under section 37(1) of the National Insurance Act 1965 (addition to weekly rate of retirement pension for widows and widowers) to the amount of such benefit."

(3) In section 155(7) of that Act (effect of alteration of rates of graduated retirement benefit) for the words following "provisions of this section" there is substituted—

"(a) to the amount of graduated retirement benefit payable for each unit of graduated contributions,
 (b) to increases of such benefit under any provisions made by virtue of section 24(1)(b) of the Social Security Pensions Act 1975 or section 62(1)(a) of the Contributions and Benefits Act, and
 (c) to any addition under section 37(1) of the National Insurance Act 1965 (addition to weekly rate of retirement pension for widows and widowers) to the amount of such benefit".

Definitions For "entitled", see the Social Security Contributions and Benefits Act 1992, s 122(1).
References See para 13.15.

132 Extension of Christmas bonus for pensioners

(1) Section 150 of the Social Security Contributions and Benefits Act 1992 (Christmas bonus: interpretation) is amended as follows.

(2) In subsection (1), after paragraph (k) there is inserted—

"(l) a mobility supplement".

(3) In subsection (2)—
   (a) after the definition of "attendance allowance" there is inserted—

""mobility supplement" means a supplement awarded in respect of disablement which affects a person's ability to walk and for which the person is in receipt of war disablement pension;",

   (b) in the definition of "retirement pension", "if paid periodically" is omitted,
   (c) in paragraph (b) of the definition of "unemployability supplement or allowance", after sub-paragraph (iv) there is inserted "or

      (v) under the Pensions (Navy, Army, Air Force and Mercantile Marine) Act 1939."

and accordingly, the "or" immediately following sub-paragraph (iii) is omitted.

References   See para 13.15.

133 Contributions paid in error

After section 61 of the Social Security Contributions and Benefits Act 1992 there is inserted—

"61A Contributions paid in error

(1) This section applies in the case of any individual if—
   (a) the individual has paid amounts by way of primary Class 1 contributions which, because the individual was not an employed earner, were paid in error, and
   (b) prescribed conditions are satisfied.

(2) Regulations may, where—
   (a) this section applies in the case of any individual, and
   (b) the Secretary of State is of the opinion that it is appropriate for the regulations to apply to the individual,

provide for entitlement to, and the amount of, additional pension to be determined as if the individual had been an employed earner and, accordingly, those contributions had been properly paid.

(3) The reference in subsection (2) above to additional pension is to additional pension for the individual or the individual's spouse falling to be calculated under section 45 above for the purposes of—
   (a) Category A retirement pension,
   (b) Category B retirement pension for widows or widowers,
   (c) widowed mother's allowance and widow's pension, and
   (d) incapacity benefit (except in transitional cases).

(4) Regulations may, where—
   (a) this section applies in the case of any individual, and
   (b) the Secretary of State is of the opinion that it is appropriate for regulations made by virtue of section 4(8) of the Social Security (Incapacity for Work) Act 1994 (provision during transition from

invalidity benefit to incapacity benefit for incapacity benefit to include the additional pension element of invalidity pension) to have the following effect in the case of the individual,
provide for the regulations made by virtue of that section to have effect as if, in relation to the provisions in force before the commencement of that section with respect to that additional pension element, the individual had been an employed earner and, accordingly, the contributions had been properly paid.

(5) Where such provision made by regulations as is mentioned in subsection (2) or (4) above applies in respect of any individual, regulations under paragraph 8(1)(m) of Schedule 1 to this Act may not require the amounts paid by way of primary Class 1 contributions to be repaid.

(6) Regulations may provide, where—
  (a) such provision made by regulations as is mentioned in subsection (2) or (4) above applies in respect of any individual,
  (b) prescribed conditions are satisfied, and
  (c) any amount calculated by reference to the contributions in question has been paid in respect of that individual by way of minimum contributions under section 43 of the Pension Schemes Act 1993 (contributions to personal pension schemes),
for that individual to be treated for the purposes of that Act as if that individual had been an employed earner and, accordingly, the amount had been properly paid.".

Definitions For "employed earner", see the Social Security Contributions and Benefits Act 1992, s 2; for "entitled" and "prescribe", see 122(1) thereof.
References See para 13.15.

134 Minor amendments

(1) In section 23(1) of the Social Security Contributions and Benefits Act 1992 (contribution conditions: supplemental), for "22(1)(a)" there is substituted "22(1)".

(2) Section 54(4) of that Act (effect on advance claims for retirement pension of deferral of entitlement) is omitted.

(3) For section 55 of that Act (deferred entitlement) there is substituted—

"55 Increase of retirement pension where entitlement is deferred

(1) Where a person's entitlement to a Category A or Category B retirement pension is deferred, Schedule 5 to this Act shall have effect for increasing the rate of pension.

(2) For the purposes of this Act a person's entitlement to a Category A or Category B retirement pension is deferred if and so long as that person—
  (a) does not become entitled to that pension by reason only—
    (i) of not satisfying the conditions of section 1 of the Administration Act (entitlement to benefit dependent on claim), or
    (ii) in the case of a Category B retirement pension payable by virtue of a spouse's contributions, of the spouse not satisfying those conditions with respect to his Category A retirement pension; or
  (b) in consequence of an election under section 54(1) above, falls to be treated as not having become entitled to that pension;
and, in relation to any such pension, "period of deferment" shall be construed accordingly.".

(4) In section 122(1) of that Act (interpretation of Parts I to VI), after the definition of "week" there is inserted—

""working life" has the meaning given by paragraph 5(8) of Schedule 3 to this Act".

(5) In paragraph 5(8) of Schedule 3 to that Act (contribution conditions: meaning of "working life") for "this paragraph" there is substituted "Parts I to VI of this Act".

Definitions For "entitled", see the Social Security Contributions Act 1992, s 122(1).
References See para 13.15.

PART III
CERTIFICATION OF PENSION SCHEMES AND EFFECTS ON MEMBERS' STATE SCHEME RIGHTS AND DUTIES

Introductory

135 The "principal appointed day" for Part III

An order under section 180 of this Act appointing a day for the coming into force of any provisions of this Part, being 6th April in any year, may designate that day as the principal appointed day for the purposes of this Part.

References See para 13.1.

New certification requirements applying as from the principal appointed day

136 New requirements for contracted-out schemes

(1) In section 7 of the Pension Schemes Act 1993 (issue of contracting-out etc certificates), after subsection (2) there is inserted—

"(2A) The regulations may provide, in the case of contracting-out certificates issued before the principal appointed day, for their cancellation by virtue of the regulations—
(a) at the end of a prescribed period beginning with that day, or
(b) if prescribed conditions are not satisfied at any time in that period,
but for them to continue to have effect until so cancelled; and the regulations may provide that a certificate having effect on and after that day by virtue of this subsection is to have effect, in relation to any earner's service on or after that day, as if issued on or after that day.

(2B) In this Part, "the principal appointed day" means the day designated by an order under section 180 of the Pensions Act 1995 as the principal appointed day for the purposes of Part III of that Act.".

(2) In section 8 of that Act (definition of terms), for subsection (1)(a)(i) there is substituted—

"(i) his service in the employment is for the time being service which qualifies him for a pension provided by an occupational pension scheme contracted out by virtue of satisfying section 9(2) (in this Act referred to as "a salary related contracted-out scheme")".

(3) In section 9 of that Act (requirements for certification of schemes: general), for subsection (2) (requirement for guaranteed minimum pension) there is substituted—

"(2) An occupational pension scheme satisfies this subsection only if—
    (a) in relation to any earner's service before the principal appointed day, it satisfies the conditions of subsection (2A), and
    (b) in relation to any earner's service on or after that day, it satisfies the conditions of subsection (2B).

(2A) The conditions of this subsection are that—
    (a) the scheme complies in all respects with sections 13 to 23 or, in such cases or classes of case as may be prescribed, with those sections as modified by regulations, and
    (b) the rules of the scheme applying to guaranteed minimum pensions are framed so as to comply with the relevant requirements.

(2B) The conditions of this subsection are that the Secretary of State is satisfied that—
    (a) the scheme complies with section 12A,
    (b) restrictions imposed under section 40 of the Pensions Act 1995 (restriction on employer-related investments) apply to the scheme and the scheme complies with those restrictions,
    (c) the scheme satisfies such other requirements as may be prescribed (which—
        (i) must include requirements as to the amount of the resources of the scheme and,
        (ii) may include a requirement that, if the only members of the scheme were those falling within any prescribed class or description, the scheme would comply with section 12A); and
    (d) the scheme does not fall within a prescribed class or description,
and is satisfied that the rules of the scheme are framed so as to comply with the relevant requirements.

(2C) Regulations may modify subsection (2B)(a) and (b) in their application to occupational pension schemes falling within a prescribed class or description."

(4) In subsection (3) of that section (requirement for protected rights, etc) after "case" in paragraph (a) there is inserted—

"(aa) the Secretary of State is satisfied that the scheme does not fall within a prescribed class or description".

(5) After section 12 of that Act there is inserted—

"Requirements for certification of occupational pension schemes applying from the principal appointed day of the Pensions Act 1995

12A The statutory standard

(1) Subject to the provisions of this Part, the scheme must, in relation to the provision of pensions for earners in employed earner's employment, and for their widows or widowers, satisfy the statutory standard.

(2) Subject to regulations made by virtue of section 9(2B)(c)(ii), in applying this section regard must only be had to—
    (a) earners in employed earner's employment, or
    (b) their widows or widowers,
collectively, and the pensions to be provided for persons falling within paragraph (a) or (b) must be considered as a whole.

(3) For the purposes of this section, a scheme satisfies the statutory standard if the pensions to be provided for such persons are broadly equivalent to, or better than, the pensions which would be provided for such persons under a reference scheme.

(4) Regulations may provide for the manner of, and criteria for, determining whether the pensions to be provided for such persons under a scheme are broadly equivalent to, or better than, the pensions which would be provided for such persons under a reference scheme.

(5) Regulations made by virtue of subsection (4) may provide for the determination to be made in accordance with guidance prepared from time to time by a prescribed body and approved by the Secretary of State.

(6) The pensions to be provided for such persons under a scheme are to be treated as broadly equivalent to or better than the pensions which would be provided for such persons under a reference scheme if and only if an actuary (who, except in prescribed circumstances, must be the actuary appointed for the scheme in pursuance of section 47 of the Pensions Act 1995) so certifies.

12B Reference scheme

(1) This section applies for the purposes of section 12A.

(2) A reference scheme is an occupational pension scheme which—
- (a) complies with each of subsections (3) and (4), and
- (b) complies with any prescribed requirements.

(3) In relation to earners employed in employed earner's employment, a reference scheme is one which provides—
- (a) for them to be entitled to a pension under the scheme commencing at a normal pension age of 65 and continuing for life, and
- (b) for the annual rate of the pension at that age to be—
    - (i) 1/80th of average qualifying earnings in the last three tax years preceding the end of service,

    multiplied by

    - (ii) the number of years service, not exceeding such number as would produce an annual rate equal to half the earnings on which it is calculated.

(4) In relation to widows or widowers, a reference scheme is one which provides—
- (a) for the widows or widowers of earners employed in employed earner's employment (whether the earners die before or after attaining the age of 65) to be entitled, except in prescribed circumstances, to pensions under the scheme, and
- (b) except in prescribed circumstances, for the annual rate of the pensions, at the time when the widows or widowers first become entitled to them, to be—
    - (i) in the case of widows or widowers of persons whose age when they died was, or was greater than, normal pension age, 50 per cent of the annual rate which a reference scheme is required to provide for persons of that age, and
    - (ii) in the case of widows or widowers of other persons, 50 per cent of the annual rate which a reference scheme would have been required to provide in respect of the persons' actual periods of service if those persons had attained that age.

(5) For the purposes of this section, an earner's qualifying earnings in any tax year are 90 per cent of the amount by which the earner's earnings—
- (a) exceed the qualifying earnings factor for that year, and
- (b) do not exceed the upper earnings limit for that year multiplied by fifty-three.

(6) Regulations may modify subsections (2) to (5).

(7) In this section—

"normal pension age", in relation to a scheme, means the age specified in the scheme as the earliest age at which pension becomes payable under the scheme (apart from any special provision as to early retirement on grounds of ill-health or otherwise),

"qualifying earnings factor", in relation to a tax year, has the meaning given by section 122(1) of the Social Security Contributions and Benefits Act 1992, and

"upper earnings limit", in relation to a tax year, means the amount specified for that year by regulations made by virtue of section 5(3) of that Act as the upper earnings limit for Class 1 contributions.

12C Transfer, commutation, etc

(1) Regulations may prohibit or restrict—
  (a) the transfer of any liability—
    (i) for the payment of pensions under a relevant scheme, or
    (ii) in respect of accrued rights to such pensions,
  (b) the discharge of any liability to provide pensions under a relevant scheme, or
  (c) the payment of a lump sum instead of a pension payable under a relevant scheme,

except in prescribed circumstances or on prescribed conditions.

(2) In this section "relevant scheme" means a scheme contracted out by virtue of section 9(2B) of this Act and references to pensions and accrued rights under the scheme are to such pensions and rights so far as attributable to an earner's service on or after the principal appointed day.

(3) Regulations under subsection (1) may provide that any provision of this Part shall have effect subject to such modifications as may be specified in the regulations.

12D Entitlement to benefit

In the case of a scheme contracted out by virtue of section 9(2B) of this Act, regulations may make provision as to the ages by reference to which benefits under the scheme are to be paid.".

Definitions For "occupational pension scheme", see the Pension Schemes Act 1993, s 1; for "contracting-out certificate", see s 7(1) of that Act, as amended by s 151, Sch 5, paras 18, 22(a) of this Act; for "guaranteed minimum pension", see s 8(2) of the 1993 Act, as amended by s 151, Sch 5, paras 18, 23(a) of this Act; for "relevant requirements", see s 9(6) of the 1993 Act; for "normal pension age", see s 180 of that Act; for "age", "employment", "modifications", "modified", "modify", "prescribed", "regulations", "resources" and "tax year", see 181(1) of that Act; as to "member", see s 181(4) thereof. By virtue of s 181(1) thereof, as to "employed earner", see the Social Security Contributions and Benefits Act 1992, s 2, for "earner" and "earnings", see ss 3, 4, 112 of that Act. Note as to "the principal appointed day", s 7(2B) of the 1993 Act, as inserted by sub-s (1) above; as to "a salary related contracted-out scheme", s 8(1) of the 1993 Act, as amended by sub-s (2) above, and s 151, Sch 5, paras 18, 21(a); as to "the statutory standard", s 12A(3) of the 1993 Act, as substituted by sub-s (5) above; as to "a reference scheme", s 12B(2), (4) of the 1993 Act, as so substituted; as to "normal pension age", "qualifying earnings factor" and "upper earnings limits", s 12B(7) of the 1993 Act, as so substituted; as to "relevant scheme", see s 12C(2) of the 1993 Act, as so substituted.
References See paras 13.2, 13.3.

Reduction in State scheme contributions, payment of rebates and reduction in State scheme benefits

137 State scheme contributions and rebates

(1) In section 40 of the Pension Schemes Act 1993 (scope of Chapter II of Part III), in paragraph (b), after "members of" there is inserted "money purchase contracted-out schemes and members of".

(2) For section 41(1) of that Act (reduced rates of Class 1 contributions for earners in contracted-out employment), including the sidenote and the preceding heading, there is substituted—

"Reduced rates of contributions for members of salary related contracted-out schemes

41   Reduced rates of Class 1 contributions

(1) Where—
  (a) the earnings paid to or for the benefit of an earner in any tax week are in respect of an employment which is contracted-out employment at the time of the payment, and
  (b) the earner's service in the employment is service which qualifies him for a pension provided by a salary related contracted-out scheme,

the amount of a Class 1 contribution in respect of so much of the earnings paid in that week as exceeds the current lower earnings limit but not the current upper earnings limit for that week (or the prescribed equivalents if he is paid otherwise than weekly) shall be reduced by the following amount.

(1A) The amount is—
  (a) in the case of a primary Class 1 contribution, an amount equal to 1.8 per cent of that part of those earnings, and
  (b) in the case of a secondary Class 1 contribution, an amount equal to 3 per cent of that part of those earnings.".

(3) In section 42 of that Act (review and alteration of rates of contributions applicable under section 41), for subsection (1)(a) there is substituted—

"(a) a report by the Government Actuary or the Deputy Government Actuary on—
  (i) the percentages for the time being applying under section 41(1A)(a) and (b), and
  (ii) any changes since the preparation of the last report under this paragraph in the factors in his opinion affecting the cost of providing benefits of an actuarial value equivalent to that of the benefits which, under section 48A, are foregone by or in respect of members of salary related contracted-out schemes".

(4) In relation to the first report under section 42(1)(a) of that Act laid after the passing of this Act, that section shall have effect as if—
  (a) in subsection (1)(a), sub-paragraph (i) and, in sub-paragraph (ii), "any changes since the preparation of the last report under this paragraph in" were omitted,
  (b) for subsection (1)(b) there were substituted—

"(b) a report by the Secretary of State stating what, in view of the report under paragraph (a), he considers the percentages under section 41(1A)(a) should be",

  (c) for subsections (3) and (4) there were substituted—

"(3) The Secretary of State shall prepare and lay before each House of Parliament with the report the draft of an order specifying the percentages; and if the draft is approved by resolution of each House the Secretary of State shall make the order in the form of the draft.

(4) An order under subsection (3) shall have effect from the beginning of the tax year which begins with the principal appointed day, not being a tax year earlier than the second after that in which the order is made.",

(d) in subsection (5), for "alteration" there were substituted "determination", and
(e) in subsection (6), for "an order making alterations in either or both of those percentages" there were substituted "such an order".

(5) After that section there is inserted—

"Reduced rates of contributions, and rebates, for members of money purchase contracted-out schemes

42A Reduced rates of Class 1 contributions, and rebates

(1) Subsections (2) and (3) apply where—
(a) the earnings paid to or for the benefit of an earner in any tax week are in respect of an employment which is contracted-out employment at the time of the payment, and
(b) the earner's service in the employment is service which qualifies him for a pension provided by a money purchase contracted-out scheme.

(2) The amount of a Class 1 contribution in respect of so much of the earnings paid in that week in respect of that employment as exceeds the current lower earnings limit but not the current upper earnings limit for that week (or the prescribed equivalents if he is paid otherwise than weekly) shall be reduced by an amount equal to the appropriate flat-rate percentage of that part of those earnings.

(3) The Secretary of State shall except in prescribed circumstances or in respect of prescribed periods pay in respect of that earner and that tax week to the trustees or managers of the scheme or, in prescribed circumstances, to a prescribed person the amount by which—

(a) the appropriate age-related percentage of that part of those earnings, exceeds
(b) the appropriate flat-rate percentage of that part of those earnings.

(4) Regulations may make provision—
(a) as to the manner in which and time at which or period within which payments under subsection (3) are to be made,
(b) for the adjustment of the amount which would otherwise be payable under that subsection so as to avoid the payment of trivial or fractional amounts,
(c) for earnings to be calculated or estimated in such manner and on such basis as may be prescribed for the purpose of determining whether any, and if so what, payments under subsection (3) are to be made.

(5) If the Secretary of State pays an amount under subsection (3) which he is not required to pay or is not required to pay to the person to whom, or in respect of whom, he pays it, he may recover it from any person to whom, or in respect of whom, he paid it.

(6) Where—
(a) an earner has ceased to be employed in an employment, and
(b) earnings are paid to him or for his benefit within the period of six weeks, or such other period as may be prescribed, from the day on which he so ceased,

that employment shall be treated for the purposes of this section as contracted-out employment at the time when the earnings are paid if it was contracted-out employment in relation to the earner when he was last employed in it.

(7) Subsection (3) of section 41 applies for the purposes of this section as it applies for the purposes of that.

42B Determination and alteration of rates of contributions, and rebates, applicable under section 42A

(1) The Secretary of State shall at intervals of not more than five years lay before each House of Parliament—
    (a) a report by the Government Actuary or the Deputy Government Actuary on the percentages which, in his opinion, are required to be specified in an order under this section so as to reflect the cost of providing benefits of an actuarial value equivalent to that of the benefits which, under section 48A, are foregone by or in respect of members of money purchase contracted-out schemes,
    (b) a report by the Secretary of State stating what, in view of the report under paragraph (a), he considers those percentages should be, and
    (c) a draft of an order under subsection (2).

(2) An order under this subsection shall have effect in relation to a period of tax years (not exceeding five) and may—
    (a) specify different percentages for primary and secondary Class 1 contributions, and
    (b) for each of the tax years for which it has effect—
        (i) specify a percentage in respect of all earners which is "the appropriate flat-rate percentage" for the purposes of section 42A, and
        (ii) specify different percentages (not being less than the percentage specified by virtue of sub-paragraph (i)) in respect of earners by reference to their ages on the last day of the preceding year (the percentage for each group of earners being "the appropriate age-related percentage" in respect of earners in that group for the purposes of section 42A).

(3) If the draft of an order under subsection (2) is approved by resolution of each House of Parliament, the Secretary of State shall make the order in the form of the draft.

(4) An order under subsection (2) shall have effect from the beginning of such tax year as may be specified in the order, not being a tax year earlier than the second after that in which the order is made.

(5) Subsection (2) is without prejudice to the generality of section 182.".

(6) In Schedule 4 to that Act (priority in bankruptcy, etc), in paragraph 2(3)—
    (a) in paragraph (a), for "4.8 per cent" there is substituted "the percentage for non-contributing earners",
    (b) in paragraph (b), for "3 per cent" there is substituted "the percentage for contributing earners".

(7) In paragraph 2(5) of that Schedule—
    (a) before the definition of "employer" there is inserted—

    ""appropriate flat-rate percentage" has the same meaning as in section 42A", and

    (b) after the definition there is inserted—

    ""the percentage for contributing earners" means—
        (a) in relation to a salary related contracted-out scheme, 3 per cent, and
        (b) in relation to a money purchase contracted-out scheme, the percentage which is the appropriate flat-rate percentage for secondary Class 1 contributions,

"the percentage for non-contributing earners" means—
    (a) in relation to a salary related contracted-out scheme, 4.8 per cent, and
    (b) in relation to a money purchase contracted-out scheme, a percentage equal to the sum of the appropriate flat-rate percentages for primary and secondary Class 1 contributions".

Definitions For "the principal appointed day", see the Pension Schemes Act 1993, s 7(2B), as inserted by s 136(1) of this Act; for "contracted-out employment", "a money purchase contracted-out scheme" and "a salary related contracted-out scheme", see s 8(1) of the 1993 Act, as amended by s 136(2), s 151, Sch 5, paras 18, 21(a) of this Act; for "employment", "prescribed", "the prescribed equivalents", "regulations", "tax year", "tax week" and "week", see s 181(1) of the 1993 Act; as to "member", see s 181(4) thereof. By virtue of s 181(1) of the 1993 Act, for "earner" and "earnings", see the Social Security Contributions and Benefits Act 1992, ss 3, 4, 112; for "lower earnings limit" and "upper earnings limit", see s 5 of the Social Security Contributions and Benefits Act 1992; (and for "current" in relation to those limits, see s 181(1) of the 1993 Act).
References See paras 14.11, 14.12.

138 Minimum contributions towards appropriate personal pension schemes

(1) Section 45 of the Pension Schemes Act 1993 (minimum contributions to personal pension schemes) is amended as follows.

(2) For subsection (1) there is substituted—

"(1) In relation to any tax week falling within a period for which the Secretary of State is required to pay minimum contributions in respect of an earner, the amount of those contributions shall be an amount equal to the appropriate age-related percentage of so much of the earnings paid in that week (other than earnings in respect of contracted-out employment) as exceeds the current lower earnings limit but not the current upper earnings limit for that week (or the prescribed equivalents if he is paid otherwise than weekly).".

(3) Subsection (2) is omitted.

(4) In subsection (3)(e), the words following "prescribed period" are omitted.

(5) After that section there is inserted—

"45A Determination and alteration of rates of minimum contributions under section 45

(1) The Secretary of State shall at intervals of not more than five years lay before each House of Parliament—
    (a) a report by the Government Actuary or the Deputy Government Actuary on the percentages which, in his opinion, are required to be specified in an order under this section so as to reflect the cost of providing benefits of an actuarial value equivalent to that of the benefits which, under section 48A, are foregone by or in respect of members of appropriate personal pension schemes,
    (b) a report by the Secretary of State stating what, in view of the report under paragraph (a), he considers those percentages should be, and
    (c) a draft of an order under subsection (2).

(2) An order under this subsection—
    (a) shall have effect in relation to a period of tax years (not exceeding five), and
    (b) may, for each of the tax years for which it has effect, specify different percentages in respect of earners by reference to their ages on the last day of the preceding year (the percentage for each group of earners being "the appropriate age-related percentage" in respect of earners in that group for the purposes of section 45).

(3) If the draft of an order under subsection (2) is approved by resolution of each House of Parliament, the Secretary of State shall make the order in the form of the draft.

(4) An order under subsection (2) shall have effect from the beginning of such tax year as may be specified in the order, not being a tax year earlier than the second after that in which the order is made.

(5) Subsection (2) is without prejudice to the generality of section 182.".

Definitions For "personal pension scheme", see the Pension Schemes Act 1993, s 1; for "appropriate personal pension scheme", see s 7(4) of that Act, as amended and repealed in part by ss 151, 177, Sch 5, paras 18, 22(b), Sch 7, Pt III of this Act; for "contracted-out employment", see s 8(1) of the 1993 Act, as amended by s 136(2), s 151, Sch 5, paras 18, 21(a) of this Act; for "age", "employment", "minimum contributions", "prescribed", "the prescribed equivalents", "regulations", "tax week", "tax year" and "week", see s 181(1) of the 1993 Act. By virtue of s 181(1) of the 1993 Act, for "earner" and "earnings", see the Social Security Contributions and Benefits Act 1992, ss 3, 4, 112; for "lower earnings limit" and "upper earnings limit", see s 5 of the 1992 Act (and for "current" in relation to those limits, see s 181(1) of the 1993 Act). Note as to "the appropriate age-related percentage", s 45A(2) of the 1993 Act, as inserted by sub-s (5) above.
References See para 14.13.

139 Money purchase and personal pension schemes: verification of ages

After section 45A of the Pension Schemes Act 1993 (inserted by section 138) there is inserted—

"45B Money purchase and personal pension schemes: verification of ages

(1) Regulations may make provision for the manner in which an earner's age is to be verified in determining the appropriate age-related percentages for the purposes of sections 42A and 45(1).

(2) Information held by the Secretary of State as to the age of any individual may, whether or not it was obtained in pursuance of regulations under subsection (1), be disclosed by the Secretary of State—
    (a) to the trustees or managers of a money purchase contracted-out scheme or an appropriate personal pension scheme, and
    (b) to such other persons as may be prescribed,
in connection with the making of payments under section 42A(3) or the payment of minimum contributions."

Definitions For "personal pension scheme", see the Pension Schemes Act 1993, s 1; for "appropriate personal pension scheme", see s 7(4) of that Act, as amended and repealed in part by ss 151, 177, Sch 5, paras 18, 22(b), Sch 7, Pt III of this Act; for "a money purchase contracted-out scheme", see s 8(1) thereof, as amended by s 136(2), s 151, Sch 5, paras 18, 21(a); for "age", "minimum contributions", "prescribed" and "regulations", see s 181(1) of the 1993 Act. By virtue of s 181(1) thereof, for "earner", see the Social Security Contributions and Benefits Act 1992, ss 3, 4, 112.
References See para 14.14.

140 Reduction in benefits for members of certified schemes

(1) After section 48 of the Pension Schemes Act 1993 there is inserted—

"Effect of reduced contributions and rebates on social security benefits

48A Additional pension and other benefits

(1) In relation to any tax week where—
    (a) the amount of a Class 1 contribution in respect of the earnings paid to or for the benefit of an earner in that week is reduced under section 41 or 42A, or

(b) an amount is paid under section 45(1) in respect of the earnings paid to or for the benefit of an earner,

section 44(6) of the Social Security Contributions and Benefits Act 1992 (earnings factors for additional pension) shall have effect, except in prescribed circumstances, as if no primary Class 1 contributions had been paid or treated as paid upon those earnings for that week and section 45A of that Act did not apply (where it would, apart from this subsection, apply).

(2) Where the whole or part of a contributions equivalent premium has been paid or treated as paid in respect of the earner, the Secretary of State may make a determination reducing or eliminating the application of subsection (1).

(3) Subsection (1) is subject to regulations under paragraph 5(3A) to (3E) of Schedule 2.

(4) Regulations may, so far as is required for the purpose of providing entitlement to additional pension (such as is mentioned in section 44(3)(b) of the Social Security Contributions and Benefits Act 1992) but to the extent only that the amount of additional pension is attributable to provision made by regulations under section 45(5) of that Act, disapply subsection (1).

(5) In relation to earners where, by virtue of subsection (1), section 44(6) of the Social Security Contributions and Benefits Act 1992 has effect, in any tax year, as mentioned in that subsection in relation to some but not all of their earnings, regulations may modify the application of section 44(5) of that Act."

(2) In section 48 of the Pension Schemes Act 1993 (effect of membership of money purchase contracted-out scheme or appropriate scheme on payment of social security benefits) in subsection (2), paragraph (b) is omitted and, in paragraph (c), "if the earner dies before reaching pensionable age" is omitted.

(3) Section 48 of that Act shall cease to have effect in relation to minimum payments made, or minimum contributions paid, on or after the principal appointed day.

Definitions For "the principal appointed day", see the Pension Schemes Act 1993, s 7(2B), as inserted by s 136(1) of this Act; for "minimum payment", see s 8(2) of the 1993 Act, as amended by s 151, Sch 5, paras 18, 23(a) of this Act; as to a "contributions equivalent premium", see s 55(2) of the 1993 Act, as substituted by s 141(1) of this Act; for "minimum contributions", "modify", "prescribed", "regulations", "tax week" and "week", see s 181(1) of the 1993 Act. By virtue of s 181(1) of the 1993 Act, for "earner" and "earnings", see the Social Security Contributions and Benefits Act 1992, ss 3, 4, 112.
References See para 13.4.

Premiums and return to State scheme

141 State scheme etc premiums and buyback into State scheme

(1) In section 55 of the Pension Schemes Act 1993 (payment of state scheme premiums on termination of certified status), for subsection (2) there is substituted—

"(2) Where—
  (a) an earner is serving in employment which is contracted-out employment by reference to an occupational pension scheme (other than a money purchase contracted-out scheme),
  (b) paragraph (a) ceases to apply, by reason of any of the following circumstances, before the earner attains the scheme's normal pension age or (if earlier) the end of the tax year preceding that in which the earner attains pensionable age, and
  (c) the earner has served for less than two years in the employment,
the prescribed person may elect to pay a premium under this subsection (referred to in this Act as a "contributions equivalent premium").

(2A) The circumstances referred to in subsection (2) are that—
- (a) the earner's service in the employment ceases otherwise than on the earner's death,
- (b) the earner ceases to be a member of the scheme otherwise than on the earner's death,
- (c) the earner's service in the employment ceases on the earner's death and the earner dies leaving a widow or widower,
- (d) the scheme is wound up,
- (e) the scheme ceases to be a contracted-out occupational pension scheme;

but paragraph (a), (b), (d) or (e) does not apply if the earner has an accrued right to short service benefit.".

(2) In Schedule 2 to that Act, in paragraph 5 (state scheme premiums)—
- (a) in sub-paragraph (3)—
  - (i) "in relation to state scheme premiums" is omitted,
  - (ii) paragraph (b) is omitted, and
  - (iii) at the end there is added—

"and in this sub-paragraph and the following provisions of this paragraph "premium" means a contributions equivalent premium",

- (b) after sub-paragraph (3) there is inserted—

"(3A) Sub-paragraph (3B) applies in relation to a member of a contracted-out occupational pension scheme which is being wound up if, in the opinion of the Secretary of State—
- (a) the resources of the scheme are insufficient to meet the whole of the liability for the cash equivalent of the member's rights under the scheme, and
- (b) if the resources of the scheme are sufficient to meet a part of that liability, that part is less than the amount required for restoring his State scheme rights.

(3B) Where this sub-paragraph applies—
- (a) regulations may provide for treating the member as if sections 46 to 48 or, as the case may be, section 48A(1) did not apply, or applied only to such extent as is determined in accordance with the regulations, and
- (b) the amount required for restoring the member's State scheme rights, or a prescribed part of that amount, shall be a debt due from the trustees or managers of the scheme to the Secretary of State.

(3C) Regulations may make provision—
- (a) for determining the cash equivalent of a member's rights under a scheme and the extent (if any) to which the resources of the scheme are insufficient to meet the liability for that cash equivalent,
- (b) for the recovery of any debt due under sub-paragraph (3B)(b), and
- (c) for determining the amount required for restoring a member's State scheme rights including provision requiring the Secretary of State to apply whichever prescribed actuarial table in force at the appropriate time is applicable.

(3D) Section 155 shall apply as if sub-paragraphs (3A) and (3B)(a), and regulations made by virtue of this sub-paragraph and sub-paragraph (3B)(b), were included among the provisions there referred to.

(3E) In sub-paragraphs (3A) and (3B), "State scheme rights", in relation to a member of a scheme, are the rights for which, if the scheme had not been a contracted-out scheme, the member would have been eligible by virtue of section 44(6) of the Social Security Contributions and Benefits Act 1992 (earnings factors for additional pension).", and

(c) sub-paragraph (5) is omitted.

Definitions For "occupational pension scheme", see the Pension Schemes Act 1993, s 1; as to "contracted-out occupational scheme", see s 7(3) of that Act; for "contracted-out employment" and "a money purchase contracted-out scheme", see s 8(1) of the 1993 Act, as amended by s 136(2), s 151, Sch 5, paras 18, 21(a) of this Act; as to an "accrued right to short service benefit", see s 56(5) of the 1993 Act, as substituted by s 151, Sch 5, paras 18, 51(b) of this Act; for "short service benefit", see s 71(2) of the 1993 Act; for "normal pension age", see s 180 of that Act; for "employment", "pensionable age", "prescribed", "regulations", "resources" and "tax year", see s 181(1) thereof, as amended by s 126(c), Sch 4, Pt III, para 17 of this Act; as to "member", see s 181(4) of the 1993 Act. By virtue of s 181(1) thereof, for "earner", see the Social Security Contributions and Benefits Act 1992, ss 3, 4, 112. Note as to a "contributions equivalent premium", s 55(2) of the 1993 Act, as substituted by sub-s (1) above; and as to "State scheme rights", see Sch 2, para 5(3E) to the 1993 Act, as inserted by sub-s (2)(b) above.
References See paras 13.4–13.6.

Protected rights

142 Interim arrangements for giving effect to protected rights

(1) Section 28 of the Pension Schemes Act 1993 (ways of giving effect to protected rights) is amended as follows.

(2) In subsection (1), after paragraph (a) there is inserted—

"(aa) in any case where subsection (1A) so requires, by the making of such payments as are mentioned in that subsection,".

(3) After that subsection there is inserted—

"(1A) In the case of a personal pension scheme, where the member so elects, effect shall be given to his protected rights—
(a) during the interim period, by the making of payments under an interim arrangement which—
(i) complies with section 28A,
(ii) satisfies such conditions as may be prescribed, and
(b) at the end of the interim period, in such of the ways permitted by the following subsections as the rules of the scheme may specify."

(4) In subsection (3)—
(a) in paragraph (b), after "the member" there is inserted "or, where section 28A(2) applies, the member's widow or widower", and
(b) in the words following that paragraph, after "subsection" there is inserted "(1A)(a) or".

(5) In subsection (4)(a), for the words from "65" to the end there is substituted—

"65 or such later date as has been agreed by him, or
(ii) in the case of a personal pension scheme, where the member has elected to receive payments under an interim arrangement, the date by reference to which the member elects to terminate that arrangement, and otherwise such date as has been agreed by him and is not earlier than his 60th birthday nor later than his 75th birthday."

(6) In subsection (5), after "subsection" there is inserted "(1A)".

(7) After subsection (7) there is added—

"(8) In this section and sections 28A, 28B and 29—
"the interim period" means the period beginning with the starting date in relation to the member in question and ending with the termination date;

"the starting date" means the date, which must not be earlier than the member's 60th birthday, by reference to which the member elects to begin to receive payments under the interim arrangement;

"the termination date" means the date by reference to which the member (or, where section 28A(2) applies, the member's widow or widower) elects to terminate the interim arrangement, and that date must be not later than—

(i) the member's 75th birthday, or

(ii) where section 28A(2) applies, the earlier of the member's widow or widower's 75th birthday and the 75th anniversary of the member's birth."

Definitions   For "personal pension scheme", see the Pension Schemes Act 1993, s 1; for "protected rights", see s 10 of that Act, as amended by s 151, Sch 5, paras 18, 25 of this Act; for "prescribed", see s 181(1) of the 1993 Act; as to "member", see s 181(4) thereof. Note as to "the interim period", "the starting date" and "the termination date", s 28(8) of the 1993 Act, as added by sub-s (7) above.
References   See paras 14.21, 14.22.

143 Requirements for interim arrangements

After section 28 of the Pension Schemes Act 1993 there is inserted—

"28A Requirements for interim arrangements

(1) An interim arrangement must provide for interim payments to be made to the member, and, where subsection (2) applies, to the member's widow or widower, throughout the interim period, at intervals not exceeding twelve months.

(2) This subsection applies where the member dies during the interim period and is survived by a widow or widower who at the date of the member's death has not yet attained the age of 75 years.

(3) The aggregate amount of payments made to a person under an interim arrangement in each successive period of twelve months must not be—

(a) greater than the annual amount of the annuity which would have been purchasable by him on the relevant reference date, or

(b) less than the prescribed percentage of that amount.

(4) The percentage prescribed under subsection (3)(b) may be zero.

(5) For the purposes of this section—

(a) the annual amount of the annuity which would have been purchasable by a person on any date shall be calculated in the prescribed manner by reference to—

(i) the value on that date, determined by or on behalf of the trustees or managers of the scheme, of the person's protected rights, and

(ii) the current published tables of rates of annuities prepared in the prescribed manner by the Government Actuary for the purposes of this section, and

(b) the relevant reference date is—

(i) in relation to payments made to the member during the three years beginning with the member's starting date, that date, and in relation to such payments made during each succeeding period of three years, the first day of the period of three years in question, or

(ii) where subsection (2) applies, in relation to payments made to the member's widow or widower during the three years beginning with the date of the member's death, that date, and in relation to such payments made during each succeeding period of three years, the first day of the period of three years in question.

28B Information about interim arrangements

(1) The trustees or managers of a personal pension scheme must, if required to do so by the Secretary of State, produce any document relevant to—
    (a) the level of payments made under any interim arrangement, or
    (b) the value of protected rights to which such an arrangement gives effect,
or otherwise connected with the making of payments under such an arrangement.

(2) In this section, "document" includes information recorded in any form, and the reference to the production of a document, in relation to information recorded otherwise than in legible form, is a reference to producing a copy of the information in legible form."

Definitions For "personal pension scheme", see the Pension Schemes Act 1993, s 1; for "protected rights", see s 10 thereof, as amended by s 151, Sch 5, paras 18, 25 of this Act; for "the interim period" and "the starting date", see s 28(8) of the 1993 Act, as added by s 142(7) of this Act; for "age" and "prescribed", see s 181(1) of the 1993 Act; as to "member", see s 181(4) thereof. Note as to "the relevant reference date", s 28A(5)(b) of the 1993 Act, as inserted by this section, and as to "document", s 28B(2) of that Act, as so inserted.
References See paras 14.23–14.25.

144 Interim arrangements: supplementary

(1) Section 29 of the Pension Schemes Act 1993 (the pension and annuity requirements) is amended as follows.

(2) In subsection (1) for paragraph (a) there is substituted—

"(a) in the case of an occupational pension scheme it commences on a date—
    (i) not earlier than the member's 60th birthday, and
    (ii) not later than his 65th birthday,
or on such later date as has been agreed by him, and continues until the date of his death, or

(aa) in the case of a personal pension scheme—
    (i) where the member has elected under section 28(1A) to receive payments under an interim arrangement, it commences on the termination date, and continues until the date of the member's death or, where section 28A(2) applies, until the death of the member's widow or widower, or
    (ii) otherwise, it commences on such a date as has been agreed by the member and is not earlier than his 60th birthday nor later than his 75th birthday, and continues until the date of his death;".

(3) In subsection (3)(b)(iii), after "member" there is inserted "or, where section 28A(2) applies, the member's widow or widower".

(4) In subsection (4), after "member" there is inserted "(or a member's widow or widower)".

Definitions For "occupational pension scheme" and "personal pension scheme", see the Pension Schemes Act 1993, s 1; for "the termination date", see s 28(8) of that Act, as added by s 142(7); as to "member", see s 181(4) of that Act.
References See para 14.26.

Pensions Act 1995, s 145

145 Extension of interim arrangements to occupational pension schemes

Regulations made by the Secretary of State may provide that sections 141 to 143 shall have effect, subject to prescribed modifications, in relation to protected rights under an occupational pension scheme as they have effect in relation to protected rights under a personal pension scheme.

Definitions By virtue of s 176, for "occupational pension scheme" and "personal pension scheme", see the Pension Schemes Act 1993; and for "protected rights", cf s 10 of that Act, as amended by s 151, Sch 5, paras 18, 25 of this Act.
References See para 14.27.

146 Discharge of protected rights on winding up: insurance policies

(1) After section 32 of the Pension Schemes Act 1993 there is inserted—

"**32A Discharge of protected rights on winding up: insurance policies**

(1) Where an occupational pension scheme is being wound up and such conditions as may be prescribed are satisfied, effect may be given to the protected rights of a member of the scheme (in spite of section 28) by—
  (a) taking out an appropriate policy of insurance, or a number of such policies, under which the member is the beneficiary, or
  (b) assuring the benefits of a policy of insurance, or a number of such policies, to the member, where the policy assured is an appropriate policy.

(2) A policy of insurance is appropriate for the purposes of this section if—
  (a) the insurance company with which it is or was taken out or entered into—
    (i) is, or was at the time when the policy was taken out or (as the case may be) the benefit of it was assured, carrying on ordinary long-term insurance business (within the meaning of the Insurance Companies Act 1982) in the United Kingdom or any other Member State, and
    (ii) satisfies, or at that time satisfied, prescribed requirements, and
  (b) it may not be assigned or surrendered except on conditions which satisfy such requirements as may be prescribed, and
  (c) it contains or is endorsed with terms whose effect is that the amount secured by it may not be commuted except on conditions which satisfy such requirements as may be prescribed, and
  (d) it satisfies such other requirements as may be prescribed.".

(2) At the end of section 28 of that Act, as amended by this Act, (ways of giving effect to protected rights) there is inserted—

"(9) This section is subject to section 32A.".

Definitions For "occupational pension scheme", see the Pension Schemes Act 1993, s 1; for "protected rights", see s 10 of that Act, as amended by s 151, Sch 5, paras 18, 25 of this Act; for "insurance company" and "prescribed", see s 181(1) of the 1993 Act; as to "member", see s 181(4) of that Act.
References See para 13.7.

Miscellaneous

147 Monitoring personal pension schemes

After section 33 of the Pension Schemes Act 1993 there is inserted—

"33A Appropriate schemes: "Blowing the whistle"

(1) If any person acting as an auditor or actuary of an appropriate scheme has reasonable cause to believe that—
> (a) any requirement which, in the case of the scheme, is required by section 9(5)(a) to be satisfied is not satisfied, and
> (b) the failure to satisfy the requirement is likely to be of material significance in the exercise by the Secretary of State of any of his functions relating to appropriate schemes,

that person must immediately give a written report of the matter to the Secretary of State.

(2) No duty to which a person acting as auditor or actuary of an appropriate scheme is subject shall be regarded as contravened merely because of any information or opinion contained in a written report under this section."

Definitions For "appropriate scheme", see the Pension Schemes Act 1993, s 7(4), as amended and repealed in part by ss 151, 177 of, and Sch 5, paras 18, 22(b), Sch 7, Pt III to, this Act.
References See paras 5.19, 5.20.

148 Earner employed in more than one employment

(1) Paragraph 1 of Schedule 1 to the Social Security Contributions and Benefits Act 1992 (Class 1 contributions where earner in more than one employment) is amended as follows.

(2) For sub-paragraph (3) there is substituted—

> "(3) The amount of the primary Class 1 contribution shall be the aggregate of the amounts determined under the following paragraphs (applying earlier paragraphs before later ones)—
> > (a) if the aggregated earnings are paid to or for the benefit of an earner in respect of whom minimum contributions are payable under section 43(1) of the Pension Schemes Act 1993 (contributions to personal pension schemes), the amount obtained by applying the rate of primary Class 1 contributions that would apply if all the aggregated earnings were attributable to employments which are not contracted-out to such part of the aggregated earnings so attributable as does not exceed the current upper earnings limit (referred to in this paragraph as "the APPS earnings"),
> > (b) if some of the aggregated earnings are attributable to COMPS service, the amount obtained by applying the rate of primary Class 1 contributions that would apply if all the aggregated earnings were attributable to COMPS service—
> > > (i) to such part of the aggregated earnings attributable to COMPS service as does not exceed the current upper earnings limit, or
> > > (ii) if paragraph (a) applies, to such part of the earnings attributable to COMPS service as, when added to the APPS earnings, does not exceed the current upper earnings limit,
> > (c) if some of the aggregated earnings are attributable to COSRS service, the amount obtained by applying the rate of primary Class 1 contributions that would apply if all the aggregated earnings were attributable to COSRS service—
> > > (i) to such part of the aggregated earnings attributable to COSRS service as does not exceed the current upper earnings limit, or
> > > (ii) if paragraph (a) or (b) applies, to such part of the earnings attributable to COSRS service as, when added to the APPS

Pensions Act 1995, s 148

> earnings or the part attributable to COMPS service (or both), does not exceed the current upper earnings limit,
>
> (d) the amount obtained by applying the rate of primary Class 1 contributions that would apply if all the aggregated earnings were attributable to employments which are not contracted-out to such part of the aggregated earnings as, when added to the part or parts attributable to COMPS or COSRS service, does not exceed the current upper earnings limit.".

(3) For sub-paragraph (6) there is substituted—

> "(6) The amount of the secondary Class 1 contribution shall be the aggregate of the amounts determined under the following paragraphs (applying earlier paragraphs before later ones)—
>
> (a) if the aggregated earnings are paid to or for the benefit of an earner in respect of whom minimum contributions are payable under section 43(1) of the Pension Schemes Act 1993, the amount obtained by applying the rate of secondary Class 1 contributions that would apply if all the aggregated earnings were attributable to employments which are not contracted-out to the APPS earnings,
>
> (b) if some of the aggregated earnings are attributable to COMPS service, the amount obtained by applying the rate of secondary Class 1 contributions that would apply if all the aggregated earnings were attributable to COMPS service to the part of the aggregated earnings attributable to such service,
>
> (c) if some of the aggregated earnings are attributable to COSRS service, the amount obtained by applying the rate of secondary Class 1 contributions that would apply if all the aggregated earnings were attributable to COSRS service to the part of the aggregated earnings attributable to such service,
>
> (d) the amount obtained by applying the rate of secondary Class 1 contributions that would apply if all the aggregated earnings were attributable to employments which are not contracted-out to the remainder of the aggregated earnings.".

(4) At the end of that paragraph there is added—

> "(9) In this paragraph—
>
> "COMPS service" means service in employment in respect of which minimum payments are made to a money purchase contracted-out scheme,
>
> "COSRS service" means service in employment which qualifies the earner for a pension provided by a salary related contracted-out scheme.".

(5) Until the principal appointed day, that paragraph, as amended by this section, shall have effect as if—

> (a) for sub-paragraph (3)(b) there were substituted—
>
> "(b) if some of the aggregated earnings are attributable to service in contracted-out employment, the amount obtained by applying the rate of primary Class 1 contributions that would apply if all the aggregated earnings were attributable to such service—
>
> (i) to such part of the aggregated earnings attributable to such service as does not exceed the current upper earnings limit, or
>
> (ii) if paragraph (a) applies, to such part of the earnings attributable to such service as, when added to the APPS earnings, does not exceed the current upper earnings limit",

(b) sub-paragraph (3)(c) were omitted,
(c) in sub-paragraph (3)(d), for "COMPS or COSRS service" there were substituted "service in contracted-out employment",
(d) for sub-paragraph (6)(b) there were substituted—

"(b) if some of the aggregated earnings are attributable to service in contracted-out employment, the amount obtained by applying the rate of secondary Class 1 contributions that would apply if all the aggregated earnings were attributable to such service to the part of the aggregated earnings attributable to such service",

(e) sub-paragraph (6)(c) were omitted, and
(f) in sub-paragraph (9) the definitions of "COMPS service" and "COSRS service" were omitted.

Definitions For "earner" and "earnings", see the Social Security Contributions and Benefits Act 1992, ss 3, 4, 112; for "upper earnings limit", see ss 5, 122(1) of that Act; for "current" and "employment", see s 122(1) of that Act. By virtue of s 122(1) of the 1992 Act, as amended by s 126(b), Sch 4, Pt II, para 13(a) of this Act, for "pensionable age", see Sch 4, para 1 to this Act. Note as to "the APPS earnings", Sch 1, para 1(3)(a) to the 1992 Act, as substituted by sub-ss (1), (2) above; and as to "COMPS service" and "COSRS service", Sch 1, para 1(9) to that Act, as added by sub-ss (1), (4) above.
References See para 13.9.

149 Hybrid occupational pension schemes

(1) In spite of anything in sections 9 and 12 of the Pension Schemes Act 1993 (requirements for certification and determination of basis on which scheme is contracted-out), the Secretary of State may by regulations provide, where the pensions provided by an occupational pension scheme include both—
    (a) such pensions that, if the scheme provided only those pensions, it would satisfy section 9(2) of that Act, and
    (b) such other pensions that, if the scheme provided only those other pensions, it would satisfy section 9(3) of that Act,
for Part III of that Act to have effect as if the scheme were two separate schemes providing, respectively, the pensions referred to in paragraphs (a) and (b).

(2) Regulations made by the Secretary of State may, in connection with any provision made by virtue of subsection (1), make such modifications of the following Acts, and the instruments made or having effect as if made under them, as appear to the Secretary of State desirable: the Social Security Contributions and Benefits Act 1992, the Pension Schemes Act 1993 and Part I of this Act.

Definitions For "occupational pension scheme", by virtue of s 176, see the Pension Schemes Act 1993, s 1.
References See para 13.8.

150 Dissolution of Occupational Pensions Board

(1) The Occupational Pensions Board (referred to in this section as "the Board") is hereby dissolved.

(2) An order under section 180 appointing the day on which subsection (1) is to come into force may provide—
    (a) for all property, rights and liabilities to which the Board is entitled or subject immediately before that day to become property, rights and liabilities of the Authority or the Secretary of State, and
    (b) for any function of the Board falling to be exercised on or after that day, or which fell to be exercised before that day but has not been exercised, to be exercised by the Authority, the Secretary of State or the Department of Health and Social Services for Northern Ireland.

Definitions For "the Authority", cf s 1 of this Act.
References See paras 2.4, 2.5.

Minor and consequential amendments

151 Minor and consequential amendments related to sections 136 to 150

Schedule 5 (which makes amendments related to sections 136 to 150) shall have effect.

References See paras 13.10, 13.11, 14.18.

PART IV
MISCELLANEOUS AND GENERAL

Transfer values

152 Extension of scope of right to cash equivalent

(1)   Section 93 of the Pension Schemes Act 1993 (scope of provisions relating to transfer values) is amended as follows.

(2)   For subsection (1)(a) there is substituted—

"(a) to any member of an occupational pension scheme—
   (i) whose pensionable service has terminated at least one year before normal pension age, and
   (ii) who on the date on which his pensionable service terminated had accrued rights to benefit under the scheme,
except a member of a salary related occupational pension scheme whose pensionable service terminated before 1st January 1986 and in respect of whom prescribed requirements are satisfied".

(3)   After subsection (1) there is inserted—

"(1A) For the purposes of this section and the following provisions of this Chapter, an occupational pension scheme is salary related if—
   (a) the scheme is not a money purchase scheme, and
   (b) the scheme does not fall within a prescribed class.

(1B) Regulations may—
   (a) provide for this Chapter not to apply in relation to a person of a prescribed description, or
   (b) apply this Chapter with prescribed modifications to occupational pension schemes—
      (i) which are not money purchase schemes, but
      (ii) where some of the benefits that may be provided are money purchase benefits."

Definitions For "occupational pension scheme", see the Pension Schemes Act 1993, s 1; for "pensionable service", see s 70(2), (3) of that Act; as to "member", see ss 93(2), 181(4) of that Act; for "normal pension age" see s 180(1) of that Act; for "modifications", "money purchase benefits", "money purchase scheme", "prescribed" and "regulations", see s 181(1) thereof. Note as to "a salary related occupational pension scheme", s 93(1A) of the 1993 Act, as inserted by sub-ss (1), (3) above.
References See paras 10.24, 10.25.

153 Right to guaranteed cash equivalent

After section 93 of the Pension Schemes Act 1993 there is inserted—

"93A Salary related schemes: right to statement of entitlement

(1)   The trustees or managers of a salary related occupational pension scheme must, on the application of statement of any member, provide the member with a written statement (in this Chapter referred to as a "statement of entitlement") of the amount of the cash equivalent at the guarantee date of any benefits which have accrued to or in respect of him under the applicable rules.

(2)   In this section—
"the applicable rules" has the same meaning as in section 94;
"the guarantee date" means the date by reference to which the value of the cash equivalent is calculated, and must be—
  (a) within the prescribed period beginning with the date of the application, and
  (b) within the prescribed period ending with the date on which the statement of entitlement is provided to the member.

(3)   Regulations may make provision in relation to applications for a statement of entitlement, including, in particular, provision as to the period which must elapse after the making of such an application before a member may make a further such application.

(4)   If, in the case of any scheme, a statement of entitlement has not been provided under this section, section 10 of the Pensions Act 1995 (power of the Regulatory Authority to impose civil penalties) applies to any trustee or manager who has failed to take all such steps as are reasonable to secure compliance with this section."

Definitions   As to "a salary related occupational pension scheme", see the Pension Schemes Act 1993, s 93(1A), as inserted by s 152(1), (3) of this Act; as to "member", see ss 93(2), 181(4) of the 1993 Act; as to "manager", see s 178(a) of that Act, as amended and repealed in part by ss 122, 177 of, and Sch 3, paras 22, 43 to, this Act; for "prescribed" and "regulations", see s 181(1) thereof. Note as to "statement of entitlement", s 93(1A) of the 1993 Act, as inserted by this section, and as to "the applicable rules" and "the guarantee date" see s 93A of that Act, as so inserted.
References   See para 10.27.

154 Right to guaranteed cash equivalent: supplementary

(1)   In paragraph (a) of section 94(1) of the Pension Schemes Act 1993—
  (a) after "occupational pension scheme" there is inserted "other than a salary related scheme", and
  (b) after "terminates" there is inserted "(whether before or after 1st January 1986)".

(2)   After that paragraph there is inserted—

"(aa) a member of a salary related occupational pension scheme who has received a statement of entitlement and has made a relevant application within three months beginning with the guarantee date in respect of that statement acquires a right to his guaranteed cash equivalent".

(3)   After that subsection there is inserted—

"(1A) For the purposes of subsection (1)(aa), a person's "guaranteed cash equivalent" is the amount stated in the statement of entitlement mentioned in that subsection."

(4)   In subsection (2) of that section, after the definition of "the applicable rules" there is inserted—

""the guarantee date" has the same meaning as in section 93A(2)".

(5) After that subsection there is inserted—

"(3) Regulations may provide that, in prescribed circumstances, subsection (1)(aa) does not apply to members of salary related occupational pension schemes or applies to them with prescribed modifications."

Definitions   As to "a salary related occupational pension scheme", see the Pension Schemes Act 1993, s 93(1A), as inserted by s 152(1), (3) of this Act; as to "statement of entitlement", see s 93A(1) of that Act, as inserted by s 153 of this Act; as to "member", see ss 93(2), 181(4) of the 1993 Act; and for "modifications", "prescribed" and "regulations", see s 181(1) thereof. Note as to "the guarantee date" s 94(2) of that Act, as amended by sub-s (4) above.
References   See para 10.27.

Penalties

155 Breach of regulations under the Pension Schemes Act 1993

(1)   For section 168 of the Pension Schemes Act 1993 (penalties for breach of regulations) there is substituted—

"168 Breach of regulations

(1)   Regulations under any provision of this Act (other than Chapter II of Part VII) may make such provision as is referred to in subsection (2) or (4) for the contravention of any provision contained in regulations made or having effect as if made under any provision of this Act.

(2)   The regulations may provide for the contravention to be an offence under this Act and for the recovery on summary conviction of a fine not exceeding level 5 on the standard scale.

(3)   An offence under any provision of the regulations may be charged by reference to any day or longer period of time; and a person may be convicted of a second or subsequent offence under such a provision by reference to any period of time following the preceding conviction of the offence.

(4)   The regulations may provide for a person who has contravened the provision to pay to the Regulatory Authority, within a prescribed period, a penalty not exceeding an amount specified in the regulations; and the regulations must specify different amounts in the case of individuals from those specified in other cases and any amount so specified may not exceed the amount for the time being specified in the case of individuals or, as the case may be, others in section 10(2)(a) of the Pensions Act 1995.

(5)   Regulations made by virtue of subsection (4) do not affect the amount of any penalty recoverable under that subsection by reason of an act or omission occurring before the regulations are made.

(6)   Where—
   (a) apart from this subsection, a penalty under subsection (4) is recoverable from a body corporate or Scottish partnership by reason of any act or omission of the body or partnership as a trustee of a trust scheme, and
   (b) the act or omission was done with the consent or connivance of, or is attributable to any neglect on the part of, any persons mentioned in subsection (7),
such a penalty is recoverable from each of those persons who consented to or connived in the act or omission or to whose neglect the act or omission was attributable.

(7)   The persons referred to in subsection (6)(b)—
   (a) in relation to a body corporate, are—

(i) any director, manager, secretary, or other similar officer of the body, or a person purporting to act in any such capacity, and
(ii) where the affairs of a body corporate are managed by its members, any member in connection with his functions of management, and
(b) in relation to a Scottish partnership, are the partners.

(8) Where the Regulatory Authority requires any person to pay a penalty by virtue of subsection (6), they may not also require the body corporate, or Scottish partnership, in question to pay a penalty in respect of the same act or omission.

(9) A penalty under subsection (4) is recoverable by the Authority and any such penalty recovered by the Authority must be paid to the Secretary of State.

(10) Where by reason of the contravention of any provision contained in regulations made, or having effect as if made, under this Act—
(a) a person is convicted of an offence under this Act, or
(b) a person pays a penalty under subsection (4),
then, in respect of that contravention, he shall not, in a case within paragraph (a), be liable to pay such a penalty or, in a case within paragraph (b), be convicted of such an offence.

(11) In this section "contravention" includes failure to comply, and "Scottish partnership" means a partnership constituted under the law of Scotland.

168A Offence in connection with the Registrar

(1) Any person who knowingly or recklessly provides the Registrar with information which is false or misleading in a material particular is guilty of an offence if the information—
(a) is provided in purported compliance with a requirement under section 6, or
(b) is provided otherwise than as mentioned in paragraph (a) above but in circumstances in which the person providing the information intends, or could reasonably be expected to know, that it would be used by the Registrar for the purpose of discharging his functions under this Act.

(2) Any person guilty of an offence under subsection (1) is liable—
(a) on summary conviction, to a fine not exceeding the statutory maximum,
(b) on conviction on indictment, to imprisonment or a fine, or both.".

(2) In section 186 of that Act (Parliamentary control of orders and regulations), in subsection (3), after paragraph (c) there is inserted "or

(d) regulations made by virtue of section 168(2)".

Definitions   For "the Registrar", see the Pension Schemes Act 1993, s 6(1)(b); for "prescribed", "regulations" and "the Regulatory Authority", see s 181(1) of that Act, as amended by s 122 of, Sch 3, paras 22, 44 to, this Act. Note as to "contravention" and "Scottish partnership", s 168(11) of the 1993 Act, as substituted by sub-s (1) above.
References   See para 2.32.

Pensions Ombudsman

156 Employment of staff by the Pensions Ombudsman

For section 145(4) of the Pension Schemes Act 1993 (staff of the Pensions Ombudsman), there is substituted—

"(4A) The Pensions Ombudsman may (with the approval of the Secretary of State as to numbers) appoint such persons to be employees of his as he thinks fit, on such terms and conditions as to remuneration and other matters as the Pensions Ombudsman may with the approval of the Secretary of State determine.

(4B) The Secretary of State may, on such terms as to payment by the Pensions Ombudsman as the Secretary of State thinks fit, make available to the Pensions Ombudsman such additional staff and such other facilities as he thinks fit.

(4C) Any function of the Pensions Ombudsman, other than the determination of complaints made and disputes referred under this Part, may be performed by any—
  (a) employee appointed by the Pensions Ombudsman under subsection (4A), or
  (b) member of staff made available to him by the Secretary of State under subsection (4B),
who is authorised for that purpose by the Pensions Ombudsman."

References   See para 4.10.

157 Jurisdiction of Pensions Ombudsman

(1) Sections 146 to 151 of the Pension Schemes Act 1993 are amended as shown in subsections (2) to (11).

(2) In section 146 (investigations concerning the trustees or managers of schemes), for subsections (1) to (4) there is substituted—

"(1) The Pensions Ombudsman may investigate and determine the following complaints and disputes—
  (a) a complaint made to him by or on behalf of an actual or potential beneficiary of an occupational or personal pension scheme who alleges that he has sustained injustice in consequence of maladministration in connection with any act or omission of a person responsible for the management of the scheme,
  (b) a complaint made to him—
    (i) by or on behalf of a person responsible for the management of an occupational pension scheme who in connection with any act or omission of another person responsible for the management of the scheme, alleges maladministration of the scheme, or
    (ii) by or on behalf of the trustees or managers of an occupational pension scheme who in connection with any act or omission of any trustee or manager of another such scheme, allege maladministration of the other scheme,
  and in any case falling within sub-paragraph (ii) references in this Part to the scheme to which the complaint relates is to the other scheme referred to in that paragraph,
  (c) any dispute of fact or law which arises in relation to an occupational or personal pension scheme between—
    (i) a person responsible for the management of the scheme, and
    (ii) an actual or potential beneficiary,
  and which is referred to him by or on behalf of the actual or potential beneficiary, and
  (d) any dispute of fact or law which arises between the trustees or managers of an occupational pension scheme and—
    (i) another person responsible for the management of the scheme, or
    (ii) any trustee or manager of another such scheme,

and which is referred to him by or on behalf of the person referred to in sub-paragraph (i) or (ii); and in any case falling within sub-paragraph (ii) references in this Part to the scheme to which the reference relates is to the scheme first mentioned in that paragraph.

(2) Complaints and references made to the Pensions Ombudsman must be made to him in writing.

(3) For the purposes of this Part, the following persons (subject to subsection (4)) are responsible for the management of an occupational pension scheme—
  (a) the trustees or managers, and
  (b) the employer;

but, in relation to a person falling within one of those paragraphs, references in this Part to another person responsible for the management of the same scheme are to a person falling within the other paragraph.

(3A) For the purposes of this Part, a person is responsible for the management of a personal pension scheme if he is a trustee or manager of the scheme.

(4) Regulations may provide that, subject to any prescribed modifications or exceptions, this Part shall apply in the case of an occupational or personal pension scheme in relation to any prescribed person or body of persons where the person or body—
  (a) is not a trustee or manager or employer, but
  (b) is concerned with the financing or administration of, or the provision of benefits under, the scheme,
as if for the purposes of this Part he were a person responsible for the management of the scheme".

(3) In subsection (7) of that section, for ""authorised complainants"" there is substituted "actual or potential beneficiaries".

(4) In section 147 (death, insolvency etc), in subsections (1) and (2), for "authorised complainant" there is substituted "actual or potential beneficiary" and for "the authorised complainant's" there is substituted "his".

(5) In subsection (3) of that section, for "an authorised complainant" there is substituted "a person by whom, or on whose behalf, a complaint or reference has been made under this Part".

(6) In section 148 (staying court proceedings), in subsection (5), for paragraphs (a) and (b) there is substituted—

  "(a) the person by whom, or on whose behalf, the complaint or reference has been made,
  (b) any person responsible for the management of the scheme to which the complaint or reference relates".

(7) In section 149 (procedure on investigation), in subsection (1)(a), for "the trustees and managers of the scheme concerned" there is substituted "any person (other than the person by whom, or on whose behalf, the complaint or reference was made) responsible for the management of the scheme to which the complaint or reference relates".

(8) In section 150 (investigations: further provisions), in subsection (1)(a), for "any trustee or manager of the scheme concerned" there is substituted "any person responsible for the management of the scheme to which the complaint or reference relates".

(9) In section 151 (determinations of Pensions Ombudsman), for subsection (1)(a) and (b) there is substituted—

"(a) to the person by whom, or on whose behalf, the complaint or reference was made, and
(b) to any person (if different) responsible for the management of the scheme to which the complaint or reference relates".

(10) In subsection (2) of that section, for "the trustees or managers of the scheme concerned" there is substituted "any person responsible for the management of the scheme to which the complaint or reference relates".

(11) In subsection (3) of that section, for paragraphs (a) to (c) there is substituted—

"(a) the person by whom, or on whose behalf, the complaint or reference was made,
(b) any person (if different) responsible for the management of the scheme to which the complaint or reference relates, and
(c) any person claiming under a person falling within paragraph (a) or (b)".

(12) In Part I of Schedule 1 to the Tribunals and Inquiries Act 1992 (tribunals under the direct supervision of the Council on Tribunals), in paragraph 35(e), for "section 146(2)" there is substituted "section 146(1)(c) and (d)".

Definitions As to "occupational pension scheme" and "personal pension scheme", see the Pension Schemes Act 1993, s 1; as to "manager", see s 178(a) of that Act, as amended and repealed in part by ss 122, 177 of, and Sch 3, paras 22, 43, Sch 7, Pt I to, this Act; for "modifications", "prescribed" and "regulations", see s 181(1) of that Act; for "employer", see s 181(1)–(3) of the 1993 Act, and, in the case of s 181(2), by s 122 of, Sch 3, paras 22, 44, to, this Act, and, in the case of s 181(3), by s 177, Sch 5, paras 22, 77(b), Sch 7, Pts III, IV. Note as to the "persons . . . responsible for the management of an occupational pension scheme", s 146(3) of the 1993 Act, as inserted by sub-ss (1), (2) above; and as to "a person . . . responsible for the management of a personal pension scheme" s 146(3A) of the 1993 Act, as so inserted.
References See paras 4.3–4.6.

158 Costs and expenses

In section 149 of the Pension Schemes Act 1993—
(a) after subsection (3)(b) there is inserted "and

(c) for the payment by the Ombudsman of such travelling and other allowances (including compensation for loss of remunerative time) as the Secretary of State may determine, to—
(i) actual or potential beneficiaries of a scheme to which a complaint or reference relates, or
(ii) persons appearing and being heard on behalf of such actual or potential beneficiaries,
who attend at the request of the Ombudsman any oral hearing held in connection with an investigation into the complaint or dispute.", and

(b) at the end of subsection (3)(a), "and" is omitted.

References See para 4.8.

159 Disclosing information

(1) In section 149 of the Pension Schemes Act 1993, after subsection (4) there is added—

"(5) The Pensions Ombudsman may disclose any information which he obtains for the purposes of an investigation under this Part to any person to whom subsection (6) applies, if the Ombudsman considers that the disclosure would enable or assist that person to discharge any of his functions.

(6) This subsection applies to the following—
  (a) the Regulatory Authority,
  (b) the Pensions Compensation Board,
  (c) the Registrar,
  (d) any department of the Government (including the government of Northern Ireland),
  (e) the Bank of England,
  (f) the Friendly Societies Commission,
  (g) the Building Societies Commission,
  (h) an inspector appointed by the Secretary of State under Part XIV of the Companies Act 1985 or section 94 or 177 of the Financial Services Act 1986,
  (j) an inspector appointed by the Department of Economic Development in Northern Ireland under Part XV of the Companies (Northern Ireland) Order 1986,
  (k) a person authorised under section 106 of the Financial Services Act 1986 to exercise powers conferred by section 105 of that Act,
  (l) a designated agency or transferee body or the competent authority within the meaning of that Act, and
  (m) a recognised self-regulating organisation, recognised professional body, recognised investment exchange or recognised clearing house, within the meaning of that Act.
(7) The Secretary of State may by order—
  (a) amend subsection (6) by adding any person or removing any person for the time being specified in that subsection, or
  (b) restrict the circumstances in which, or impose conditions subject to which, disclosure may be made to any person for the time being specified in that subsection."

(2) In section 151 of that Act, in subsection (7)(a), after "this section" there is inserted—

"(aa) in disclosing any information under section 149(5)".

Definitions For "the Registrar", see the Pension Schemes Act 1993, s 6(1)(b); "the Regulatory Authority", see s 181(1) of that Act, as amended by s 122 of, Sch 3, paras 22, 44 to, this Act.
References See para 4.9.

160 Interest on late payment of benefit

After section 151 of the Pension Schemes Act 1993 there is inserted—

"151A Interest on late payment of benefit

Where under this Part the Pensions Ombudsman directs a person responsible for the management of an occupational or personal pension scheme to make any payment in respect of benefit under the scheme which, in his opinion, ought to have been paid earlier, his direction may also require the payment of interest at the prescribed rate".

References See para 4.7.

Modification and winding up of schemes

161 Repeal of sections 136 to 143 of the Pension Schemes Act 1993

Sections 136 to 141 (modification) and 142 and 143 (winding up) of the Pension Schemes Act 1993 are repealed.

References See paras 2.39, 9.13.

Personal pensions

162 Annual increase in rate of personal pension

(1) This section applies to any pension provided to give effect to protected rights of a member of a personal pension scheme if—
  (a) there is in force, or was in force at any time after the appointed day, an appropriate scheme certificate issued in accordance with Chapter I of Part III (certification) of the Pension Schemes Act 1993, and
  (b) apart from this section, the annual rate of the pension would not be increased each year by at least the appropriate percentage of that rate.

(2) Where a pension to which this section applies, or any part of it, is attributable to contributions in respect of employment carried on on or after the appointed day—
  (a) the annual rate of the pension, or
  (b) if only part of the pension is attributable to contributions in respect of employment carried on on or after the appointed day, so much of the annual rate as is attributable to that part,
must be increased annually by at least the appropriate percentage.

Definitions For "annual rate", "appropriate percentage", "pension" and "protected rights", see s 163(3). By virtue of s 176, for "personal pension scheme", see the Pension Schemes Act 1993, s 1. For "employment" cf s 181(1) of the 1993 Act, and for "member", cf s 11(4) thereof.
References See paras 6.13, 14.15.

163 Section 162: supplementary

(1) The first increase required by section 162 in the rate of a pension must take effect not later than the first anniversary of the date on which the pension is first paid; and subsequent increases must take effect at intervals of not more than twelve months.

(2) Where the first such increase is to take effect on a date when the pension has been in payment for a period of less than 12 months, the increase must be of an amount at least equal to one twelfth of the amount of the increase so required (apart from this subsection) for each complete month in that period.

(3) In section 162 and this section—
  "annual rate", in relation to a pension, means the annual rate of the pension, as previously increased under the rules of the scheme or under section 162,
  "the appointed day" means the day appointed under section 180 for the commencement of section 162,
  "appropriate percentage", in relation to an increase in the whole or part of the annual rate of a pension, means the revaluation percentage for the revaluation period the reference period for which ends with the last preceding 30th September before the increase is made (expressions used in this definition having the same meaning as in paragraph 2 of Schedule 3 to the Pension Schemes Act 1993 (methods of revaluing accrued pension benefits)),
  "pension", in relation to a scheme, means any pension in payment under the scheme and includes an annuity,
  "protected rights" has the meaning given by section 10 of the Pension Schemes Act 1993 (money purchase benefits).

References See paras 6.13, 14.15.

164 Power to reject notice choosing appropriate personal pension scheme

In section 44 of the Pension Schemes Act 1993 (earner's chosen scheme)—

(a) in subsection (1), after paragraph (b) there is inserted—

"then, unless the Secretary of State rejects the notice on either or both of the grounds mentioned in subsection (1A)", and

(b) after that subsection there is inserted—

"(1A) The grounds referred to in subsection (1) are that the Secretary of State is of the opinion—
    (a) that section 31(5) is not being complied with in respect of any members of the scheme,
    (b) that, having regard to any other provisions of sections 26 to 32 and 43 to 45, it is inexpedient to allow the scheme to be the chosen scheme of any further earners".

Definitions   For "earner", see by virtue of the Pension Schemes Act 1993, s 181(1), the Social Security Contributions and Benefits Act 1992, ss 3, 4, 112.
References   See para 14.16.

Levy

165 Levy

For section 175 of the Pension Schemes Act 1993 (levies towards meeting certain costs and grants) there is substituted—

"175 Levies towards certain expenditure

(1) For the purpose of meeting expenditure—
    (a) under section 6,
    (b) under Part X and section 174, or
    (c) of the Regulatory Authority (including the establishment of the authority and, if the authority are appointed as Registrar under section 6 of this Act, their expenditure as Registrar),
regulations may make provision for imposing levies in respect of prescribed occupational or prescribed personal pension schemes.

(2) Any levy imposed under subsection (1) is payable to the Secretary of State by or on behalf of—
    (a) the administrators of any prescribed public service pension scheme,
    (b) the trustees or managers of any other prescribed occupational or prescribed personal pension scheme, or
    (c) any other prescribed person,
at prescribed rates and at prescribed times.

(3) Regulations made by virtue of subsection (1)—
    (a) in determining the amount of any levy in respect of the Regulatory Authority, must take account (among other things) of any amounts paid to the Secretary of State under section 168(4) of this Act or section 10 of the Pensions Act 1995, and
    (b) in determining the amount of expenditure in respect of which any levy is to be imposed, may take one year with another and, accordingly, may have regard to expenditure estimated to be incurred in current or future periods and to actual expenditure incurred in previous periods (including periods ending before the coming into force of this subsection).

(4) Regulations may make provision for imposing a levy in respect of prescribed occupational pension schemes for the purpose of meeting expenditure of the Pensions Compensation Board (including the establishment of the Board).

(5) Any levy imposed under subsection (4) is payable to the Board by or on behalf of—
  (a) the trustees of any prescribed occupational pension scheme, or
  (b) any other prescribed person,
at prescribed times and at a rate, not exceeding the prescribed rate, determined by the Board.

(6) In determining the amount of expenditure in respect of which any levy under subsection (4) is to be imposed, the Board, and regulations made by virtue of subsection (5), may take one year with another and, accordingly, may have regard to expenditure estimated to be incurred in current or future periods and to actual expenditure incurred in previous periods (including periods ending before the coming into force of this subsection).

(7) Notice of the rates determined by the Board under subsection (5) must be given to prescribed persons in the prescribed manner.

(8) An amount payable by a person on account of a levy imposed under this section shall be a debt due from him to the appropriate person, that is—
  (a) if the levy is imposed under subsection (1), the Secretary of State, and
  (b) if the levy is imposed under subsection (4), the Board,
and an amount so payable shall be recoverable by the appropriate person accordingly or, if the appropriate person so determines, be recoverable by the Registrar on behalf of the appropriate person.

(9) Without prejudice to the generality of subsections (1) and (4), regulations under this section may include provision relating to—
  (a) the collection and recovery of amounts payable by way of levy under this section, or
  (b) the circumstances in which any such amount may be waived."

Definitions For "occupational pension scheme", "personal pension scheme" and "public service pension scheme", see the Pension Schemes Act 1993, s 1; for "the registrar", s 6(1)(b) of that Act; for "prescribed", "regulations" and "the Regulatory Authority", see s 181(1) of that Act, as amended by s 122 of, Sch 3, paras 22, 44 to, this Act.
References See paras 2.10, 2.11, 11.6, 14.10.

Pensions on divorce, etc

166 Pensions on divorce etc

(1) In the Matrimonial Causes Act 1973, after section 25A there is inserted—

"25B Pensions

(1) The matters to which the court is to have regard under section 25(2) above include—
  (a) in the case of paragraph (a), any benefits under a pension scheme which a party to the marriage has or is likely to have, and
  (b) in the case of paragraph (h), any benefits under a pension scheme which, by reason of the dissolution or annulment of the marriage, a party to the marriage will lose the chance of acquiring,
and, accordingly, in relation to benefits under a pension scheme, section 25(2)(a) above shall have effect as if "in the foreseeable future" were omitted.

(2) In any proceedings for a financial provision order under section 23 above in a case where a party to the marriage has, or is likely to have, any benefit under a pension scheme, the court shall, in addition to considering any other matter which it is required to consider apart from this subsection, consider—

(a) whether, having regard to any matter to which it is required to have regard in the proceedings by virtue of subsection (1) above, such an order (whether deferred or not) should be made, and
(b) where the court determines to make such an order, how the terms of the order should be affected, having regard to any such matter.

(3) The following provisions apply where, having regard to any benefits under a pension scheme, the court determines to make an order under section 23 above.

(4) To the extent to which the order is made having regard to any benefits under a pension scheme, the order may require the trustees or managers of the pension scheme in question, if at any time any payment in respect of any benefits under the scheme becomes due to the party with pension rights, to make a payment for the benefit of the other party.

(5) The amount of any payment which, by virtue of subsection (4) above, the trustees or managers are required to make under the order at any time shall not exceed the amount of the payment which is due at that time to the party with pension rights.

(6) Any such payment by the trustees or managers—
   (a) shall discharge so much of the trustees or managers liability to the party with pension rights as corresponds to the amount of the payment, and
   (b) shall be treated for all purposes as a payment made by the party with pension rights in or towards the discharge of his liability under the order.

(7) Where the party with pension rights may require any benefits which he has or is likely to have under the scheme to be commuted, the order may require him to commute the whole or part of those benefits; and this section applies to the payment of any amount commuted in pursuance of the order as it applies to other payments in respect of benefits under the scheme.

25C Pensions: lump sums

(1) The power of the court under section 23 above to order a party to a marriage to pay a lump sum to the other party includes, where the benefits which the party with pension rights has or is likely to have under a pension scheme include any lump sum payable in respect of his death, power to make any of the following provision by the order.

(2) The court may—
   (a) if the trustees or managers of the pension scheme in question have power to determine the person to whom the sum, or any part of it, is to be paid, require them to pay the whole or part of that sum, when it becomes due, to the other party,
   (b) if the party with pension rights has power to nominate the person to whom the sum, or any part of it, is to be paid, require the party with pension rights to nominate the other party in respect of the whole or part of that sum,
   (c) in any other case, require the trustees or managers of the pension scheme in question to pay the whole or part of that sum, when it becomes due, for the benefit of the other party instead of to the person to whom, apart from the order, it would be paid.

(3) Any payment by the trustees or managers under an order made under section 23 above by virtue of this section shall discharge so much of the trustees, or managers, liability in respect of the party with pension rights as corresponds to the amount of the payment.

25D Pensions: supplementary

(1) Where—
 (a) an order made under section 23 above by virtue of section 25B or 25C above imposes any requirement on the trustees or managers of a pension scheme ("the first scheme") and the party with pension rights acquires transfer credits under another pension scheme ("the new scheme") which are derived (directly or indirectly) from a transfer from the first scheme of all his accrued rights under that scheme (including transfer credits allowed by that scheme), and
 (b) the trustees or managers of the new scheme have been given notice in accordance with regulations,

the order shall have effect as if it has been made instead in respect of the trustees or managers of the new scheme; and in this subsection "transfer credits" has the same meaning as in the Pension Schemes Act 1993.

(2) Regulations may—
 (a) in relation to any provision of sections 25B or 25C above which authorises the court making an order under section 23 above to require the trustees or managers of a pension scheme to make a payment for the benefit of the other party, make provision as to the person to whom, and the terms on which, the payment is to be made,
 (b) require notices to be given in respect of changes of circumstances relevant to such orders which include provision made by virtue of sections 25B and 25C above,
 (c) make provision for the trustees or managers of any pension scheme to provide, for the purposes of orders under section 23 above, information as to the value of any benefits under the scheme,
 (d) make provision for the recovery of the administrative expenses of—
  (i) complying with such orders, so far as they include provision made by virtue of sections 25B and 25C above, and
  (ii) providing such information,
  from the party with pension rights or the other party,
 (e) make provision for the value of any benefits under a pension scheme to be calculated and verified, for the purposes of orders under section 23 above, in a prescribed manner,

and regulations made by virtue of paragraph (e) above may provide for that value to be calculated and verified in accordance with guidance which is prepared and from time to time revised by a prescribed person and approved by the Secretary of State.

(3) In this section and sections 25B and 25C above—
 (a) references to a pension scheme include—
  (i) a retirement annuity contract, or
  (ii) an annuity, or insurance policy, purchased or transferred for the purpose of giving effect to rights under a pension scheme,
 (b) in relation to such a contract or annuity, references to the trustees or managers shall be read as references to the provider of the annuity,
 (c) in relation to such a policy, references to the trustees or managers shall be read as references to the insurer,

and in section 25B(1) and (2) above, references to benefits under a pension scheme include any benefits by way of pension, whether under a pension scheme or not.

(4) In this section and sections 25B and 25C above—
 "the party with pension rights" means the party to the marriage who has or is likely to have benefits under a pension scheme and "the other party" means the other party to the marriage,

"pension scheme" means an occupational pension scheme or a personal pension scheme (applying the definitions in section 1 of the Pension Schemes Act 1993, but as if the reference to employed earners in the definition of "personal pension scheme" were to any earners),
"prescribed" means prescribed by regulations, and
"regulations" means regulations made by the Lord Chancellor;

and the power to make regulations under this section shall be exercisable by statutory instrument, which shall be subject to annulment in pursuance of a resolution of either House of Parliament."

(2) In section 25(2)(h) of that Act (loss of chance to acquire benefits), "(for example, a pension)" is omitted.

(3) In section 31 of that Act (variation, discharge, etc of orders)—
  (a) in subsection (2), after paragraph (d) there is inserted—

"(dd) any deferred order made by virtue of section 23(1)(c) (lump sums) which includes provision made by virtue of—
  (i) section 25B(4), or
  (ii) section 25C,
(provision in respect of pension rights)", and

  (b) after subsection (2A) there is inserted—

"(2B) Where the court has made an order referred to in subsection (2)(dd)(ii) above, this section shall cease to apply to the order on the death of either of the parties to the marriage".

(4) Nothing in the provisions mentioned in subsection (5) applies to a court exercising its powers under section 23 of the Matrimonial Causes Act 1973 (financial provision in connection with divorce proceedings, etc) in respect of any benefits under a pension scheme (within the meaning of section 25B(1) of the Matrimonial Causes Act 1973) which a party to the marriage has or is likely to have.

(5) The provisions referred to in subsection (4) are—
  (a) section 203(1) and (2) of the Army Act 1955, 203(1) and (2) of the Air Force Act 1955, 128G(1) and (2) of the Naval Discipline Act 1957 or 159(4) and (4A) of the Pension Schemes Act 1993 (which prevent assignment, or orders being made restraining a person from receiving anything which he is prevented from assigning),
  (b) section 91 of this Act,
  (c) any provision of any enactment (whether passed or made before or after this Act is passed) corresponding to any of the enactments mentioned in paragraphs (a) and (b), and
  (d) any provision of the scheme in question corresponding to any of those enactments.

(6) Subsections (3) to (7) of section 25B, and section 25C of the Matrimonial Causes Act 1973, as inserted by this section, do not affect the powers of the court under section 31 of that Act (variation, discharge, etc) in relation to any order made before the commencement of this section.

Definitions   For the meaning of "the court" in the Matrimonial Causes Act 1973, see s 52(1) of that Act. For "enactment" see s 176 of this Act. Note as to "the first scheme" and "the new scheme", s 25D(1) of the 1973 Act, as inserted by sub-s (1) above; as to "a pension scheme" and "trustees or managers", s 25D(3) of that Act, as so inserted, and as to "the party with pension rights", "the other party", "pension scheme", "prescribed" and "regulations", s 25D(4) of the 1973 Act, as so inserted.
References   See paras 12.1–12.9, 12.19.

167 Pensions on divorce, etc: Scotland

(1) In section 8(1) (orders for financial provision) of the Family Law (Scotland) Act 1985 ("the 1985 Act"), after paragraph (b) there is inserted—

"(ba) an order under section 12A(2) or (3) of this Act;".

(2) In section 10 of the 1985 Act (sharing of value of matrimonial property)—
    (a) in subsection (5)—
        (i) after "party" there is inserted "(a)"; and
        (ii) for "or occupational pension scheme or similar arrangement" there is substituted—

"or similar arrangement; and
(b) in any benefits under a pension scheme which either party has or may have (including such benefits payable in respect of the death of either party),
which is"; and

    (b) after subsection (7) there is inserted—

"(8) The Secretary of State may by regulations make provision—
    (a) for the value of any benefits under a pension scheme to be calculated and verified, for the purposes of this Act, in a prescribed manner;
    (b) for the trustees or managers of any pension scheme to provide, for the purposes of this Act, information as to that value, and for the recovery of the administrative expenses of providing such information from either party,

and regulations made by virtue of paragraph (a) above may provide for that value to be calculated and verified in accordance with guidance which is prepared and from time to time revised by a prescribed body and approved by the Secretary of State.

(9) Regulations under subsection (8) above shall be made by statutory instrument which shall be subject to annulment in pursuance of a resolution of either House of Parliament.

(10) In this section—
    "benefits under a pension scheme" includes any benefits by way of pension, whether under a pension scheme or not;
    "pension scheme" means—
        (a) an occupational pension scheme or a personal pension scheme (applying the definitions in section 1 of the Pension Schemes Act 1993, but as if the reference to employed earners in the definition of "personal pension scheme" were to any earners);
        (b) a retirement annuity contract; or
        (c) an annuity, or insurance policy, purchased or transferred for the purpose of giving effect to rights under a pension scheme falling within paragraph (a) above; and
    "prescribed" means prescribed by regulations.

(11) In this section, references to the trustees or managers of a pension scheme—
    (a) in relation to a contract or annuity referred to in paragraph (b) or (c) of the definition of "pension scheme" in subsection (10) above, shall be read as references to the provider of the annuity;
    (b) in relation to an insurance policy referred to in paragraph (c) of that definition, shall be read as a reference to the insurer.".

(3) After section 12 of the 1985 Act there is inserted—

"12A Orders for payment of capital sum: pensions lump sums

(1) This section applies where the court makes an order under section 8(2) of this Act for payment of a capital sum (a "capital sum order") by a party to the marriage ("the liable party") in circumstances where—
- (a) the matrimonial property within the meaning of section 10 of this Act includes any rights or interests in benefits under a pension scheme which the liable party has or may have (whether such benefits are payable to him or in respect of his death); and
- (b) those benefits include a lump sum payable to him or in respect of his death.

(2) Where the benefits referred to in subsection (1) above include a lump sum payable to the liable party, the court, on making the capital sum order, may make an order requiring the trustees or managers of the pension scheme in question to pay the whole or part of that sum, when it becomes due, to the other party to the marriage ("the other party").

(3) Where the benefits referred to in subsection (1) above include a lump sum payable in respect of the death of the liable party, the court, on making the capital sum order, may make an order—
- (a) if the trustees or managers of the pension scheme in question have power to determine the person to whom the sum, or any part of it, is to be paid, requiring them to pay the whole or part of that sum, when it becomes due, to the other party;
- (b) if the liable party has power to nominate the person to whom the sum, or any part of it, is to be paid, requiring the liable party to nominate the other party in respect of the whole or part of that sum;
- (c) in any other case, requiring the trustees or managers of the pension scheme in question to pay the whole or part of that sum, when it becomes due, to the other party instead of to the person to whom, apart from the order, it would be paid.

(4) Any payment by the trustees or managers under an order under subsection (2) or (3) above—
- (a) shall discharge so much of the trustees' or managers' liability to or in respect of the liable party as corresponds to the amount of the payment; and
- (b) shall be treated for all purposes as a payment made by the liable party in or towards the discharge of his liability under the capital sum order.

(5) Where the liability of the liable party under the capital sum order has been discharged in whole or in part, other than by a payment by the trustees or managers under an order under subsection (2) or (3) above, the court may, on an application by any person having an interest, recall any order under either of those subsections or vary the amount specified in such an order, as appears to the court appropriate in the circumstances.

(6) Where—
- (a) an order under subsection (2) or (3) above imposes any requirement on the trustees or managers of a pension scheme ("the first scheme") and the liable party acquires transfer credits under another scheme ("the new scheme") which are derived (directly or indirectly) from a transfer from the first scheme of all his accrued rights under that scheme; and
- (b) the trustees or managers of the new scheme have been given notice in accordance with regulations under subsection (8) below,

the order shall have effect as if it had been made instead in respect of the trustees or managers of the new scheme; and in this subsection "transfer credits" has the same meaning as in the Pension Schemes Act 1993.

(7) Without prejudice to subsection (6) above, the court may, on an application by any person having an interest, vary an order under subsection (2) or (3) above by substituting for the trustees or managers specified in the order the trustees or managers of any other pension scheme under which any lump sum referred to in subsection (1) above is payable to the liable party or in respect of his death.

(8) The Secretary of State may by regulations—
   (a) require notices to be given in respect of changes of circumstances relevant to orders under subsection (2) or (3) above;
   (b) make provision for the recovery of the administrative expenses of complying with such orders from the liable party or the other party.

(9) Regulations under subsection (8) above shall be made by statutory instrument which shall be subject to annulment in pursuance of a resolution of either House of Parliament.

(10) Subsection (10) (other than the definition of "benefits under a pension scheme") and subsection (11) of section 10 of this Act shall apply for the purposes of this section as those subsections apply for the purposes of that section.".

(4) Nothing in the provisions mentioned in section 166(5) above applies to a court exercising its powers under section 8 (orders for financial provision on divorce, etc) or 12A (orders for payment of capital sum: pensions lump sums) of the 1985 Act in respect of any benefits under a pension scheme which fall within subsection (5)(b) of section 10 of that Act ("pension scheme" having the meaning given in subsection (10) of that section).

References See paras 12.1–12.9, 12.19.

168 War pensions for widows: effect of remarriage

(1) In determining whether a pension is payable to a person as a widow under any of the enactments mentioned in subsection (3) in respect of any period beginning on or after the commencement of this section, no account may be taken of the fact that the widow has married another if, before the beginning of that period, the marriage has been terminated or the parties have been judicially separated.

(2) For the purposes of this section—
   (a) the reference to the termination of a marriage is to the termination of the marriage by death, dissolution or annulment, and
   (b) the reference to judicial separation includes any legal separation obtained in a country or territory outside the British Islands and recognised in the United Kingdom;

and for those purposes a divorce, annulment or legal separation obtained in a country or territory outside the British Islands must, if the Secretary of State so determines, be treated as recognised in the United Kingdom even though no declaration as to its validity has been made by any court in the United Kingdom.

(3) The enactments referred to in subsection (1) are—
   (a) The Naval, Military and Air Forces Etc (Disablement and Death) Service Pensions Order 1983, and any order re-enacting the provisions of that order,
   (b) The Personal Injuries (Civilians) Scheme 1983, and any subsequent scheme made under the Personal Injuries (Emergency Provisions) Act 1939,
   (c) any scheme made under the Pensions (Navy, Army, Air Force and Mercantile Marine) Act 1939 or the Polish Resettlement Act 1947 applying the provisions of any such order as is referred to in paragraph (a),
   (d) the order made under section 1(5) of the Ulster Defence Regiment Act 1969 concerning pensions and other grants in respect of disablement or death due to service in the Ulster Defence Regiment.

Definitions For "enactment", see s 176. Note as to "termination of a marriage" and "judicial separation", sub-s (2) above.
References See para 12.10.

169 Extensions of Pensions Appeal Tribunals Act 1943

(1) The Pensions Appeal Tribunals Act 1943 is amended as follows.

(2) In section 1 (appeals against rejection of war pension claims made in respect of members of armed forces)—
   (a) in subsection (1), after "administered by the Minister" there is inserted "or under a scheme made under section 1 of the Polish Resettlement Act 1947", and
   (b) in subsections (3) and (3A), for "or Order of His Majesty" there is substituted ", Order of Her Majesty or scheme".

(3) In section 7 (application of Act to past decisions and assessments)—
   (a) in subsection (2), at the beginning there is inserted "Subject to subsection (2A) of this section,", and
   (b) after that subsection, there is inserted—

"(2A) Subsection (2) of this section shall not apply in relation to any decision given by the Minister before the passing of this Act which corresponds, apart from any difference of the kind referred to in that subsection, with such a decision as is referred to in section 1 of this Act in respect of claims made under the scheme referred to in that section.".

(4) In section 10 (power to modify sections 1 to 4 by Order in Council), in subsections (1) and (2), for "or Order of His Majesty" there is substituted ", Order of Her Majesty or scheme".

(5) In section 12 (interpretation), in the definition of "relevant service"—
   (a) for "or Order of His Majesty" there is substituted ", Order of Her Majesty or scheme", and
   (b) for "or Order" there is substituted ", Order or scheme".

(6) In the Schedule (constitution, jurisdiction and procedure of Pensions Appeal Tribunals), in paragraph 3(2), after paragraph (b) there is inserted—

   "(ba) if the claim was made under the scheme referred to in section 1 of this Act in respect of a person who is treated under the scheme as an officer, shall be a retired or demobilised officer of Her Majesty's naval, military or air forces;
   (bb) if the claim was made under the aforesaid scheme in respect of a person who is treated under the scheme as a soldier, shall be a discharged or demobilised member of any of the said forces who was not at the time of his discharge or demobilisation an officer;".

Definitions For "Her Majesty's naval, military or air forces" and "the minister", see the Pensions Appeals Tribunals Act 1943, s 12(1), as amended by sub-s (5) above.
References See para 12.10.

Official and public service pensions

170 Pensions for dependants of the Prime Minister etc

(1) Section 27 of the Parliamentary and Other Pensions Act 1972 (application of certain provisions with modifications in relation to the Prime Minister and the Speaker) is amended as follows.

(2) For subsection (1)(b) (amount by reference to which dependant's pension calculated) there is substituted—

"(b) for the purposes of that scheme, that person's basic or prospective pension were of an amount equal to his section 26 entitlement".

(3) After subsection (1) there is inserted—

"(1A) For the purposes of subsection (1)(b), the amount of a person's section 26 entitlement—
   (a) where at the time of his death he was entitled to receive a pension under section 26 of this Act (whether or not, by virtue of subsection (2) of that section, the pension was payable), is the annual amount of the pension to which he was entitled under that section at the time when he ceased to hold that office or (if later) on 28th February 1991, and
   (b) where at the time of his death he held office as Prime Minister and First Lord of the Treasury or as Speaker of the House of Commons, is the annual amount of the pension to which he would have been entitled under that section if he had ceased to hold office immediately before his death,
but in either case, any provision which deems such a pension to have begun on a day earlier than the day referred to in section 8(2) of the Pensions (Increase) Act 1971 shall be disregarded."

(4) For the purposes of the Pensions (Increase) Act 1971, a pension payable under section 27 of the Parliamentary and Other Pensions Act 1972 in respect of a person who ceased to hold the office of Prime Minister and First Lord of the Treasury or Speaker of the House of Commons before 28th February 1991 shall be deemed to have begun on that date.

(5) Where a person—
   (a) is entitled to receive a pension under that section by reason of the death of a person who, at any time before the commencement of this section, held the office of Prime Minister and First Lord of the Treasury or Speaker of the House of Commons, and
   (b) the amount of that pension determined in accordance with subsection (6) is greater than the amount of the pension determined in accordance with subsections (1) to (4),
it shall be determined in accordance with subsection (6).

(6) The annual amount of the pension shall be determined as if—
   (a) subsections (1) to (3) had not been enacted, and
   (b) for the purposes of the Pensions (Increase) Act 1971, the pension had begun on the day following the date of the death.

(7) This section has effect, and shall be treated as having had effect, in relation to any person who becomes entitled to a pension payable under section 27 of the Parliamentary and Other Pensions Act 1972 on or after 15th December 1994.

References   See paras 1.21, 13.18.

171 Equal treatment in relation to official pensions

(1) Section 3 of the Pensions (Increase) Act 1971 (qualifying conditions for pensions increase) is amended as follows.

(2) In subsection (2)(c), "is a woman who" is omitted.

(3) In subsection (10)—
   (a) for "woman is in receipt of a pension" there is substituted "person is in receipt of a pension the whole or any part of", and
   (b) for "woman and that pension" there is substituted "person and that pension or part".

(4) In subsection (11)—
   (a) for "woman's" there is substituted "person's", and
   (b) for "woman" there is substituted "person",

and accordingly for "she" there is substituted "he".

(5) This section shall have effect, and shall be deemed to have had effect, in relation to pensions commencing after 17th May 1990, and in relation to so much of any such pension as is referable to service on or after that date.

Definitions For "pension", see the Pensions (Increase) Act 1971, s 8.
References See paras 1.21, 8.14.

172 Information about public service schemes

(1) In prescribed circumstances, the Secretary of State may provide information to any prescribed person in connection with the following questions—
   (a) whether an individual who during any period—
      (i) has been eligible to be an active member of an occupational pension scheme under the Superannuation Act 1972, but
      (ii) has instead made contributions to a personal pension scheme,
   has suffered loss as a result of a contravention which is actionable under section 62 of the Financial Services Act 1986 (actions for damages in respect of contravention of rules etc made under the Act), and
   (b) if so, what payment would need to be made to the occupational scheme in respect of the individual to restore the position to what it would have been if the individual had been an active member of the occupational scheme throughout the period in question,

and may impose on that person reasonable fees in respect of administrative expenses incurred in providing that information.

(2) Where—
   (a) such an individual as is mentioned in subsection (1) is admitted or readmitted as an active member of an occupational pension scheme under the Superannuation Act 1972, or
   (b) a payment is made to the Secretary of State in respect of such an individual for the purpose mentioned in paragraph (b) of that subsection,

the Secretary of State may impose on any prescribed person reasonable fees in respect of administrative expenses incurred in connection with the admission, readmission or payment.

(3) In the case of an occupational pension scheme under section 1 of the Superannuation Act 1972 (superannuation of civil servants), the references in subsections (1) and (2) to the Secretary of State shall be read as references to the Minister for the Civil Service, or such person as may be prescribed.

(4) In the case of an occupational pension scheme under section 7 of the Superannuation Act 1972 (superannuation of persons employed in local government etc), the references in subsections (1) and (2) to the Secretary of State shall be read as references to a prescribed person.

(5) In this section—
   "prescribed" means—

Pensions Act 1995, s 172

        (i)   in the case of a scheme made under section 1 of the Superannuation Act 1972, prescribed by a scheme made by the Minister for the Civil Service, or

        (ii) in any other case, prescribed by regulations made by the Secretary of State, and

"active member", in relation to an occupational pension scheme, has the same meaning as in Part I.

Definitions   By virtue of s 176, for "occupational pension scheme" and "personal pension scheme", see the Pension Schemes Act 1993, s 1. Note as to "prescribed" and "active member", sub-s (5) above.
References   See para 14.19.

General minor and consequential amendments

173 General minor and consequential amendments

Schedule 6, which makes general minor and consequential amendments, shall have effect.

Definitions   For "the Authority", cf s 1(1).
References   See para 10.28.

Subordinate legislation etc

174 Orders and regulations (general provisions)

(1) Any power under this Act to make regulations or orders (except a power of the court or the Authority to make orders) shall be exercisable by statutory instrument.

(2) Except in so far as this Act provides otherwise, any power conferred by it to make regulations or an order may be exercised—

    (a) either in relation to all cases to which the power extends, or in relation to those cases subject to specified exceptions, or in relation to any specified cases or classes of case,

    (b) so as to make, as respects the cases in relation to which it is exercised—

        (i)   the full provision to which the power extends or any less provision (whether by way of exception or otherwise),

        (ii) the same provision for all cases in relation to which the power is exercised, or different provision for different cases or different classes of case or different provision as respects the same case or class of case for different purposes of this Act, or

        (iii) any such provision either unconditionally or subject to any specified condition,

and where such a power is expressed to be exercisable for alternative purposes it may be exercised in relation to the same case for any or all of those purposes; and any power to make regulations or an order for the purposes of any one provision of this Act shall be without prejudice to any power to make regulations or an order for the purposes of any other provision.

(3) Any power conferred by this Act to make regulations or an order includes power to make such incidental, supplementary, consequential or transitional provision as appears to the authority making the regulations or order to be expedient for the purposes of the regulations or order.

(4) Regulations made by the Secretary of State may, for the purposes of or in connection with the coming into force of any provisions of this Act, make any such provision as could be made, by virtue of subsection (4)(a) of section 180, by an order bringing those provisions into force.

References   See para 1.24.

175 Parliamentary control of orders and regulations

(1) Subject to subsections (2) and (3), a statutory instrument which contains any regulations or order made under this Act shall be subject to annulment in pursuance of a resolution of either House of Parliament.

(2) A statutory instrument which contains any regulations made by virtue of—
    (a) section 64(4),
    (b) section 78(6),
    (c) section 116(1), or
    (d) section 149

or order under section 10(2) must not be made unless a draft of the instrument has been laid before and approved by a resolution of each House of Parliament.

(3) Subsection (1) does not apply to an order under section 180.

References   See para 1.24.

General

176 Interpretation

In this Act—
    "enactment" includes an enactment comprised in subordinate legislation (within the meaning of the Interpretation Act 1978),
    "occupational pension scheme" and "personal pension scheme" have the meaning given by section 1 of the Pension Schemes Act 1993,

and the definition of "enactment" shall apply for the purposes of section 114 as if "Act" in section 21(1) of the Interpretation Act 1978 included any enactment.

References   See para 1.22.

177 Repeals

The enactments shown in Schedule 7 are repealed to the extent specified in the third column.

References   See para 1.26.

178 Extent

(1) Subject to the following provisions, this Act does not extend to Northern Ireland.

(2) Sections 1, 2, 21(3), 68(5), 78, 79, 80(4), 150, 168, 170(4) to (7), 172 and 179 extend to Northern Ireland.

(3) The amendment by this Act of an enactment which extends to Northern Ireland extends also to Northern Ireland.

Definitions   For "enactment", see s 176.
References   See para 1.21.

179 Northern Ireland

An Order in Council under paragraph 1(1)(b) of Schedule 1 to the Northern Ireland Act 1974 (legislation for Northern Ireland in the interim period) which states that it is made only for purposes corresponding to those of this Act—

(a) shall not be subject to paragraph 1(4) and (5) of that Schedule (affirmative resolution of both Houses of Parliament), but
(b) shall be subject to annulment in pursuance of a resolution of either House.

References See para 1.21.

180 Commencement

(1) Subject to the following provisions, this Act shall come into force on such day as the Secretary of State may by order made by statutory instrument appoint and different days may be appointed for different purposes.

(2) The following provisions shall come into force on the day this Act is passed—
  (a) subject to the provisions of Schedule 4, Part II,
  (b) section 168,
  (c) sections 170 and 171,
  (d) section 179,
and any repeal in Schedule 7 for which there is a note shall come into force in accordance with that note.

(3) Section 166 shall come into force on such day as the Lord Chancellor may by order made by statutory instrument appoint and different days may be appointed for different purposes.

(4) Without prejudice to section 174(3), the power to make an order under this section includes power—
  (a) to make transitional adaptations or modifications—
    (i) of the provisions brought into force by the order, or
    (ii) in connection with those provisions, of any provisions of this Act, or the Pension Schemes Act 1993, then in force, or
  (b) to save the effect of any of the repealed provisions of that Act, or those provisions as adapted or modified by the order,
as it appears to the Secretary of State expedient, including different adaptations or modifications for different periods.

References See para 1.20.

181 Short title

This Act may be cited as the Pensions Act 1995.

SCHEDULES

SCHEDULE 1

Section 1

OCCUPATIONAL PENSIONS REGULATORY AUTHORITY

General

1. The Authority shall not be regarded as the servant or agent of the Crown, or as enjoying any status, privilege or immunity of the Crown; and its property shall not be regarded as property of, or property held on behalf of, the Crown.

2. The Authority may do anything (except borrow money) which is calculated to facilitate the discharge of their function

Tenure of members

3. Subject to the following provisions, a person shall hold and vacate office as chairman or other member of the Authority in accordance with the terms of the instrument appointing him.

4. If a member of the Authority becomes or ceases to be chairman, the Secretary of State may vary the terms of the instrument appointing him to be a member so as to alter the date on which he is to vacate office.

5. A person may at any time resign office as chairman or other member of the Authority by giving written notice of his resignation signed by him to the Secretary of State.

6.—(1) The chairman of the Authority may at any time be removed from office by notice in writing given to him by the Secretary of State.

(2) If a person ceases to be chairman by virtue of sub-paragraph (1), he shall cease to be a member of the Authority.

7.—(1) If the Secretary of State is satisfied that a member of the Authority other than the chairman—
    (a) has been absent from meetings of the Authority for a period longer than three consecutive months without the Authority's permission,
    (b) has become bankrupt or made an arrangement with his creditors, or
    (c) is unable or unfit to discharge the functions of a member, the Secretary of State may remove that member by notice in writing.

(2) In the application of sub-paragraph (1) to Scotland—
    (a) the reference to a member's having become bankrupt shall be read as a reference to sequestration of the member's estate having been awarded, and
    (b) the reference to a member having made an arrangement with his creditors shall be read as a reference to his having made a trust deed for the behoof of his creditors or a composition contract.

Expenses, remuneration, etc

8.—(1) The Secretary of State may pay the Authority such sums as he thinks fit towards their expenses.

(2) The Authority may pay, or make provision for paying, to or in respect of the chairman or any other member such salaries or other remuneration, and such pensions, allowances, fees, expenses or gratuities, as the Secretary of State may determine.

(3) Where a person ceases to be a member of the Authority otherwise than on the expiration of his term of office and it appears to the Secretary of State that there are circumstances which make it right for that person to receive compensation, the Authority may make to that person a payment of such amount as the Secretary of State may determine.

Parliamentary disqualification

9. In Part II of Schedule 1 to the House of Commons Disqualification Act 1975, and in Part II of Schedule 1 to the Northern Ireland Assembly Disqualification Act 1975 (bodies all members of which are disqualified), there is inserted at the appropriate place—

"The Occupational Pensions Regulatory Authority".

The Ombudsman

10. In the Parliamentary Commissioner Act 1967, in Schedule 2 (departments and authorities subject to investigation), there is inserted at the appropriate place—

"The Occupational Pensions Regulatory Authority".

Staff

11.—(1) There shall be a chief executive and, with the approval of the Secretary of State as to numbers, other employees of the Authority.

(2) The first chief executive shall be appointed by the Secretary of State on such terms and conditions as to remuneration and other matters as the Secretary of State may determine.

(3) Any reappointment of the first chief executive, and the appointment of the second and any subsequent chief executive, shall be made by the Authority, with the approval of the Secretary of State, on such terms and conditions as to remuneration and other matters as the Authority may, with the approval of the Secretary of State, determine.

(4) The other employees shall be appointed by the Authority on such terms and conditions as to remuneration and other matters as the Authority may, with the approval of the Secretary of State, determine.

(5) The Secretary of State may, on such terms as to payment by the Authority as he thinks fit, make available to the Authority such additional staff and such other facilities as he thinks fit.

The Superannuation Act 1972 (c 11)

12.—(1) Employment with the Authority shall be included among the kinds of employment to which a scheme under section 1 of the Superannuation Act 1972 can apply, and accordingly in Schedule 1 to that Act (in which those kinds of employment are listed), at the end of the list of Other Bodies there is inserted—

"The Occupational Pensions Regulatory Authority"

(2) The Authority must pay to the Treasury, at such times as the Treasury may direct, such sums as the Treasury may determine in respect of the increase attributable to this paragraph in the sums payable out of money provided by Parliament under the Superannuation Act 1972.

Proceedings

13.—(1) The Secretary of State may make regulations generally as to the procedure to be followed by the Authority in the exercise of their functions and the manner in which their functions are to be exercised.

(2) Such regulations may in particular make provision—
  (a) as to the hearing of parties, the taking of evidence and the circumstances (if any) in which a document of any prescribed description is to be treated, for the purposes of any proceedings before the Authority, as evidence, or conclusive evidence, of any prescribed matter,
  (b) as to the time to be allowed for making any application or renewed application to the Authority (whether for an order or determination of the Authority or for the review of a determination, or otherwise),
  (c) as to the manner in which parties to any proceedings before the Authority may or are to be represented for the purposes of the proceedings.

(3) Regulations under sub-paragraph (1) may provide for enabling the Authority to summon persons—
  (a) to attend before them and give evidence (including evidence on oath) for any purposes of proceedings in connection with an occupational pension scheme,
  (b) to produce any documents required by the Authority for those purposes, or
  (c) to furnish any information which the Authority may require relating to any such scheme which is the subject matter of proceedings pending before them.

14.—(1) The Authority may establish a committee for any purpose.

(2) The quorum of the Authority shall be such as they may determine, and the Authority may regulate their own procedure and that of any of their committees.

(3) The Authority may authorise the chairman or any other member, the chief executive or any committee established by the Authority to exercise such of the Authority's functions as they may determine.

(4) This paragraph is subject to regulations made by virtue of paragraph 13 and to section 96(5).

Validity

15. The validity of any proceedings of the Authority, or of any of their committees, shall not be affected by any vacancy among the members or by any defect in the appointment of any member.

Accounts

16.—(1) It shall be the duty of the Authority—
   (a) to keep proper accounts and proper records in relation to the accounts,
   (b) to prepare in respect of each financial year of the Authority a statement of accounts, and
   (c) to send copies of the statement to the Secretary of State and to the Comptroller and Auditor General before the end of the month of August next following the financial year to which the statement relates.

(2) The statement of accounts shall comply with any directions given by the Secretary of State with the approval of the Treasury as to—
   (a) the information to be contained in it,
   (b) the manner in which the information contained in it is to be presented, or
   (c) the methods and principles according to which the statement is to be prepared,

and shall contain such additional information as the Secretary of State may with the approval of the Treasury require to be provided for the information of Parliament.

(3) The Comptroller and Auditor General shall examine, certify and report on each statement received by him in pursuance of this paragraph and shall lay copies of each statement and of his report before each House of Parliament.

(4) In this paragraph, "financial year" means the period beginning with the date on which the Authority is established and ending with the next following 31st March, and each successive period of twelve months.

Other expenses

17. The Authority may—
   (a) pay to persons attending meetings of the Authority at the request of the Authority such travelling and other allowances (including compensation for loss of remunerative time) as the Secretary of State may determine, and
   (b) pay to persons from whom the Authority may decide to seek advice, as being persons considered by the Authority to be specially qualified to advise them on particular matters, such fees as the Secretary of State may determine.

Fees

18. Regulations made by the Secretary of State may authorise the Authority to charge fees for their services in respect of the modification of an occupational pension scheme on an application made under section 69, or under any corresponding provision in force in Northern Ireland, including services in connection with the drawing up of any order of the Authority made on application.

Application of seal and proof of instruments

19.—(1) The fixing of the common seal of the Authority shall be authenticated by the signature of the secretary of the Authority or some other person authorised by them to act for that purpose.

(2) Sub-paragraph (1) does not apply in relation to any document which is or is to be signed in accordance with the law of Scotland.

20. A document purporting to be duly executed under the seal of the Authority shall be received in evidence and shall, unless the contrary is proved, be deemed to be so executed.

Definitions   For "the Authority", see s 1(1); for "prescribed" and "regulations", see s 124(1). By virtue of s 176, for "occupational pension scheme" and "personal pension scheme", see the Pension Schemes Act 1993, s 1. Note as to "financial year", para 16(4) above.
References   See Chapter 2.

SCHEDULE 2

Section 78

PENSIONS COMPENSATION BOARD

General

1. The Compensation Board shall not be regarded as the servant or agent of the Crown, or as enjoying any status, privilege or immunity of the Crown; and their property shall not be regarded as property of, or property held on behalf of, the Crown.

2. The Compensation Board may do anything which is calculated to facilitate the discharge of their functions, or is incidental or conducive to their discharge, including in particular—
  (a) giving guarantees or indemnities in favour of any person, or
  (b) making any other agreement or arrangement with or for the benefit of any person.

Tenure of members

3. Subject to the following provisions, a person shall hold and vacate office as chairman or other member of the Compensation Board in accordance with the terms of the instrument appointing him.

4. If a member of the Compensation Board becomes or ceases to be chairman, the Secretary of State may vary the terms of the instrument appointing him to be a member so as to alter the date on which he is to vacate office.

5. A person may at any time resign office as chairman or other member of the Compensation Board by giving written notice of his resignation signed by him to the Secretary of State.

6. The chairman or any other member of the Compensation Board may at any time be removed from office by notice in writing given to him by the Secretary of State.

Expenses, remuneration, etc

7.—(1) The Compensation Board may pay, or make provision for paying, to or in respect of the chairman or any other member such salaries or other remuneration, and such pensions, allowances, fees, expenses or gratuities, as the Secretary of State may determine.

(2) Where a person ceases to be a member of the Compensation Board otherwise than on the expiration of his term of office and it appears to the Secretary of State that there are circumstances which make it right for that person to receive compensation, the Compensation Board may make to that person a payment of such amount as the Secretary of State may determine.

Parliamentary disqualification

8. In Part II of Schedule 1 to the House of Commons Disqualification Act 1975, and in Part II of Schedule 1 to the Northern Ireland Assembly Disqualification Act 1975 (bodies all members of which are disqualified), there is inserted at the appropriate place—

"The Pensions Compensation Board".

The Ombudsman

9. In the Parliamentary Commissioner Act 1967, in Schedule 2 (departments and authorities subject to investigation), there is inserted at the appropriate place—

"The Pensions Compensation Board".

Staff

10.—(1) The Compensation Board may (with the approval of the Secretary of State as to numbers) appoint such persons to be employees of theirs as the Board think fit, on such terms and conditions as to remuneration and other matters as the Board may with the approval of the Secretary of State determine.

(2) The Secretary of State may, on such terms as to payment by the Compensation Board as he thinks fit, make available to the Compensation Board such additional staff and such other facilities as he thinks fit.

(3) The Pensions Ombudsman may, on such terms as to payment by the Compensation Board as he thinks fit, make available to the Compensation Board such of his employees as he thinks fit.

The Superannuation Act 1972 (c 11)

11.—(1) Employment with the Compensation Board shall be included among the kinds of employment to which a scheme under section 1 of the Superannuation Act 1972 can apply, and accordingly in Schedule 1 to that Act (in which those kinds of employment are listed), at the end of the list of Other Bodies there is inserted—

"The Pensions Compensation Board".

(2) The Compensation Board must pay to the Treasury, at such times as the Treasury may direct, such sums as the Treasury may determine in respect of the increase attributable to this paragraph in the sums payable out of money provided by Parliament under the Superannuation Act 1972.

Proceedings

12. The Secretary of State may make regulations generally as to the procedure to be followed by the Compensation Board in the exercise of their functions and the manner in which their functions are to be exercised.

13. The Compensation Board must meet at least once in the first twelve months of their existence, and at least once in each succeeding period of twelve months.

14.—(1) The Compensation Board may (subject to sub-paragraph (2)) authorise any of their members to exercise such of the Compensation Board's functions as the Board may determine.

(2) The Compensation Board may not authorise any of their members to—
   (a) determine whether section 81 applies to an application for compensation under section 82 in respect of any occupational pension scheme,
   (b) determine the amount of any payment under section 83,
   (c) determine whether any payment should be made under section 84 or the amount of any such payment, or
   (d) exercise such functions of the Compensation Board as may be prescribed.

(3) The quorum of the Compensation Board shall be such as they may determine, and the Board may regulate their own procedure.

(4) The decisions of the Compensation Board must be taken by agreement of a majority of the members of the Compensation Board who are present at the meeting where the decision is taken.

(5) This paragraph is subject to regulations made by virtue of paragraph 12.

15.—(1) Where the Compensation Board notify any person of a decision on any matter dealt with by them by means of a formal hearing, or on review, they shall furnish a written statement of the reasons for the decision.

(2) Any statement by the Compensation Board of their reasons for a decision, whether the statement is given by them in pursuance of this paragraph or otherwise, shall be taken to form part of the decision, and accordingly to be incorporated in the record.

Validity

16. The validity of any proceedings of the Compensation Board shall not be affected by any vacancy among the members or by any defect in the appointment of any member.

Accounts

17.—(1) The Compensation Board must—
   (a) keep proper accounts and proper records in relation to the accounts,
   (b) prepare in respect of each financial year of the Compensation Board a statement of accounts, and
   (c) send copies of the statement to the Secretary of State and to the Comptroller and Auditor General before the end of the month of August next following the financial year to which the statement relates.

(2) The statement of accounts must comply with any directions given by the Secretary of State with the approval of the Treasury as to—
   (a) the information to be contained in it,
   (b) the manner in which the information contained in it is to be presented, or
   (c) the methods and principles according to which the statement is to be prepared,

and must contain such additional information as the Secretary of State may with the approval of the Treasury require to be provided for the information of Parliament.

(3) The Comptroller and Auditor General must examine, certify and report on each statement received by him in pursuance of this paragraph and must lay copies of each statement and of his report before each House of Parliament.

(4) In this paragraph, "financial year" means the period beginning with the date on which the Board is established and ending with the next following 5th April, and each successive period of twelve months.

Other expenses

18.—(1) The Compensation Board may—
  (a) pay to persons attending meetings of the Compensation Board at the request of the Board such travelling and other allowances (including compensation for loss of remunerative time) as the Board may determine, and
  (b) pay to persons from whom the Compensation Board may decide to seek advice, as being persons considered by the Board to be specially qualified to advise them on particular matters, such fees as the Board may determine.

(2) A determination under sub-paragraph (1) requires the approval of the Secretary of State.

Application of seal and proof of instruments

19.—(1) The fixing of the common seal of the Compensation Board shall be authenticated by the signature of the chairman of the Compensation Board or some other person authorised by them to act for that purpose.

(2) Sub-paragraph (1) above does not apply in relation to any document which is or is to be signed in accordance with the law of Scotland.

20. A document purporting to be duly executed under the seal of the Compensation Board shall be received in evidence and shall, unless the contrary is proved, be deemed to be so executed.

Definitions For "the Compensation Board", see s 78(1); for "prescribed" and "regulations", see s 124(1). By virtue of s 176, for "occupational pension scheme", see the Pension Schemes Act 1993, s 1. Note as to "financial year", para 17(4) above.
References See Chapter 11.

SCHEDULE 3

Section 122

AMENDMENTS CONSEQUENTIAL ON PART I

The Employment Protection (Consolidation) Act 1978 (c 44)

1. The Employment Protection (Consolidation) Act 1978 is amended as follows.

2. In section 60A(4) (dismissal on grounds of assertion of statutory right), after paragraph (c) there is added—

   "(d) the rights conferred by sections 42, 43 and 46 of the Pensions Act 1995."

3. In section 71(2B) (compensation award for failure to comply with section 69 not to be made), at the end there is added "of this Act or section 46 of the Pensions Act 1995."

4. In section 72(2) (special award), at the end there is added "of this Act or section 46 of the Pensions Act 1995."

5. In section 73(6B) (calculation of basic award), at the end there is added "of this Act or section 46 of the Pensions Act 1995."

6. In section 77(1) (interim relief), after "57A(1)(a) and (b)" there is inserted "of this Act or section 46 of the Pensions Act 1995".

7. In section 77A(1) (procedure on application for interim relief), after "57A(1)(a) and (b)" there is inserted "of this Act or section 46 of the Pensions Act 1995".

8. In section 133(1) (conciliation officers), after paragraph (e) there is added—

   "or

   (ea) arising out of a contravention, or alleged contravention, of section 42, 43 or 46 of the Pensions Act 1995."

9. In section 136(1) (appeals to Employment Appeal Tribunal), alter paragraph (f) there is added—

"(g) the Pensions Act 1995;"

10. In section 138 (application of Act to Crown employment), in subsection (1), after "and section 53" there is inserted "of this Act and sections 42 to 46 of the Pensions Act 1995;"

The Insurance Companies Act 1982 (c 50)

11.—(1) In the Table in sub-paragraph (1) of paragraph 3 of Schedule 2B to the Insurance Companies Act 1982, after the entry relating to the Building Societies Commission there is inserted—

"The Occupational Pensions Regulatory Authority.	Functions under the Pension Schemes Act 1993 or the Pensions Act 1995, or any enactment in force in Northern Ireland corresponding to either of them."

(2) In sub-paragraph (9) of that paragraph, after paragraph (b) there is added—

"or

(c) persons involved in the operation of occupational pension schemes (within the meaning of the Pension Schemes Act 1993 or, in Northern Ireland, the Pension Schemes (Northern Ireland) Act 1993)",

and accordingly the "or" after paragraph (a) is omitted.

The Companies Act 1985 (c 6)

12. In section 449(1) of the Companies Act 1985, after paragraph (df) there is inserted—

"(dg) for the purpose of enabling or assisting the Occupational Pensions Regulatory Authority to discharge their functions under the Pension Schemes Act 1993 or the Pensions Act 1995 or any enactment in force in Northern Ireland corresponding to either of them,".

The Bankruptcy (Scotland) Act 1985 (c 66)

13. In section 31(1) of the Bankruptcy (Scotland) Act 1985 (vesting in permanent trustee of debtor's estate on sequestration), after "Act" there is inserted "and section 91(3) of the Pensions Act 1995".

14. In section 32 of that Act (vesting of estate, and dealings of debtor, after sequestration), after subsection (2) there is inserted—

"(2A) The amount allowed for the purposes specified in paragraphs (a) and (b) of subsection (2) above shall not be less than the total amount of any income received by the debtor—
 (a) by way of guaranteed minimum pension; and
 (b) in respect of his protected rights as a member of a pension scheme,
"guaranteed minimum pension" and "protected rights" having the same meanings as in the Pension Schemes Act 1993.".

The Insolvency Act 1986 (c 45)

15. In section 310 of the Insolvency Act 1986 (income payments orders)—
 (a) in subsection (2), after "income of the bankrupt" there is inserted "when taken together with any payments to which subsection (8) applies", and
 (b) at the end of subsection (7), there is added—

"and any payment under a pension scheme but excluding any payment to which subsection (8) applies.

(8) This subsection applies to—
 (a) payments by way of guaranteed minimum pension; and
 (b) payments giving effect to the bankrupt's protected rights as a member of a pension scheme.

(9) In this section, "guaranteed minimum pension" and "protected rights" have the same meaning as in the Pension Schemes Act 1993.".

The Building Societies Act 1986 (c 53)

16. In section 53(15) of the Building Societies Act 1986, after paragraph (b) there is added—

"or

(c) persons involved in the operation of occupational pension schemes (within the meaning of the Pension Schemes Act 1993 or, in Northern Ireland, the Pension Schemes (Northern Ireland) Act 1993)",

and accordingly the "or" after paragraph (a) is omitted.

The Financial Services Act 1986 (c 60)

17. In section 180(1) of the Financial Services Act 1986, after paragraph (m) there is inserted—

"(mm) for the purpose of enabling or assisting the Occupational Pensions Regulatory Authority or the Pensions Compensation Board to discharge their functions under the Pension Schemes Act 1993 or the Pensions Act 1995 or any enactment in force in Northern Ireland corresponding to either of them;"

The Banking Act 1987 (c 22)

18.—(1) In the Table in subsection (1) of section 84 of the Banking Act 1987, at the end there is added—

"20. The Occupational Pensions Regulatory Authority. | Functions under the Pension Schemes Act 1993 or the Pensions Act 1995 or any enactment in force in Northern Ireland corresponding to either of them."

(2) In subsection (10) of that section, after paragraph (b) there is added—

"or

(c) persons involved in the operation of occupational pension schemes (within the meaning of the Pension Schemes Act 1993 or, in Northern Ireland, the Pension Schemes (Northern Ireland Act 1993)",

and accordingly the "or" after paragraph (a) is omitted.

The Companies Act 1989 (c 40)

19. In the Table in section 87(4) of the Companies Act 1989, after the entry relating to the Building Societies Commission there is inserted—

"The Occupational Pensions Regulatory Authority. | Functions under the Pension Schemes Act 1993 or the Pensions Act 1995 or any enactment in force in Northern Ireland corresponding to either of them.

The Friendly Societies Act 1992 (c 40)

20. In the Table in section 64(5) of the Friendly Societies Act 1992, after the entry relating to the Building Societies Commission there is inserted—

"The Occupational Pensions Regulatory Authority. | Functions under the Pension Schemes Act 1993 or the Pensions Act 1995 or any enactment in force in Northern Ireland corresponding to either of them.

The Tribunals and Inquiries Act 1992 (c 53)

21. The Tribunals and Inquiries Act 1992 is amended as follows—
    (a) in section 7(2) (concurrence required for removal of tribunal members), after "(e)" there is inserted "(g) or (h)",
    (b) in section 10 (reasons to be given on request), at the end of subsection (5) there is added—

    "(ba) to decisions of the Pensions Compensation Board referred to in paragraph 35(h) of Schedule 1",

    (c) in section 14 (restricted application of the Act in relation to certain tribunals), after subsection (1) there is inserted—

    "(1A) In this Act—
    (a) references to the working of the Occupational Pensions Regulatory Authority referred to in paragraph 35(g) of Schedule 1 are references to their working so far as relating to matters dealt with by them by means of a formal hearing or on review, and
    (b) references to procedural rules for the Authority are references to regulations under—
        (i) section 96(5) of the Pensions Act 1995 (procedure to be adopted with respect to reviews), or
        (ii) paragraph 13 of Schedule 1 to that Act (procedure of the Authority), so far as the regulations relate to procedure on any formal hearing by the Authority.", and

    (d) in paragraph 35 of Schedule 1 (tribunals under the direct supervision of the Council on Tribunals: pensions), after paragraph (f) there is inserted—

    "(g) the Occupational Pensions Regulatory Authority established by section 1 of the Pensions Act 1995;
    (h) the Pensions Compensation Board established by section 78 of that Act".

The Pension Schemes Act 1993 (c 48)

22. The Pension Schemes Act 1993 is amended as follows.

23. In section 6 (registration)—
    (a) after subsection (5) there is inserted—

    "(5A) The regulations may make provision for information obtained by or furnished to the Registrar under or for the purposes of this Act to be disclosed to the Regulatory Authority or the Pensions Compensation Board", and

    (b) in subsection (7), for "(5)" there is substituted "(5A)".

24. Sections 77 to 80 (assignment, forfeiture etc of short service benefit) are repealed.

25. Sections 102 to 108 (annual increase in pensions in payment) are repealed.

26. Section 112 (restriction on investment in employer-related assets) is repealed.

27. Section 114 (documents for members etc) is repealed.

28. Section 116 (regulations as to auditors) is repealed.

29. Section 118 (equal access) is repealed.

30. Sections 119 to 122 (independent trustees) are repealed.

31. In section 129 (overriding requirements)—
    (a) in subsection (1), "Chapter I of Part V", "sections 119 to 122", "under Chapter I of Part V or" and "or sections 119 to 122" are omitted,
    (b) in subsection (2), for the words from "Chapter III" to "section 108)" there is substituted "and Chapter III of that Part", and
    (c) subsection (3)(a) is omitted.

32. In section 132 (conformity of schemes with requirements), "the equal access requirements" is omitted.

33. In section 133(1) (advice of the Board), "the equal access requirements" is omitted.

34. In section 134 (determination of questions)—
    (a) in subsection (3), "the equal access requirements", and
    (b) in subsection (4), "or the equal access requirements" and "or , as the case may be, section 118(1)",

are omitted.

35. In section 136(2)(e)(iv) (applications to modify schemes), "or the equal access requirements" is omitted.

36. In section 139(2) (functions of the Board), "the equal access requirements" is omitted.

37. In section 140(4) (effect of orders), paragraph (c) and the "and" immediately preceding it are omitted.

38. Section 144 (deficiencies in assets on winding up) is repealed.

39. In section 153 (power to modify Act)—
    (a) in subsection (1), the words from "and Chapter I" to "section 108" are omitted,
    (b) subsections (3) and (4) are omitted,
    (c) in subsection (5), "Chapter I of Part VII" is omitted, at the end of paragraph (b) there is inserted "or", and paragraph (d) and the preceding "or" are omitted, and
    (d) subsections (6) and (7) are omitted.

40. In section 154(1) (application of provisions to personal pension schemes), after "provision of this Act" there is inserted "or of sections 22 to 26 and 40 of the Pensions Act 1995".

41. In section 159 (inalienability of certain pensions), after subsection (4) there is inserted—

"(4A) Where a person—
    (a) is entitled or prospectively entitled as is mentioned in subsection (1), or
    (b) is entitled to such rights or to such a payment as is mentioned in subsection (4),

no order shall be made by any court the effect of which would be that he would be restrained from receiving anything the assignment of which is or would be made void by either of those subsections.

(4B) Subsection (4A) does not prevent the making of an attachment of earnings order under the Attachment of Earnings Act 1971."

42. In section 170 (determination of questions by Secretary of State), subsections (5) and (6) are omitted.

43. In section 178 (meaning of "trustee" and "manager") in paragraph (a), after "Administration Act 1992" there is inserted "or of sections 22 to 26 of the Pensions Act 1995", and the "or" after "Social Security Acts 1975 to 1991" is omitted.

44. In section 181 (general interpretation)—
    (a) in subsection (1)—
        (i) the definition of "equal access requirements" is omitted, and
        (ii) after the definition of "regulations" there is inserted—

    ""the Regulatory Authority" means the Occupational Pensions Regulatory Authority;", and

    (b) in subsection (2), for the words from "160" to "requirements" there is substituted "and 160".

45. In section 183 (sub-delegation), in subsection (3)—
    (a) for "97(1), 104(8) and 144(5)" there is substituted "and 97(1)",
    (b) the words from "or, in the case of" to "determined" are omitted, and
    (c) the words following paragraph (b) are omitted.

46. In section 185(1) (consultation about regulations), "I or" is omitted.

47. In Schedule 7 (re-enactment or amendment of certain provisions not in force), paragraphs 1 and 3 are omitted.

Definitions For the meaning of "bankrupt" in the Insolvency Act 1986, see s 381 thereof. For the meaning of "decision" in the Tribunals and Inquiries Act 1992, see s 14 thereof. For the meaning of "occupational pension scheme" in the Pension Schemes Act 1993, see s 1 thereof; for "protected rights", see s 10 of the 1993 Act, as amended by s 151 of, Sch 5, paras 18, 25 to, this Act; for "regulations" and "the Regulatory Authority", see 181(1) of that Act, as amended by paras 22, 44 above.
References See paras 6.4, 8.4, 12.12.

SCHEDULE 4

Section 126

EQUALISATION

PART I

PENSIONABLE AGES FOR MEN AND WOMEN

Rules for determining pensionable age

1. The following rules apply for the purposes of the enactments relating to social security, that is, the following Acts and the instruments made, or having effect as if made, under them: the Social Security Contributions and Benefits Act 1992, the Social Security Administration Act 1992 and the Pension Schemes Act 1993.

Rules

(1) A man attains pensionable age when he attains the age of 65 years.

(2) A woman born before 6th April 1950 attains pensionable age when she attains the age of 60.

(3) A woman born on any day in a period mentioned in column 1 of the following table attains pensionable age at the commencement of the day shown against that period in column 2.

(4) A woman born after 5th April 1955 attains pensionable age when she attains the age of 65.

TABLE

(1) *Period within which woman's birthday falls*	*(2)* *Day pensionable age attained*
6th April 1950 to 5th May 1950	6th May 2010
6th May 1950 to 5th June 1950	6th July 2010
6th June 1950 to 5th July 1950	6th September 2010
6th July 1950 to 5th August 1950	6th November 2010
6th August 1950 to 5th September 1950	6th January 2011
6th September 1950 to 5th October 1950	6th March 2011
6th October 1950 to 5th November 1950	6th May 2011
6th November 1950 to 5th December 1950	6th July 2011

Pensions Act 1995, Sch 4

(1) Period within which woman's birthday falls	(2) Day pensionable age attained
6th December 1950 to 5th January 1951	6th September 2011
6th January 1951 to 5th February 1951	6th November 2011
6th February 1951 to 5th March 1951	6th January 2012
6th March 1951 to 5th April 1951	6th March 2012
6th April 1951 to 5th May 1951	6th May 2012
6th May 1951 to 5th June 1951	6th July 2012
6th June 1951 to 5th July 1951	6th September 2012
6th July 1951 to 5th August 1951	6th November 2012
6th August 1951 to 5th September 1951	6th January 2013
6th September 1951 to 5th October 1951	6th March 2013
6th October 1951 to 5th November 1951	6th May 2013
6th November 1951 to 5th December 1951	6th July 2013
6th December 1951 to 5th January 1952	6th September 2013
6th January 1952 to 5th February 1952	6th November 2013
6th February 1952 to 5th March 1952	6th January 2014
6th March 1952 to 5th April 1952	6th March 2014
6th April 1952 to 5th May 1952	6th May 2014
6th May 1952 to 5th June 1952	6th July 2014
6th June 1952 to 5th July 1952	6th September 2014
6th July 1952 to 5th August 1952	6th November 2014
6th August 1952 to 5th September 1952	6th January 2015
6th September 1952 to 5th October 1952	6th March 2015
6th October 1952 to 5th November 1952	6th May 2015
6th November 1952 to 5th December 1952	6th July 2015
6th December 1952 to 5th January 1953	6th September 2015
6th January 1953 to 5th February 1953	6th November 2015

Pensions Act 1995, Sch 4

(1) *Period within which woman's birthday falls*	(2) *Day pensionable age attained*
6th February 1953 to 5th March 1953	6th January 2016
6th March 1953 to 5th April 1953	6th March 2016
6th April 1953 to 5th May 1953	6th May 2016
6th May 1953 to 5th June 1953	6th July 2016
6th June 1953 to 5th July 1953	6th September 2016
6th July 1953 to 5th August 1953	6th November 2016
6th August 1953 to 5th September 1953	6th January 2017
6th September 1953 to 5th October 1953	6th March 2017
6th October 1953 to 5th November 1953	6th May 2017
6th November 1953 to 5th December 1953	6th July 2017
6th December 1953 to 5th January 1954	6th September 2017
6th January 1954 to 5th February 1954	6th November 2017
6th February 1954 to 5th March 1954	6th January 2018
6th March 1954 to 5th April 1954	6th March 2018
6th April 1954 to 5th May 1954	6th May 2018
6th May 1954 to 5th June 1954	6th July 2018
6th June 1954 to 5th July 1954	6th September 2018
6th July 1954 to 5th August 1954	6th November 2018
6th August 1954 to 5th September 1954	6th January 2019
6th September 1954 to 5th October 1954	6th March 2019
6th October 1954 to 5th November 1954	6th May 2019
6th November 1954 to 5th December 1954	6th July 2019
6th December 1954 to 5th January 1955	6th September 2019
6th January 1955 to 5th February 1955	6th November 2019
6th February 1955 to 5th March 1955	6th January 2020
6th March 1955 to 5th April 1955	6th March 2020

References   See paras 8.15, 8.16, 13.14–13.17.

PART II

ENTITLEMENT TO CERTAIN PENSION AND OTHER BENEFITS

Pension increases for dependent spouses

2.—(1) For sections 83 and 84 of the Social Security Contributions and Benefits Act 1992 (pension increases for dependent wife or husband) there is substituted—

"83A Pension increase for spouse

(1) Subject to subsection (3) below, the weekly rate of a Category A or Category C retirement pension payable to a married pensioner shall, for any period mentioned in subsection (2) below, be increased by the amount specified in relation to the pension in Schedule 4, Part IV, column (3).

(2) The periods referred to in subsection (1) above are—
    (a) any period during which the pensioner is residing with the spouse, and
    (b) any period during which the pensioner is contributing to the maintenance of the spouse at a weekly rate not less than the amount so specified, and the spouse does not have weekly earnings which exceed that amount.

(3) Regulations may provide that for any period during which the pensioner is residing with the spouse and the spouse has earnings there shall be no increase of pension under this section".

(2) This paragraph shall have effect on or after 6th April 2010.

Category B retirement pensions

3.—(1) For sections 49 and 50 of the Social Security Contributions and Benefits Act 1992 (Category B retirement pensions for women) there is substituted—

"48A Category B retirement pension for married person

(1) A person who—
    (a) has attained pensionable age, and
    (b) on attaining that age was a married person or marries after attaining that age,
shall be entitled to a Category B retirement pension by virtue of the contributions of the other party to the marriage ("the spouse") if the following requirement is met.

(2) The requirement is that the spouse—
    (a) has attained pensionable age and become entitled to a Category A retirement pension, and
    (b) satisfies the conditions specified in Schedule 3, Part I, paragraph 5.

(3) During any period when the spouse is alive, a Category B retirement pension payable by virtue of this section shall be payable at the weekly rate specified in Schedule 4, Part I, paragraph 5.

(4) During any period after the spouse is dead, a Category B retirement pension payable by virtue of this section shall be payable at a weekly rate corresponding to—
    (a) the weekly rate of the basic pension, plus
    (b) half of the weekly rate of the additional pension,
determined in accordance with the provisions of sections 44 to 45A above as they apply in relation to a Category A retirement pension, but subject to section 46(2) above and the modification in section 48C(4) below.

(5) A person's Category B retirement pension payable by virtue of this section shall not be payable for any period falling before the day on which the spouse's entitlement is to be regarded as beginning for that purpose by virtue of section 5(1)(k) of the Administration Act.

48B Category B retirement pension for widows and widowers

(1) A person ("the pensioner") whose spouse died—
    (a) while they were married, and
    (b) after the pensioner attained pensionable age,

shall be entitled to a Category B retirement pension by virtue of the contributions of the spouse if the spouse satisfied the conditions specified in Schedule 3, Part I, paragraph 5.

(2) A Category B retirement pension payable by virtue of subsection (1) above shall be payable at a weekly rate corresponding to—
    (a) the weekly rate of the basic pension, plus
    (b) half of the weekly rate of the additional pension,
determined in accordance with the provisions of sections 44 to 45A above as they apply in relation to a Category A retirement pension, but subject to section 46(2) above and the modifications in subsection (3) below and section 48C(4) below.

(3) Where the spouse died under pensionable age, references in the provisions of sections 44 to 45A above as applied by subsection (2) above to the tax year in which the pensioner attained pensionable age shall be taken as references to the tax year in which the spouse died.

(4) A person who has attained pensionable age ("the pensioner") whose spouse died before the pensioner attained that age shall be entitled to a Category B retirement pension by virtue of the contributions of the spouse if—
    (a) where the pensioner is a woman, the following condition is satisfied, and
    (b) where the pensioner is a man, the following condition would have been satisfied on the assumption mentioned in subsection (7) below.

(5) The condition is that the pensioner—
    (a) is entitled (or is treated by regulations as entitled) to a widow's pension by virtue of section 38 above, and
    (b) became entitled to that pension in consequence of the spouse's death.

(6) A Category B retirement pension payable by virtue of subsection (4) above shall be payable—
    (a) where the pensioner is a woman, at the same weekly rate as her widow's pension, and
    (b) where the pensioner is a man, at the same weekly rate as that of the pension to which he would have been entitled by virtue of section 38 above on the assumption mentioned in subsection (7) below.

(7) The assumption referred to in subsections (4) and (6) above is that a man is entitled to a pension by virtue of section 38 above on the same terms and conditions, and at the same rate, as a woman.

48C Category B retirement pension: general

(1) Subject to the provisions of this Act, a person's entitlement to a Category B retirement pension shall begin on the day on which the conditions of entitlement become satisfied and shall continue for life.

(2) In any case where—
    (a) a person would, apart from section 43(1) above, be entitled both to a Category A and to a Category B retirement pension; and
    (b) section 47(1) above would apply for the increase of the Category A retirement pension,
section 47(1) above shall be taken as applying also for the increase of the Category B retirement pension, subject to reduction or extinguishment of the increase by the application of section 47(2) above or section 46(5) of the Pensions Act.

(3) In the case of a pensioner whose spouse died on or before 5th April 2000, sections 48A(4)(b) and 48B(2)(b) above shall have effect with the omission of the words "half of".

(4) In the application of the provisions of sections 44 to 45A above by virtue of sections 48A(4) or 48B(2) above, references in those provisions to the pensioner shall be taken as references to the spouse".

(2) Section 48A of that Act (as inserted by this paragraph) does not confer a right to a Category B retirement pension on a man by reason of his marriage to a woman who was born before 6th April 1950.

(3) Section 48B of that Act (as inserted by this paragraph) does not confer a right to a Category B retirement pension on a man who attains pensionable age before 6th April 2010; and section 51 of that Act does not confer a right to a Category B retirement pension on a man who attains pensionable age on or after that date.

Home responsibilities protection

4.—(1) In paragraph 5 of Schedule 3 to the Social Security Contributions and Benefits Act 1992 (contribution conditions for entitlement to retirement pension), in sub-paragraph (7)(a) (condition that contributor must have paid or been credited with contributions of the relevant class for not less than the requisite number of years modified in the case of those precluded from regular employment by responsibilities at home), "(or at least 20 of them, if that is less than half)" is omitted.

(2) This paragraph shall have effect in relation to any person attaining pensionable age on or after 6th April 2010.

Additional pension

5. In section 46(2) of the Social Security Contributions and Benefits Act 1992 (benefits calculated by reference to Category A retirement pension), for the words following "45(4)(b) above—" there is substituted—

""N"=
  (a) the number of tax years which begin after 5th April 1978 and end before the date when the entitlement to the additional pension commences, or
  (b) the number of tax years in the period—
    (i) beginning with the tax year in which the deceased spouse ("S") attained the age of 16 or if later 1978–79, and
    (ii) ending immediately before the tax year in which S would have attained pensionable age if had not died earlier,
whichever is the smaller number".

Increments

6.—(1) In section 54(1) of the Social Security Contributions and Benefits Act 1992 (election to defer right to pension), in paragraph (a), the words from "but" to "70" are omitted.

(2) In Schedule 5 to that Act—
  (a) in paragraph 2(2), the definition of "period of enhancement" (and the preceding "and") are omitted, and
  (b) for "period of enhancement" (in every other place in paragraphs 2 and 3 where it appears) there is substituted "period of deferment".

(3) In paragraph 2(3) of that Schedule, for "1/7th per cent" there is substituted "1/5th per cent"

(4) In paragraph 8 of that Schedule, sub-paragraphs (1) and (2) are omitted.

(5) Sub-paragraph (1) above shall come into force on 6th April 2010; and sub-paragraphs (2) to (4) above shall have effect in relation to incremental periods beginning on or after that date.

Graduated retirement benefit

7. In section 62(1) of the Social Security Contributions and Benefits Act 1992 (graduated retirement benefit continued in force by regulations)—
  (a) in paragraph (a), for "replacing section 36(4) of the National Insurance Act 1965" there is substituted "amending section 36(2) of the National Insurance Act 1965 (value of unit of graduated contributions) so that the value is the same for women as it is for men and for replacing section 36(4) of that Act", and
  (b) at the end of paragraph (b) there is added "and for that section (except subsection (5)) so to apply as it applies to women and their late husbands".

Christmas bonus for pensioners

8. In section 149(4) of that Act (Christmas bonus: supplementary), for "70 in the case of a man or 65 in the case of a woman" there is substituted "65".

Definitions For "earnings", see the Social Security Contributions and Benefits Act 1992, ss 3, 4, 112; note as to "the spouse", s 48A(1) of the 1992 Act, as substituted by para 3(1) above; and as to "the pensioner", ss 48B(1), 48C(4) of that Act, as so substituted; for "period of deferment", see s 55(2) thereof, as substituted by s 134(3) of this Act; for "entitled" and "tax year", see the 1992 Act, s 122(1). By virtue of s 122(1) of that Act, as amended by para 13(a) of Pt III to this Schedule, for "pensionable age", see Sch 4, para 1 to this Act; for "incremental period", see Sch 5, para 2(2) to the 1992 Act, as amended by para 6(2) above.
References See paras 8.15, 8.16, 13.14–13.17.

PART III

CONSEQUENTIAL AMENDMENTS

Pensionable age

9. In section 50 of the London Regional Transport Act 1984 (travel concessions), for subsection (7)(a) there is substituted—

"(a) persons who have attained pensionable age (within the meaning given by the rules in paragraph 1 of Schedule 4 to the Pensions Act 1995)".

10. In section 93 of the Transport Act 1985 (travel concessions), for subsection (7)(a) there is substituted—

"(a) persons who have attained pensionable age (within the meaning given by the rules in paragraph 1 of Schedule 4 to the Pensions Act 1995)".

11. In section 73B(2)(b)(ii) of the Housing (Scotland) Act 1987 (rent loan scheme), for "of the Social Security Act 1975" there is substituted "given by the rules in paragraph 1 of Schedule 4 to the Pensions Act 1995)".

12. In the Income and Corporation Taxes Act 1988—
  (a) in section 187(2) (interpretation), the definition of "pensionable age" is omitted,
  (b) in the words following paragraph (d) of paragraph 2 of Schedule 10 (retention of shares in connection with profit sharing schemes), for "to pensionable age" there is substituted "in the case of a man, to the age of 65, and in the case of a woman, to the age of 60".
  (c) in sub-paragraph (2) of paragraph 3A of that Schedule, for "pensionable age" there is substituted—

  "(a) in the case of a man, 65, and
  (b) in the case of a woman, 60.", and

  (d) in sub-paragraph (4) of that paragraph, for "pensionable age" there is substituted "in the case of a man, 65, and in the case of a woman, 60."

13. In the Social Security Contributions and Benefits Act 1992—
  (a) in section 122(1) (interpretation of Parts I to VI), for the definition of "pensionable age" there is substituted—

  ""pensionable age" has the meaning given by the rules in paragraph 1 of Schedule 4 to the Pensions Act 1995", and

  (b) in section 150(2) (interpretation of Part X), for the definition of "pensionable age" there is substituted—

  ""pensionable age" has the meaning given by the rules in paragraph 1 of Schedule 4 to the Pensions Act 1995".

14. In section 191 of the Social Security Administration Act 1992 (interpretation), for the definition of "pensionable age" there is substituted—

""pensionable age" has the meaning given by the rules in paragraph 1 of Schedule 4 to the Pensions Act 1995".

15. In section 58 of the Trade Union and Labour Relations (Consolidation) Act 1992 (exemption from requirement for election), in subsection (3)(b), for the words following

"pensionable age" there is substituted "(within the meaning given by the rules in paragraph 1 of Schedule 4 to the Pensions Act 1995)".

16. For section 49 of the Pension Schemes Act 1993 (married women and widows), including the cross heading preceding it, there is substituted—

"Women, married women and widows

49   Women, married women and widows

The Secretary of State may make regulations modifying, in such manner as he thinks proper—

    (a)   this Chapter in its application to women born on or after 6th April 1950, and

    (b)   sections 41, 42, 46(1), 47(2) and (5) and 48, in their application to women who are or have been married".

17. In section 181(1) of that Act (interpretation), for the definition of "pensionable age" there is substituted—

""pensionable age"—

    (a)   so far as any provisions (other than sections 46 to 48) relate to guaranteed minimum pensions, means the age of 65 in the case of a man and the age of 60 in the case of a woman, and

    (b)   in any other case, has the meaning given by the rules in paragraph 1 of Schedule 4 to the Pensions Act 1995".

Pension increases for dependent spouses

18. In the Social Security Contributions and Benefits Act 1992—

    (a)   in section 25(6)(c) (unemployment benefit), for "83" there is substituted "83A",

    (b)   in section 30B(3) (incapacity benefit: rate, inserted by the Social Security (Incapacity for Work) Act 1994), for "83" there is substituted "83A",

    (c)   in section 78(4)(d) (benefits for the aged), for "83" there is substituted "83A",

    (d)   in section 85(4) (pension increase: care of children), for "83(3)" there is substituted "83A(3)",

    (e)   in section 88 (pension increase: supplementary), for "83" there is substituted "83A",

    (f)   in section 114(4) (persons maintaining dependants, etc), for "84" there is substituted "83A", and

    (g)   in section 149(3)(b) (Christmas bonus), for "83(2) or (3)" there is substituted "83A(2) or (3)".

19. In the Social Security (Incapacity for Work) Act 1994, in Schedule 1, paragraphs 20 and 21 are omitted.

20. Paragraphs 18 and 19 shall have effect on or after 6th April 2010.

Category B retirement pensions

21. In section 20(1)(f) of the Social Security Contributions and Benefits Act 1992 (general description of benefits), for sub-paragraph (ii) there is substituted—

"(ii) Category B, payable to a person by virtue of the contributions of a spouse (with increase for child dependants)".

(2) In section 25(6) of that Act, in paragraph (b), for "(for married women) under section 53(2)" there is substituted "(for married people) under section 51A(2)".

(3) In section 30B of that Act (incapacity benefit), in paragraph (a) of the proviso to subsection (3), for "(for married women) under section 53(2)" there is substituted "(for married people) under section 51A(2)".

(4) In section 41(5)(a) of that Act (long-term incapacity benefit for widowers), for "section 51 below" there is substituted "the contributions of his wife".

(5) In section 46(2) of that Act (calculation of additional pension in certain benefits), for "50(3)" there is substituted "48A(4) or 48B(2)".

(6) After section 51 of that Act there is inserted—

"51A Special provision for married people

(1) This section has effect where, apart from section 43(1) above, a married person would be entitled both—
  (a) to a Category A retirement pension, and
  (b) to a Category B retirement pension by virtue of the contributions of the other party to the marriage.

(2) If by reason of a deficiency of contributions the basic pension in the Category A retirement pension falls short of the weekly rate specified in Schedule 4, Part I, paragraph 5, that basic pension shall be increased by the lesser of—
  (a) the amount of the shortfall, or
  (b) the amount of the weekly rate of the Category B retirement pension.

(3) This section does not apply in any case where both parties to the marriage attained pensionable age before 6th April 1979",

and section 53 of that Act (special provision for married women) is omitted.

(7) In section 52 of that Act (special provision for surviving spouses), for subsection (1)(b) there is substituted—

"(b) to a Category B retirement pension by virtue of the contributions of a spouse who has died".

(8) In section 54 of that Act (supplemental provisions), for subsection (3) there is substituted—

"(3) Where both parties to a marriage (call them "P" and "S") have become entitled to retirement pensions and—
  (a) P's pension is Category A, and
  (b) S's pension is—
    (i) Category B by virtue of P's contributions, or
    (ii) Category A with an increase under section 51A(2) above by virtue of P's contributions,
P shall not be entitled to make an election in accordance with regulations made under subsection (1) above without S's consent, unless that consent is unreasonably withheld".

(9) In section 60 of that Act (complete or partial failure to satisfy contribution conditions)—
  (a) in subsection (2), for "him" (in paragraph (b)) there is substituted "the employed earner" and for "his widow's entitlement" there is substituted "the entitlement of the employed earner's widow or widower", and
  (b) for subsection (3)(d) there is substituted—

"(d) a Category B retirement pension payable by virtue of section 48B above".

(10) In section 85 of that Act (pension increase for person with care of children), in subsection (3), for "man whose wife" there is substituted "person whose spouse".

(11) In Schedule 4 to that Act (rates of benefit, etc), in paragraph 5 of Part I, for "section 50(1)(a)(i)" there is substituted "section 48A(3)".

(12) In Schedule 5 to that Act (increased pension where entitlement deferred), in paragraph 2(5)(a), for "5 or 6" there is substituted "5, 5A or 6".

(13) In paragraph 4 of that Schedule, for sub-paragraphs (1) and (2) there is substituted—

"(1) Subject to sub-paragraph (3) below, where—
  (a) a widow or widower (call that person "W") is entitled to a Category A or Category B retirement pension and was married to the other party to the marriage (call that person "S") when S died, and

(b) S either—
　　(i) was entitled to a Category A or Category B retirement pension with an increase under this Schedule, or
　　(ii) would have been so entitled if S's period of deferment had ended on the day before S's death,
the rate of W's pension shall be increased by an amount equal to the increase to which S was or would have been entitled under this Schedule apart from paragraphs 5 to 6".

(14) Paragraph 4(1) of that Schedule (as inserted by sub-paragraph (13) above) shall have effect where W is a man who attains pensionable age before 6th April 2010 as if paragraph (a) also required him to have been over pensionable age when S died.

(15) For paragraphs 5 and 6 of that Schedule there is substituted—

"5.—(1) Where—
　(a) a widow or widower (call that person "W") is entitled to a Category A or Category B retirement pension and was married to the other party to the marriage (call that person "S") when S died, and
　(b) S either—
　　(i) was entitled to a guaranteed minimum pension with an increase under section 15(1) of the Pensions Act, or
　　(ii) would have been so entitled if S had retired on the date of S's death,
the rate of W's pension shall be increased by the following amount.

(2) The amount is—
　(a) where W is a widow, an amount equal to the sum of the amounts set out in paragraph 5A(2) or (3) below (as the case may be), and
　(b) where W is a widower, an amount equal to the sum of the amounts set out in paragraph 6(2), (3) or (4) below (as the case may be).

5A.—(1) This paragraph applies where W (referred to in paragraph 5 above) is a widow.

(2) Where the husband dies before 6th April 2000, the amounts referred to in paragraph 5(2)(a) above are the following—
　(a) an amount equal to one-half of the increase mentioned in paragraph 5(1)(b) above,
　(b) the appropriate amount, and
　(c) an amount equal to any increase to which the husband had been entitled under paragraph 5 above.

(3) Where the husband dies after 5th April 2000, the amounts referred to in paragraph 5(2)(a) above are the following—
　(a) one-half of the appropriate amount after it has been reduced by the amount of any increases under section 109 of the Pensions Act, and
　(b) one-half of any increase to which the husband had been entitled under paragraph 5 above.

6.—(1) This paragraph applies where W (referred to in paragraph 5 above) is a widower.

(2) Where the wife dies before 6th April 1989, the amounts referred to in paragraph 5(2)(b) above are the following—
　(a) an amount equal to the increase mentioned in paragraph 5(1)(b) above,
　(b) the appropriate amount, and
　(c) an amount equal to any increase to which the wife had been entitled under paragraph 5 above.

(3) Where the wife dies after 5th April 1989 but before 6th April 2000, the amounts referred to in paragraph 5(2)(b) above are the following—
　(a) the increase mentioned in paragraph 5(1)(b) above, so far as attributable to employment before 6th April 1988,
　(b) one-half of that increase, so far as attributable to employment after 5th April 1988,
　(c) the appropriate amount reduced by the amount of any increases under section 109 of the Pensions Act, and
　(d) any increase to which the wife had been entitled under paragraph 5 above.

(4) Where the wife dies after 5th April 2000, the amounts referred to in paragraph 5(2)(b) above are the following—
　(a) one-half of the increase mentioned in paragraph 5(1)(b) above, so far as attributable to employment before 6th April 1988,

(b) one-half of the appropriate amount after it has been reduced by the amount of any increases under section 109 of the Pensions Act, and
(c) one-half of any increase to which the wife had been entitled under paragraph 5 above".

(16) Paragraph 5(1) of that Schedule (inserted by sub-paragraph (15) above) shall have effect, where W is a man who attained pensionable age before 6th April 2010, as if paragraph (a) also required him to have been over pensionable age when S died.

(17) In paragraph 7 of that Schedule—
(a) in sub-paragraph (1), for "paragraphs 5 and 6" there is substituted "paragraphs 5 to 6", and
(b) in sub-paragraph (2), for "paragraph 5 or 6" there is substituted "paragraph 5, 5A or 6".

(18) In paragraph 8 of that Schedule, for sub-paragraphs (3) and (4) there is substituted—

"(3) In the case of the following pensions (where "P" is a married person and "S" is the other party to the marriage), that is—

(a) a Category B retirement pension to which P is entitled by virtue of the contributions of S, or
(b) P's Category A retirement pension with an increase under section 51A(2) above attributable to the contributions of S,

the reference in paragraph 2(3) above to the pension to which a person would have been entitled if that person's entitlement had not been deferred shall be construed as a reference to the pension to which P would have been entitled if neither P's nor S's entitlement to a retirement pension had been deferred.

(4) Paragraph 4(1)(b) above shall not apply to a Category B retirement pension to which S was or would have been entitled by virtue of W's contributions ("W" and "S" having the same meaning as in paragraph 4(1)); and where the Category A retirement pension to which S was or would have been entitled includes an increase under section 51A(2) above attributable to W's contributions, the increase to which W is entitled under that paragraph shall be calculated as if there had been no increase under that section".

22. In section 46 of the Pension Schemes Act 1993 (effect of entitlement to guaranteed minimum pension on payment of benefits), in subsection (6)(b)(iii), for "section 49" there is substituted "section 48A or 48B".

Definitions For "employed earner", see the Social Security Contributions and Benefits Act 1992, s 2; for "period of deferment", see s 55(2) of the 1992 Act, as substituted by s 134(3) of this Act; for "employment", "entitled" and "tax year", see s 122(1) of the 1992 Act; for "the appropriate amount", see para 7(1) of Sch 5 to that Act; for "guaranteed minimum pension", see 8(2) of the Pension Schemes Act 1993, as amended by s 151, Sch 5, paras 18, 23(a) of this Act, for "modifying" and "regulations", see s 181(1) of the 1993 Act, as amended by para 17 above.
References See paras 8.15, 8.16, 13.14–13.17.

SCHEDULE 5

AMENDMENTS RELATING TO PART III

Section 151

The Public Records Act 1958 (c 51)

1. In Schedule 1 to the Public Records Act 1958 (definition of "Public Record"), in the Table—
(a) in Part I, the entry relating to the Occupational Pensions Board is omitted, and
(b) in Part II—
(i) after the entry relating to the Nature Conservancy Council for England, there is inserted—

"Occupational Pensions Regulatory Authority.", and

Pensions Act 1995, Sch 5

(ii) after the entry relating to the Office of the Director General of Fair Trading, there is inserted—

"Pensions Compensation Board."

The Administration of Justice Act 1970 (c 31)

2. In Schedule 4 to the Administration of Justice Act 1970 (taxes, social insurance contributions, etc subject to special enforcement provisions), in paragraph 3, for "State scheme premiums" there is substituted "Contributions equivalent premiums".

The Attachment of Earnings Act 1971 (c 31)

3. In Schedule 2 to the Attachment of Earnings Act 1971 (taxes, social security contributions, etc relevant for purposes of section 3(6)), in paragraph 3, for "State scheme premiums" there is substituted "Contributions equivalent premiums".

The House of Commons Disqualification Act 1975 (c 24)

4. In Part II of Schedule 1 to the House of Commons Disqualification Act 1975 (bodies of which all members are disqualified), the entry relating to the Occupational Pensions Board is omitted.

The Northern Ireland Assembly Disqualification Act 1975 (c 25)

5. In Part II of Schedule 1 to the Northern Ireland Assembly Disqualification Act 1975 (bodies of which all members are disqualified), the entry relating to the Occupational Pensions Board is omitted.

The Social Security Pensions Act 1975 (c 60)

6.—(1) In section 61 of the Social Security Pensions Act 1975 (consultation about regulations) for the words from "refer the proposals" in subsection (2) to the end of subsection (3) there is substituted "consult such persons as he may consider appropriate".

(2) In section 61B(1) of that Act (orders and regulations: general provisions), "except any power of the Occupational Pensions Board to make orders" is omitted.

(3) In section 64(3) of that Act (expenses and receipts), for "state scheme premium" there is substituted "contributions equivalent premium".

The European Parliament (Pay and Pensions) Act 1979 (c 50)

7. In section 6(4) of the European Parliament (Pay and Pensions) Act 1979 (provision for payment of block transfer value into another pension scheme), "and the Occupational Pensions Board" is omitted.

The Justices of the Peace Act 1979 (c 55)

8. In section 55(6)(b)(ii) of the Justices of the Peace Act 1979 (duties of local authorities), for "state scheme premiums" there is substituted "contributions equivalent premiums".

The Judicial Pensions Act 1981 (c 20)

9. In section 14A(2) of the Judicial Pensions Act 1981 (modifications of that Act in relation to personal pensions), in the definition of "personal pension scheme", for the words from "by" to the end there is substituted "in accordance with section 7 of the Pension Schemes Act 1993;".

The Insurance Companies Act 1982 (c 50)

10. In the Table in paragraph 3(1) of Schedule 2B to the Insurance Companies Act 1982 (restriction on disclosure of information), the entry relating to the Occupational Pensions Board is omitted.

The Companies Act 1985 (c 6)

11. In Schedule 2 to the Companies Act 1985 (interpretation of references to "beneficial interest"), in paragraphs 3(2)(b) and 7(2)(b), for "state scheme premium" there is substituted "contributions equivalent premium".

The Income and Corporation Taxes Act 1988 (c 1)

12.—(1) In section 649 of the Income and Corporation Taxes Act 1988 (minimum contributions towards approved personal pension schemes), in subsection (2), for the definition of "the employee's share" there is substituted—

> ""the employee's share" of minimum contributions is the amount that would be the minimum contributions if, for the reference in section 45(1) of the Pension Schemes Act 1993 to the appropriate age-related percentage, there were substituted a reference to the percentage mentioned in section 41(1A)(a) of that Act".

(2) This paragraph does not extend to Northern Ireland.

The Social Security Act 1989 (c 24)

13.—(1) Section 29(7) of the Social Security Act 1989 (regulations and orders) is omitted.

(2) In Schedule 5 to that Act (equal treatment in employment related schemes for pensions etc), paragraph 4 is omitted.

The Social Security Contributions and Benefits Act 1992 (c 4)

14. In Schedule 1 to the Social Security Contributions and Benefits Act 1992 (supplementary provisions), in paragraph 8(1)(g), for "state scheme premium" there is substituted "contributions equivalent premium".

The Social Security Administration Act 1992 (c 5)

15.—(1) The Social Security Administration Act 1992 is amended as follows.

(2) In section 110 (appointment and powers of inspectors)—
   (a) in subsections (2)(c)(ii) and (6)(a)(ii), for "state scheme premium" there is substituted "contributions equivalent premium", and
   (b) ink subsection (7)(e)(i), for "state scheme premiums" there is substituted "contributions equivalent premiums".

(3) In section 120 (proof of previous offences), in subsections (3) and (4), for "state scheme premiums" there is substituted "contributions equivalent premiums".

(4) In Schedule 4 (persons employed in social security administration etc), the entries in Part I relating to the Occupational Pensions Board are omitted.

The Tribunals and Inquiries Act 1992 (c 53)

16.—(1) The Tribunals and Inquiries Act 1992 is amended as follows.

(2) In section 7(2) (concurrence needed for removal of members of certain tribunals), "(d) or" is omitted.

(3) In section 10(5) (reasons to be given for decisions of tribunals and Ministers), paragraph (c) is omitted.

(4) In section 13(5)(a) (power to amend), "and (d)" is omitted.

(5) In section 14 (restricted application of Act in relation to certain tribunals), subsection (2) is omitted.

(6) In Schedule 1 (Tribunals under the direct supervision of the Council on Tribunals), paragraph 35(d) is omitted.

The Judicial Pensions and Retirement Act 1993 (c 8)

17. In section 13(9) of the Judicial Pensions and Retirement Act 1993 (election for personal pension), in the definition of "personal pension scheme", "by the Occupational Pensions Board" is omitted.

The Pension Schemes Act 1993 (c 48)

18. The Pension Schemes Act 1993 is amended as follows.

19. Sections 2 to 5 (constitution, membership etc of the Board) are repealed.

20. For section 6(8) (Board may be appointed as Registrar), there is substituted—

"(8) Nothing in this Act or the Pensions Act 1995 shall be taken to imply that the Regulatory Authority may not be appointed as the Registrar."

21. In the provisions listed in the first column of the table—
   (a) in each place where the word appears, for "Board" there is substituted "Secretary of State", and
   (b) the additional amendments listed in the second column of the table in relation to those provisions shall have effect.

TABLE

Provision	Additional amendments
Section 8 (meaning of terms)	—
Section 9 (requirements for certification)	In subsection (4), for "they think" there is substituted "he thinks"
Section 11 (employer's right to elect as to contracting-out)	In subsection (4), for "consider" and "they" there is substituted, respectively, "considers" and "he"
	In subsection (5)(d), for "they are" there is substituted "he is".
Section 30 (protected rights)	—
Section 34 (cancellation etc of certificates)	In subsection (2)(a), for "they have" there is substituted "he has"
	In subsections (4) and (5), for "they consider" (in both places) and "they" (in both places) there is substituted, respectively, "he considers" and "he"
Section 50 (schemes ceasing to be certified)	In subsection (2), for "have" (in both places) and "their" there is substituted, respectively, "has" and "his"
	In subsection (3), for "they subsequently approve" there is substituted "he subsequently approves"
	In subsection (4), for the first "have" there is substituted "has"
Section 57 (contribution equivalent premiums)	In subsection (4) for "consider" and "they" there is substituted, respectively, "considers" and "he"
Section 163 (rule against perpetuities)	In subsection (6), for "consider" there is substituted "considers"

22. In section 7—
   (a) in subsections (1) and (6), for "Board" there is substituted "Secretary of State", and
   (b) in subsection (4), "by the Board" is omitted.

23. In section 8 (definition of terms)—
   (a) in subsection (2), for the words following the definition of "minimum payment" there is substituted—

"and for the purposes of this subsection "rebate percentage" means the appropriate flat rate percentage for the purposes of section 42A(2)", and

   (b) subsection (5) is omitted.

Pensions Act 1995, Sch 5

24. In section 9 (requirements for certification), in subsection (3) "22 and" is omitted.

25. In section 10 (protected rights), in subsection (2)(a), after "minimum payments" there is inserted "and payments under section 42A(3)".

26. In section 13 (minimum pensions for earners), in subsection (2)(a), the words from "and does" to the end are omitted.

27. In section 14 (earner's guaranteed minimum)—
    (a) subsection (3) is omitted,
    (b) in subsection (8) after "1978–79" there is inserted "or later than the tax year ending immediately before the principal appointed day".

28. In section 16 (revaluation of earnings factors)—
    (a) in subsection (3), for the words following "at least" there is substituted "the prescribed percentage for each relevant year after the last service tax year; and the provisions included by virtue of this subsection may also conform with such additional requirements as may be prescribed", and
    (b) for the definition of "final relevant year" in subsection (5) there is substituted—

""final relevant year" means the last tax year in the earner's working life".

29. In section 17 (minimum pensions for widows and widowers), at the end of subsection (7) there is added "or widows".

30. Section 22 (financing of benefits) is repealed.

31. In section 23 (securing of benefits)—
    (a) subsections (1) and (5) are omitted,
    (b) in subsection (4), for "(1) to (3)" there is substituted "(2) and (3)";

and subsections (2) and (3) of that section do not apply where the winding up is begun on or after the principal appointed day.

32. Section 24 (sufficiency of resources) is repealed.

33. In section 25 (conditions as to investments, etc)—
    (a) subsections (1) and (3) are repealed, and
    (b) for subsection (2) there is substituted—

"(2) A salary related contracted-out scheme must, in relation to any earner's service before the principal appointed day, comply with any requirements prescribed for the purpose of securing that—
    (a) the Secretary of State is kept informed about any matters affecting the security of the minimum pensions guaranteed under the scheme, and
    (b) the resources of the scheme are brought to and are maintained at a level satisfactory to the Secretary of State".

34. In section 28 (ways of giving effect to protected rights)—
    (a) in subsection (4)(d), for "a manner satisfactory to the Board" there is substituted "the prescribed manner", and
    (b) subsection (7) is omitted.

35. In section 29 (the pension and annuity requirements), in subsection (1)(b)(ii), for "a manner satisfactory to the Board" there is substituted "the prescribed manner".

36. In section 31 (investment and resources of schemes)—
    (a) subsection (1) is omitted,
    (b) in subsection (3)(a), after "minimum payments" there is inserted "and payments under section 42A(3)", and
    (c) at the end of that section there is added—

"(5) Any minimum contributions required by reason of this section to be applied so as to provide money purchase benefits for or in respect of a member of a scheme must be so applied in the prescribed manner and within the prescribed period".

37. In section 34 (cancellation, etc of certificates)—
    (a) in subsection (1), for paragraph (a) there is substituted—

"(a) in the case of a contracting-out certificate—
   (i) on any change of circumstances affecting the treatment of an employment as contracted-out employment, or
   (ii) where the scheme is a salary related contracted-out scheme and the certificate was issued on or after the principal appointed day, if any employer of persons in the description or category of employment to which the scheme in question relates, or the actuary of the scheme, fails to provide the Secretary of State, at prescribed intervals, with such documents as may be prescribed for the purpose of verifying that the conditions of section 9(2B) are satisfied",

(b) subsection (6) is omitted, and
(c) for subsection (7) there is substituted—

"(7) Without prejudice to the previous provisions of this section, failure of a scheme to comply with any requirements prescribed by virtue of section 25(2) shall be a ground on which the Secretary of State may, in respect of any employment to which the scheme relates, cancel a contracting-out certificate".

38. Sections 35 (surrender, etc issue of further certificates) and 36 (surrender etc cancellation of further certificates) are repealed.

39. For section 37 (alteration of rules of contracted-out schemes) there is substituted—

"37 Alteration of rules of contracted-out schemes

(1) Except in prescribed circumstances, the rules of a contracted-out scheme cannot be altered unless the alteration is of a prescribed description.

(2) Regulations made by virtue of subsection (1) may operate so as to validate with retrospective effect any alteration of the rules which would otherwise be void under this section.

(3) References in this section to a contracted-out scheme include a scheme which has ceased to be contracted-out so long as any person is entitled to receive, or has accrued rights to, any benefits under the scheme attributable to a period when the scheme was contracted-out.

(4) The reference in subsection (3) to a person entitled to receive benefits under a scheme includes a person so entitled by virtue of being the widower of an earner only in such cases as may be prescribed."

40. In section 38 (alteration of rules of appropriate schemes)—
   (a) in subsection (1), the words from "unless" to the end are omitted,
   (b) in subsection (3), the words from "if" to the end are omitted,
   (c) in subsection (4), for the words from the beginning to "direct" there is substituted "Regulations made by virtue of subsection (2) may", and
   (d) subsection (7) is omitted.

41. In section 42 (review of reduced rates of contributions), in subsection (3), for "41(1)(a)" there is substituted "41(1A)(a)".

42. In section 43 (payment of minimum contributions), in subsection (1), after "circumstances" there is inserted "or in respect of such periods".

43. In section 45 (minimum contributions towards personal pension schemes), subsection (3)(d) is omitted.

44. In section 46(1) (effect of entitlement to guaranteed minimum pensions on payment of social security benefits), for sub-paragraph (i) there is substituted—

"(i) to that part of its additional pension which is attributable to earnings factors for any tax years ending before the principal appointed day".

45. In section 50 (powers to approve arrangements for scheme ceasing to be certified)—

(a) in subsection (1)(a)—
  (i) at the end of sub-paragraph (i) there is inserted "or accrued rights to pensions under the scheme attributable to their service on or after the principal appointed day", and
  (ii) in sub-paragraph (ii), for "guaranteed minimum pensions under the scheme" there is substituted "such pensions",

(b) after subsection (1) there is inserted—

"(1A) The power of the Secretary of State to approve arrangements under this section—
  (a) includes power to approve arrangements subject to conditions, and
  (b) may be exercised either generally or in relation to a particular scheme.

(1B) Arrangements may not be approved under this section unless any prescribed conditions are met", and

(c) subsection (7) is omitted.

46. In section 51 (calculation of GMPs preserved under approved arrangements), in subsection (1)(a), for "are subject to approved arrangements" there is substituted "satisfy prescribed conditions".

47. In section 52 (supervision of schemes which have ceased to be certified)—
  (a) in subsection (2), for paragraphs (a) and (b) there is substituted—

"(a) the scheme has ceased to be a contracted-out scheme, and
(b) any persons remain who fall within any of the following categories.

(2A) Those categories are—
  (a) any persons entitled to receive, or having accrued rights to—
    (i) guaranteed minimum pensions, or
    (ii) pensions under the scheme attributable to service on or after the principal appointed day but before the scheme ceased to be contracted-out,
  (b) any persons who have protected rights under the scheme or are entitled to any benefit giving effect to protected rights under it",

  (b) in subsection (3), for paragraphs (a) and (b) there is substituted—

"(a) the scheme has ceased to be an appropriate scheme, and
(b) any persons remain who have protected rights under the scheme or are entitled to any benefit giving effect to protected rights under it", and

  (c) subsections (4) to (6) are omitted.

48. In section 53 (supervision: former contracted-out schemes)—
  (a) for subsection (1) there is substituted—

"(1) The Secretary of State may direct the trustees or managers of the scheme, or the employer, to take or refrain from taking such steps as the Secretary of State may specify in writing; and such a direction shall be final and binding on the person directed and any person claiming under him.

(1A) An appeal on a point of law shall lie to the High Court or, in Scotland, the Court of Session from a direction under subsection (1) at the instance of the trustees or managers or the employer, or any person claiming under them.

(1B) A direction under subsection (1) shall be enforceable—
  (a) in England and Wales, in a county court as if it were an order of that court, and
  (b) in Scotland, by the sheriff, as if it were an order of the sheriff and whether or not the sheriff could himself have given such an order",

  (b) subsection (2) is omitted,
  (c) for subsection (3) there is substituted—

"(3) If a certificate has been issued under subsection (2) of section 50 and has not been cancelled under subsection (3) of that section, any liabilities in respect of such entitlement or rights as are referred to in section 52(2A)(a) or (b) must, except in prescribed circumstances, be discharged (subject to any directions under subsection (1)) in a prescribed manner and within a prescribed period or such longer period as the Secretary of State may allow", and

(d) subsections (4) and (5) are omitted.

49. In section 54 (supervision: former appropriate personal pension schemes)—
    (a) for subsections (1) and (2) there is substituted—

"(1) The Secretary of State may direct the trustees or managers of the scheme to take or refrain from taking such steps as the Secretary of State may specify in writing; and such a direction shall be final and binding on the person directed and any person claiming under him.

(1A) An appeal on a point of law shall lie to the High Court or, in Scotland, the Court of Session from a direction under subsection (1) at the instance of the trustees or managers or the employer, or any person claiming under them.

(1B) A direction under subsection (1) shall be enforceable—
  (a) in England and Wales, in a county court as if it were an order of that court, and
  (b) in Scotland, by the sheriff, as if it were an order of the sheriff and whether or not the sheriff could himself have given such an order.

(2) If a certificate has been issued under subsection (2) of section 50 and has not been cancelled under subsection (3) of that section, any liabilities in respect of such entitlement or rights as are referred to in section 52(3)(b) must, except in prescribed circumstances, be discharged (subject to any directions under subsection (1)) in a prescribed manner and within a prescribed period or such longer period as the Secretary of State may allow", and

(b) subsection (3) is omitted.

50. In section 55 (state scheme premiums), subsections (1) and (3) to (6) are omitted.

51. In section 56 (provisions supplementary to section 55)—
    (a) subsection (1), in subsection (2) the words following "the prescribed period" and subsection (3) are omitted, and
    (b) for subsections (5) and (6) there is substituted—

"(5) The references in section 55(2A) to an accrued right to short service benefit include an accrued right to any provision which, under the preservation requirements, is permitted as an alternative to short service benefit (other than provision for return of contributions or for benefit in the form of a lump sum).

(6) Subject to regulations under paragraph 1 of Schedule 2, service in any employment which ceases with the death of the employer shall be treated for the purposes of section 55(2A) as ceasing immediately before the death".

52. In section 58 (amount of premiums under section 55), subsections (1) to (3), (5) and (6) are omitted.

53. Section 59 (alternative basis for revaluation) is repealed.

54. In section 60 (effect of payment of premiums on rights)—
    (a) subsections (1) to (3) are omitted,
    (b) in subsection (4)—
        (i) for "55(2)(i)" there is substituted "55(2A)(a) and (b), (d) and (e)", and
        (ii) at the end there is added "or (in relation to service on or after the principal appointed day) rights to pensions under the scheme so far as attributable to the amount of the premium", and

(c) in subsection (5), for "55(2)(ii)" there is substituted "55(2A)(c)", and after "widow" there is added "or widower", and

(d) subsections (6) to (10) are omitted.

55. In section 61 (deduction of contributions equivalent premium from refund of scheme contributions)—
  (a) in subsection (1), for paragraph (a) there is substituted—

  "(a) an earner's service in contracted-out employment ceases or his employment ceases to be contracted-out employment, and",

  (b) in subsection (8)—
    (i) for paragraph (a) there is substituted—

    "(a) an earner's service in contracted-out employment ceases or his employment ceases to be contracted-out employment", and

    (ii) for "termination" there is substituted "cessation", and
  (c) in subsection (9), for "termination" (in both places) there is substituted "cessation".

56. In section 62 (no recovery of premiums from earners)—
  (a) in subsection (1), for "state scheme" there is substituted "contributions equivalent", and
  (b) subsection (2) is omitted.

57. In section 63 (further provisions concerning calculations relating to premiums)—
  (a) in subsection (1)—
    (i) paragraph (a) is omitted,
    (ii) in paragraph (b), for "that section" there is substituted "section 58", and
    (iii) paragraph (c) is omitted,
  (b) subsection (2) is omitted,
  (c) in subsection (3)—
    (i) paragraph (a) is omitted,
    (ii) in paragraph (b), for "subsection (4) of that section" there is substituted "section 58(4)", and
    (iii) the words following sub-paragraph (ii) are omitted, and
  (d) subsection (4) is omitted.

58. Section 64 (actuarial tables) is repealed.

59. Section 65 (former and future earners) is repealed.

60. Section 66 (widowers) is repealed.

61. In sections 67 and 68 (non-payment of state scheme premiums), for "state scheme premium" (in each place) there is substituted "contributions equivalent premium".

62. In section 84(5), paragraph (b) and the preceding "or" are omitted.

63. In section 96 (right to cash equivalent: exercise of options)—
  (a) in subsection (2)(a), after "guaranteed minimum pensions" there is inserted "his accrued rights so far as attributable to service in contracted-out employment on or after the principal appointed day", and
  (b) in subsection (3)(a), for "guaranteed minimum pensions" there is substituted "pensions, being guaranteed minimum pensions or pensions so far as attributable to service in contracted-out employment on or after the principal appointed day".

64. Sections 133 to 135 (advice and determinations as to conformity of schemes with requirements) are repealed.

65. In section 155 (requirement to give information to the Secretary of State or the Board)—
  (a) "or the Board" is omitted,
  (b) for "or they require" there is substituted "requires", and
  (c) for the words from "sections 7" to "premiums" there is substituted "Part III".

66. In section 158 (disclosure of information between government departments)—
   (a) subsections (2) and (3) are omitted,
   (b) in subsection (6), "(2) or (3)", paragraph (d) and the "or" immediately preceding it are omitted,
   (c) in subsection (7)—
      (i) for "the Inland Revenue and the Board", there is substituted "and the Inland Revenue",
      (ii) after paragraph (a), there is inserted "or", and
      (iii) paragraph (c) and the "or" immediately preceding it are omitted, and
   (d) subsection (8) is omitted.

67. In section 164(1)(b)(i) (Crown employment), "2 to 5", "172, 173" and "and Schedule 1" are omitted.

68. In section 165 (application of certain provisions to case with foreign element), in subsection (2)(a), for the words from "sections 7" to "premiums)" there is substituted "Part III".

69. In section 166(5) (reciprocity with other countries), "sections 2 to 5", "172, 173" and "and Schedule 1" are omitted.

70. In section 170 (determinations by the Secretary of State)—
   (a) in subsection (1)—
      (i) in paragraph (b) for "state scheme premium" (in both places) there is substituted "contributions equivalent premium",
      (ii) the "and" at the end of paragraph (c) is omitted, and
      (iii) for the words following paragraph (d) there is substituted

      "and
      (e) any question whether an employment is, or is to be treated, for the purposes of the Pension Schemes Act 1993 as contracted-out employment or as to the persons in relation to whom, or the period for which, an employment is, or is to be treated, for the purposes of that Act as such employment",

   (b) subsections (3) and (4) are omitted, and
   (c) at the end of that section there is added—

   "(7) Sections 18 and 19 of the Social Security Administration Act 1992 (appeals and reviews) shall have effect as if the questions mentioned in subsection (1) of section 17 of that Act included—
      (a) any question arising in connection with the issue, cancellation or variation of contracting-out certificates or appropriate scheme certificates, not being a question mentioned in subsection (1)(e) above, and
      (b) any other question arising under this Act which falls to be determined by the Secretary of State, not being a question mentioned in that subsection.

   (8) Regulations may make provision with respect to the procedure to be adopted on any application for a review made under section 19 of that Act by virtue of subsection (7) above and generally with respect to such applications and reviews, but may not prevent such a review being entered upon without an application being made".

71. In section 171 (questions arising in proceedings), in subsection (1)(b), for "state scheme premium" there is substituted "contributions equivalent premium".

72. Sections 172 and 173 (reviews and appeals) are repealed.

73. In section 174 (grants), for "Board" (in both places) there is substituted "Regulatory Authority".

74. In section 176 (fees), for "either by the Secretary of State or by the Board on his behalf" there is substituted "by the Secretary of State".

75. In section 177 (general financial arrangements)—
   (a) in subsection (3)(b)—
      (i) in sub-paragraph (i), "sections 2 to 5", "172, 173" and "and Schedule 1" are omitted, and
      (ii) in sub-paragraph (ii), the words from "sections 55" to "premiums)" are omitted, and
   (b) subsection (7)(b) is omitted.

76. In section 178(b) (meaning of "trustee" and "manager"), "sections 2 to 5", "172, 173" and "and Schedule 1" are omitted.

77. In section 181 (general interpretation)—
   (a) in subsection (1)—
      (i) the definitions of "accrued rights premium", "the Board", "contracted-out protected rights premium", "limited revaluation premium", "pensioner's rights premium", "personal pension protected rights premium", "state scheme premium" and "transfer premium" are omitted, and
      (ii) in the definition of "contributions equivalent premium", for "section 55(6)(e)" there is substituted "section 55(2)",
   (b) in subsection (3), for "sections 2 to" there is substituted "section", and "172, 173" and "and Schedule 1" are omitted, and
   (c) in subsection (7), "and Schedule 1" is omitted.

78. In section 182(1) (orders and regulations), "the Board or" is omitted.

79. In section 183 (sub-delegation), in subsection (1), "sections 2 to 5", "172, 173" and "or Schedule 1", and subsection (2) are omitted.

80. In section 185 (consultation about regulations)—
   (a) in subsection (1), for the words from the beginning to "make" there is substituted "Subject to subsection (2), before the Secretary of State makes", and for the words from "refer the proposals" to the end there is substituted "consult such persons as he may consider appropriate",
   (b) in subsection (2), at the end of paragraph (c) there is added—

   "(d) regulations in the case of which the Secretary of State considers consultation inexpedient because of urgency, or
      (e) regulations which—
         (i) state that they are consequential upon a specified enactment, and
         (ii) are made before the end of the period of six months beginning with the coming into force of that enactment,"

   (c) subsections (3) and (4) are omitted,
   (d) in subsection (5), for "subsections (1) to (4)" there is substituted "subsection (1)",
   (e) subsection (6) is omitted, and
   (f) in subsection (8), for "172(4)" there is substituted "170(8)".

81. In section 186(5) (Parliamentary control of regulations and orders), "or section 185(4)" is omitted.

82. In section 192(2) (extent), for "sections 1 to 5" there is substituted "section 1" and "section 172(4) and (5)" is omitted.

83. Schedule 1 (the Occupational Pensions Board) is repealed.

84. In Schedule 2 (certification regulations)—
   (a) in paragraph 2(1), for "the Board" there is substituted "the Secretary of State",
   (b) in paragraph 4(3), for the words from "does not cease" to the end there is substituted "which, apart from the regulations, would not be contracted-out employment is treated as contracted-out employment where any benefits provided under the scheme are attributable to a period when the scheme was contracted-out",

(c) in paragraph 5(1)—
  (i) "or the Board" and "or, as the case may be, the Board" are omitted, and
  (ii) for "65" there is substituted "63",
(d) in paragraph 5(2), "to 65" is omitted, and
(e) in paragraph 9, for sub-paragraphs (3) to (5) there is substituted—

"(2A) Sub-paragraphs (3) and (4) shall be omitted".

85. In Schedule 4 (priority in bankruptcy), in paragraph 3(1), for "state scheme premium" there is substituted "contributions equivalent premium".

86. In Schedule 6 (transitional provisions and savings), paragraph 11 is omitted.

Definitions   For "the principal appointed day" in the Pension Schemes Act 1993, see s 7(2B) of that Act, as inserted by s 136(1) of this Act; as to "appropriate scheme certificate" and "contracting-out certificate", see s 7(1) of the 1993 Act, as amended by paras 18, 22(a) above; as to "appropriate scheme", see s 7(4) of that Act, as amended and repealed in part by s 177, paras 18, 22(b) above, and Sch 7, Pt III of this Act; for "contracted-out employment" and "a salary related contracted-out scheme", see s 8(1) of the 1993 Act, as amended by s 136(2), paras 18, 21(a) above; for "guaranteed minimum pension", see s 8(2) of the 1993 Act, as amended by paras 18, 23(a) above; for "protected rights", see s 10 thereof, as amended by paras 18, 25 above; for "the last service tax year", see s 16(2) thereof; for "relevant year", see, by virtue of s 16(5) of that Act, as amended by paras 18, 28(b) above, s 14(8) of that Act, as amended by paras 18, 27(b) above; as to a "contributions equivalent premium", see s 55(2) of that Act, as substituted by s 141(1) hereof; for "the preservation requirements", see s 69(2) of the 1993 Act; for "short service benefit", see s 71(2) of that Act; for "employment", "minimum contributions", "money purchase benefits", "prescribed", "regulations", "the Regulatory Authority", "resources" and "tax year", see s 181(1) of the 1993 Act, as amended by s 122 of, Sch 3, paras 22, 44 to, this Act; for "employer", see s 181(1)Đ(3) of the 1993 Act, as amended, in the case of s 181(2), by s 122 of, Sch 3, paras 22, 44(b) to, this Act, and, in the case of s 181(3), by s 177, paras 22, 77(b) above, Sch 7, Pts III, IV hereof; as to "member", see s 181(4) of the 1993 Act. By virtue of s 181(1) thereof, for "earner", see the Social Security Contributions and Benefits Act 1992, ss 3, 4, 112, and for "earnings factors", see ss 22, 23 of that Act.
References   See paras 2.4, 13.10, 14.16–14.18.

SCHEDULE 6

Section 177

GENERAL MINOR AND CONSEQUENTIAL AMENDMENTS

The Public Records Act 1958 (c 51)

1. In Schedule 1 to the Public Records Act 1958 (definition of "Public Record"), in Part II of the Table, there is inserted at the appropriate place—

"Pensions Ombudsman."

The Pension Schemes Act 1993 (c 48)

2. The Pension Schemes Act 1993 is amended as follows.

3. In section 95(1) (ways of taking right to cash equivalent), for "this Chapter" there is substituted "paragraph (a), (aa) or (b) of section 94(1)".

4. In section 97 (calculation of cash equivalents)—
  (a) in subsection (2)(a) after "cash equivalents" there is inserted "except guaranteed cash equivalents",
  (b) in subsection (3)(b), for the words from "the date" to the end there is substituted "the appropriate date", and
  (c) after that subsection there is inserted—

"(3A) For the purposes of subsection (3), the "appropriate date"—
  (a) in the case of a salary related occupational pension scheme, is the guarantee date (within the meaning of section 93A), and
  (b) in any other case, is the date on which the trustees receive an application from the member under section 95."

5. In section 98 (variation and loss of rights to cash equivalents)—
   (a) in subsection (1), after "occupational pension scheme" there is inserted "other than a salary related scheme",
   (b) after that subsection there is inserted—

   "(1A) Regulations may provide that a member of a salary related occupational pension scheme who continues in employment to which the scheme applies after his pensionable service in that employment terminates—
   (a) acquires a right to only part of his guaranteed cash equivalent, or
   (b) acquires no right to his guaranteed cash equivalent.",

   (c) in subsection (2), after "(1)" there is inserted "or (1A)", and
   (d) in subsection (3)—
      (i) in paragraph (a), after "occupational pension scheme" there is inserted "other than a salary related scheme", and
      (ii) for paragraph (b) and the "and" immediately preceding it there is substituted—

   "or
   (aa) by virtue of regulations under subsection (1A) or (2), a member of a salary related occupational pension scheme does not, on such a termination, acquire a right to the whole or any part of his guaranteed cash equivalent,

   and his employment terminates at least one year before normal pension age".

6. In section 99 (trustee's duties after exercise of an option under section 95)—
   (a) in subsection (2), for paragraphs (a) and (b) there is substituted—

   "(a) in the case of a member of a salary related occupational pension scheme, within 6 months of the guarantee date, or (if earlier) by the date on which the member attains normal pension age,
   (b) in the case of a member of any other occupational pension scheme, within 6 months of the date on which they receive the application, or (if earlier) by the date on which the member attains normal pension age, or
   (c) in the case of a member of a personal pension scheme, within 6 months of the date on which they receive the application.",

   (b) after subsection (3) there is inserted—

   "(3A) In this section, "guarantee date" has the same meaning as in section 93A.",

   (c) for subsections (4) and (5) there is substituted—

   "(4) The Regulatory Authority may, in prescribed circumstances, grant an extension of the period within which the trustees or managers of the scheme are obliged to do what is needed to carry out what a member of the scheme requires.

   (4A) Regulations may make provision in relation to applications for extensions under subsection (4).",

   (d) in subsection (6), for "Board" there is substituted "Regulatory Authority", and
   (e) after that subsection there is added—

   "(7) Where the trustees or managers of an occupational pension scheme have not done what is needed to carry out what a member of the scheme requires within six months of the date mentioned in paragraph (a) or (b) of subsection (2)—
   (a) they must, except in prescribed cases, notify the Regulatory Authority of that fact within the prescribed period, and
   (b) section 10 of the Pensions Act 1995 (power of the Regulatory Authority to impose civil penalties) shall apply to any trustee or manager who has failed to take all such steps as are reasonable to ensure that it was so done.

   (8) Regulations may provide that in prescribed circumstances subsection (7) shall not apply in relation to an occupational pension scheme."

7. In section 145 (Pensions Ombudsman), in subsection (5) "with the approval of the Treasury" is omitted.

8. In section 151(5)(b) (enforcement in Scotland of Pensions Ombudsman's determinations), for the words from "Scotland," to the end there is substituted "in like manner as an extract registered decree arbitral bearing warrant for execution issued by the sheriff court of any sheriffdom in Scotland.".

9. After section 158 there is inserted—

"158A Other disclosures by the Secretary of State

(1) The Secretary of State may, in spite of any obligation as to secrecy or confidentiality imposed by statute or otherwise on him or on persons employed in the Department of Social Security, disclose any information received by him in connection with his functions under this Act or the Pensions Act 1995 to any person specified in the first column of the following Table if he considers that the disclosure would enable or assist the person to discharge the functions specified in relation to the person in the second column of the Table.

TABLE

Persons	Functions
The Treasury.	Functions under the Financial Services Act 1986.
The Bank of England.	Functions under the Banking Act 1987 or any other functions.
The Regulatory Authority.	Functions under this Act or the Pensions Act 1995, or any enactment in force in Northern Ireland corresponding to either of them.
The Pensions Compensation Board.	Functions under the Pensions Act 1995 or any corresponding enactment in force in Northern Ireland.
The Friendly Societies Commission.	Functions under the enactments relating to friendly societies.
The Building Societies Commission.	Functions under the Building Societies Act 1986.
An inspector appointed by the Secretary of State.	Functions under section 94 or 177 of the Financial Services Act 1986.
A person authorised to exercise powers under section 106 of the Financial Services Act 1986.	Functions under that section.
A designated agency or transferee body or the competent authority (within the meaning of the Financial Services Act 1986).	Functions under the Financial Services Act 1986.
A recognised self-regulating organisation, recognised professional body, recognised investment exchange or recognised clearing house (within the meaning of the Financial Services Act 1986).	Functions in its capacity as an organisation, body, exchange or clearing house recognised under the Financial Services Act 1986.

(2) The Secretary of State may by order—
  (a) amend the Table in subsection (1) by—
    (i) adding any person exercising regulatory functions and specifying functions in relation to that person,

(ii) removing any person for the time being specified in the Table, or
(iii) altering the functions for the time being specified in the Table in relation to any person, or
(b) restrict the circumstances in which, or impose conditions subject to which, disclosure may be made to any person for the time being specified in the Table".

10. In section 164(1)(b)(i) (Crown employment), the words from "136" to "143" are omitted.

11. In section 166(5) (reciprocity with other countries), the words from "136" to "143" are omitted.

12. In section 177 (general financial arrangements), in subsection (3)(b)(i), the words from "136" to "143" are omitted.

13. In section 178 (meaning of "trustee" and "manager"), in paragraph (b), the words from "136" to "143" are omitted.

14. In section 181 (general interpretation), in subsection (3), the words from "136" to "143" are omitted.

15. In section 183 (sub-delegation)—
    (a) in subsection (1), the words from "136" to "143" are omitted, and
    (b) in subsection (3)(b), after "prepared" there is inserted "and from time to time revised".

16.—(1) Schedule 9 (transitory modifications) is amended as follows.

(2) In paragraph 1—
    (a) in sub-paragraph (1), sub-paragraphs (ii) to (v) are omitted,
    (b) in sub-paragraph (3)(a)(i), for "provisions mentioned in paragraphs (i) to (v)" there is substituted "provision mentioned in paragraph (i)", and
    (c) sub-paragraph (5) is omitted.

(3) Paragraphs 3 and 4 are omitted.

Definitions For "occupational pension scheme" and "personal pension scheme", see the Pension Schemes Act 1993, s 1; for "pensionable service", see s 70(2), (3) of that Act; as to "a salary related occupational pension scheme", see s 93(1A) of the 1993 Act, as inserted by s 152(1), (3) hereof; as to "member", see ss 93(2), 181(4) of that Act; as to "manager", see s 178(a) of that Act, as amended and repealed in part by s 122 of, Sch 3, paras 22, 43 to, this Act, and by s 177, Sch 7, Pt I hereof; for "normal pension age", see s 180(1) of the 1993 Act; for "employment", "prescribed", "regulations" and "the Regulatory Authority", see s 181(1) of that Act, as amended by s 122 of, Sch 3, paras 22, 44 to, this Act.
References See para 10.28.

SCHEDULE 7

Section 177

REPEALS

PART I

OCCUPATIONAL PENSIONS

Chapter	Short title	Extent of repeal
1982 c 50	The Insurance Companies Act 1982	In Schedule 2B, in paragraph 3(9), the "or" after paragraph (a)
1986 c 53	The Building Societies Act 1986	In section 53(15), the "or" after paragraph (a)
1987 c 22	The Banking Act 1987	In section 84(10), the "or" after paragraph (a)

Chapter	Short title	Extent of repeal
1989 c 24	The Social Security Act 1989	In Schedule 5, paragraph 14
1993 c 48	The Pension Schemes Act 1993	Sections 77 to 80
		Sections 102 to 108
		In section 110, subsections (2) to (4)
		Section 112
		Section 114
		Section 116
		Section 118
		Sections 119 to 122.
		In section 129, in subsection (1), "Chapter I of Part V", "sections 119 to 122", "under Chapter I of Part V or" and "or sections 119 to 122", and subsection (3)(a)
		In section 132, "the equal access requirements"
		In section 133(1), "the equal access requirements"
		In section 134, in subsection (3), "the equal access requirements" and, in subsection (4), "or the equal access requirements" and "or, as the case may be, section 118(1)"
		In section 136(2)(e)(iv), "or the equal access requirements"
		In section 139(2), "the equal access requirements"
		In section 140(4), paragraph (c) and the "and" immediately preceding it
		Section 144
		In section 153, in subsection (1), the words from "and Chapter I" to "section 108", subsections (3) and (4), in subsection (5), "Chapter I of Part VII", paragraph (d) and the preceding "or", and subsections (6) and (7)
		In section 170, subsections (5) and (6)

Chapter	Short title	Extent of repeal
1993 c 48—*contd*	The Pension Schemes Act 1993—*contd*	In section 178, in paragraph (a), the second "or"
		In section 181(1), the definition of "equal access requirements"
		In section 183, in subsection (3), the words from "or, in the case of" to "determined" and the words following paragraph (b)
		In section 185, in subsection (1), "I or"
		In Schedule 7, paragraphs 1 and 3
		In Schedule 8, paragraph 3

References See para 1.26.

PART II

STATE PENSIONS

Chapter	Short title	Extent of repeal
1988 c 1	The Income and Corporation Taxes Act 1988	In section 187, in subsection (2), the definition of "pensionable age"
1992 c 4	The Social Security Contributions and Benefits Act 1992	Section 53
		In section 54, in subsection (1)(a), the words from "but" to "70", and subsection (4)
		In Schedule 3, in paragraph 5(7)(a), "(or at least 20 of them, if that is less than half"
		In Schedule 5, in paragraph 2(2), the definition of "period of enhancement" and the previous "and", and in paragraph 8, sub-paragraphs (1) and (2)
1994 c 18	The Social Security (Incapacity for Work) Act 1994	In Schedule 1, paragraphs 20 and 21

These repeals have effect in accordance with Schedule 4 to this Act.

References See para 1.26.

PART III

CERTIFICATION OF PENSION SCHEMES ETC

Chapter	Short title	Extent of repeal
1958 c 51	The Public Records Act 1958	In Schedule 1, in the Table, the entry relating to the Occupational Pensions Board
1975 c 24	The House of Commons Disqualification Act 1975	In Part II of Schedule 1, the entry relating to the Occupational Pensions Board
1975 c 25	The Northern Ireland Assembly Disqualification Act 1975	In Part II of Schedule 1, the entry relating to the Occupational Pensions Board
1975 c 60	The Social Security Pensions Act 1975	In section 61B(1), "except any power of the Occupational Pensions Board to make orders"
1979 c 50	The European Parliament (Pay and Pensions) Act 1979	In section 6(4), "and the Occupational Pensions Board"
1982 c 50	The Insurance Companies Act 1982	In Schedule 2B, in paragraph 3(1), in the Table, the entry relating to the Occupational Pensions Board
1989 c 24	The Social Security Act 1989	Section 29(7)
		In Schedule 5, paragraph 4
1992 c 5	The Social Security Administration Act 1992	In Schedule 4, the entries in Part I relating to the Occupational Pensions Board
1992 c 53	The Tribunals and Inquiries Act 1992	In section 7(2), "(d) or"
		In section 10(5), paragraph (c)
		In section 13(5)(a), "and (d)"
		In section 14, subsection (2)
		In Schedule 1, paragraph 35(d)
1993 c 8	The Judicial Pensions and Retirement Act 1993	In section 13(9), in the definition of "personal pension scheme", "by the Occupational Pensions Board"
1993 c 48	The Pension Schemes Act 1993	Sections 2 to 5
		In section 7(4), "by the Board"
		Section 8(5)
		In section 9(3), "22 and".
		In section 13(2)(a), the words from "and does" to the end

Chapter	Short title	Extent of repeal
1993 c 48—*contd*	The Pension Schemes Act 1993—*contd*	In section 14, subsection (3)
		Section 22
		In section 23, subsections (1) and (5)
		Section 24
		In section 25, subsections (1) and (3)
		Section 28(7)
		Section 31(1)
		Section 34(6)
		Sections 35 and 36
		In section 38, in subsection (1), the words from "unless" to the end, in subsection (3), the words from "if" to the end, and subsection (7)
		In section 45, subsection (2) and, in subsection (3), paragraph (d) and, in paragraph (e), the words following "prescribed period"
		In section 48(2), paragraph (b) and, in paragraph (c), "if the earner dies before reaching pensionable age"
		Section 50(7).
		In section 52, subsections (4) to (6)
		In section 53, subsections (2), (4) and (5)
		Section 54(3)
		In section 55, subsection (1) and subsections (3) to (6)
		In section 56, subsection (1), in subsection (2), the words following "the prescribed period", and subsection (3)
		In section 58, subsections (1) to (3), (5) and (6)
		Section 59
		In section 60, subsections (1) to (3) and (6) to (10)
		In section 62, subsection (2). In section 63, in subsection (1), paragraphs (a) and (c), subsection (2), in subsection (3), paragraph (a) and the words following sub-paragraph (ii), and subsection (4).

Chapter	Short title	Extent of repeal
1993 c 48—*contd*	The Pension Schemes Act 1993—*contd*	Sections 64 to 66
		In section 84, in subsection (5), paragraph (b) and the preceding "or"
		Sections 133 to 135
		In section 155, "or the Board"
		In section 158, subsections (2) and (3), in subsection (6), "(2) or (3)", paragraph (d) (and the "or" immediately preceding it), in subsection (7), paragraph (c) (and the "or" immediately preceding it) and subsection (8)
		In section 164(1)(b)(i), "2 to 5", "172, 173" and "and Schedule 1"
		In section 166(5), "sections 2 to 5", "172, 173" and "and Schedule 1"
		In section 170, in subsection (1), the "and" at the end of paragraph (c) and subsections (3) and (4)
		Sections 172 and 173
		In section 177, in subsection 3(b)(i), "sections 2 to 5", "172, 173" and "and Schedule 1" in subsection (3)(b)(ii), the words from "sections 55" to "premiums)", and in subsection (7), paragraph (b)
		In section 178, in paragraph (b), "sections 2 to 5", "172, 173" and "and Schedule 1"
		In section 181, in subsection (1), the definitions of "accrued rights premium,", "the Board", "contracted-out protected rights premium", "limited revaluation premium","pensioner's rights premium", "personal pension protected rights premium", "state scheme premium" and "transfer premium", in subsection (3) "172, 173" and "and Schedule 1", and in subsection (7) "and Schedule 1"

Pensions Act 1995, Sch 7

Chapter	Short title	Extent of repeal
1993 c 48—*contd*	The Pension Schemes Act 1993—*contd*	In section 182(1), "the Board or"
		In section 183, in subsection (1), "sections 2 to 5", "172, 173", and "or Schedule 1" and subsection (2)
		In section 185, subsections (3), (4) and (6)
		In section 186(5), "or section 185(4)"
		In section 192(2), "section 172(4) and (5)"
		Schedule 1
		In Schedule 2, in paragraph 5, in sub-paragraph (1), "or the Board" and "or, as the case may be, the Board", in sub-paragraph (2), "to 65", in sub-paragraph (3), "in relation to state scheme premiums" and paragraph (b), and sub-paragraph (5)
		In Schedule 6, paragraph 11
		In Schedule 8, paragraph 44(a) and (b)(i) and the "and" immediately following it

References   See para 1.26.

PART IV

MISCELLANEOUS AND GENERAL

Chapter	Short title	Extent of repeal
1971 c 56	The Pensions (Increase) Act 1971	In section 3, in subsection (2)(c), "is a woman who"
1993 c 48	The Pension Schemes Act 1993	Sections 136 to 143
		In section 145, "with the approval of the Treasury".
		In section 149, in subsection (3), at the end of paragraph (a), "and"
		In section 164(1)(b)(i), the words from "136" to "143"
		In section 166(5), the words from "136" to "143"

Pensions Act 1995, Sch 7

Chapter	Short title	Extent of repeal
1993 c 48—*contd*	The Pension Schemes Act 1993—*contd*	Section 172(1)(b)
		In section 177, in subsection (3)(b)(i), the words from "136" to "143"
		In section 178, in paragraph (b), the words from "136" to "143"
		In section 181, in subsection (3), the words from "136" to "143"
		In section 183, in subsection (1), the words from "136" to "143"
		In Schedule 9, in paragraph 1, in sub-paragraph (1), sub-paragraphs (ii) to (v), and sub-paragraph (5), and paragraphs 3 and 4

The repeal in the Pensions (Increase) Act 1971 shall come into force on the day this Act is passed.

References   See para 1.26.

Index

Accrued rights
entitlement distinguished from, 9.3
Active members
winding-up priorities, 10.7
Actuary
duty to appoint, 5.1–5.2
whistleblowing, 5.11–5.12
Additional voluntary contributions
indexation, 6.9
priorities, 10.4–10.5
Administration
OPRA, of, 2.9
Pensions Compensation Board, of, 11.7–11.8
Advisers. *See* Professional advisers
Age related rebates
generally, 14.11
money purchase scheme, 14.12
personal pension scheme, 14.13
verification of ages, 14.14
Agreement
schedule of contributions, on, 7.14
Annuity deferral
personal pensions, 14.20–14.27
Appointment
independent trustees, of, 3.12–3.18
trustees, of, 2.22–2.25
Assignment
attachment of earnings, 12.16
bankruptcy, 12.18
divorce, 12.19
generally, 12.13–12.14
new provisions, 12.12
previous position, 12.11
Attachment of earnings, 12.16
Auditor
duty to appoint, 5.1–5.2
whistleblowing, 5.11–5.12

Background to 1995 Act, 1.1, 1.15–1.16
Bank accounts
trustees, powers of, 3.37
Bankruptcy
Scotland, 12.18
Blowing whistle. *See* Whistleblowing
Budget
OPRA, of, 2.8
Pensions Compensation Board, of, 11.6

Case law, 1.7–1.9, 1.17
Cash equivalents
guaranteed, 10.26–10.27

Certificates
minimum funding requirement, 7.8–7.11
schedule of contributions, 7.15
Choice of investments, 3.31
Civil offences, 2.30–2.31
Closed funds
winding-up priorities, 10.20–10.21
Compensation. *See* Pensions Compensation Board (PCB)
Complaints
procedure, 4.1–4.2
Compliance
member-nominated trustees, 3.11
Confidentiality
duty of, 2.45
Contracting-out
equal treatment, 8.12
hybrid schemes, 13.8–13.9
indexation, 6.12
new certification requirements,
generally, 13.1–13.2
reference scheme, 13.3
rule changes, 13.10–13.11
SERPS, breaking link with,
generally, 13.4
state scheme premiums, 13.5–13.7
Contribution holiday, 1.10
Contributions
additional voluntary, 6.9
MFR. *See* Minimum funding requirement
member, 3.38
money purchase scheme, 14.3
rates of, 7.12
state pensions, changes to, 13.15
Corporate trustees
nature of, 3.3–3.4
Costs
divorce orders, 12.7
equal treatment, 8.13
pensions Ombudsman, of, 4.8
Criminal offences, 2.26–2.29
Crown application, 3.42

Debt on employer
money purchase scheme, 14.5
schedule of contributions, 7.18
Deferred pensioners
winding-up priorities, 10.7
Defined benefit (final salary) schemes
growth of, 1.1
indexation, 6.5

257

Index

Defined benefit (final salary) schemes—*contd*
  member-nominated trustees, 3.1
Delegation
  investment powers, of, 3.25–3.26
  sub-delegation, 3.27
Department of Social Security
  contracting-out legislation, responsibility for, 2.5
Dependent spouses
  pension increases for, 13.16
Detrimental amendments, 9.1–9.2
Directions
  OPRA, by, 2.35–2.37
Directors
  member-nominated, 3.3
Disability working allowance
  state pensions, changes to, 13.12
Disclosure of information
  divorce, relating to, 12.7
  OPRA, powers of, 2.44–2.45
  Pensions Compensation Board, powers of, 11.22–11.24
  Pensions Ombudsman, by, 4.9
  professional advisers, relating to, 5.6
  regulations, 3.34–3.35
Dispute resolution
  complaints procedure, 4.1–4.2
  Pensions Ombudsman,
    costs, 4.8
    disclosure, 4.9
    expanded jurisdiction, 4.3–4.6
    expenses, 4.8
    interest, 4.7
    staff, 4.10
Disqualification of trustees, 2.17–2.21
Divorce
  assignment, 12.19
  calculation, 12.6
  costs, 12.7
  disclosure, 12.7
  earmarking, 12.3–12.4
  historic position, 12.1–12.2
  pension splitting, 12.5
  personal pension schemes and policies, 12.8
  retrospection, 12.9

Early retirement
  indexation, 6.10
Earmarking, 12.3–12.4
Earnings
  attachment of, 12.16
  factors, calculation of surplus in, 13.13
Eligibility
  professional advisers, of, 5.8–5.10

Employees
  funded pension benefits, tax reliefs relating to, 1.1
Employers
  contribution holiday, 1.10
  debt on,
    money purchase scheme, 14.5
    schedule of contributions, 7.18
  funded pension benefits, tax reliefs relating to, 1.1
Employment
  equal treatment, 8.8
Entitlement
  accrued rights distinguished from, 9.3
  pension already arisen, to, 10.6
Equal treatment
  bringing claim, 8.9–8.11
  contracting-out, 8.12
  cost, 8.13
  employment legislation, interaction with, 8.8
  exceptions, 8.5–8.6
  implementation, 8.7
  new rule, 8.2–8.4
  official pensions, for, 8.14
  Social Security Act 1989, 8.1
  state pension age equalisation, 8.15–8.16
European Community (EC)
  membership, effects of, 1.17
European Court of Justice
  case law, 1.17
Exoneration
  investment powers, relating to, 3.28
Expenses
  Pensions Ombudsman, of, 4.8
Family credit
  state pensions, changes to, 13.12
Final salary schemes. *See* Defined benefit (final salary) schemes
Flexible deferment, 13.14
Forfeiture
  generally, 12.16–12.17
  new provisions, 12.12
  previous position, 12.11
Fund manager
  duty to appoint, 5.1–5.2

Goode, Professor Roy, 1.13
Government White Paper, 1.14
Guaranteed minimum pensions (GMPs)
  winding-up priorities, 10.11

Home responsibilities protection, 13.17

Index

House of Commons
  Select Committee on Social Security, 1.13
Hybrid schemes, 13.8–13.9

Implementation of 1995 Act
  interpretation, 1.22
  overriding legislation, 1.25
  regulations, 1.23–1.24
  repeals, 1.26
  timetable, 1.20–1.21
Independent trustees
  appointment of, 3.12–3.18
Indexation
  additional voluntary contributions, 6.9
  contracting-out, 6.12
  early retirement, 6.10
  final salary scheme, 6.5
  limited price, 6.2–6.3
  money purchase scheme, 6.6–6.8
  new provisions, 6.4–6.11
  personal pensions, 6.13, 14.15
  preservation precedents, 6.1
  repeals, 6.4
  revaluation precedents, 6.1
  scope, 6.4
  set-offs, 6.11
  surplus, refunds of, 6.14–6.17
Information. *See* Disclosure of information
Injunctions
  power to grant, 2.34
Inland Revenue
  OPRA, disclosure of tax information to, 2.45
  Practice Notes, 1.4–1.6
Interest
  Pensions Ombudsman, powers of, 4.7
Interpretation, 1.22
Investigation
  OPRA, powers of, 2.41–2.43
  Pensions Compensation Board, powers of, 11.19–11.21
Investments
  choice of, 3.31
  delegation of powers, 3.25–3.26
  exoneration, 3.28
  new powers, 3.23
  self-investment, 3.32
  skill and care, duty of, 3.24
  statement of investment principles, 3.29–3.30
  sub-delegation, 3.27
Levy
  money purchase scheme, 14.10
  OPRA, management of, 2.10–2.11
  Pensions Compensation Board, 11.6

Maxwell pension schemes, 1.10–1.12
Meetings
  records of, 3.36
Member-nominated directors, 3.3
Member-nominated trustees. *See* Trustees
Memoranda
  Inland Revenue, issued by, 1.5–1.6
Minimum funding requirement
  certificates, 7.8–7.11
  PLRC recommendations, 7.1–7.3
  schedule of contributions,
    agreement, 7.14
    certification, 7.15
    debt on employer, 7.18
    notice of breach, 7.16–7.17
    rates of contributions, 7.12
    timetable, 7.13
  serious underprovision, 7.19–7.20
  skeleton procedures, 7.4–7.7
  valuations, 7.8–7.11
Mis-selling of personal pensions, 14.19
Modification of scheme rules
  accrued rights, 9.3
  amendment by OPRA, 9.8–9.13
  detrimental amendments, 9.1–9.2
  overriding amendments, 9.6–9.7
  public service schemes, 9.14
  special circumstances, 9.4–9.5
Money purchase schemes
  age related rebates, 14.12
  contribution rates, agreement of, 14.3
  debt on employer, 14.5
  indexation, 6.6–6.8
  levy, 14.10
  member-nominated trustees, 3.1
  notice of breach, 14.4
  payment schedules, 14.1–14.2
  penalties, 14.6–14.7
  serious underprovision, 14.8–14.9

Non-reimbursement
  penalties, 2.33
Numbers of member-nominated trustees, 3.7

Occupational Pensions Board (OPB)
  dissolution of, 2.4–2.5
  transfer of functions to OPRA, 2.5
Occupational Pensions Regulatory Authority (OPRA)
  administration, 2.9
  amendment by, 9.8–9.13
  board, appointment of, 2.3
  body corporate, as, 2.2
  budget, 2.8

Index

Occupational Pensions Regulatory Authority (OPRA)—*contd*
creation of, 2.1–2.3
directions, 2.35–2.37
disclosure of information, 2.44–2.45
investigative powers, 2.41–2.43
levy, 2.10–2.11
management of, 2.6–2.11
OPB, transfer of functions from, 2.5
penalties,
   civil offences, 2.30–2.31
   criminal offences, 2.26–2.29
   directions, 2.35–2.37
   injunctions, 2.34
   non-reimbursement, 2.33
   Pension Schemes Act 1993, offences under, 2.32
   restitution, 2.34
personnel, 2.6–2.7
review of decisions, 2.40
trustees,
   appointment of, 2.22–2.25
   disqualification, 2.17–2.21
   removal of, 2.12–2.13
   suspension of, 2.14–2.16
winding-up schemes, 2.38–2.39
Offences
civil, 2.30–2.31
criminal, 2.26–2.29
Pension Schemes Act 1993, under, 2.32
Official pensions, 13.18
Overriding legislation, 1.25

PLRC. *See* Pension Law Reform Committee (PLRC)
Penalties
civil offences, 2.30–2.31
criminal offences, 2.26–2.29
directions, 2.35–2.37
injunctions, 2.34
money purchase scheme, relating to, 14.6–14.7
non-reimbursement, 2.33
Pensions Schemes Act 1993, offences under, 2.32
professional advisers, relating to, 5.3–5.5
restitution, 2.34
whistleblowing, relating to, 5.17
winding-up, surplus on, 10.19
Pension Law Reform Committee (PLRC)
appointment of, 1.13
minimum funding requirement, recommendations on, 7.1–7.3
Pension schemes
six-sided fortress of protection for, 1.15

Pension schemes—*contd*
winding-up, 2.38–2.39
Pension splitting, 12.5
Pensioneer trustees
small self-administered schemes, 3.6
Pensions Compensation Board (PCB)
amount of compensation, 11.13–11.15
creation of, 11.2–11.3
disclosure of information, 11.22–11.24
excluded schemes, 11.11
investigative powers, 11.19–11.21
management of,
   administration, 11.7–11.8
   budget, 11.6
   levy, 11.6
   special powers, 11.4–11.5
new scheme, 11.1
notification, 11.16
qualifying schemes, 11.10
review of decisions, 11.9
surplus funds, 11.17–11.18
time limits, 11.12
Pensions legislation
previous, 1.1
statutory, 1.2–1.3
Pensions Ombudsman
costs, 4.8
disclosure by, 4.9
expanded jurisdiction, 4.3–4.6
expenses, 4.8
interest, powers relating to, 4.7
role of, 1.2
staff, 4.10
Pensions Regulator
role of, 1.13, 1.14
Period of office
member-nominated trustees, 3.9–3.10
Personal benefit of trustees, 3.19–3.20
Personal pensions
age related rebates, 14.13
annuity deferral for, 14.20–14.27
divorce, effect of, 12.8
indexation, 6.13, 14.15
mis-selling of, 14.19
providers, control over, 14.16–14.18
whistleblowing, 5.19–5.20
Personnel of OPRA, 2.6–2.7
Political implications of 1995 Act, 1.18–1.19
Practice Notes
contents, 1.4
memoranda, supplemented by, 1.5–1.6
Premiums
state scheme, 13.5–13.7
Professional advisers
actuary, appointment of, 5.1–5.2
auditor, appointment of, 5.1–5.2

Index

Professional advisers—*contd*
  disclosure, 5.6
  exceptions, 5.7
  fund manager, appointment of, 5.1–5.2
  ineligibility, 5.8–5.10
  penalties, 5.3–5.5
  whistleblowing, 5.11–5.13
Public service schemes
  changes to, 13.18
  modification of rules, 9.14

Records of meetings, 3.36
Reference scheme
  contracting-out, 13.3
Regulations
  power to make, 1.23–1.24
Removal of trustees, 2.12–2.13
Repeals, 1.26, 6.4
Restitution
  court, application to, 2.34
Review of decisions, 2.40

SERPS. *See* State Earnings Related Pension Scheme (SERPS)
Scotland
  bankruptcy, 12.18
Selection of member-nominated trustees, 3.8
Self-investment
  trustees, powers of, 3.32–3.33
Set-offs
  indexation, 6.11
Skill and care, duty of
  investments, relating to, 3.24
Small self-administered schemes
  pensioneer trustees, 3.6
Spouses
  dependent, pension increases for, 13.16
Staff
  Pensions Ombudsman, of, 4.10
State Earnings Related Pension Scheme (SERPS)
  breaking link with,
    generally, 13.4
    state scheme premiums, 13.5–13.7
  contracting-out. *See* Contracting-out
State pensions
  changes to,
    contribution conditions, 13.15
    dependent spouses, pension increases for, 13.16
    disability working allowance, 13.12
    earnings factors, calculation of surplus in, 13.13
    family credit, 13.12
    flexible derefment of retirement pension, 13.14

State pensions—*contd*
  changes to—*contd*
    home responsibilities protection, 13.17
    official pensions, 13.18
    public service pensions, 13.18
  equal treatment, 8.15–8.16
  SERPS. *See* State Earnings Related Pension Scheme (SERPS)
State retirement pension
  flexible deferment of, 13.14
Statement of investment principles, 3.29–3.30
Statutory discharge
  winding-up priorities, 10.22–10.23
Statutory legislation, 1.2–1.3
Sub-delegation, 3.27
Surplus funds
  asset-stripping of, 1.9
  ownership of, 1.11
  Pensions Compensation Board, 11.17–11.18
  refunds of, indexation requirements, 6.14–6.17
Suspension of trustees, 2.14–2.16

Time limits
  Pensions Compensation Board, relating to, 11.12
  transfers, 10.28
Time off work and training, 3.39–3.41
Timetable
  implementation of 1995 Act, 1.20–1.21
  schedule of contributions, 7.13
Transfers
  extension of rights, 10.24–10.25
  guaranteed cash equivalents, 10.26–10.27
  time limits, 10.28
Trustees
  appointment of, 2.22–2.25
  bank account, 3.37
  Crown application, 3.42
  disclosure regulations, 3.34–3.35
  disqualification, 2.17–2.21
  independent, 3.12–3.18
  investments,
    choice of, 3.31
    delegation, 3.25–3.26
    exoneration, 3.28
    new powers, 3.23
    self-investment, 3.32–3.33
    skill and care, duty of, 3.24
    statement of investment principles, 3.29–3.30
    sub-delegation, 3.27

Index

Trustees—*contd*
member contributions, responsibility for, 3.38
member-nominated,
  appointment of, 3.1–3.2
  compliance, 3.11
  corporate trustees, 3.3–3.4
  equal status, 3.5
  exemptions, 3.1
  numbers, 3.7
  period of office, 3.9–3.10
  selection, 3.8
  small self-administered schemes, 3.6
personal benefit of, 3.19–3.20
records of meetings, 3.36
removal of, 2.12–2.13
suspension, 2.14–2.16
time off work and training, 3.39–3.41
voting, 3.21–3.22

Trusts
law of, 1.7–1.9
political implications of 1995 Act, 1.18–1.19

Unapproved schemes
tax treatment of, 1.3

Valuation
minimum funding requirement, 7.8–7.11

Verification of ages, 14.14

Voting
trustees, powers of, 3.21–3.22

War widow's pensions, 12.10

Welfare benefits
state pension, relationship with, 1.2

Whistleblowing
actuary, by, 5.11–5.12
auditor, by, 5.11–5.12
penalties, 5.17
personal pensions, 5.19–5.20
professional advisers, 5.11–5.13
statutory protection, 5.14–5.16
Whistleblower Protection Bill, 5.18

White Paper, 1.14

Winding-up
closed funds, 10.20–10.21
deficit on, 10.12
OPRA, powers of, 2.38–2.39
preferential liabilities on, 10.3
priorities,
  AVC priorities, 10.4–10.5
  active members, 10.7
  deferred pensioners, 10.7
  entitlement to pension already arisen, 10.6
  guaranteed minimum pensions, 10.11
  interaction with scheme rules, 10.9–10.10
  pension increases, 10.8
  preferential liabilities, 10.3
  reasons for change, 10.1–10.2
statutory discharge, 10.22–10.23
surplus on,
  generally, 10.13–10.18
  penalties, 10.19